...uure du coste de la court

The great ages of architecture

The great ages of architecture

from ancient Greece to the present day

by BODO CICHY

G. P. PUTNAM'S SONS · NEW YORK

Translated into English by Susan McMorran
This edition copyright © 1964 by Oldbourne Press, London

Published in Germany in 1959 as *Architektur und Baustile* by Schuler Verlagsgesellschaft
© 1959 by Schuler Verlagsgesellschaft, Stuttgart

Published in France in 1961 as *Art et Secrets des Bâtisseurs* by Editions du Pont-Royal
© 1961 by Librairie Hachette, Paris

Library of Congress Catalog Card Number: 64–13517

Printed in West Germany

CONTENTS

PLATES

GOTHIC ARCHITECTURE

RENAISSANCE ARCHITECTURE

BAROQUE AND ROCOCO ARCHITECTURE

ARCHITECTURE DURING THE LATE EIGHTEENTH AND NINETEENTH CENTURIES

TWENTIETH-CENTURY ARCHITECTURE

I
INTRODUCTION

———

Architecture—like painting and sculpture—is an art involving perception and touch through the materials at its disposal; it makes no direct appeal to the ear, as do poetry or music. However, the concepts of architecture, like its artistic means, are different from those of painting and sculpture. Painting is concerned with the world of objects that surrounds us. Its aim is to create an illusion of reality with colors arranged upon a flat surface (canvas, wall, wood, paper) and is therefore limited to two dimensions, for only by an optical trick can it give an impression of relief.

Sculpture and architecture, on the other hand, command the third dimension and actually exist in space, giving concrete shape to design, bulk to the flat image, and volume to plan.

Sculpture, then, consists in setting up a definable, tangible object in space, the outer surface of which alone is significant. The fundamental principle of architecture is to define space itself by enclosing it within a solid—to construct a form having primary significance in the interior volume. The two arts are obviously related, however, for both are three-dimensional, and architecture cannot ignore the outer aspect of a work, even though the first concern is the enclosed space. A building's outward appearance, its form and dimensions, will all be related to its interior construction.

All building is not necessarily architecture. A structure that is merely the end product of a technical undertaking cannot aspire to such a claim. Architecture means more than this: technical means and the will to build must be accompanied by a regard for beauty and perfectly finished forms. We may say that a building becomes a work of art when it surpasses functional limitations and can be considered on an esthetic level. But it is not always easy to distinguish clearly between the strictly functional building and the work of art, which itself must have a purpose; every building should fulfill the needs it was built to serve. Perhaps the decisive factor is that a work of art should not only provide for basic needs but ennoble the status of man by giving him an ideal environment. It is no coincidence that many of the finest and most beautiful buildings have been those created in the service of religion, and that religion has been among the chief inspirations for great art.

The architect's aim is not solely to carry out a plan of construction. He must continually seek to inspire and give pleasure with the beauty of the forms he uses; appealing to man's innate artistic sense is the very *raison d'être* of architecture. Art stems from our ability to recognize beauty when we see it and our desire to leave beautiful creations as a heritage for humanity — a need that the architect appreciates when he sets out to transform ideas into the tangible substance of his buildings. Moved by the creative impulse, he takes the raw materials of nature — the formless lumps of stone, wood, iron, etc. — and reveals their inner life and mysterious strength by incorporating them within a vital whole. Form, order and harmony are attained by the careful arranging, balancing and piecing together of each part of a construction. The forces that comprise a building — the dead weight of a block of stone . . . the lateral thrust of an arch or a vault — require that the supporting and supported parts exactly correspond, and the need for perfect equilibrium is a discipline to which architecture must submit. In spite of this, man has refused to be defeated by the physical forces that he tackles, and in the course of the centuries he has tried to devise ways of overcoming them. But the fundamental problems still remain. Though submission to the peculiar demands of architecture's materials naturally imposes technical limitations, architectural features have been evolved to reveal the existence of the forces of thrust and counterthrust — supporting walls, buttresses, vaulting ribs — elements which need not necessarily serve a functional purpose, though they are often thought to be technically indispensable.

From the battle with the different forces and the desire to exploit them came architectural ornament. In building, man has also tended to imitate the forms of Nature. Painting and sculpture are sometimes a building's only decoration, and architecture has often been called the mother of the arts because they are put to her service and used to enhance her grandeur. In many cases, instead of emphasizing the static forces in his building, an architect will deliberately try to disguise them or deny their existence altogether by using lavish ornament. He may have ceilings decorated to give the illusion of lightness and the appearance of being suspended in mid-air, or walls painted to give an impression of vast space.

The character of a building and its ornamentation (painting and sculpture) will be dependent on contemporary tastes and culture. Like all true art, architecture is a product of the spiritual climate of a particular age and is a reflection of human endeavor, thoughts and aspirations. Through an understanding of architecture we can come near to understanding the mind of man, for the aim of the historian of art is to reveal not only the structural principles of buildings but the intellectual background that produced them and made them what they are. It goes without saying that painting, sculpture, literature and music, too, are mirrors of society, sharing with architecture a common basis of artistic forms and principles. Thus only from a study of the masterpieces of all the arts can we derive a clear picture of the age that gave them birth.

The characteristics of one period are called its "style" — a word derived from the Latin *stilus* or writing tool. Therefore the original meaning is: a manner of writing. In the course of history many styles have come into being and together they form a picture of the development of architecture and art in general. Every style has its own vitality and — like the human mind itself — is in a state of perpetual flux. Each strong current of thought is accompanied by its artistic equivalent — a new style that follows an identical course of growth and decay.

The purpose of this book is to trace the progress and development of human ideas as they were translated, century by century, into the material terms of architecture.

II
GREEK ARCHITECTURE

Historical Background

The lands where East meets West around the Aegean Sea and the Eastern Mediterranean were the setting for the founding of the Western architecture that developed during the two thousand years before the birth of Christ. Within the compass of this civilization were Egypt, Greece, Crete, countless islands (Delos, Paros, Naxos, Melos, Lesbos, Chios, Samos, Rhodes, etc.) and the shores of Asia Minor.

During the Neolithic age and for the first part of the Bronze Age (from the fifth to the end of the third millennium B.C.) these lands were thinly inhabited by a primitive people called by the ancients the Pelasgi or Carians. From their culture, little survives but tools, pieces of pottery and the scattered remains of a few settlements or towns. We only know that they belonged to no Indo-European race and therefore cannot have been ancestors of the Greeks. But they were to be of great importance to the Greek invaders, for the Indo-European tribes who streamed into Greece from the second millennium brought the old race to subjection but did not obliterate it. The Pelasgi must be considered as a vital part of the racial substrata that formed the character of the Greek people.

Even before the wave of Indo-European invasion broke upon them, the men of the Aegean lands had acquired great cultural advances from the civilizations of Mesopotamia — not only a knowledge of stone and brick construction, of copper and bronze work (c. 2600 B.C.), but also a complete system of agriculture and horticulture. These discoveries had an overwhelming effect on the lives of the simple peasants and nomadic shepherds. They were able to enjoy all the advantages of a highly civilized life: stability, the introduction of permanent settlements, division of labor, an organized society and agricultural development. Questions of soil fertility and the power of natural forces gained a hold on men's minds. The religion that developed therefrom was eventually strong enough to influence that of the incoming Greeks and to survive into recorded history. It is surely no coincidence that only the father of the Greek gods, Zeus, has a Greek name, while the names of the others — Apollo, Dionysus, Hermes, Athena, Aphrodite — are all taken from the old Aegean language.

The same applies to numerous place names, of which the most important examples are Athens, Corinth and Thebes, and to many names of plants and implements. It is especially interesting that technical terms applied to architecture were also frequently of Aegean origin. Behind this transmission of words from one language to another lies more than mere borrowing. The hypothesis that the invaders simply took over the native words for places, plants and tools, the nautical and architectural terms, is probable, for these would have been new and unfamiliar. But it is more difficult to accept the fact that for the same reason they abandoned their own ancient deities and adopted those of the Pelasgi. The greatest of all the gods worshiped by the peoples of the Mesopotamian civilizations — and consequently by the Aegean race also — was the female god (the Great Mother) of agricultural fertility, but henceforth it was the patriarchal figure of Zeus that took first place in the areas occupied by the newcomers. Here we are witnesses to a profound process of assimilation. It serves no real purpose to dwell at greater length on this phenomenon, and the field of research is extremely limited, for there is little substantial evidence and a total lack of written documents. However, we should keep in mind that the direction of Greek culture was decided in the first place by this meeting, intermingling and fusion of Aegean and Hellenic elements.

About 1800 B.C., when the first tide of Indo-Europeans from the Balkans moved toward Greece, the invaders conquered large areas in the middle of the country and in Peloponnesian territory and encouraged the spread of their own language, Greek; but Aegean civilization was left undisturbed in the hands of the indigenous dwellers. Their seamanship and knowledge of Eastern culture, acquired during the third millennium, had enabled them to build up a flourishing civilization (since c. 2000 B.C.) under Cretan supremacy — the Minoan dynasty that reached its height about 1600 B.C. The humblest craftsmen were producing work of considerable artistic value in pottery, precious

1. *Plan of the Palace of Knossos, c.* 1500 B.C.

metals and other crafts. Painting was not limited to vase decoration but came to be used in architecture, and buildings would be completely covered in wall paintings.

Following upon smaller establishments came the great palaces of Knossos and Phaestos, with their innumerable rectangular rooms, several stories high and often furnished with staircases (a feature that does not occur in Greek architecture until 300 B.C.). A maze of long narrow corridors, halls for dramatic or theatrical presentations, and stockrooms, surrounds a large inner courtyard. These palaces served a double purpose as dwellings and trading houses, and their apparently incoherent pattern of nooks and corners and complex plans (Fig. 1) formed the basis of the Greek legend of the minotaur and the labyrinth. These Cretan buildings had flat roofs and the supporting columns that were to take on such deep significance in Greek architecture. The Cretans had probably borrowed the columnar form from Egyptian temples, and it can hardly be doubted that they in turn influenced the character of the columnar buildings of the Greeks.

Whatever the case, the affinity between the capital of a Cretan column — rounded echinus and square abacus — and a Doric capital betrays an influence that was to spread through the channel of the Mycenaean culture of the mainland, which was dependent on Crete, and where similar columns are to be found. But in all probability this was only a foretaste of the Doric capital, for the stage was not yet set for the coming of the columnar architecture of the Greeks, with its infinite refinements of the structural theme.

At the height of its power (1600–1400 B.C.) Cretan civilization — courtly in the true sense of the word — spread to the mainland of Greece in the form of merchandise of high artistic value. The inhabitants of the mainland, who were used to a simpler way of life, were ready to acknowledge the superiority of the island dwellers but not to accord them political supremacy. Independently of Crete, the Greek villages grew into fortified towns and strongholds from which powerful warriors would trade and plunder to acquire more land. Contrasting with the palaces of Crete, which were open and almost defenseless, the dwellings of these half-barbarian warlike princes were equipped with great defensive walls and were in fact fortified castles. Those at Mycenae and Tiryns are the best known, and the lords who once held them are the warriors of Greek legend, of the *Iliad* and the *Odyssey,* appearing in the guise of mythical heroes: Achilles, Patroclus, Ajax, Ulysses. It is important to notice a certain feature at the center of these Mycenaean castles — the megaron, where the lord of the castle would reside — for it will later reappear as the inner sanctuary of Greek temples. The megaron is a long rectangular structure with side walls stretching beyond the entrance façade, to form a small vestibule. Two columns are set between the ends of these extended side walls, as can be seen at the palace of Tiryns.

About 1500 B.C. an influx of new immigrants — the Achaeans — augmented the strength of the mainland dwellers, who then felt themselves powerful enough to challenge the sovereignty of the Minoan dynasty. Their capture of the islands of Melos and Paros was followed (about 1400 B.C.) by the looting and destruction of Cretan towns and palaces as they forced their way toward Asia Minor (Trojan War, *c.*1200 B.C.) and even into Egypt (1171 B.C.). Minoan civilization was replaced by a less advanced and

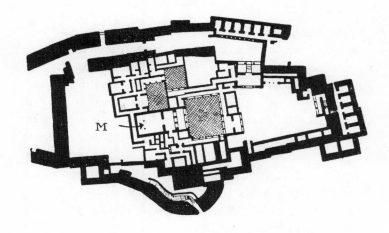

2. *Plan of the fortress of Tiryns, c.* 1400 B.C.

more cruel civilization, distinguished not for reaching new heights of grandeur but for bringing about a steady decline in artistic standards. Internal strife was hastening the process of ruin when the last crucial immigration of Greek tribes — the Dorian invasion — reached the Peloponnesus and southern Greece (about 1100 B.C.). Here the Dorians settled, probably drawn by a desire to conquer new territories and attracted by the riches of the Mycenaean rulers. The Dorians threw out their allied races, the Ionians and the Aeolians. Large numbers of these went inland, while the majority fled to the coasts of Asia Minor and neighboring islands, living there as exiles — and later, colonists — and building rich and prosperous cities (Ephesus and Miletus, for example). They took part in the creation of the Ionic culture which was to equal in beauty and importance that evolved by the Dorians in their newly conquered land.

The Origins
of Greek Architecture

The Dorian invasion and all its repercussions struck at the very roots of the Aegean world. The collapse of Mycenaean civilization had been followed by no cultural rebirth, but had set in motion a gradual decline in traditions (post-Mycenaean age). This period is like a dark interval before the brilliant dawn of true Greek art, for not until the ninth century B.C. do we once again find fresh vigor and hope for the future. Even then, until the seventh century B.C., the only signs of a renewed artistic impulse are minor works of art in pottery or bronze and terra cotta statuettes. Vases often standing higher than a man, were made to place on tombs and were decorated with minutely regular geometrical patterns. These vases already express that feeling for the monumental which was to be such a decisive factor in the coming developments. With archaic Greek art (c. 650–480 B.C.), a new chapter opens and artists began to seek inspiration in the human figure. Life-size statues of nude youths (kouroi)—probably dedicated to young athletes who had won acclaim in the Olympic Games (instituted in 776 B.C.)—and votive statues of women (korai) appeared all over the Greek world. These were truly monumental sculptures demanding an equally monumental architecture, and thus great houses were built for them. But it is remarkable that these first monumental sculptures did not represent the gods whose temples now stand on hallowed ground. There is no doubt that the temples must once have held images of gods, since destroyed by fire, earthquake or other misfortune or perhaps replaced by more beautiful figures. The tradition of dedicating a building to a particular god must be very much older, but the desire to distinguish it by architectural splendor originates in the eighth century.

The Greeks had no inclination to undertake huge palaces like those of the Cretans or fortresses like those of Tiryns and Mycenae. They were mainly concerned with creating an architecture that would serve their religion, building temples and temple precincts with their porticoes or propylaea. It was only in the Hellenistic age that secular architecture achieved any degree of importance. Temples and sanctuaries certainly figured in Minoan and Mycenaean architecture, but were never given the monumental form of their Greek counterparts. Perhaps the underlying reason for this indifference is that men judged it proper to worship the gods of Nature at altars beneath the open sky, giving them the form of effigies, sacred columns and other idols. But Greek gods more and more tended to be represented as human beings endowed with the same desires, virtues and weaknesses as the people who worshiped them. Temples were needed to house these gods, where their images might always be accessible for worship.

Certainly the Greeks, too, paid homage to their gods at altars in the open air. The sacred precincts of the Heraeum at Olympia (dedicated to Hera, mother of the gods), are quite distinct from the temple of the same name erected later (about 590 B.C.). In the sanctuary of Hera at Samos

3. *Terra cotta model. Discovered in the Heraeum of Argos, middle of the eighth century* B.C. *Restored.*

and in several other places, a large number of these altars has been found (dating from between 950 and 625 B.C.). There were also small sanctuary chapels modeled on human habitations, where the image was housed. The appearance of these buildings is known to us through two terra cotta models discovered in the Heraeum of Argos, which, judging by their painted decoration, must date from 750 B.C. (Fig. 3). These little buildings are rectangular in plan. Two columns (or pillars) in the line of the side walls stand before the entrance wall, separated from it by a short interval. This projecting part has a flat roof and forms a kind of covered porch, while the building itself has a steeply pitched roof and a rectangular opening in the front gable, providing for internal lighting. Several of the most important features of Greek architecture are here anticipated: rectangular plan, porched entrance and gable roof. We have before us a type of building—the megaron—which, in a modified form, was first brought from the East (to the Danube region and into the Aegean) by the Indo-European invaders. It appears in the East (Jericho, Byblos) and a little later in the oldest strata of Troy (c. 2700 B.C.). Many

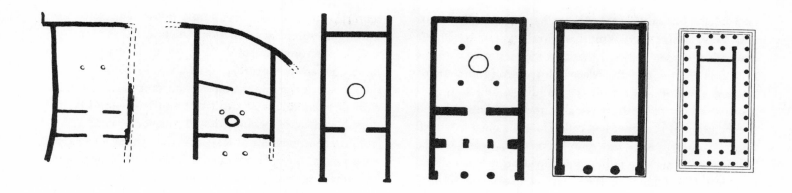

4. *Megara, temples* in antis *and peripteral temples. Left to right: Jericho, fourth century* B.C.; *Dimini, c. 2800* B.C.; *Troy II, c. 2500* B.C.; *Tiryns, c. 1400* B.C.; *temple* in antis; *peripteral temple.*

of these houses left by the Indo-European invaders are to be found in the Danube region and in Thessaly (Dimini). This type was unknown in Crete, where buildings have flat roofs and are never gabled. The same must apply to the earliest buildings of the East, for the gable roof is a typically northern phenomenon, dependent on climatic conditions and on the widespread use of timber in these regions. The megaron at Tiryns, with its gable roof of about the second millennium B.C., is representative of the type used in the north and brought by the early Greeks from their land of origin.

The megaron is illustrated by the two Argos models, but not in its purest form—normally the anteroom is formed by an extension of the side walls, and there is a second smaller compartment behind the principal room. It was in this form that the megaron took its place in Greek temple architecture. In the temple *in antis* (Fig. 4), the side walls extend forward and terminate in rectangular pilasters called antae, between which there are usually two columns (as at Tiryns), and the megaron preserves its independence insofar as it is an isolated unity. However, there is no small inner room. The second and most important form to be used by the Greeks from the seventh century onward is the peripteral temple (Glossary), where the megaron lies within a surrounding colonnade but retains its classical form with porch (pronaos), principal room (cella or secos)

and inner room (adytum). The Greek temples of Sicily are good examples of this type. As a general rule the adytum is replaced by the opisthodome, which gives no access to the cella.

The development of the megaron into the peripteral temple is an entirely Greek phenomenon. It is not even possible to detect the influence of columned Egyptian temples. Nor can Crete and Mycenae, where the column was also well known, offer anything similar. But it would be a mistake to regard the colonnade purely as decoration or embellishment. Its existence is due to sound practical considerations. The first temples of megaron form had walls of brick or clay set on a stone foundation and were completely exposed to the weather. For this reason, the most vulnerable parts—the projecting ends of the side walls—were faced with wood. The wood was subsequently replaced by stone and the protective covering thus lost its original meaning and became an esthetic and decorative element. The same applies to the colonnade. This was originally a row of wooden posts which surrounded a building and allowed for an extension of the roof to shelter the temple proper. The first accounts of peripteral temples only approach the truth when they describe the colonnade as a sort of ornamental afterthought. A megaron at Thermon, far to the north (megaron B), was surrounded by a ring of wooden columns in horseshoe formation. Excavations have proved these to be a later addition (Fig. 5). The archaic temples at Samos and Locri Epizephyrii (southern Italy) present similar cases. It was soon realized that a colonnade was a means of giving the temple an added architectural grandeur, of distinguishing it from ordinary buildings, and setting it apart as a holy place. In particular, these columns stressed the seclusion of the sanctified cella from the outside world. Right of entry into the temple was restricted to the initiated few, and the public worshiped at open-air altars outside the building. For these various reasons, peripteral temples became increasingly popular during the great

5. Sanctuary of Thermos. *(A) Aegean hairpin megaron; (B) megaron with ring of posts, c. tenth century* B.C *Superimposed, peripteral Doric Temple of Apollo, c. 620* B.C.

centuries to follow, while simple house temples *in antis* were given subsidiary functions (such as treasuries).

Columned Greek temples were not originally built in stone. The central feature, the cella, was first constructed of rubble or brick, while the most important parts — columns with their entablature (architrave and frieze) and double-sloped roof with pediments and cornice — were derived from timber models or at least owe their character to forms essential to timber construction. The Greek geographer Pausanias (second century A.D.) in his account of his travels reports that the opisthodome of the Heraeum at Olympia (second construction, c. 600 B.C.) still contained the remains of an old oak column. Like so many other temples, this Heraeum has come down to us in a state of ruin, and the surviving stone columns are so varied in type (many are monolithic shafts; others are made up of superimposed drums; some have 16 flutes and others 20; their diameters and the Doric capitals also vary considerably) that there can be only one possible explanation: they must have gradually replaced original wooden columns. Moreover, contrary to the rule for stone constructions, the intercolumniation is so wide that the columns could only have carried a wooden entablature, never one of stone.

The peripteral temple of Apollo at Thermon was built during the second half of the seventh century B.C. over the remains of megaron B, and is believed to be one of the earliest Doric temples (Fig. 5). This also originally had timber columns and entablature. The wooden columns have disappeared but are implied by the surviving flat stone slabs on which they once rested, like those of the Mycenaean era which are still preserved. There were 5 columns on each façade and 5 on each flank. As in the Olympian Heraeum, the distance between columns was so great that it presupposes a wooden entablature, now also lost. This is confirmed by the existence of several painted terra cotta tablets that formerly served to fill the gaps between the crossbeams of the roof as they rested on the architrave. As a whole, this construction constitutes the Doric order and was precisely adopted in later Doric buildings of stone, together with other structural forms peculiar to timber buildings. It is generally agreed that this structure represents the earliest form of wooden entablature as used in the archaic temples (Fig. 6).

Two heavy, squared beams, smooth and without decoration (the architrave), rest side by side upon the columns. Each supporting column is placed at the meeting point of two pairs of beams. A square plate called the abacus is interposed between the rounded head (capital) of the column and the beams, in order to strengthen the structure at this point. The beams are held together by

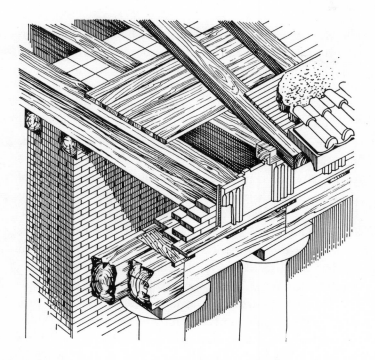

6. Timber prototype of the Doric entablature.

of terra cotta tablets with vertical grooves that probably served to drain off the rain water. These reappear as the triglyphs (three grooves) in stone temples, and with the metopes comprise the characteristic frieze of Doric architecture. Finally, above the frieze one or more smaller beams run parallel to the architrave; notched into these are the sloping members of the roof trusses. This structure is preserved in stone cornices below which sloping mutules (thin slabs) take the place of rafters. The pegs used to secure the roof covering in timber construction also reappear as stone guttae. Thus all the characteristics of columned Doric construction are ultimately derived from wooden prototypes. This is also true of Ionic construction, although different forms are used.

small planks that lie across their entire width at the juncture of each pair, and are secured with wood or metal pegs. These small planks project slightly beyond the face of the architrave and are covered by a layer of long planks running parallel to the architrave and projecting from it to form a narrow band. Both features—cross planks and terminating band—are faithfully adopted in stone construction and are called respectively the regulae and the taenia. Even the peg heads that secure these parts in a wooden temple are imitated in stone: these are the guttae (page 33). On this substructure lie heavy crossbeams which span the whole building and carry the wooden ceiling and rafters. In the largest temples one or two rows of columns inside the cella give the beams added support. As a rule there is one crossbeam to every column and one to every space between the columns. The spaces between the ends of the beams as they rest on the architrave are filled in with clay bricks faced with painted terra cotta tablets (metopes), as at Thermon. As these were replaced by stone, painted decoration soon gave way to relief sculpture. The ends of the beams themselves, particularly exposed to the weather, were given a protective covering

The Orders:
The Development
of Greek Architecture

At the beginning of the sixth century B. C., monumental temples in stone began to appear all over the Greek world. But the methods by which they were built were different, and whether a temple is Doric or Ionic in form depends on regional locations and on the people who, in creating them, gave them their peculiar characteristics. The Doric and the Ionic are both based on the megaron and wooden prototypes; the column is an essential feature in both styles and each is rectangular in form. Later, toward the end of the fifth century, the Corinthian order appeared, but it did not achieve importance until the third century B. C., although it later became predominant in Roman architecture.

THE DORIC ORDER

The Doric order originated in the lands occupied by the Dorians (from *c.* 1100 B.C.) and especially in the Peloponnesus. But it was taken much farther afield when, before the building of the first great temples, branches of the Dorian people settled in southern Italy and Sicily (Syracuse in 733; Tarentum in 705; Gela in 688; Paestum and Selinus in 627). These Greek colonies erected magnificent temples (at the same time as the Greeks in the homeland) which have come down to us better preserved than those of Greece itself; they are often more impressive and afford a better opportunity of studying the Doric order in its essence. To examine every detail would be beyond the scope of this book, and it is sufficient here to point out that the general design remains the same, though several variations do occur, notably in sixth-century temples. It was not simply a question of taking the old forms evolved during the seventh century and reproducing them in stone, but of freeing the whole building, as well as its constructional details, from the spirit of improvisation.

This meant establishing a system: an *order* whereby, according to size and scale, all parts of the temple would be fixed by strict rules of proportion, and closely interrelated. Straight lines predominate and verticals and horizontals balance one another in perfect unity. These are vital characteristics of Doric temple architecture. Where violent contrasts are sought, vertical (column, triglyph) is juxtaposed with horizontal (stylobate, architrave). Transitional elements (favored by the Ionic, where columns rest on molded bases) are deliberately avoided. Even the cushionlike echinus of a Doric capital cannot be considered as a transitional feature, for its rounded form set beneath the square abacus is the source of yet another contrast. Nevertheless Doric makes use of compromise in the play of forces. With its level row of columns, triglyphs and metopes, the Doric temple would seem to be dominated by the horizontal, strongly stressed again in the cornice and architrave. But balance is maintained by the vertical sweep of the columns and the answering uprights of the triglyphs and especially by the pediment that gathers up the horizontals at the point where the verticals also reach their climax. The Doric temple is an embodiment of a rich and ordered system of design where opposing forces are reconciled and achieve total harmony.

The classical formula of the Doric order found its ultimate expression during the fifth century B.C. The first monument to which the term classical may be applied is the Temple of Zeus at Olympia (*c.* 480–430 B.C.). One of the greatest Doric temples ever to be built in Greece, this was the work of Libon, who came from the nearby town of Elis. It is peripteral and demonstrates the classical canon of proportion for the first time—the arithmetical relationship between the columns on the front and those on the flanks being as 6 to 13, that is, on each side the number of columns is double that on the façade, plus 1. Thus the proportions of the Parthenon are also classical, being as 8 to 17. Archaic temples usually have a greater number of side columns (Thermon, *c.* 620 B.C., 5 by 15; Heraeum at Olympia, *c.* 590 B.C., 6 by 16; Temple of Apollo at Syracuse, *c.* 560 B.C., 6 by 17). During the fourth century B.C. —the post-classical period—and in the Hellenistic age, it became usual to reduce the length of the side colonnades, and classical proportions were abandoned. For the Temple of Zeus, Libon strove to set up an ideal system of proportion that would apply not only to the number of parts in the building but to dimensions also. The height of the columns is 32 Doric feet (1 Doric foot = 32.5 cms); the intercolumniation is 16 feet, center to center. The abaci are 8 feet wide and consequently the width of the roof tiles is 2 feet. But the Doric style always had to contend with a problem that did not concern either Ionic or Corinthian, a problem that—like architects before and after him— Libon had to face. This was the arrangement of the triglyphs at the ends of the frieze. According to the Doric rule, there should be one triglyph to each column and one to each intercolumniation, but by this scheme the frieze would have had to end with a half metope on each side (Fig. 7)— an esthetically unsatisfactory arrangement. For the same esthetic reasons, it was impossible to enlarge the last metopes by one and a half times the normal size, even though this would have allowed the frieze to end with triglyphs. Finally a means of overcoming this problem was found—one which seems small and insignificant to the untrained eye. The space between the two outer columns on each side was reduced so that by widening the last metope slightly, the last triglyphs could be placed not on the center of the outer columns but at the angles, thus stopping the frieze.

The Temple of Zeus at Olympia owes its historical importance to the fact that it was a symbol of unity between the different branches of the Greek people. This awakening of national pride was dearly bought, for until the fifth century the Greeks had been engaged in a desperate struggle, often amounting to fratricide, against the system of self-government that their geographical position seemed to dictate for them. It was only under the threat of Persian aggression that the Hellenic world was driven to unite in self-defense. In 499 B.C., the Ionian towns on the coasts of

7. *The adjustment of the triglyphs on a Doric temple.*

Asia Minor revolted against Persian oppression but the rebellion was put down (Miletus was recaptured by Darius in 494 B.C.). The Athenians — that is, the inhabitants of Attica — soon had to defend themselves against the same invaders. At Marathon in 490 B.C., though greatly outnumbered, they successfully repulsed the aggressors. When Xerxes I, King of the Persians, set out to conquer Greece in 480 B.C., he met with the opposition of a united people. In mortal danger, the Greeks realized that for the first time in their history they were bound by a common destiny. But the heroic battle fought by the Spartans under Leonidas at Thermopylae was not enough to save them. The gateway to Greece was open, Attica was lost, and Athens and all the temples of the Acropolis were about to be sacked. Greece was nearing the end of her strength when the Athenian Themistocles destroyed the entire Persian fleet at Salamis (480 B.C.). The following year the Greeks gained a resounding victory at the battle of Plataea and the Persians were finally ejected. Meanwhile (in 480 B.C.) the Greek colonies had foiled an attempt by the Carthaginians to conquer Sicily and had defeated them at the battle of Himera.

This life struggle of the Greek people had spared the Western world from being overwhelmed by the East and is therefore of considerable historical importance. Their triumph is symbolized in the Temple of Zeus at Olympia. The decision to build this temple was taken with one accord at the first Olympic Games to be held after the war (476 B.C.). Like the games themselves, in which young Greeks had taken part in peaceful athletic contests every four years since 776, it was a symbol of the reawakening of Hellenic pride. In Athens, however — now the leading power among the Greek city-states — no great monument was undertaken for a period of ten years. There was a specific reason for this. After the battle of Plataea in 479 B.C., the Greeks had sworn never to rebuild the sanctuaries burned and ravaged by the barbarians; their ruins should always bear witness to the godlessness of the enemy. Thus no temples were built in the areas that had been laid waste during the Persian wars. The ban was lifted — for Athens at least — when it was proposed to rebuild the sacred precincts of the Acropolis, and the Parthenon was begun in 447 B.C. The Parthenon (page 33) is with good cause the most celebrated of all Greek temples, for it is not only the supreme example of classical temple architecture, but proof that temple design is not, as one might imagine, tied to a rigid mathematical formula. The Parthenon is a pure artistic creation imbued with an inner life revealed only to those who search for it. The work of the most renowned artists of their time — Ictinus (architect) and Phidias (sculptor) — this temple is peripteral Doric with classical proportions, having 8 columns on the front and 17 on the sides. Even the manner of solving the triglyph problem betrays something of the vitality that pervades the whole building. Though the angle intercolumniations are contracted, as in the old temples, not only do the final metopes become slightly larger but this enlarging process is extended to all the metopes, so that each is a little bigger than the one before it, going toward the center, and no triglyph falls exactly on the axis of a column.

A fairly convincing attempt has been made to explain the narrower angle intercolumniations and progressive diminution of metopes as a device for achieving an effect of perspective. The eye does not perceive the differences in proportion, and will judge the row of columns and frieze of triglyphs to be longer than they actually are. This would also explain why, on measurement, the columns at the angles prove to be thicker than the others. The Roman architect Vitruvius (first century B.C.), to whom we owe much of our knowledge of Greek architecture, gives the following explanation: because the angle columns, seen against a background of sky, would look thinner than the others that are backed by the building itself, they were made proportionately thicker. Even the shape of the column shafts plays an optical part in the perspective. Not only in the Parthenon, but from the very beginning, a Doric column does not taper upward from the bottom at a uniform rate; it is worked with an outward curve, with its widest point in the lower half. This entasis is at once a means of expressing the strength of the load-bearing element and of correcting the impression of slight concavity given by columns with straight sides. The numerous shallow flutes (generally 20 during the classical period) meet in sharp edges and create a pattern of light and shade (page 33).

The Parthenon is full of other subtle refinements. The effects so laboriously sought during the building of other temples are achieved here with scientific precision and logic: none of the columns is exactly perpendicular. All have a slight inclination toward the interior of the temple, and those at the angles are inclined toward the angles of the cella. In this way the whole building conveys a greater impression of stability. Neither the stylobate nor the entablature are precisely horizontal, but rise toward the center with a delicate curvature that again accentuates the sense of firmness and balance.

The Parthenon is the sum of all the discoveries and achievements of past ages. The old forms, being perfectly integrated, are given new meaning. Passing within the colonnade, in front of the cella we find a row of 6 columns which is repeated before the opisthodome at the opposite end (Fig. 8). Right around the top of the outer wall of the cella runs a continuous frieze of relief sculptures representing the Panathenaic procession. This, too, is a new feature in Doric architecture. The figurative decoration of a Doric temple had been invariably confined to the metopes and the two pediments — that is to the outside of the building. The cella itself differs from the usual type. Previously in archaic temples, the cella took the form of a long and fairly narrow gallery the length of which was emphasized by two rows of columns supporting the ceiling. Now it becomes proportionately wider, owing to the presence of the opisthodomes, and the two rows of columns no longer reach to the end wall but are discontinued in front of it by another row placed transversely. Thus a form of colonnade was evolved which divides the cella, deprives it of the character of a gallery, and makes it a self-sufficient compartment.

The increased number of columns, the frieze decoration and the formation of separate rooms, are new features in Doric architecture, but they were not invented by Ictinus. They originated in Ionic architecture and here for the first

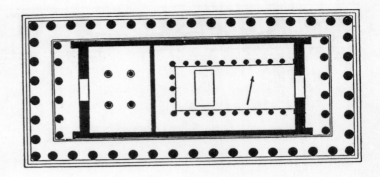

8. *Plan of the Parthenon, begun 447 B.C.; completed 482. On the Acropolis, Athens.*

time are fused with the Doric tradition. That this should have happened at precisely this moment seems to indicate that the revival of communal spirit among the Greeks was not least among its causes.

THE IONIC ORDER

The Ionic order originated on the coasts of Asia Minor and the adjacent islands to which (about 1100 B.C.) the Aeolians and Ionians had retreated after the Dorian invasion. The Ionic style, like the Doric, is expressed in two main types — the temple *in antis* and the great peripteral temple still reminiscent of the megaron in plan — and many of its features similarly may be traced to wooden prototypes. But the methods by which these types were interpreted in Ionic building were, from the beginning, quite different from those adopted in Doric temples. The first great monuments of the sixth century B.C. (Samos, Ephesus) already display the characteristic use of numerous columns. Whereas a peripteral Doric temple has a single colonnade, in these a second was added within the first, thus creating a new type — the dipteral temple. There is no doubt that such a development was accelerated by the example of Egyptian temples with their distinctive forests of columns. Egyptian influence was especially to be felt in the Aegean, probably as a result of the flourishing sea trade.

At the same time there appears the tendency to give graceful and delicate proportions to temples and their decoration, contrasting vividly with the sheer mass of Doric building. Columns become appreciably more slender, and proportionately to their width, considerably taller than those of Doric temples. The smooth bulk of the Doric architrave gives way to three horizontal bands producing lines of shade that detract from the heaviness of the entablature. Instead of the ponderous rhythm of triglyphs, there is a frieze—plain or decorated with reliefs—finished above with a row of dentils. Moreover, the whole entablature is much narrower than that of the Doric and conveys an impression of lightness appropriate to the slenderness of the columns. Harsh contrasts are scrupulously avoided in relating one element to another, in particular by setting the columns upon molded bases.

The capital is a characteristic element of the Ionic order. In its classical form, it consists of a flat rectangular plate resting horizontally on the column, with its loose ends wound up (like paper) into spiral-shaped volutes on either side of the shaft. Between the volutes is a convex molding carved with an Ionic leaf pattern (usually the egg and dart) which constitutes the joint between shaft and capital. The capital is crowned by a very shallow abacus with an undercut profile. Unlike the Doric which has no one face because it has a circular echinus, the Ionic capital differs according to whether it is seen from the front or from the side. It has two frontal faces and two side faces. This design constituted a problem, for the external side face of the capitals on the angle columns needed special treatment. The solution adopted was to give these capitals a third frontal aspect by bending out the volutes at an angle of 45 degrees.

While the Doric capital is closely connected with Minoan and Mycenaean forms, where columns are terminated by a round slab like an echinus set beneath an abacus, the chain of development of the Ionic capital may be traced back through forms used in Nearer Asia to the capitals on the columns of Egyptian temples. The last link in the chain— and one which is already Greek—is the proto-Ionic or Aeolic capital discovered in several small temples dating from the beginning of the sixth century B.C. (at Neandria, near Troy; at Nape, on Lesbos; at Larissa, near Smyrna). As shown (Fig. 9), a ring of hanging leaves projects from a circular molding above which is another convex molding, also adorned with leaves, that is probably the prototype of the Ionic egg-and-dart motif. The volutes spring up from the shaft and curl outward into spirals. In the true Ionic capital which replaced the Aeolic type about 550 B.C. and

was never modified, the volute member becomes a horizontal cushion and the vegetable forms (from Egypt) are replaced by a more architectonic terminal.

The archaic temples of Ionia—the largest to be built on Greek soil—have all disappeared, not least because of the uprising against the Persians in 499 B.C. Nevertheless the remains which have been brought to light—like those of

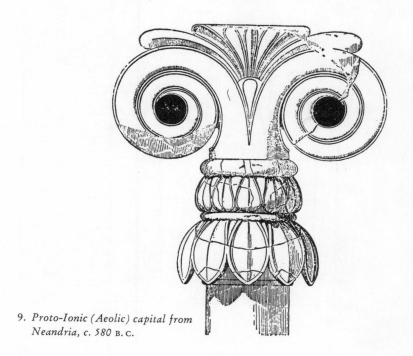

9. *Proto-Ionic (Aeolic) capital from Neandria, c. 580 B.C.*

their Hellenistic successors (at Ephesus, Didyma and Sardis)—during excavations are enough to reveal their structural characteristics and to show that these temples had a different arrangement from their Doric counterparts. Doric temples have an air of massive grandeur arising from the sheer ponderous weight and contrast of the various parts and their closely knit construction; they seem to forbid the outside world the right of entry to their innermost precincts. Ionic temples, on the other hand, invite our approach, for their columns are slim and tall, and a second colonnade is introduced, creating a space between the exterior and the cella (Fig. 10). The desire of these architects to emphasize the accessibility of the cella would also explain why, in some small buildings (treasuries at Delphi, porch of caryatids of the Erechtheum, Athens, page 35), column shafts are replaced by figures of maidens (caryatids) or other statues implying the importance of the space between cella and colonnade as a constituent part of the building. It is in this light that one may appreciate why the cella of Ionic temples was always closely related to the

10. *The Artemision at Ephesus, sixth–fifth century* B.C.
Restoration columnar arrangement, Köpf.

portico, its side walls being on the same axis as the columns of the portico. A similar relationship appears in Doric temples, though much later and then only under Ionic influence. Previously the cella tended to float like an independent entity, with no relation to the surrounding girdle of columns (Fig. 11). The Ionic cella becomes more and more like a room, whereas that in a Doric temple is narrow and like a long passageway. The Erechtheum (421–405 B.C.) and Temple of Victory (427–424 B.C.)—the two Ionic monuments on the Acropolis of Athens—have cellae that are actually wider than they are long.

This problem of relating the temple as a whole to the outside world soon gave rise to a new attitude toward the façade: during the Hellenistic period façade decoration became a matter of principal concern.

While the Doric temple remains an impenetrable entity presenting no welcoming front, in spite of its decorated pediment, the façade of the archaic Heraeum of Samos (burned *c*. 520 B.C.) is emphasized and its function clearly established by means of the intercolumniation. The columns of the entrance portico are more widely spaced than those at the back of the temple. This frontality is substantiated by the peculiar nature of Ionic capitals, for they, too, demand to be seen directly from the front.

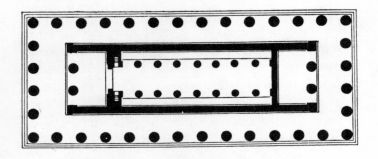

11a. *Plan of the Temple of Poseidon, Paestum, c. 460* B.C.
Example of the floating Doric cella.

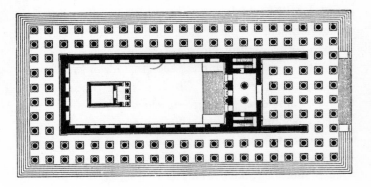

11b. *Plan of the Temple of Apollo, Didyma, 332* B.C.
Example of an aligned Ionic cella.

THE CORINTHIAN ORDER

One might easily come to suppose that all Greek temples are alike or at the most distinguishable only by subtle variations of proportion in their parts. This is largely true, for Greek architecture is essentially traditional, holding fast to the approved forms. But in the Parthenon we have already seen how Doric architecture—of all styles the most closely bound to tradition at the height of its maturity— was receptive to forms that were not Doric but Ionic: evidence of a real transmutation. It may be that the political situation and recent revival of patriotism had something to do with this phenomenon. Whatever the cause, the event is of considerable significance, together with the fact that from then on such tendencies gathered force and became widespread.

The fusion of Doric and Ionic may be seen in the Propylaea on the Acropolis at Athens, begun in 437 B.C. and contemporary with the Parthenon. This monumental portico is externally Doric and has Ionic columns on the inside. The same combination occurs in the Temple of Apollo at Bassae, near Phigalia (c. 430 B.C.), built by Ictinus, architect of the Parthenon. Like the Parthenon, this temple had an Ionic frieze, though this time it was within the cella. The cella had engaged columns and Ionic forms and capitals. A single column stood on the central axis near the back wall. This free column and the two engaged columns flanking it had capitals that correspond neither with Doric nor Ionic forms and which were to be the germ of a new order—the Corinthian. This capital is shaped like a bell. At the bottom of the bell and rising up its sides are two overlapping rows of acanthus leaves. From these emerge fine stems that form volutes beneath the angles of the concave-sided abacus, and on the face of the bell are two other more slender volutes (spirals) coiling inward toward each other. This prototype was to receive only minor modifications during the centuries to follow, while the idea from which it originated was never forgotten: the vegetable forms of nature are used to symbolize structural forces. With this transmutation of plant forms into the vocabulary of architectural ornament, we are for the first time witnessing a process that will be repeated in Western architecture (in Romanesque and Gothic), where naturalistic ornament takes the place of abstract decoration. That this process can be reversed we have already seen in the example of an Ionic capital—an abstract transformation of the wholly naturalistic Egyptian capital. It would not yet be true to say that the Corinthian column now completely replaced Doric and Ionic, for at first this new order re-mained an isolated phenomenon. Even in the fourth century, the post-classical period when Corinthian columns constituted a complete order for the first time, they were only used for the interiors of traditional temples. Their use as an exterior feature begins with a secular building—the Monument of Lysicrates at Athens (334 B.C., page 36). They attained an independent status as a monumental order during the Hellenistic age (third–first century B.C.) as may be seen in the Olympieum at Athens (page 36), the second largest of all Greek temples, built on old foundations between 174 and 131 B.C. In other respects, Corinthian temples retain the forms of the Ionic order (column bases, entablature).

The Corinthian capital is a purely Greek invention. Egyptian palm columns, with their similar carved-leaf motif, cannot be regarded as a convincing source, for columns of this type did not appear until about a hundred years after the capital at Phigalia. The name Corinthian is probably derived from a legend handed down by Vitruvius —that the form of the column was invented by Callimachus, a metalworker of Corinth. According to Pausanias, he also made the gold lamp for the Erechtheum in the shape of a Corinthian capital. Certainly the form of the capital is not, properly speaking, architectonic, but wholly plastic in character, and the delicacy of its design would seem to suggest that its origins do indeed lie in metal sculpture.

The Fourth Century
and the Hellenistic Age

The period covering the end of the fifth century and the whole of the fourth century B.C. was of vital significance for the Hellenic world. After some ten prosperous years around 450 B.C., the old antagonism between rival cities flared up once more. The Peloponnesian War broke out between the bitter opponents, Athens and Sparta, resulting in the eclipse of Athens. During the same period the Carthaginians invaded Sicily, taking Selinus, Himera, Agrigentum, Gela and Camarina. Syracuse alone was able to preserve her independence by negotiating a treaty to that effect. All this meant the end of monumental architecture in Magna Graecia. Persian aggression was resumed in Asia

Minor. Fighting ended with the peace of Antalcidas (386) by which the Greek cities of Asia Minor, together with Cyprus, were surrendered to the Persians. But then came a surprising development. The building of great temples (which had practically ceased in the fifth century) began anew and Ionic architecture became subject to a grand revival.

The demands of grandiloquent Persian rulers hastened the restoration of temples that had been destroyed and resulted in much new building. Though the old forms were again brought into play, there appeared everywhere a tendency to elaborate these forms and to give buildings a much richer decoration. The dipteral temple, with its host of columns, was given supreme expression in the rebuilding of the Artemision at Ephesus (from 356 B.C.; over a hundred columns) and in the gigantic temple of Apollo at Didyma (page 35), begun about 332 B.C. and still incomplete in 41 A.D. These forests of columns no longer stand on the traditional three-stepped platform still used for the Erechtheum and the temple of Victory (both built about 430 B.C.), but on an elevated podium that isolates the building from its surroundings. At the Artemision the podium is actually duplicated! Massive square plinths are now set below the column bases, accentuating the play of concave and convex moldings.

On the mainland of Greece, however, Sparta's power was broken by the Thebans (362 B.C.). Smaller uprisings ensued against the Macedonian enemies in the north. Philip, King of Macedon, finally brought Greece to subjection by his victory at Chaeronea (338 B.C.). His successor, Alexander the Great, accomplished what the con-

13. *Theatre of Oropus, c. 150 B.C. Restored, Fiechter.*

tinually striving Greek city-states had never been able to achieve — the union of all powers in the struggle against the everlasting threat from the East.

It is self-evident that the turmoil of the fourth century was hardly favorable to architecture and not surprising that during this time a few isolated temples were built in Greece. Particularly popular was the round building or tholos. The tholos is peripteral and circular in plan, having an exterior peristyle and cella with internal colonnade. The tholos of Delphi (beginning of the fourth century) and those of Epidaurus (c. 350 B.C.) and Olympia (c. 320 B.C.) are the best-known examples.

At the same time secular buildings began to be conceived on a monumental scale. Columns, previously reserved for temple architecture alone, formed long colonnades flanking single-story halls or were introduced inside public buildings. Gymnasiums or palaestrae, meeting places for athletic practice, were constructed around rectangular porticoes. Theatres and stadiums, the seats of culture and sport, were given a truly monumental status. Drama had long been an integral part of Greek life but until now had consisted simply of recitations and other histrionic entertainment. During the fourth century, with the coming of theatre architecture, drama was provided with a scenic setting for the first time. About 325 B.C., Polyclitus the Younger built the theatre at Epidaurus. This incorporates all the most essential features that with slight alterations were to hold good for later enterprises and are still the basis of our modern theatres (Fig. 12). Tiers of seats are arranged in concentric semicircles around a circular space (orchestra) where the chorus would perform. In the middle of the orchestra is an altar (thymele). The auditorium is divided

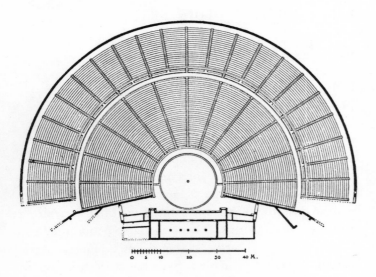

12. *Plan of the Theatre at Epidaurus, c. 325 B.C.*

by radiating rows of steps, and facing it is a platform (skene), a long, narrow rectangular structure accessible by ramps. Though here it is still only one story high, in Hellenistic times the skene was composed of two more stories and richly decorated with colonnades (Fig. 13). Sometimes these theatres held as many as 20,000 spectators.

The stadium, where athletic competitions took place, consisted of tiered seats surrounding a hairpin track. At the entrance to the track was a colonnade.

The Hellenistic Age

The three centuries between the reign of Alexander the Great and the birth of Christ are collectively known as the Hellenistic age. This description explicitly refers to the historical event that characterizes the epoch — the Hellenization of the vast areas of Nearer Asia brought under Alexander's rule from 334 B.C. onward and so becoming subject to the influence of Greek thought and culture. After the death of Alexander (323), this first world empire, stretching to the borders of India and to Nubia in Egypt, broke up into different camps that were governed by his generals and their successors (the Diadochi) and became totally autonomous kingdoms (Pergamum, Cappadocia, the Kingdom of the Seleucids and the Ptolemaic Kingdom of Egypt). Nevertheless, despite Asiatic trends, Greek tradition prevailed everywhere. It was spread by books and by scholars and artists visiting the courts of the Diadochi. Ancient works of art were collected and displayed in museums, to serve as models and incentives. Nor were the old centers of Greek civilization forgotten, though left behind by these developments. The Attalids of Pergamum, the Seleucids of Antioch, and Ariobarzanes of Cappadocia, built and restored porticoes, temples and many other buildings in Athens at their own expense. This was but a gesture of homage to the great stronghold of tradition, for elsewhere — at Pergamum in particular — at that very moment new enterprises were already pointing to the future.

Architects now turned their attention to secular tasks — with good reason, for their patrons were princes whose courts became centers of learning and culture. Because of this, Hellenistic art has been called a court art. The purpose

behind many works of art, even temples designed for the worship of a god, was largely the glorification of a prince or patron. The towns that now sprang up in Asia Minor provided this creative spirit with a rich field of action. While most ancient Greek towns, developed in the course of centuries, were accommodated to the natural environment and followed no predetermined design, the foundations of the new towns almost invariably comply with an established plan: residential areas are disposed in checkerboard pattern; the roads intersect at right angles and are much wider.

Some of the finest sites are given to those buildings most necessary to urban life, the market place (agora), council house *(bouleuterion)*, theatre, gymnasium etc., and each is conceived according to a careful architectural scheme. Sometimes the agora has long porticoes and these will often be applied on two or three stories, thus constituting one of the architectural innovations of Hellenism — the storied structure said to have been invented by Sostratus of Cnidus (third century B.C.). Palaces and assembly halls also receive a much richer architectural treatment and the simultaneous use of two orders is resolved into a system: the lower story generally has Doric columns, while those on the upper story are usually Ionic.

In temple construction, the combination of two orders of columns was retained, though the Doric order was now much less used. There are no great changes to be seen in the general form of temples, but a new type was invented during the Hellenistic age — the pseudodipteral temple. The plan is like that of an Ionic temple with two colonnades, except that the interior side rows disappear and the width of the peristasis (Glossary) is consequently doubled.

Most important is the fact that order and symmetry were imposed on temple precincts. Ancient precincts like those at Athens and Olympia, for example, have no such organized plan. The buildings on the temenos (sacred precincts) were scattered here and there, haphazardly juxtaposed with no apparent relationship except that all temples faced east. Henceforth, however, the monuments and their surroundings are conceived in relation to each other, forming a homogeneous whole grouped around a central axis, often at the cost of sacrificing the old rules of worship that dictated the East-West orientation. For instance, none of the eight temples on the Acropolis at Pergamum is orientated in this way; they and their surrounding walls are simply built in accordance with topographical and architectural requirements. How logically this principle could be applied may be seen perfectly in the Aesculapion at Cos (page 39). Three terraces are cut into the slope of the hill, like huge steps. The first two serve as forecourts to the third on which stands the temple as the spiritual center and climax of the whole composition. Entrance portico and steps to the terraces are centered on the axis of the temple. An imposing portico forming a three-sided gallery provides the temple with a rectangular frame and also defines the limits of the sacred precincts.

These elements — axiality, symmetry and the building up to a dominant point — are certainly the greatest achievements of Hellenistic architecture. They were adopted in Roman architecture where they found their logical development and consummation.

When the last sovereign of Pergamum bequeathed his empire to the Roman people in 133 B.C., a political phe-nomenon — the effects of which had already been pro-foundly felt in Greece ten years earlier — was finally real-ized. This was the rise of Rome to become a world power. The prosperous Greek towns of southern Italy had already fallen into Roman hands before the first Punic War (264 – 241 B.C.); after four military campaigns, Macedonia be-came a Roman province; in 146, Corinth was destroyed. The capture of Athens in 86 B.C. only confirmed the fact that a long process had reached its inevitable conclusion, and Greece at last became a dependency of Rome. But her glory was undimmed, for in spite of political defeat, the culture of Greece lived on and gave birth to the art of Rome.

GREEK ARCHITECTURE

ILLUSTRATIONS

a

b

c

THE PARTHENON, ATHENS
On the Acropolis, 447–438 B.C. *Ictinus.*
View from the northeast.

Here the elements of the Doric order are easily recognizable: fluted columns with capitals consisting of a completely smooth square block (the abacus) supported on a round cushion (the echinus); above, the single undecorated beam of the architrave (the epistyle) terminated on its upper edge by a projecting plank (taenia) with little bands attached to it (regulae); then the frieze consisting of three-grooved plaques (triglyphs) and panels with relief decoration (metopes); finally the cornice, beneath which are sloping mutules carrying guttae. Above the cornice, the remains of the triangular pediment that once crowned the entablature. But traces of painted decoration such as that used in most Doric temples are no longer visible. Triglyphs, regulae and mutules were blue; the taenia and the spaces between the mutules were red; the guttae were left white and so were the metopes, though the reliefs were painted. (Facing page.)

a) TEMPLE OF CONCORD, AGRIGENTUM
Sicily, c. 420 B.C.

Standing on a four-stepped platform, this peripteral temple well expresses the heavy, closed character of the Doric order. Clearly to be seen are the sharp contrasts of horizontal and vertical elements, and the balancing force of the triangular pediment whose sloping lines prevent the verticals from being crushed by the horizontals stressed in the row of columns, the architrave and frieze.

b) TEMPLE OF SEGESTA
Sicily, begun c. 420 B.C., *unfinished.*

The building of this temple was interrupted when the Carthaginians invaded Sicily in 409 B.C. It was never completed and therefore provides us with some knowledge of the stages of construction. The lifting bosses used for setting the heavy blocks of stone into place may still be seen in the lower parts. These projections would eventually have been chiseled away. The columns are still unfluted. The carving was always left until the whole of the shaft, consisting of superimposed drums, had been erected. This temple presents a colonnade with entablature and pediment, but there is no sign of a cella within, which proves that the construction procedure was to build the exterior features first and then erect the internal structure.

c) TEMPLE OF POSEIDON, PAESTUM
Southern Italy, c. 460 B.C.

The bulkiness and squat form of Doric columns are characteristic of the order. There is a perceptible swelling of the shaft (entasis) that gives an impression of weight-bearing power. The flutes enhance this effect with their chiaroscuro pattern. The columns spring directly from the top step (stylobate) of the substructure, without bases, and are terminated beneath the capital with three deep and narrow necking grooves. In many temples built of limestone or other "inferior" material, the columns were afterward covered with a sort of stucco dressing, to give them the look of marble and to hide the joints between the drums.

TEMPLE OF VICTORY, ATHENS
On the Acropolis, 427–424 B.C.

This beautiful temple is a splendid example of the use of the Ionic order and its differences from the Doric. Slender columns rest on bases that soften the juncture between stylobate and shaft. Their capitals, with Ionic volutes, support an architrave composed of three horizontal bands (fasciae) that has none of the sheer bulk of a Doric architrave. Here, instead of triglyphs, the frieze has a decoration of figures in relief, while in some other Ionic temples it may be completely smooth. The cornice and pediment that must once have covered the temple are no longer extant. (Facing page.)

a) AN IONIC CAPITAL
One of the capitals of the Propylaea on the Acropolis, Athens, c. 435 B.C.

This detail shows how the rectangular plate of an Ionic capital is placed horizontally on the shaft, with its ends rolled up like paper or parchment. These spiral curves are called volutes and end in a central eye. They form the frontal faces of the capital, while the two side faces are simply adorned with the rolled motif. Between the volutes runs a band decorated with egg and dart. The abacus of an Ionic column is much more shallow than its Doric equivalent and has an undercut profile.

b) THE PORCH OF CARYATIDS, ERECHTHEUM, ATHENS
On the Acropolis, 421–405 B.C.

In several small Ionic temples, statues of young women (korai or caryatids) replace columns as supports for the entablature. This must be regarded as evidence that the masters of the Ionic style considered the column to be much too powerful an element for the purpose it would serve here and saw that it could profitably be replaced by a statue. The row of dentils above the architrave is a typically Ionic decorative device.

c) THE TEMPLE OF APOLLO, DIDYMA
332 B.C.–*41* A.D.   *Restored, Knackfuss.*

The thick array of columns presented by ancient temples is found again, even more accentuated, in the late Ionic temples of Asia Minor. In this example, not only does a double colonnade surround the cella but columns penetrate the pronaos itself. Their slenderness and easy spacing imply a fusion with the outside world that is absent from Doric temples, with their forbidding mass and tightly spaced columns.

d) THE ARTEMISION, EPHESUS
Later construction, c. 356–236 B.C.
Restored, Henderson.

The penetration of exterior space between tall, slender columns and lightness of structure (especially evident in the shallow entablature that looks almost elegant by comparison with Doric forms) are characteristic features of dipteral Ionic temples. Particularly noticeable is the fact that the intercolumniations before the entrance to the cella are enlarged, thus stressing the function of this façade as an entrance portico. Like all great Ionic monuments of the later period, the Artemision stands, not on a three-stepped substructure, but on a raised platform with four flights of steps that enhance its effect of grand isolation.

a

b

c

d

a

b

c

OLYMPIEUM, ATHENS
174 B.C.–*13* A.D.

Of this, the second largest of all Greek temples, only a few columns and fragments of architrave remain. It is evident (Fig. a) that the Corinthian order consists of all the forms used in Ionic, with the exception of the capital — its one peculiarity. (Facing page.)

a) OLYMPIEUM, ATHENS

As in an Ionic temple, the slender, graceful columns stand on bases, and their shafts have deep-hollowed flutes divided by flat strips. Each flute is rounded off beneath the capital (Fig. b). The flutes of a Doric column are shallow, separated by sharp edges and finished with a horizontal line. The massive quality of these great Corinthian capitals betrays their late date. Upon them rests a shallow architrave that has the three superimposed Ionic fasciae.

b) A CORINTHIAN CAPITAL
Detail from the tholos of Epidaurus, c. 350 B.C.

Unlike Doric and Ionic capitals, the Corinthian is composed of plant forms suggestive of the invisible forces that work within the column. The characteristic bell-shaped block is surrounded by two overlapping rows of acanthus leaves from which spring four stems that form volutes beneath the corners of the abacus. Between these volutes, two other smaller stems form face-to-face spirals on each side of the bell. Above these spirals is a rosette placed centrally on each side of the abacus, whose profile is curvilinear, not rectilinear, as in the earlier orders.

c) THE CHORAGIC MONUMENT OF LYSICRATES, ATHENS
334 B.C.

The Corinthian order did not become truly independent until the Hellenistic period. Previously — since the invention of the capital by the metalworker Callimachus of Corinth (end of the fifth century B.C.) it had only been used for the interiors of Doric and Ionic buildings. The order made its first appearance on secular work, the first example being the monument that Lysicrates erected to commemorate a victory in a Dionysian contest of 334 B.C. Particularly to be noticed is the treatment of the entablature, with the typically Ionic features of architrave fasciae, frieze and line of dentils.

THE THEATRE OF SYRACUSE
Third – second century B.C.

Theatres built in stone are a product of the fourth century. In the Hellenistic age, much care was devoted to theatre construction, and the forms that were evolved are still in use today. The chorus would perform in the orchestra which was spread out before a long rectangular structure — at first only one story high and subsequently of two or more stories (the skene). The orchestra, where all action took place, was originally a circular space but later became semi-circular, as it is in this example. Of the skene at Syracuse, only the foundations are still extant. Facing the skene and orchestra are the tiers of seats of the auditorium, linked by radiating stairways. (Facing page.)

a

a) THE BOULEUTERION AT MILETUS
c. 170 B.C. *Restored, Knackfuss.*

In the Hellenistic age, the same care was given to secular architecture that in preceding centuries had been almost entirely devoted to the building of temples. Assembly halls, gymnasiums, houses of council (*bouleuterion*), etc. received exceptionally rich architectural decoration, though it is a striking fact that this decoration was confined to interiors. The *Bouleuterion* of Miletus, for example, with the stark severity of its walls, presents a forbidding face to the world. Each feature (temple entrance, porticoed quadrangle with the tomb, and — if not externally, at least on the inside — the council house itself) is axially planned. This axial design and ordered symmetry of the scheme as a whole are characteristic of Hellenistic architecture.

b

b) THE AESCULAPION OF COS
Second century B.C. *Restored, Schazmann.*

The axiality and symmetry of Hellenistic architecture are even more rigorously applied in the terracing of the precincts of this temple. Each terrace is like a prologue to the last, on which the great temple stands as the point of climax and spiritual centerpiece. The principal axis, rising from the entrance block and following the stairways, also achieves its consummation in the temple. The symmetrical design and organization of the temenos is essentially a Hellenistic achievement. Ancient precincts present an accumulation of isolated buildings, each independently conceived and with no apparent relation to the others. The reason for this difference is probably that whereas ancient precincts were developed gradually in the course of centuries, those of Hellenistic times were designed, so to speak, in one piece.

c) THE MARKET PLACE OF ASSOS
Third – second century B.C. *Restored, Bacon.*

Market places are always the focal point of urban life, and during the Hellenistic age the agora was given a new architectural splendor. The agora of the little town of Assos, though it does not show the regularity of design found in other towns, conveys some idea of the richness of treatment once common to many such market places.

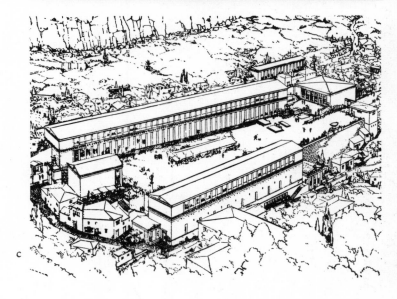

c

III
ROMAN ARCHITECTURE

Historical Background

Roman civilization, and consequently Roman art itself, differed widely from the civilization and the art of Greece.

The very phrase Roman art implies fundamental differences. The Greeks were a hybrid race. Their cities, often competing for power, each maintained an individual character, and art for them was a bond of contact and a common ground for the expression of their national genius. Roman art, on the other hand, was from the beginning the product of one city — Rome. It was imposed as the official art and adopted in every outpost of the empire.

Wherever it is found — in Gaul, Germania, Britain or Spain, in North Africa, Egypt, Syria, Asia Minor or Greece — it is not to be regarded as a spontaneous expression of the people but as an importation of the native art of the ruling class: the Roman conquerors.

As the art of the empire, it became the symbol and manifestation of a political situation: the world supremacy of

Rome. It is no coincidence that Roman art took root at the moment when the Roman Empire began to expand and cover not only extensive regions hitherto uncivilized but also the Mediterranean states, with their Hellenic culture—in short, at the moment when the Romans' thirst for power and conquest found fulfillment. Only then, influenced by treasures snatched at random from conquered provinces and accumulated in Rome, did men begin to feel the need to cultivate those very arts and sciences they had scorned in the past.

But the growth and realization of this need did not stem from true appreciation or genuine interest, and still less from any deep feeling for these things. The Romans saw art merely as a means of confirming and advertising their own leadership. Their attitude to art had always been different from that of the Greeks. To them, art was not valuable for its own sake but only for its potentialities as propaganda. It is significant that the poet Virgil (70–19 B.C.) once said that other races (referring particularly to the Greeks) might surpass the Romans in casting bronze and carving marble and be more skilled, too, in rhetoric, but "... *tu regere imperio populos, Romane, memento!*" ("Thou, O Roman, remember that thy destiny is to rule over all peoples!") That is, Rome's purpose lay not in promoting the arts but in steadfastly carrying out her political program. For centuries the history of the Roman people was colored by this dictum, and art never became an end in itself. This attitude is perhaps even more vividly expressed by Cicero, the great orator and statesman (106–43 B.C.), when he said that any move to gain the favor of the Roman people must, by word or deed, be distinguished by the grandeur and the great practical advantages of its motives.

This love of splendor—this craving for the grandiose and feeling for the practical so characteristic of Roman civilization—is reflected in Roman art. It is not surprising that architecture took the lead over the other arts, for its range of possibilities gave the Romans an opportunity to satisfy their taste for the practical and at the same time to exploit their love of magnificence. It could also provide the scope for painted and sculptural decoration. Here, however, lay the danger of lapsing into grandiloquence and pomposity, for the temptation to overelaborate was one the Romans found difficult to resist.

The Greeks, even during the Hellenistic age, sought to make their buildings works of art by means of pure architectural form, by simplicity and breadth of style, but the Romans were easily seduced by purely decorative effects, and in this respect their use of ornament is particularly revealing. In Greek building, ornament is always organi-cally related to the construction and often demonstrates unseen static forces. Even when used solely as decoration in frieze or molding, ornament is strictly controlled and never allowed to become obtrusive. Now the Roman love of flamboyance regarded ornament principally as a decorative adjunct, with no deep significance. It would be applied where, for the Greeks, it would have had no justification. Equally significant is the fact that the column—originally conceived as a supporting member and a structural necessity in temple architecture—was now also treated as a decorative element. Whether freestanding in front of a building or in the form of an engaged half column, its sole purpose was to delight the eye. It may be said without exaggeration that while the Greeks sought inner meaning, the Romans were content with outward appearance. Being concerned with superficial effects and eager to give their buildings an air of luxury and richness, the Romans would not hesitate to hide inferior materials behind a coating of stucco jointed to look like ashlar masonry.

However, in making these comparisons, it would be wrong to deprecate the quality of Roman art which, irrespective of esthetic merit, is valuable because it reflects the spirit of an age and the character of the Roman people. Moreover, in spite of the license with which the Romans treated architectural forms, their buildings never lacked nobility of concept. The luxurious grandeur so dear to the Roman heart was achieved with no loss of structural integrity. The astonishing impact still made by Roman monuments—an impact not only due to their colossal scale and antiquity—is surely proof in itself of the greatness of this architecture. Discovery of new forms played little part in the artistic achievement of the Romans, for, as will be seen, the Greeks and Etruscans provided most of their prototypes. To their credit, however, is the fact that they did not limit their architectural activity to a few selected channels but applied it to every aspect of their lives: an achievement which was to have profound consequences and was to produce works of art with functions that would have been unknown to the Greeks. It is important to remember that the Romans regarded art as an essential part of life and they consequently encouraged artistic activity wherever they went within their vast empire. Though the monuments scattered over the empire only rarely attained to the richness of those built in Roman cities and by comparison were modest and provincial, they were to be of vital importance. Through these buildings, a knowledge of stone construction spread across large areas of Europe. Without their example, the development of architecture in this part of the world might have taken a very different course, following the tradition of timber construction.

It has already been observed that the emergence of Roman art coincided with the beginnings of her empire. Until that time the Romans had been preoccupied with military conquests. Rome had developed from a small community founded on the banks of the Tiber in 753 B.C. by a few resolute and now legendary men and had become a great city — the heart of a vast empire. At first the Romans concentrated on establishing their supremacy in Italy, conquering the Etruscan communities and taking over what is now Tuscany (fourth–third century B.C.).

Next followed the subjugation of southern Italy, with its prosperous Greek cities, all of which still belonged to the Carthaginian enemy overseas (Sicily in 241; Spain in 201 B.C.). Simultaneously, driven on by ambition, the Romans turned eastward. After several attempts, they finally defeated Macedonia, and under pretext of arbitrating internal quarrels, took command of the Greek cities. Corinth and Carthage fell in 146 B.C. When the Hellenistic kingdoms of Asia Minor, Syria and eventually Egypt came under her rule, Rome's triumph was complete and her mastery of the world established. The Romans continued to extend their frontiers into northern Europe, though they failed to subjugate the Teutonic tribes protected by the dense forests of Germany.

Roman conquest brought the Mediterranean peoples into servitude but it also brought peace. Formerly, kingdoms, cities and confederations had coexisted in ill-disguised antagonism, indulging in terrible warfare from time to time. The Pax Romana, once instituted, put an end to strife but did not at first result in prosperity, for the Romans were merciless in their plundering of conquered lands and took full possession of the vast wealth that poured in from every quarter. At the height of their power, they were suddenly exposed to the influence of Greece, and having the necessary means, felt the need to form some sort of cultural background for their own political achievements. Having no tradition worthy of the name upon which to base this creative ambition, the Romans took the line of least resistance by adopting the Greek tradition and making themselves the inheritors of Greek culture.

At first this process was conducted somewhat crudely: Marcellus ordered that the most beautiful works of art from Syracuse (conquered 212 B.C.) be brought to Rome to adorn the capital; Aemilius Paulus, after his crowning victory over Philip of Macedon, carried off war plunder of more than 250 chariotloads of sculptures and *objets d'art*. Not until the first century B.C., when this blind lust for riches was appeased, did the Romans fully appreciate the true value of their heritage.

Then the poet Horace (65–8 B.C.) was able to declare that vanquished Greece had prevailed over the barbarians because she had planted the seed of art in the land of her conquerors.

The process of assimilation was certainly made easier by the fact that the Romans took late Hellenistic, not classical, art as their model, finding the richer decorative forms more sympathetic than the stark simplicity of the classical style. Inevitably they left the mark of their own character on this artistic revival. During the age of Augustus (27 B.C. – 14 A.D.) the influence of classical Greek art was felt more strongly, especially in the field of sculpture. This must first be explained in the light of the many-sided character of Roman art, formed of numerous interpenetrating stylistic trends of widely differing origins. Ultimately, however, this transitory enthusiasm for classical Greece was a result of the prevailing taste of that time when a style had to be found that would be worthy of the emperor and the new era of peace and order he had introduced. The classical style was manifestly more suited to express the new ideals than were the baroque forms of Hellenistic art. The emperor's own attitude to architecture is clearly revealed in his account of the rebuilding of Rome, when he proudly tells how he transformed a town of brick into a marble city equal in splendor to those of the Hellenistic East.

Rome soon became a rallying point for numerous Greek artists, for the new regime offered untold opportunities. There were no artists of merit among the Romans themselves and Greek sculptors and architects were much in demand. The Romans were not satisfied with the countless works of art brought home by the conquerors and eagerly began to have these copied and reproduced. There is no doubt that at first and for some time to come Greek artists were employed to do this work, and it may be assumed that both architecture and sculpture were produced in this way. In fact, the two earliest marble temples in Rome — the Temple of Jupiter Stator and that of Juno Regina on the Capitol (146 B.C.) — were built by the Greek architect Hermodorus of Salamis. However, it is curious to find that the buildings and particularly the works of sculpture produced in Rome are quite different in character, not only from their Greek prototypes but also from works executed in Greece during the same period, and already betray a marked Roman quality. The Greeks themselves, living in Rome, absorbed something of its peculiar vitality and power, and meanwhile more and more Roman artists were taking part in its artistic activity. Proving excellent pupils, they soon equaled their masters and in many respects eventually outstripped them.

Rome's assimilation of Greek art was of momentous significance, for this formal language became the basis of all Roman art and was to remain so throughout the centuries. The Early Christian churches were a product of Roman architectural forms, and themselves paved the way for the buildings of the Middle Ages. When Renaissance artists took Roman antiquity as their ideal, they were nonetheless returning ultimately to Greek art, which thus lived on and was perpetuated in other styles. The true ancestor of all Western architecture is that of Greece, and Roman architecture must be regarded as the great intermediary force by whose means those ancient forms were handed down to posterity.

Roman Construction

From the second century B. C. and to an even greater extent during the first century, Roman architects were faced with a program of building such as had never been known before. Their works were to be unprecedented in grandeur of scale and in sheer richness of decoration. There is no need to dwell at length on the construction of the world-famous aqueducts or the Colosseum in Rome to realize that the structural techniques introduced and disseminated by the Hellenistic Greeks — their ashlar masonry and columnar architecture — by no means provided the solidity and firmness required for the vast constructional feats of the Romans. One of the aims of Roman architects was to give their buildings a grandeur that would be a proud expression of their own power, but their chief concern was to make their work immortal through structural perfection. Throughout their ancient empire, the scattered ruins that still defy the ravages of time are enough to show how close the Romans came to achieving their purpose. Ashlar masonry construction in the Greek and Etruscan traditions was employed for buildings of normal size, while stone rubble was also frequently used at the beginning of the empire. However, it was not long before the Romans turned to the general use of concrete for the sake of its strength and durability. This technique was first used at the end of the second century B. C.

The external faces of concrete walls were finished in various ways to give them a more pleasing appearance. For example, walls were often covered with a layer of carefully cut stones, with the joints emphasized by specially worked margins (Fig. 14). The stones themselves were seldom brought to a smooth finish but were left with a rock-faced or rusticated effect. The lively texture produced by this technique was more congenial to the Roman temperament than the immaculate masonry of the Greeks, who produced joints so fine as to be scarcely visible and whose walls still have a monolithic appearance. Although the Romans did not use smooth masonry as such, they were able to produce a similar effect by rough-and-ready means. One of these was the so-called *opus incertum* or *antiquum*, a description by which the Romans implied a primitive or rough technique. This consisted of pieces of stone embedded in concrete, with their irregularities brought to a flush face with mortar. In this system, carefully dressed stones

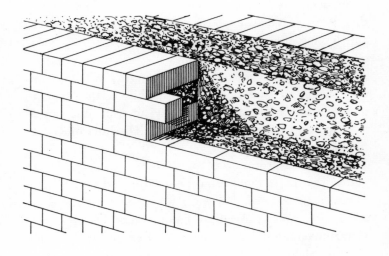

14. *Stone facing to a concrete wall.*

were used only for the quoins, while narrow band courses of bricks were used both to give variety and to contribute to the strength of the work.

Brickwork first appeared in Roman building at the end of the Republican era, about 50 B. C. Bricks were at first of irregular shapes, but later, when made in molds, were produced as rectangular blocks from 1 to 2 inches thick and from 8 to 12 inches long. They proved to be an excellent building material, being cheap and easy to make, and were soon widely adopted. Nevertheless, Roman buildings made entirely of brick (opus testaceum) are comparatively rare.

As an economy of time and material and in order to obtain greater strength, it was usual to build a brick facing consisting of poured concrete on either side of a central mass. The facings were keyed into the core by allowing the bricks to tail into the concrete, the bricks themselves lying on beds of mortar often as much as 1½ inches thick. The finished appearance was lively and attractive, with the contrast of pale joints and the deep red of the bricks. There were several other facing systems. One of the most popular was the opus reticulatum (reticulate scheme). This consisted of wide bands faced with small squared stones set diamond fashion so that in the finished work the joints formed a lattice pattern from which the name derives. In the opus spicatum (herringbone system) — a relatively late development — the decorative bands are made up of stones lying diagonally in alternate directions, producing a herringbone design.

It is because of the strong connection with Greece, where the column had had such supreme importance, that one inevitably thinks first of columnar building when considering the elements of construction in Roman architecture. Though the Romans adopted columnar architecture with important modifications, it was only in building temples that they were able to keep to the simple Greek system. The reason for this was that the column, being the principal element of temple construction, could here retain its function as a supporting member. But in larger buildings of several stories such as theatres and amphitheatres, with their ever-increasing size, columns alone could no longer carry the great weights involved. That is why the column lost its functional role and became solely a decorative device, often taking the form of an engaged half column. Deprived of any practical purpose, it might well have disappeared altogether, but it did survive and flourish in a decorative capacity. Moreover, it was used to express structural forces otherwise hidden within the building. Similarly, the entablature, also borrowed from Greek temple construction, was deprived of its structural im-

portance by the Romans and while basically retaining its Greek form, was chiefly treated as a horizontal molding and compositional motif. For example, it might be used on the exterior of a building to stress the internal divisions between the stories. Both column and cornice were now treated with a new freedom. Later, columns were placed on pedestals to increase their height and thus accentuate their decorative quality, while the projection of entablature over columns was greatly exaggerated. Complete entablatures, with architrave, frieze and cornice, were sometimes placed over freestanding columns supporting a row of arches. Clearly these elements had lost their original significance and were no longer structural necessities but ornamental motifs that could be omitted.

The Roman predilection for the arch and the vault also had far-reaching effects. It was these features rather than those borrowed from Greek temples which determined the character of Roman architecture. Though they were the first to exploit fully and to standardize these structural systems, the Romans did not invent them. Both arch and barrel vault (the simplest kind of vault, equivalent to a series of arches placed one behind the other) had been known in the ancient civilizations of Egypt and Mesopotamia, where gateways, narrow passageways and canals were frequently spanned in this way (a drainage canal discovered at Nippur, Mesopotamia, must date from about 4000 B. C.). The remains of these early constructions show that the method of building an arch with wedge-shaped blocks or voussoir had already been evolved. Stone was seldom used in Mesopotamia, where sun-dried bricks were the common material. Positive evidence is supplied by the interesting representations of vaulting in several Assyrian bas-reliefs (dating from between 1000 B. C. and 600 B. C.) which show houses of circular, polygonal or, more rarely, square plan, roofed by hemispherical or similarly shaped domes (Glossary). It is unlikely, however, that the Romans knew of these early vaults of Mesopotamia, which, after this modest first appearance, followed an independent and steady course of development culminating in the domed Byzantine basilicas (sixth–seventh century A. D.) and in the great Moslem mosques. Nor are there sufficient grounds for supposing that the Hellenistic Greeks ever showed any inclination to develop this aspect of architecture. Though they were familiar with arch, barrel vault and dome, and occasionally carried them out to perfection — as in their town gateways (Priene) and in several tombs at Pergamum — the Greeks never gave true architectural importance to this structural system; compared with the columnar style which took precedence over all, these forms remained rare.

It was quite otherwise with the Etruscans — a people whose history is still shrouded in mystery. Probably coming from Asia Minor, they arrived in Central Italy about 1000 B.C., where between the eighth and the fourth centuries they established a number of prosperous towns, only to be subjugated finally and absorbed by their neighbors the Romans in the third century B.C. Long before the Romans, these Etruscans had made use of the arch and vault and may well have learned these structural methods in their native land. Arched, barrel-vaulted and domed construction was employed in their town gates (Volterra, Porta Marzia in Perugia), small bridges (bridge at Bulicame, Viterbo), underground canals, and above all in their tombs, which resembled houses and had sumptuously decorated interiors. The Etruscans did not at first use wedge-shaped blocks but corbeled out each course of stones from the one beneath until an arch was formed when the two sides met — the "false" vaulting system (Glossary). Under the influence of the Greeks, who had settled in southern Italy, wedge-shaped stones were adopted at a relatively early date.

The Romans were not slow to profit by the skill of the Etruscans. The Temple of Jupiter on the Capitol in Rome (completed 509 B.C.) is known to have been decorated by an Etruscan artist, Volca da Veii, and it is probable that the architects, too, were chosen from among his fellow countrymen. There is no doubt that the Romans acquired their knowledge of arched and vaulted construction from the Etruscans. The first systematic use of this method of building occurred at a time when the rich architectural forms of the Greek style had hardly begun to arouse interest among the Roman people.

The first known examples of monumental arches were those which bore the colossal Aqua Marcia over the hills as it carried water fifty-six miles from the Sabine Mountains to Rome. These were built between 144 and 140 B.C. The great arches of the Pons Aemilius, the first stone bridge to be built in Rome, were erected in 142 B.C. Subsequently arches and vaults were used for other types of building and the Romans exploited every technical and esthetic possibility of the arcuated system.

Although they brought to it the added resources of poured concrete, they frequently carried out their vaults in cut stone or brick masonry. A remarkable example is the great stone barrel vault which survives in part at the Temple of Diana, Nîmes, and which was probably built in the second century B.C. But for various reasons concrete construction was favored — two early examples of this method are the vaults of the thermae at Pompeii (end of the second century B.C.) and those of the Tabularium in Rome (completed 78 B.C.) — the primary advantage being the greater speed of erection as compared with masonry vaulting. Furthermore, the use of concrete made possible the covering of wide spans, and greater stability could be obtained through the continuity and compactness of the material. In stone vaulting, the material exerts a powerful lateral, as well as a downward, thrust; each stone acts on the one below and tends to overturn the supporting walls, which must be made heavy enough to resist this force or (as in Gothic architecture) be supported on the outside by buttressing. But in concrete vaulting, this lateral thrust is considerably reduced, with the result that the maximum thrust is the downward one. The constructional problem is therefore more easily resolved. Moreover, the Roman builders reduced the dead weight of their great vaults by making their concrete of light volcanic stones (tufa), broken bricks or even hollow clay pots. But even by these methods lateral thrusts could not be eliminated and they were familiar with the need for buttressing. The semiliquid condition of newly poured concrete presents one of the major practical difficulties in vault construction. From the first century B.C., the Romans met this problem by introducing a reinforcement of regularly spaced brick arches built on the timber centering, the intervening spaces being filled with poured concrete (Fig. 15). There is little doubt that these brick ribs were mainly designed, not to strengthen the vault, but to assist in the handling of concrete while it was still fresh and liquid, and to keep the mass under control until it had set, when they became superfluous. It was only in later Roman work that "true" vaulting ribs made their appearance.

Much later in development than barrel vaults and domes, the cross or groined vault came into use during the second century A.D. This is formed by two barrel vaults of equal height intersecting at right angles, producing sharp edges or groins from which the name derives. The Romans used this vaulting method on an enormous scale, to roof their thermae and basilicas. One of the practical advantages of the cross vault and one of the chief reasons for its use was that its weight and thrust were concentrated almost exclusively on the four points on which the vault rested and not on the whole length of the side walls, as is the case with barrel vaults and domes. Thus the walling between the supporting piers could be made lighter, with more and larger openings. The possibilities of this new discovery were to be fully realized in the course of the Middle Ages.

Vaulted roofs were predominantly used for public buildings and palaces and seldom employed for temples except in the case of later monuments of circular form. The great barrel vault adopted by the Emperor Diocletian at the beginning of the fourth century A. D. for the temple of his palace at Spalato is a late and important exception. It was only in the decline of the empire that Roman builders ventured to break away from the traditional trabeated form for the design of temples, their love of splendor finding an alternative means of expression in the rich modeling and coloring of coffered vaults.

Architectural Character

The architectural system of the Greeks was suited neither to the monumental scale on which the Romans, equipped with new technical means, were to build, nor to the expression of the national love of power. It has already been observed that the essential elements of Greek temple architecture (column and entablature) were adopted by the Romans for their own temples and retained their original significance, but that in other types of building these features were given little more than a decorative function. Column and entablature were still treated as a unity but were handled with new freedom. While the Greeks distinguished clearly between the three orders, the Romans would unhesitatingly combine the elements of one with those of another. For example, the Doric entablature might receive the Ionic architrave with three fasciae and row of dentils, and similarly the elements of a Doric entablature might surmount Corinthian columns and capitals.

Ornamental motifs such as the frieze of triglyphs lost their original structural significance — a process that had already begun during the Hellenistic period. In a classical Greek temple there is one triglyph to each column and one to every intercolumniation, whereas in a Roman frieze there may be as many as three to every intercolumniation.

The delicate problem of triglyph adjustment was now disregarded and in general it mattered little to Roman builders if the frieze was terminated by a half metope (Fig. 16).

Doric columns themselves were subject to several important changes. The Romans added a base or a simple fillet and gave them the height and elegance of Ionic or Corinthian columns. They were sometimes unfluted and had no entasis. A projecting astragal took the place of the narrow grooved rings at the necking. The capital was resolved into a shallow ovolo occasionally enriched with

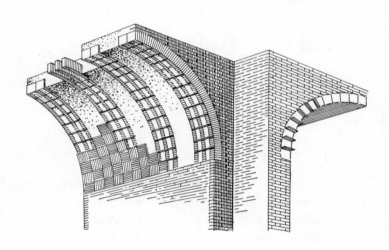

15. Construction of a concrete wall with brick ribs.

the egg and dart or egg and tongue and carrying a molded abacus (Fig. 16). The Roman Doric order and its simplified version known as Tuscan were used occasionally and sparingly. Doric forms were too severely simple to be compatible with the Roman passion for decorative splendor, and the more ornate Ionic and Corinthian orders were favored. Under the empire, the Corinthian order flourished everywhere. The capitals (Fig. 17) were carved with an abundance of foliage, not always with happy effect. During the first century A. D. on the Arch of Titus in Rome appeared the first example of the combination of Corinthian capital with the volutes and egg-and-dart decoration

16. The Roman Doric order.

of the Ionic order, comprising the typically Roman Composite capital. In their desire for richness of effect, the Romans lost sight of the original significance of the Corinthian capital which to the Greeks had justified its use: the stems that had sprung up to the angles of the abacus — perfectly expressing the relationship between the column

and the load on the abacus — were now suppressed. When, in the second and third centuries, human figures and even animals were carved on the capital, pure ornament had finally taken the place of strictly architectural decoration.

The arch, rather than column and entablature, became the characteristic feature of Roman construction. It was impossible to abandon the traditional trabeated form altogether, particularly in the design of temples, but wherever columns could no longer serve as supporting members — as in structures several stories high — arches were used and column and entablature became merely decorative elements. Even in the second and first centuries B. C. during the Republican period, the arcade was the type of construction most in evidence. Used in the first place for bridges and aqueducts, it was later employed as a decorative motif on the outer walls of the Tabularium in Rome (completed 78 B.C.). Here the arches are framed with engaged columns carrying an entablature, and all later theatres and amphitheatres, as well as many porticoes and basilicas, are externally decorated with several rows of arches separated by engaged columns. From the outset, the Romans pursued a regular system for superimposing the orders, the lowest story receiving the Doric, the second the Ionic, the third the Corinthian. In some Hellenistic work also, an Ionic colonnade was sometimes used above a range of Doric columns, but it was for the Romans to elaborate this invention hinted at by the Greeks, and to found a tradition which was to form the character of columnar architecture, not only during the classical age, but through the Renaissance and into modern times. The system appears for the

17. Development of the Roman Corinthian capital: left to right — Corinthian; Composite; elaborated form of the Composite capital.

first time in the Theatre of Marcellus in Rome (13–11 B.C.) and is to be seen in its most complete form in the Flavian Amphitheatre (the Colosseum, inaugurated 80 A.D.) where the fourth story is decorated with Corinthian pilasters (Fig. 18).

Arches were used less freely on the interiors of buildings. There are examples of arches resting on detached columns and forming continuous arcades, but this treatment was never given a prime importance. Here was an opportunity for the column to play a new part as supporting member,

but the Romans preferred to retain the ancient trabeated forms. This may have been for practical rather than esthetic reasons, since beamed construction was probably cheaper and easier to achieve.

18. The Colosseum, Rome, showing superimposed orders, 80 A.D.

The Development of Roman Architecture

The development of Roman architecture may be divided into three stages which correspond with the three great periods of Rome's history:

1. *The Republic.* The Republican government was introduced in 509 B.C. and lasted until the accession of Augustus, the first emperor, in 27 B.C. Until Rome's world supremacy had been established by the conquest of the Hellenistic states of Greece, Asia Minor, Syria and Egypt in the second century B.C., there were apparently no great developments in architecture. From what remains, it is evident that during this period methods of building and the builders themselves were of Etruscan origin. From the second half of the second century, Hellenistic elements began to exert a more powerful influence, and in the course of the first century the old Etruscan forms underwent a reinterpretation in the light of the Greek style. At the same time, the first great monuments were erected: aqueducts, bridges, theatres, basilicas and temples, and concrete and brick began to be used commonly.

2. *The Empire.* This extended from Augustus (27 B.C.) to the first Christian emperor, Constantine (306 A.D.). From the point of view of architectural development, it may be subdivided into separate periods: the Augustan, the Flavian, that of the Emperors Trajan and Hadrian, and finally that of Antoninus and the third century. The Augustan age (until 14 A.D.) was a period of intense architectural activity when there was a conscious return to the

style of classical Greece. It was the boast of Augustus that he had found Rome a town of brick and had left it a city of marble. Now, to an increasing extent, marble was employed in place of travertine and brick, while stucco was also widely used. Stately, massive forms and structural solidity were the characteristics of this somewhat coldly derivative architecture. During the Flavian period (Vespasian, Titus, Domitian, 70–96), classic severity was abandoned for a richer and more decorative style. Under the Emperors Trajan (98–117) and Hadrian (117–138), there was again a tendency toward a more rigid classicism (exemplified in the Pantheon, Rome), but side by side with this flourished the baroque element (Hadrian's Villa at Tivoli which was to gather force during the reign of Antoninus in the last sixty years of the second century and to lead to the extravagance and overdecoration of third-century architecture. There followed a decline in craftsmanship and a degeneration of architectural forms that coincided with and was accelerated by the growing provincialism of the empire which saw the erection of many large monuments in cities far from the center of power. The Emperor Diocletian (284–305) built his palace, not in Rome but at Spalato. By this time there was mounting unrest within the empire and the supremacy of Rome already hung in the balance.

3. *The Byzantine Empire.* During the two centuries between the reigns of Constantine (306–337) and Justinian (527–565) the Roman Empire was divided into east and west. In 330, the capital was removed from Rome to Constantinople (Byzantium). Architects were no longer required to attempt the monumental projects of former times, and in the west — adopting the forms of Roman architecture — they undertook new tasks, chief among which was the construction of the Early Christian churches. The spirit of these works was very different from that which had inspired the great monuments of Roman antiquity. The same situation prevailed in the Eastern empire where (from the fifth century onward) the Byzantine style was to be evolved.

Structures

Far from being limited to Rome itself, the architectural style of the Romans spread to every corner of the empire, and so many monuments have survived that it would be impossible to describe them all. The past grandeur of Rome is still reflected in many great buildings, but these consti-

tute only a fragment of the splendors of the city in the time of Constantine (beginning of the fourth century). With a population of one million, the capital abounded in temples, theatres, amphitheatres and porticoes. There were 1,790 palaces of differing sizes, 11 vast thermae and 856 smaller baths. Eight bridges spanned the Tiber and 11 aqueducts supplied the city with water. In the large provincial centers the situation must have been much the same, though neither in number nor size can the buildings have ever compared with those of the "golden city." The remains that have come down to us are comparatively few, but the 70 amphitheatres still extant show the extent to which the Romans propagated their art and their way of life. The following is a brief and general description of the various aspects of Roman architecture, illustrated with reference to several of the most outstanding examples.

TEMPLES

From the outset, Roman temple architecture was different from that of Greece. In its pure form, the cella was not enclosed within a colonnade. At the beginning of the Republican period, Roman temples — like their Etruscan prototypes — had a simple portico in front of the entrance and this was sometimes continued around the sides of the cella. But there was no colonnade on the rear façade. The plan of the Temple of Jupiter Capitolinus (509 B.C.), of which only the foundations remain, demonstrates this distinctive feature (Fig. 19). The rear wall of the cella itself formed the back elevation. It was evidently felt that there was no

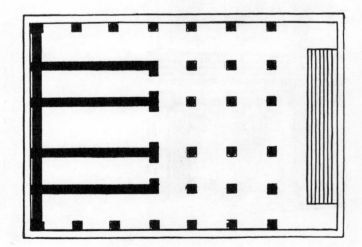

19. Plan of the Temple of Jupiter, Rome, Capitol, 509 B.C.

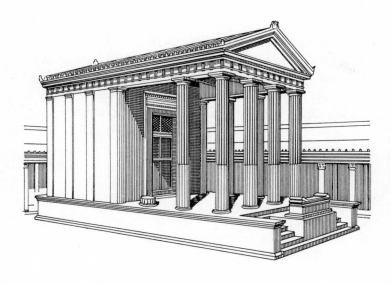

20. Doric Temple at Cori, beginning of first century B.C. *Restored by Delbrueck.*

need to attract attention at this point, once the cella had been enclosed. This insistence on the directional plan of the temple was further emphasized by the fact that the building stood, not on a continuous stylobate like those of Greek temples, but on a high podium with steps only in front of the entrance. Similarly the deep portico, with its three bays of columns, underlined the building's axiality. Even when (second century B.C.) the influence of Greece led to certain external alterations and the Romans abandoned the short Etruscan plan of the Temple of Jupiter for the more elongated Greek type or gave the cella a surrounding colonnade, these features — podium, steps, deep portico and positive alignment — remained characteristic of their temple architecture.

Little is known of the construction methods used in Etruscan or Etrusco-Roman temples, for their superstructures were built entirely or almost entirely of wood. However, according to Vitruvius and as revealed by a number of Etruscan funerary urns in the form of houses, these temples were of trabeated design and bore some resemblance to Greek temples, on which they were probably based. Numerous discoveries have shown that they were externally decorated with a rich covering of terra cotta which, in spite of some detailing reminiscent of Greek work, had a positive national character. At the end of the Republican period, a decisive change took place in Roman temples when the more primitive exterior treatment was replaced by Greek elements.

The Doric temple at Cori (beginning of the first century B.C., Fig. 20) illustrates this change. The podium, the steps

and the portico, which is almost as long as the square cella, keep their Etruscan character. The inner rows of columns before the entrance have now disappeared. The columns are a variation on Doric (Fig. 16); there is a Doric entablature with triglyph frieze and shallow architrave, and the triangular pediment is Greek in feeling. However, it is important to notice that the basic Greek forms have already undergone a transformation. Not only are the columns set on small bases but they have the slender grace of the Ionic or Corinthian. The entablature, where the frieze of triglyphs has also been treated in an unorthodox fashion, is so shallow that the effect is one of elegance in comparison with Greek prototypes. Furthermore, the pediment is higher than those of Greek temples. Important also is the fact that at the temple at Cori the cella walls are flush with the sides of the podium and are decorated with pilasters in line with the columns of the portico, so that the whole temple is enclosed. This is the pseudoperipteral form, manifestly derived from Greek models, which the Romans subsequently used for many of their temples. It was most perfectly expressed in the temple at Nîmes, known as the Maison Carrée, which was built in 16 B.C. (page 65). That the Romans were deeply influenced by the Greeks is again indicated by the fact that several of their large temples with podia have a complete peristyle. The Temple of Castor and Pollux (the Dioscuri) on the Forum Romanum (rebuilt by Tiberius) is one example (page 66). Nevertheless, these temples were not mere copies of the Greek peripteral form; they retained their distinctive Roman features, as well as the deep portico in the Etruscan manner.

It was also toward the end of the Republican era that an important change took place in temple interiors. The side walls were enriched with columns and niches containing statues (page 68 a) — in later examples orders of columns being superimposed — and frequently the rear wall, where the cult image was placed, received a domed semicircular apse. This never formed a projection on the exterior, as was usually the case in Early Christian churches, but was embedded in the wall thickness or independently constructed within the building. Thus the whole interior space was given a positive direction and the principle which had been applied to the exterior was extended throughout the plan.

Small circular temples similar to the Greek tholoi of the fourth century B.C. were particularly popular with the Romans. Usually these, too, stood on a podium and had steps in front of the entrance, giving access to the circular portico and cella (page 71). The Pantheon, temple of all the gods, completed in Hadrian's time (c. 120–130 A.D.), must be regarded as the consummation of circular building construction and is one of the noblest works of Roman architecture. The building comprises a vast rotunda with a rectangular portico of columns like that of a conventional temple. Externally, the Pantheon has hardly any ornament and is simply divided by horizontal moldings expressing the disposition of the interior. All the architectural richness of this temple is concentrated on the interior where marble columns, niches, great semicircular recesses and exedrae within the wall thickness — and above all the vast coffered dome — contribute to a truly magnificent effect. Now the building is shorn of the marble sheathing and stucco decoration which in the days of Imperial Rome glowed richly as daylight streamed in through the oculus in the top of the dome.

The future development of architecture is foretold in the growing emphasis on interior decoration and disregard for the exterior which had formerly been of such importance in religious buildings. After tentative beginnings, this trend was to culminate in the architectural concept of the fourth-century Christian basilicas, where the emphasis was placed entirely on the interior.

THEATRES, AMPHITHEATRES AND CIRCUSES

The Romans, a practical and worldly people, did not give religious building the importance accorded it by the Greeks. They merely acknowledged the presence of the gods whom the Greeks had believed to rule their destinies. It is not surprising that religious feeling had no strong hold on a people who regarded their emperors rather than the gods as the source of all well-being — hence the popular cry of *"panem et circenses."* The emperors met these demands by building great monuments such as theatres, amphitheatres and circuses where the Romans could fully indulge their passion for spectacular entertainment.

From the outset, Roman theatres were modeled on their Hellenistic Greek counterparts and consisted of a rectangular scaena, often several stories high and decorated with colonnades, and a semicircular orchestra surrounded by tiers of seats. However, the Romans diverged from Greek models both by increasing the amount of decoration on the scaena wall (page 75, c and d) and in their method of constructing the auditorium. Instead of hollowing it out of a hillside, they built up the tiers of seats on a level site like the scaena itself. This forced them to find a suitable expression for the exposed exterior, several stories high, and a system of roundheaded arches between engaged columns or pilas-

ters was devised, as in the Theatre of Marcellus at Rome (11 B.C., page 75 b). The stage was raised and brought into immediate architectural connection with the auditorium, so that it was possible to cover the smaller theatres with a single timber roof. These formed the prototypes for present-day theatres. The largest structures, like the first stone theatre in Rome (which held 40,000 spectators and was built by Pompey, 61–51 B.C.), were left uncovered. Vast canvas awnings suspended from ropes sheltered the spectators from the sun, and the stage was protected by a wooden covering. The whole of the scaena wall of the great theatre at Orange (c. 50 A.D.) is still extant, and on it remain the corbel stones and notches which once held the velarium poles and secured the scaena roof (page 75 c).

Typical of Roman life and character are the great amphitheatres where terrible displays of mortal combat took place, including animal baiting, gladiatorial contests, and later, the martyrdom of Christians. Though even in ruin these monuments compel awe and admiration and reflect the grandeur of conception of which the Romans were capable, it should not be forgotten that they were built to satisfy a brutal and barbaric streak in the Roman character. There was no need for an enclosed stage for spectacles like these, and huge crowds of spectators necessitated the enlargement of the seating space. The orchestra therefore took the form of an elliptical arena surrounded on all sides by rising tiers of seats. This plan was adopted for the oldest known amphitheatre, built in Pompeii about 70 B.C. (page 76 b), and for the remaining sixty-nine that have been discovered in the Roman Empire.

The most magnificent example is the Flavian Amphitheatre, known as the Colosseum, which was solemnly inaugurated by Titus in 80 A.D. and remains, even in ruins, one of the most impressive works of Roman architecture (pages 76 a and 77). The external façade shows the same system of decoration as that developed for theatres. The three lower stories are pierced with round arches forming a continuous arcade around the building and divided by attached columns of the Doric, Ionic and Corinthian orders superimposed on the respective stories. The top story, added later, has Corinthian pilasters. Inside, each story corresponded to an established stratum of Roman society. Staircases connected the tiers and gave access to the seats. The approaches were so arranged that nearly 60,000 spectators were able to take their seats and later vacate the amphitheatre in a very short time. Below the arena were dens for the wild beasts, cells and rooms for the gladiators. An ingenious flooding system allowed the arena to be used for naval displays (naumachiae) or crocodile hunts. It is by stupendous proportions and structural splendor alone that the Colosseum creates such an impression today, for it was used as a fortress and plundered during the following centuries and has lost all its decorative richness. Formerly, bronze medallions glittered on the wall surfaces and marble statues stood out of the shadows of the arcades on the two upper stories. The interior, too, was rich with marble sheathing.

The Roman circus was a long hairpin-shaped structure based on the Greek hippodrome and was designed for chariot and horse races. Tiers of seats like those of an amphitheatre surrounded a narrow arena, down the middle of which ran a dividing wall (the spina) adorned with statues and obelisks. At one end of the arena was an architectural screen forming an entrance for contestants, and at the other the tiers of seats followed the plan of the track. The Circus Maximus in Rome, rebuilt in the first century B.C. and subsequently much altered, measured about 2,000 feet long and 650 feet wide and held 250,000 spectators. This great building has long since disappeared (page 76 c).

BASILICAS

The community life of Roman towns centered around the market square or forum — in Rome itself the ancient center was the Forum Romanum, followed by the forums of succeeding emperors — and the principal civic building was the basilica, used as a hall of justice and commercial exchange. The origin of this type of building is somewhat obscure, but the name clearly derives from the Stoa Basileios, the portico at the west side of the agora of ancient Athens. Like their Greek prototype, Roman basilicas were of columniated design but soon took on the character of Roman architecture because of the use of arches in place of the post and beams of the Greeks.

No remains of the earliest basilicas have come down to us, though there is circumstantial evidence for their existence. Of the Basilica Porcia (built in Rome by the elder Cato, 184 B. C.) and three similar buildings erected in the second and early first centuries B.C., nothing now exists. The plan of the oldest known basilica (built at Pompeii, c. 80 B.C., Fig. 21) shows certain features common to those of later date which cannot be traced to Greek origins. The elongated rectangle of the exterior is repeated on the interior by a colonnade around all four sides, dividing the central nave from the side aisles. If it may be assumed that the nave of the Pompeian basilica was covered, as in all later examples, it was certainly carried to a greater height than the aisles and provided with clerestory windows. This basilican, stepped cross section remained an essential characteristic of these buildings in Roman times and was adopted by the early Christians. The two ends of the Pompeian basilica seem to have had a definite relationship to each other. At one end was the main entrance; at the other a raised rectangular podium enclosed by columns. This tribunal, which in other buildings took the form of a

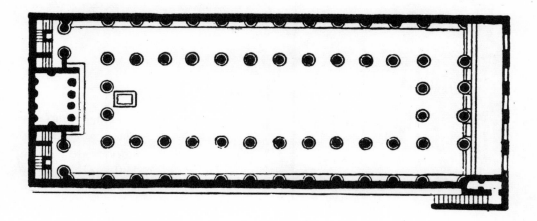

21. Plan of the Pompeian Basilica, c. 80 B.C.

semicircular apse, served as a court of law, and its position opposite the entrance was designed to give the interior of the basilica a directional emphasis similar to that of the temples. The fact, however, that a uniform architectural treatment was accorded to the sides as well as to the ends of the nave somewhat reduced the importance of the longitudinal axis in the basilica. In the Basilica Julia on the Forum Romanum (begun by Julius Caesar, completed in the reign of Augustus, 14 A.D.), no emphasis was given to the tribunal. On the other hand, the importance of the central nave was accentuated by the two-storied aisles with which it was surrounded (Fig. 22). The five-aisled Basilica Ulpia, also of two stories, was built on the Forum of Trajan about 112 A.D. Lying across the forum (Fig. 24), this basilica had its entrances in the centers of the long sides, and the ends were symmetrically terminated by two large apsidal exedrae. These, lying behind the double colonnades of the side aisles, had no specific function.

It was only with the construction of the basilica begun by Maxentius on the Forum Romanum and completed by Constantine in 313 that a plan was made with the deliberate object of opposing the entrance and the apse at either end of a major axis. The awe-inspiring scale of this gigantic basilica may be judged from the fact that its plan would comfortably contain that of Cologne Cathedral. The nave was covered by three great cross vaults, while the side aisles were each divided into three bays, barrel vaulted at right angles to the nave (Fig. 23). Thus no colonnades were interposed between entrance and apse. In completing the

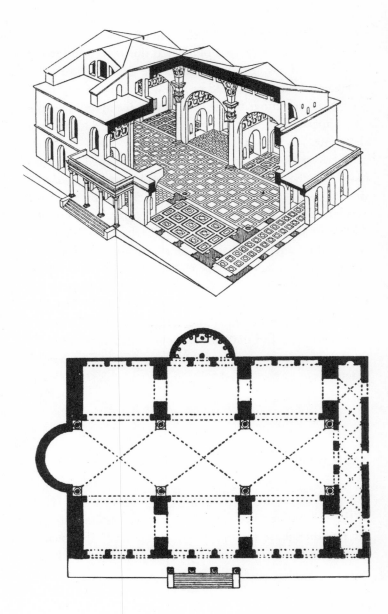

23. Basilica of Maxentius, sectional view and plan. Forum Romanum, completed 313 A.D.

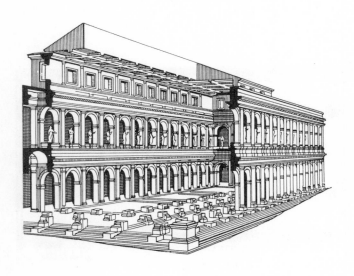

22. Sectional view of the Basilica Julia, Forum Romanum, c. 14 A.D.

building, Constantine — disregarding the original axis — placed a second entrance in the middle of one of the long sides, with a second apse opposite to it, thus giving the building another axis at right angles to the first. This development, however, did not mean the general abandonment of the typical basilica plan, with its directional emphasis, which was to achieve its most perfect expression in the Early Christian churches of the fourth century.

THE IMPERIAL FORUMS

At the end of the Republican period and especially during the empire, the Romans adopted the principles evolved by the Hellenistic Greeks for the ordering of groups of public buildings and their surroundings. The most fundamental of these principles — axiality, symmetry and the subordination of all parts to some central dominant feature — retained their importance and were particularly applied to the planning of temple precincts and the imperial forums in Rome, while they also governed the arrangement of Roman bathing establishments (thermae) and palaces.

The ancient market place of Rome, the Forum Romanum, had no predetermined plan but gradually developed in the course of time, and the buildings grouped around it were not architecturally related to each other (page 79 a). The site of the Forum, laid out in the valley between the Seven Hills of Rome, was relatively small and eventually became so overcrowded with buildings that it could no longer accommodate the imposing new monuments which were to serve the needs of a steadily increasing population. Julius Caesar was the first to take steps to resolve this dilemma by building (54 B. C.) a new forum on the north side of the Forum Romanum. This was a large open square surrounded on all four sides by a porticus containing shops. The plan of the Forum of Julius Caesar was followed in those built by succeeding emperors, though the temple was subsequently placed at the farthest end, thus accentuating the strictly axial planning. Characteristic examples are the Forum of Augustus, the temple of which was dedicated in the year 2 B.C.; that of Nerva, completed about 98 A.D.; and the Forum of Trajan. That built by Vespasian is believed to have followed the same scheme, though no remains of the temple have yet been found.

The Forum of Trajan (Fig. 24), designed by Apollodorus of Damascus and solemnly inaugurated in 113, was the last imperial forum to be built and was the largest and by far the most magnificent. It was entered through a triumphal gateway on which stood the bronze horses that are now above the portal of St. Mark's in Venice. Beyond lay a great rectangular court in the middle of which was a bronze equestrian monument to the emperor. There were covered porticoes on each long side, and to right and left — separated from the main court by avenues — were two immense hemicycles, several stories high, of shops and offices. The farther side of the forum was occupied by the great five-aisled Ulpian basilica, which is particularly remarkable because its main axis lies at right

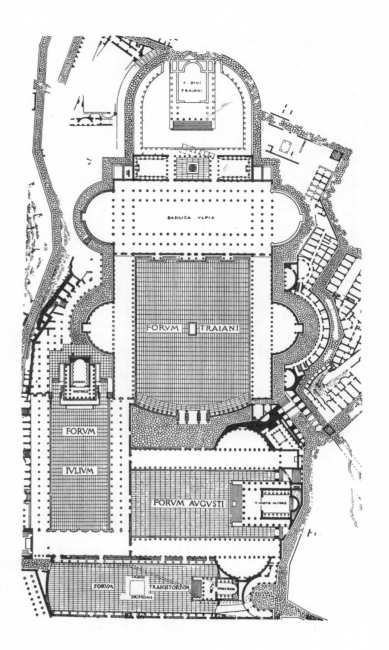

24. Plan of the imperial forums in Rome.

angles to that of the forum, thus apparently disrupting the axial relationship between the forum entrance and the temple. Though it is conceived as an independent entity and forms a break in the vast scheme, the basilica is an essential and enriching part of a complex architectural composition, for it gives the secular section of the forum a

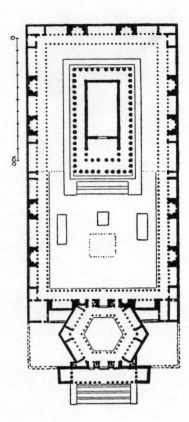

25. *Plan of the temple precincts at Heliopolis (Baalbek), Syria, second century* A.D.

THERMAE

No public buildings, whether theatres, amphitheatres, basilicas or temples, were given a more sumptuous architectural treatment than the empire's great bathing establishments known as thermae. Every town was provided with its own baths, and even in the colder provinces of the north, where the climate did not necessitate frequent bathing, the utmost care was given to their construction. Though these vast establishments were primarily built to serve a practical need, the thermae of Imperial Rome far exceeded their original purpose. The central structure containing the baths themselves was usually surrounded by a large open court (often as much as 24 acres) containing grass plots and shaded alleys. Parts of this area were reserved for various athletic sports and games, and opposite the entrance there would sometimes be raised seats for spectators (as in the Thermae of Caracalla, Rome). Disposed symmetrically to left and right of this enclosure were various apartments including libraries, lecture rooms, conference halls, rooms for games and entertainments, and even galleries for paintings and sculpture collections. The thermae were thus not only designed for bathing but served as centers for a social life which included bacchanalian orgies as well as more intellectual pleasures.

new relationship to the temple. The tendency (revealed in the Forum of Trajan) to enhance the impression of vastness and magnificence by greater complexity of planning was to become increasingly evident in Roman architecture.

Secular and sacred precincts were interrelated on the forum, and the temple formed an architectural and spiritual climax to the whole concept. However, to understand the full significance of the Roman forum and its relationship to the temple, it is important to remember that the temple in the Forum of Julius Caesar was dedicated to the emperor's own family goddess, Venus Genetrix, and that after his death, the Emperor Trajan was himself worshiped as a god in the temple on his forum. Thus the forum, too, was the material expression of Roman rule in which the emperor held the supreme position and the temple itself became a glorification, not of religion but of imperial power. The gigantic temple group at Heliopolis (Baalbek, Syria, 980 by 380 feet), erected during the second century, demonstrates that the precincts of true temples were sometimes planned on a scale as grand as that of the forums (Fig. 25).

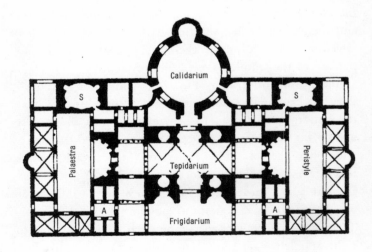

26. *Plan of the Baths of Caracalla, Rome, c. 215* A.D.

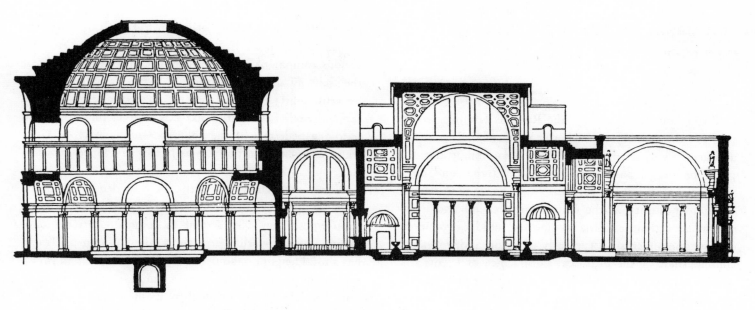

27. *The Baths of Caracalla, Rome, c. 215* A.D. *Section, restored by Köpf.*

Little now remains of the countless thermae once scattered over the whole of the empire or of the vast and magnificent establishments built in Rome by Nero, Titus, Trajan, Caracalla, Diocletian and Constantine. However, enough exists to show that the central structure always followed the same plan, though in size and degree of splendor the thermae varied considerably — those of Diocletian being the largest of all and those of Caracalla the most sumptuously decorated. When the Stabian Baths at Pompeii were first built (*c.* 120 B.C.), the rooms devoted to bathing were arranged side by side in no apparent order. Under the empire, they were rearranged according to the more usual plan, clearly illustrated in the Thermae of Caracalla (*c.* 215). The baths were entered through two halls on either side of a huge unheated swimming bath (the frigidarium), and opening off these halls were the dressing rooms (apodyteria). Beyond subsidiary rooms for washing and oiling lay a warm lounge containing small tepid baths (the tepidarium). At the far end of the central block was the circular hall of the hot room with hot-water baths (the calidarium). From the calidarium, bathers would return to the frigidarium and thence to the apodyteria. Both calidarium and tepidarium were heated by hypocausts, spaces contrived under the floor of the hall and connected to furnaces. The floor was generally raised on small brick pillars, and the heated air was directed along the walls in terra cotta channels, so that the whole room could be kept at a high temperature (Fig. 27).

As shown (Fig. 26), the three chief apartments were grouped together across the whole width of the thermae, forming a central axis about which all the other rooms were arranged with mechanical symmetry. On each side there would be a steam bath (sudatorium), rooms for oiling and massage, and a palaestra, used for physical exercise, particularly before bathing. The whole vast scheme was thus subordinated to a main axis formed by the alignment of the principal rooms. Each room was conceived as part of an architectural sequence culminating in the calidarium (Fig. 27) where the great dome gave added importance to the central axis. The frigidarium was covered with a flat roof or was left open to the sky. The tepidarium (183 by 79 feet) was roofed with an immense cross vault in three compartments, while the calidarium had a great dome about 110 feet in diameter. The section illustrated (Figure 27) shows how the progression from frigidarium to calidarium was consciously expressed in the heights of the rooms, which mount to a climax in the dome. Roman thermae may be compared with the imperial forums, for, like these, they comprised an elaborate assemblage of parts brought into relationship through their organization about the main axes. Like the basilica on the Forum of Trajan, the frigidarium and calidarium have their lengths at right angles to the directional axis of the scheme. The decoration of the interiors was of the utmost richness. Floors paved with mosaics and inlaid with marble, walls encrusted with painted stucco, vaults ornamented with deep coffering, and statues and marble colonnades gave these great halls an opulence that was never to be surpassed.

TRIUMPHAL ARCHES AND PILLARS
OF VICTORY

Throughout their history, the Romans felt the need to preserve the memory of the heroic deeds of their emperors and generals. Contemporary events were immortalized in panel paintings, bas-reliefs, triumphal arches and decorated commemorative columns, and were thus handed down to posterity as the material expression and living examples of greatness. The passion for building commemorative monuments is typically Roman and reveals a consciousness of the historical significance of events that would have been completely foreign to the Greeks, who gave more importance to myth and legend.

Nothing remains of Roman historical painting, and the only relief sculptures extant are those which decorate triumphal arches and columns. Monumental arches are known to have existed in the Republican period. They took the form of great wooden gateways, and their original function was to provide an entrance to the formal route taken by victorious armies and their generals proceeding in triumph through the Forum to the Temple of Jupiter Capitolinus. In the days of Imperial Rome, these arches came to be built of stone, in order to achieve their permanence as commemorative monuments and symbols of triumph, and the habit of erecting them to current heroes soon spread to all parts of the empire. About one hundred triumphal arches have come down to us, of which the most important are in Rome itself. They are among the best works of Roman architecture, and their forms derive from their original role as monumental gateways. The Arch of Titus (pages 86 and 87), erected by the senate and people of Rome in 81 A.D. after the death of the emperor, is barrel vaulted and coherent and simple in design. Above a high plinth on each side, engaged Composite columns and entablature articulate the decorative scheme. Above the cornice is a small upper story called the attic, which balances the composition and bears the dedicatory inscription on its front face. The monument, like all other triumphal arches, was originally surmounted by a bronze quadriga with the emperor's statue or figures of Victory.

The arch with three openings, where the central vault is flanked by smaller passageways, was more frequently employed than the single-opening type. The Arches of Septimius Severus (203) and Constantine (c. 315) are of the triple-arch type (page 87 a, b). The richness of their decoration and their structure in general indicate that a development from the classical simplicity of the Arch of Titus was already taking place. In the Arch of Titus, the adornment of bas-reliefs representing the emperor's victorious campaigns had been confined to the side walls of the archway and to the spandrels. In the Arch of Septimius Severus, while the fundamental conception remains the same, the relief decoration extends all over the façade and onto the pedestals of the columns. In the Arch of Constantine, even the attic story is partly enveloped in sculpture.

Pillars of victory were usually intended to hold the emperor's cinerary urn and were based on ancient Oriental prototypes. They also served as commemorative monuments. These towerlike structures (the Column of Trajan has a total height of about 150 feet) were set on high pedestals which contained the tomb chamber, and at the summit — on a platform reached by a spiral staircase within the shaft — stood the bronze statue of the emperor. The two well-preserved columns of Trajan (c. 113) and Marcus Aurelius (c. 180) are decorated with bands of bas-reliefs (over 800 feet long) which wind around their great shafts and represent the victorious campaigns of the emperors in the utmost detail and with an almost unbelievable realism (page 88).

HOUSES AND PALACES

With their love of luxury and all the benefits of civilization, it was to be expected that the Romans would decorate their houses with the greatest care and elaboration. Not content with mere convenience, they used every resource of art to enhance the domestic scene. Remarkable evidence of this has been provided by the excavations at Pompeii. Once a flourishing provincial town, Pompeii was buried under deposits of volcanic ash at the eruption of Vesuvius (79 A.D.). The upper parts, as well as the foundations of many of the houses, have thus been preserved almost intact, making a precise reconstruction possible. These houses are to be considered as typical examples of Roman domestic building, but it should be remembered that they represent only the form that was prevalent until 79 A.D. and that there may well have been later unknown modifications to the type, though these are not likely to have been significant.

The Roman house differed radically from the accepted standards of today in that it was detached from the outside world, having no façade decoration and very little window lighting. All effects were concentrated on the interior, and in this respect Roman houses recall those of the Greeks and Etruscans, from which they derive. The rooms of the earliest Pompeian dwellings, dating from the third century B.C., were symmetrically arranged around a central, uncovered court or atrium in the middle of which was a tank (the impluvium) to catch rain water. The atrium was always the most important feature of a Roman house and had its origin in Etruscan models, as seen, for example, in the cinerary urn in the form of a house found at Chiusi (Fig. 28).

From the second century B.C., this early plan underwent a vital change under Hellenistic influence. Although the atrium surrounded by living quarters retained its importance, a second open court was added behind the tablinum or open living room. This rear portion or peristyle was surrounded by a colonnaded walk, following Greek precedent (Fig. 29), and enclosed a garden with flower beds and fountains. Around the peristyle were grouped various apartments, including a reception room (oecus), dining rooms (triclinia), parlors (exedrae), the lararium,

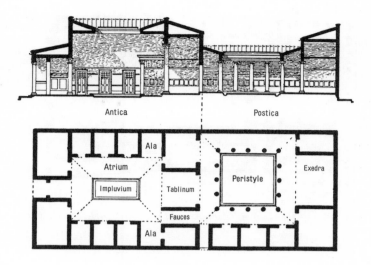

Antica   Postica

Ala

Atrium   Peristyle   Exedra

Impluvium   Tablinum

Fauces

Ala

29. *Section and plan of a Pompeian house.*

where the effigies of the household gods were placed, and rooms for games and play. Thus the fully developed Roman house consisted of two main sections — the forepart derived from the Etruscans (antica) and the rear portion from the Greeks (postica). It must not be assumed on the evidence of Pompeian examples that Roman houses were never more than one or two stories high, for it has been shown that there were multistoried apartment blocks in Rome. The height of these can be assessed from the fact that Augustus once placed a restriction of 68 feet upon them. The Roman tenement, however, is not important in the history of architecture. Even in the two-storied Pompeian "villa," the upper section was of little significance and all architectural interest was concentrated on the ground floor.

Living rooms and reception rooms were richly decorated: floors were laid with patterned mosaics of colored marble, and delicately painted frescoes covered the walls. Roman fresco decoration is important to this study because it constituted a vital and characteristic part of the house and served to broaden and enrich the whole architectural conception. This type of painting is found chiefly at Pompeii, and is thus commonly known as Pompeian wall painting, but it was also widely employed in Rome and the provinces. There are four distinct styles of decoration. The first belongs to the second century B.C. and was derived directly from Greece, consisting of the division of the wall surface into panels of painted or modeled stucco. After about 100 B.C., stucco decoration was abandoned

28. *Etruscan cinerary urn in the form of a house, Chiusi.*

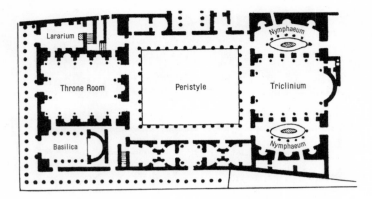

30. Plan of the Flavian Palace, Rome, Palatine. Completed 81–96 A.D.

and the second style shows panels of paintings framed in realistic architectural elements such as colonnades and entablatures, and complete spatial scenes with glimpses of the sky beyond. These paintings are strikingly modern in character. They give the illusion of a view seen through a window, breaking down the enclosing walls of the room to reveal illimitable vistas.

By the middle of the first century B.C. with the advent of the third style, walls were no longer dissolved with *trompe-l'oeil* effects but were painted with a frame of slender and insubstantial architectural elements, as artificial as the human figures which appear here and there among them. In the fourth phase (from *c.* 50 A.D.), there was a return to the *trompe-l'oeil* decoration of the second style, though the former colored line-drawing technique gave way to the heightened realism of soft, impressionistic painting. The whole body of the wall is treated in architectural terms, infused with atmosphere and peopled with figures, while there are often vistas onto garden landscapes of an almost magical charm. The background architecture is sometimes accidentally asymmetrical, giving an added realism to these paintings, though more often a strict balance of elements is maintained.

As might be expected, the villas of the richest Roman officials and the imperial palaces were on a far grander scale than the houses of ordinary citizens. Almost invariably, however, they followed the same general plan and had a similar arrangement of rooms. The entrance became an imposingly spacious vestibule, and the atrium an ample, colonnaded courtyard. The peristyle enclosed magnificent gardens, and in addition to the ordinary rooms there were often large libraries, picture galleries and theatres. Almost every villa was equipped with its own bathroom suite, and many also had a palaestra. The plan of the Flavian Palace (Fig. 30) on the Palatine Hill (com-

pleted by the Emperor Domitian, 81–96 A.D.) is very similar to that of a Roman house but on a grand scale. The state suite was begun by Augustus. Beyond the portico, raised on a massive substructure, lay three great entrance portals, that on the left leading to the lararium and that on the right to the basilica where the emperors administered justice. In the center was the entrance to a magnificent throne room (135 by 117 feet) roofed by a coffered barrel vault and decorated with niches and colonnades on the side walls. The emperor's throne stood in a recess in the end wall. Directly beyond the throne room lay a vast peristyle (188 by 172 feet) with private apartments opening off it on either side. The emperor's own apartment was situated, with the great triclinium or banqueting hall, in the rear of the palace. The triclinium was flanked by arcades looking out onto fountains.

Not all palaces corresponded to this rigid pattern plan. That of Diocletian (built at Spalato after his retirement, *c.* 300) in no way resembles an ordinary Roman villa (Fig. 31). The emperor, famous for his military achievements, gave his palace the character of a Roman camp. A vast rectangle occupying eight acres was divided into four portions by two broad avenues crossing at right angles (*cardo et decumanus*). An imposing arcaded gallery faced the Adriatic, and the other three sides were heavily fortified by walls and towers. Each square formed by the crossing streets was wholly or partly surrounded by colonnades. The two northern sections consisted of living quarters for

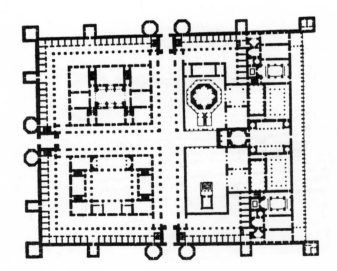

31. Plan of the Palace of Diocletian, Spalato, c. 300 A.D.

the guards and the imperial retinue, while the southern portion was devoted to the imperial apartments. These were disposed with perfect symmetry about a large atrium and splendid vestibule preceded by a porch. Projecting beyond the porch on either side were two courts, that on the right containing a temple, and that on the left Diocletian's Mausoleum. The Palace of Diocletian offers yet another example of Roman axial planning.

TOMBS

The Roman feeling for the monumental is manifest even in tomb architecture. It was the custom of the poor to bury their dead in subterranean vaults, in use chiefly during the later period. The ashes of the deceased were contained in urns placed within small rectangular or semi-circular niches in the rock. They were called columbaria because of their resemblance to dovecotes. Wealthy citizens were not usually buried in underground tombs but built themselves grand mausoleums that had more value as status symbols. These tombs lined the main roads outside the town gates, as on the Street of Tombs in Pompeii — a characteristic example of such Roman cemeteries. The Romans had several classes of burial places, largely due to the fact that they so readily assimilated the customs and habits of conquered races, including different funeral customs. Thus, in addition to tombs in the form of temples and altars, there are simple funerary columns like those of the East, direct versions or variations on Egyptian pyramids (Pyramid of Cestius at Rome) and massive tombs descended from the sepulchral tumuli of the Etruscans. These tumuli consisted of large cylindrical stone blocks containing the burial chamber, surmounted by a conical mound of earth or stone (page 91 a). This was the form given to the Mausoleum of Augustus, which he erected for himself in Rome in 28 B.C. Only the shell of the drum still exists, but from ancient descriptions it is known to have supported a mound of earth planted with cypresses and evergreens and crowned with a colossal statue of the emperor.

Another interesting example of this type is the Tomb of Caecilia Metella (c. 10 B.C.) on the Via Appia (page 90), converted into a battlemented fortress during the Middle Ages. One of the most important of these tumulus tombs is the Mausoleum of Hadrian (erected by him in Rome, c. 135), now known as the Castle of S. Angelo. The drum-shaped mass rising from a high square podium is still visible (page 91 c). It was once surrounded by a colonnade and marble statues and surmounted by a stone mound. The whole edifice was capped by a cylindrical tower which served as a platform for the gilded bronze quadriga of the emperor.

AQUEDUCTS, BRIDGES AND FORTIFICATIONS

Roman works of an engineering or purely utilitarian character are significant. These structures, in which ornament plays little part, are of timeless importance because they reveal the full extent of Roman constructional skill. The great aqueducts, sometimes formed of several tiers of arches, are landmarks in the valleys and plains of the empire. They supplied water for countless public fountains and thermae, often stretching considerable distances (the Aqua Marcia was over 30 miles long). The nobility of scale which the Romans achieved in their aqueducts may be seen in the Pont du Gard near Nîmes (dating probably from the first century A.D.), its magnificent, perfectly proportioned arches opening out like monumental gateways (the total height is about 160 feet), or in the Aqueduct at Segovia in Spain, supported on massive, closely spaced arches for over half a mile (page 92).

Roman bridges are also notable for their simple and solid construction. The Romans were the first to use masonry arches for the purpose of river crossings, though they attempted this only when arches had been successfully employed in the building of the Aqua Marcia (144 B.C.). Of the Pons Aemilius in Rome (142 B.C.), the first bridge to be supported on such arches in place of the early timber construction, only the foundations exist in the Ponte Rotto. But the Pons Mulvius, now known as the Ponte Molle (built 109 B.C.), is in an excellent state of preservation and provides the basis for our knowledge of early Roman bridge construction.

Roman fortifications built for the protection of towns throughout the empire are also of considerable architectural significance. As might be expected, the defensive gateway was the most notable architectural feature of these structures. A splendid example of Roman town gateways is the Porta Nigra (page 94), erected at Trèves about 300 A.D., which forms part of the protective wall surrounding an area of about one square mile.

Historical Significance
of Roman Architecture

Any evaluation of the architecture of ancient Rome would be incomplete without some appraisal of its effects on the future development of the art. Enough has already been said to indicate that the Roman contribution was not on a high level of esthetic originality. In this respect, they were content to draw from the work of other peoples, notably the Greeks, adapting it to their own needs. They excelled the Greeks in their practical application of architecture to a variety of purposes, in their feeling for the monumental and the magnificent, and in their devotion to utility and efficiency. Their arched and vaulted constructions were to provide the canon for the future of European architecture. Their wide-ranging invention and the variety of the motifs they employed have inspired architects ever since, and have provided a vocabulary of architectural forms that was to serve Europe for 2,000 years. This was their primary achievement. Moreover, it was

Rome that inspired the revival of architecture after the Dark Ages and in the fifteenth century, while the monuments of Greek antiquity remained unknown or disregarded until the end of the eighteenth century.

In addition, the Romans mastered a task the Greeks had never attempted: the enclosure and architectural modeling of space. The Greeks had always devoted their attention to the refinement of architectural forms and to the sculptural quality of their buildings, but the Romans were absorbed in the problems of structure and the creation of noble interiors. The spatial effects attained in the thermae and the great villas and palaces were unknown to the Greeks, whose interest was centered on simplifying and perfecting the vertical and horizontal elements (column and entablature) with which they enclosed spaces, without much concern for the quality of the space enclosed. This space was a mere foil for the architectural fabric. The Romans, on the other hand, ceaselessly and indefatigably took space itself as their medium, giving it a character dominating that of the enclosing shell. The Romans, who inherited a plastic architecture from the Greeks, transformed it into an art of space and so determined the role that it was to play throughout European history.

ROMAN ARCHITECTURE

ILLUSTRATIONS

a

b

c

MAISON CARRÉE, NÎMES
16 B.C.

This temple is in an excellent state of preservation and demonstrates all those qualities which distinguish Roman temples from those of Greece. Before the entrance is a flight of steps flanked by walls formed by the extended sides of a high podium. There is a deep porch, like those of Etruscan temples, in front of the cella entrance. But at the sides and at the back the cella walls are brought forward to the edge of the podium, leaving no room for the surrounding portico always found in Greek peripteral temples. However, the column motif is retained out of respect for Greek models, and the effect of a peripteros is produced by the engaged columns attached to the walls of the cella. Nevertheless, this building does not have the self-contained character of a Greek peripteral temple, where every side appears to be of equal importance. The flight of steps and the fusion of the porch with the cella (manifestly closed on all but one side) give the temple an unmistakable directional emphasis. In detail and as a whole, the Maison Carrée has the clarity and simplicity of Greek architecture, comparing favorably in this respect with later Roman temples. It may be considered a typical product of the Augustan age. The style of this time was powerful enough to spread to the provinces of the empire, though it later gave way to more decorative baroque forms. (Facing page and Fig. a.)

b) THE TEMPLE OF MINERVA, ASSISI
c. 40 B.C.

The temple stands on a podium and has a hexastyle porch of the Corinthian order which completely replaced Roman Doric and Ionic at the outset of the Imperial age. The columns, capitals, entablature and pediment are treated with a simplicity that reveals a close attachment to Greek prototypes, and the whole is conceived in the same spirit as the Maison Carrée — the spirit of the Augustan era, when Rome was most open to the influence of classical Greece. The fact that the temple at Assisi was built while Rome was still under the republic would seem to prove that this spirit was not exclusively fostered in the courtly circles of imperial Rome but had already taken root during the preceding decades. The pedestals on which the columns are set are a typically Roman feature. Between them, the steps of the podium lead up to the platform proper where the cella stands, thus destroying any organic relationship between substructure and column.

c) THE TEMPLE OF ANTONINUS AND FAUSTINA, ROME
Forum Romanum, 141 A.D.

The temple stands on a high podium and was built by the Emperor Antoninus in memory of his wife Faustina. Thus it was not strictly a religious building, but like many other Roman temples, was a monument erected to the memory of a person whose rank had entitled him to be deified. Cut on the architrave which surmounts the six unfluted monolithic columns of the façade is the inscription DIVAE FAVSTINAE EX S.C., another characteristically Roman feature.

COLUMNS AND ENTABLATURE
OF A ROMAN TEMPLE

*Left: part of the Temple of the Dioscuri, Forum Romanum,
dedicated 6 A.D.; restored c. 119;
right: part of the Temple of Apollo, from the Theatre of Marcellus, built 433 B.C.; entirely restored 32 B.C.*

The rendering of columns and entablature in both these temples exemplifies the rich treatment of the Corinthian order common in Roman architecture from the end of the first century B.C. Particularly noticeable is the exuberant decoration of frieze and cornice, even more elaborate than late Hellenistic examples (Figs. a, b); this treatment also extends to the capitals, though these are considerably damaged and most of the acanthus leaves have been broken away. Deep flute hollows enhance the light-and-shade effects on the column shafts of the Temple of Apollo. The high podium on which the columns stands is typically Roman. (Facing page.)

a, b) DETAILS OF ROMAN ENTABLATURES

*Above: Entablature of the Temple of Concord,
Forum Romanum, 7 B.C. – 10 A.D.;
below: Entablature of the Temple of Vespasian,
Forum Romanum, end of the second century A.D.*

In their temple architecture and especially in the working of entablatures, the Romans gave free rein to their taste for luxuriant decoration. The Greeks had always striven to keep decoration at a minimum, using it only where it could be given some architectural meaning. If pure ornament ever appears in Greek architecture, it is always restrained and unobtrusive. The Romans were less fastidious. The basic form of the entablature is undoubtedly inspired by Greek prototypes, for it consists of architrave, frieze and cornice, though the frieze was occasionally filled out with an elaborate decorative system, as in the Temple of Vespasian. The much earlier entablature of the Temple of Concord already demonstrates the characteristic avoidance of smooth surfaces, that *horror vacui* which led the Romans to decorate wherever it was possible. Ionic and Corinthian ornaments were most commonly used (egg and dart, dentils, palmettes, frets and modillions), but these were recklessly combined with Doric moldings and motifs and were richly elaborated and transformed.

In its later development, entablature decoration became increasingly complicated, as may be seen in the Temple of Vespasian. The surfaces between the modillions — left smooth in the Temple of Concord — are now covered with a double row of laurel leaves. Below the dentil course is a frieze adorned with trophies in relief, set between ox skulls. These ornaments are no longer carved in stone, but are modeled in stucco, a particularly popular material during the later period.

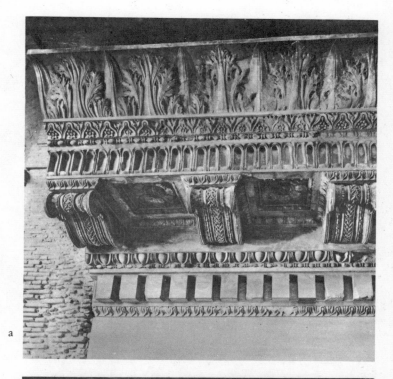

a

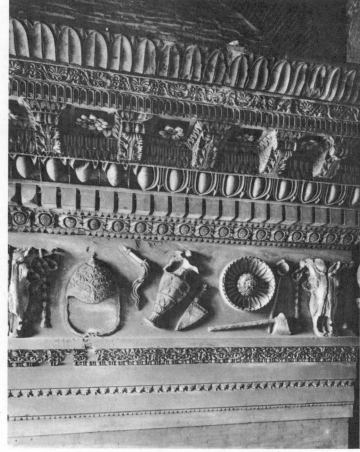

b

a

b

TEMPLE OF JUPITER, BAALBEK
Syria, first half of the first century A.D.

Temples and temple precincts built in the Roman provinces soon rivaled those of Rome itself in the grandeur and richness of their architecture. By far the most important of these precincts was that of Jupiter Optimus Maximus Heliopolitanus at Baalbek, where a gigantic peripteral temple formed the central feature (Fig. 25, page 56). The columns surrounding the cella proclaim that the ancient Greek ideals still exerted a powerful influence on this Hellenistic soil. The temple, however, was raised on a typically Roman podium. The size of the Temple of Jupiter, now almost totally destroyed, may be assessed from the scale of the few remaining columns and several other fragments. The columns are Corinthian and unfluted: including bases and capitals, they are about 65 feet high, and the entablature is more than 16 feet deep. The Temple of Bacchus (a, b below), built close by at a later date, is manifestly a close copy of the Temple of Jupiter and may provide some clue as to the construction of the cella, now utterly vanished. (Facing page.)

a, b) TEMPLE OF BACCHUS, BAALBEK
Syria, middle of the second century A.D.

From the end of the first century A.D., the cella walls of Roman temples were treated more and more elaborately. In this temple, for example, immense half columns were engaged to pilasters along each side wall, dividing the wall surfaces into vertical bands. Each band was articulated by two tiers of decoration, arched niches below and pedimental niches above. The back wall, too, was broken up with a mass of restless decorative elements. This reconstruction shows the cella covered with a flat roof, but the surviving fragments seem to indicate that it may once have had a huge barrel vault with a span of nearly 65 feet. This would be a rare example; temples were usually spanned by beams of wood. The adytum of Syrian temples is a characteristic feature. This was a recess in the end wall of the cella, where the cult statue stood. A staircase led up to it, and only priests were allowed to enter. In other Roman temples, the adytum consisted of an ordinary semicircular apse — a feature which does not occur in Greek temples and which was a means of giving the interior a directional emphasis equivalent to that of the outside of the building.

THE ROUND TEMPLE OF PORTUNUS, ROME
Forum Boarium, c. 31 B.C.

The tholos form was developed by the Greeks in the fourth century B.C. and consisted of a round cella within a colonnade. It was to this that the Romans returned when they built their small circular temples. The round temple on the Tiber, supposedly dedicated to Portunus (known to have had a temple in this neighborhood), is a particularly beautiful and characteristic example of the type. The whole of the entablature is unfortunately lost, making dating extremely hazardous. However, the working of the columns is in pure Greek tradition, and contrary to Roman custom, there is no podium, but a circular stepped base like those of the Greek tholoi — features which seem to point to a late Republican or early Imperial date. On the other hand, the ashlars in the wall of the cella, with their depressed edges, are typically Roman in treatment. (Facing page.)

a) THE TEMPLE OF VESTA, TIVOLI
c. 80 B.C.

The treatment of the Corinthian columns and especially the decoration of their capitals is inspired by Greek models. The entablature, too, is Greek in form. The frieze, a particularly characteristic feature, is adorned with ox skulls connected by heavy garlands, both Hellenistic motifs. The cella was possibly once roofed, with a low thin concrete dome.

b) THE TEMPLE OF VESTA, ROME
Forum Romanum, c. 200 A.D.

One of the most venerated of all Roman temples, this was traditionally founded in the pre-Republican era. It was rebuilt by Julia Domna, wife of Septimius Severus (193–212), and the temple as it now stands was part of this latest construction. There are a number of interesting variations on traditional forms. As usual the temple is raised on a podium, but this has been treated as a series of dies forming pedestals to the columns. The outer circular colonnade is echoed by engaged columns attached to the cella wall, giving an added richness to the scheme. The sacred fire of Vesta, goddess of the hearth, burned continually within the cella and was kept lighted by the Vestal Virgins. It was to this temple that the Romans came on New Year's Day, to light torches with which to rekindle the fires in their own homes.

c) THE ROUND TEMPLE AT BAALBEK
Syria, c. 250 A.D.

This small, round temple is the last stage in a development which began with the Temple of Vesta at Tivoli. The podium and entablature are designed in a series of concave loops, and deep niches are set into the outside wall of the cella. The building is no longer concentrated about its own center, but is a lively complex of advancing and receding forms. It exemplifies the elaborate picturesque style of late Roman architecture, a style that has no precedent in antiquity and was not seen again until the late baroque phase of the eighteenth century.

a

b

c

a

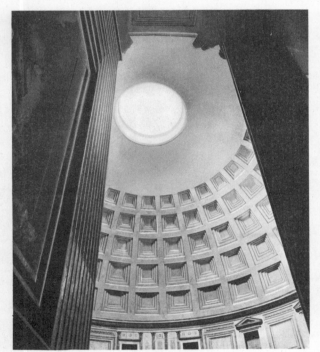

b

c

THE PANTHEON, ROME
Begun by Agrippa, c. 27 B.C.;
completed under Hadrian, c. 120 A.D.

Apart from the Temple of Fortuna Virilis, the Pantheon is the only monument in Rome that still stands intact. With the Colosseum, it is the best known of all the works of Roman antiquity. Almost nothing remains of the original structure. After a fire, the restoration was begun in Hadrian's time (*c.* 120 A.D.). The building owes its present appearance to this restoration and to several alterations carried out under Septimius Severus and Caracalla (beginning of the third century). There were no alterations when it was converted into the Church of Sta Maria ad Martyres by Pope Boniface IV in 609 A.D. The name Pantheon seems to imply that the temple was originally dedicated to several gods, probably to the seven planetary deities.

The exterior (Fig. a) shows a remarkable combination of two differently shaped building masses: the great portico, similar in treatment to those of rectangular temples, is set off against the principal circular mass. Giant monolithic columns on the façade support a low and almost graceful entablature. On the frieze, an inscription: M[arcus] AGRIPPA, L[ucii] F[ilius], CO[n]S[ul] TERTIVM FECIT, recalls the earlier structure. The façade, surmounted by an abnormally steep pediment, is remarkably simple and yet seems richly ornate when compared with the stark form of the rotunda rising above it. The rotunda is undecorated except for two horizontal bands which run around the walls like plain cornices and express the divisions between the interior stories. All the architectural splendor of the Pantheon is concentrated on the interior, one of the boldest and most perfect achievements in the whole history of architecture. The air of solemn calm and grandeur which pervades the great rotunda, as impressive today as it has ever been, is due as much to its perfect circularity as to the pure simplicity of its details and the magnificent proportions. Height and diameter correspond exactly — about 141 feet. Dome and substructure are both about 70 feet high — that is, each is equal to half the total height. The problem of lighting was overcome with ingenious skill: there are no windows to light this vast space, but the light streams in through a great circular opening (oculus) at the top of the coffered dome (Fig. b) and is thus ideally and evenly distributed throughout the building.

One can still visualize the beautiful effect of the Pantheon in its original state, with the light sparkling on the gilt bronze surfaces of the coffers in the dome, shining on the colored marble inlay of the substructure, and playing on the statues standing in the shadows of their niches. These niches are alternately curved and rectangular, with alternate semicircular and triangular pediments, and are flanked by Corinthian columns. The smaller niches higher up under the dome also once held statues. (Facing page and Fig. c.)

THEATRE AT SABRATA, NORTH AFRICA
Scaena wall, beginning of the third century A.D.

The theatre at Sabrata seated some 5,000 spectators and was probably built by Septimius Severus. The scaena wall was restored early in this century and is a magnificent example of the several-storied columnar architecture used for the scaenae of large theatres (Fig. d). The scheme of the three-storied colonnade is almost baroque in conception, and a lively and deliberately picturesque effect is achieved by a pattern of light and shade against the wall behind a gay variety of column shafts. All these features are characteristic of late Roman architecture. (Facing page.)

a) THE SMALL THEATRE AT POMPEII
c. 75 B.C.

The oldest surviving Roman theatre. Even in its fragmentary state, it throws much light on early Roman theatre construction. As shown, scaena and auditorium are closely linked together and form a single architectural whole, whereas in Greek theatres there was a complete break between them and they were treated as independent entities. When (as here) the two parts were united and built to the same height, it was possible — in smaller theatres — for the whole structure to be completely roofed in.

b) THE THEATRE OF MARCELLUS, ROME
Outer wall, completed 11 B.C.

Roman theatres were always conceived as freestanding structures and differ in this respect from their models, for Greek theatres were generally excavated in the side of a hill, so that no substructure was needed for the rising tiers of seats. The Romans, therefore, had to devise an architectural scheme to enclose tiers of corridors and staircases leading to the seats of the auditorium. Until the first century, Roman theatres were built of wood. The earliest stone construction, the theatre at Pompeii, is no longer extant, but much still remains of the exterior wall of the Theatre of Marcellus (begun under Caesar; completed by Augustus, 11 B.C.). This is especially significant because for the first time it demonstrates the use of an architectural system that was to have a far-reaching effect: the engaged columns on the lowest story are Doric, those on the second Ionic, and those on the third — now lost — were Corinthian. This sequence is not an arbitrary decorative device but shows that the Romans were aware of the different stages in the evolution of Greek styles and were deliberately bringing them together in a unified composition.

c, d) THE THEATRE AT ORANGE
c. 50 B.C.

Large theatres such as that at Orange in the South of France cannot have been completely roofed in. The scaena had a great wooden roof carried on the two return walls of the stage and on projecting piers in the scaena wall. Traces of this roof and the sinkings in which the timbers rested are still visible. The spectators were sheltered by enormous awnings hanging from cables.

a

b

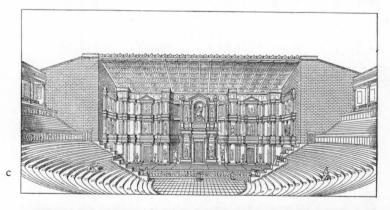

c

d

a

b

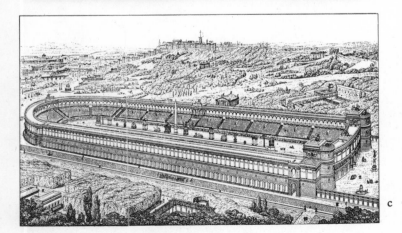

c

THE COLOSSEUM, ROME
Inaugurated 80 A.D.

This Flavian amphitheatre, begun by Vespasian and solemnly inaugurated by Titus, is one of the most important architectural enterprises of Roman antiquity and is the largest of the 70 amphitheatres known to have existed in the empire. The great oval structure, with tiers of seats rising all around the elliptical arena, is 617 feet long and 512 feet wide, with a circumference of 1,703 feet. The external façade — 157 feet 6 inches high — is divided into 4 stories, the first 3 of which (like those of the theatres already seen) are pierced with semicircular arches flanked by columns of different orders, while the fourth is a solid wall. The Colosseum is a perfect expression of the idea (practiced also in the Theatre of Marcellus) of using superimposed orders. The repetition of Corinthian on the top story is an added refinement. Here, characteristically, columns are replaced by pilasters, resulting in a much less plastic effect. The consoles projecting from the wall between these pilasters once held wooden masts driven into openings in the upper cornice and serving to secure the long ropes on which the awnings were hung across the auditorium. Statues stood in the arcaded openings of the two central stories, and the smooth wall surfaces were decorated with gilt bronze medallions. Inside, each story corresponded to a different class of society. Barrel-vaulted corridors ran all around the building, and numerous staircases connected the various levels and led to the seats. Today the vast and somewhat grotesque ruins betray almost nothing of the former decorative splendor of this extraordinary building. (Facing page and Fig. a.)

b) THE AMPHITHEATRE AT POMPEII
c. 70 B.C.

The earliest surviving amphitheatre. Its plan formed the type which was followed throughout the whole of the Roman period: oval arena, with huge entrances, surrounded on all sides by tiers of seats. Staircases radiating outward from the arena gave access to all parts of the auditorium. The lowest rows of seats were reserved for the more distinguished spectators and were rigidly segregated from those allocated to the middle classes and the poor.

c) CIRCUS MAXIMUS, ROME
Restored view.

Until the fourth century, the Circus Maximus was restored and enlarged many times. It measured about 2,000 feet long and 650 feet wide, and after its restoration in the first century, could accommodate 250,000 people, increasing to 385,000 in the fourth century. Like all other circuses, it was designed for chariot and horse races, sports for which the arenas of amphitheatres did not provide sufficient space. The hairpin track was surrounded by tiers of seats and divided down the middle by a wall adorned with obelisks and statues. At one end of the racecourse was the Porta Triumphalis.

THE BASILICA OF MAXENTIUS, ROME
Forum Romanum, 306–312 A.D.

a,b) THE FORUM ROMANUM
Restoration L. Levy and present state.

The civic life of Roman towns centered on the market place or forum. During the little-known period under the kings (eighth–sixth century B.C.), the market place of Rome was laid out in the narrow valley between the Palatine, Caelian, Esquiline, Quirinal and Capitoline hills, a marshy meadowland that in the course of the following centuries was to become the Forum Romanum.

From the second century B.C., as the power of Rome increased, the city's most important monuments were built on the Forum and became the symbols of Rome's dominance. Here, too, affairs of commerce were conducted and public questions debated. In the Curia Julia (I), the senate assembled to take vital decisions in time of crisis, and it was in the Forum that the first Roman Emperor, Augustus, received his title of Princeps. The public archives were preserved in the Tabularium (II), and in the little Temple of Vesta (III) the sacred fire was kept lighted (page 71 b). The sites of the early temples of wood were occupied by splendid marble buildings which popularized the worship of the gods and of the deified emperors. Among the most interesting buildings on the Forum (from the point of view of form and structure) are the Basilica Aemilia (X) and the Basilica Julia (XI). These great monuments served as commercial exchanges, with shops (tabernae) attached, and as halls of justice. The restoration shows them to be elongated rectangular structures, three stories high, externally decorated like theatres and amphitheatres, with semicircular arches resting on engaged columns. It must be observed that, unlike temples, the basilicas were not covered by a single roof span. The central aisle, which was carried to a greater height, was given a pitched roof, the side aisles being roofed at a lower level. This allowed the introduction of windows in the upper part of the nave — the clerestory. Colonnades separated nave and aisles. The basilican plan varied considerably and reached its greatest magnificence in the basilica commenced by Maxentius in the Forum Romanum (306) and finished by Constantine (after 312 A.D.).

Even in ruins, this is one of the most impressive of all Roman monuments. The great barrel vaults of the north aisle (illustrated here) were placed transversely, to resist the thrust of the main groined vault, parts of the springing of which are still visible. Today the Forum Romanum reveals nothing of its former splendor but is a moving reflection of the tragic fate of Roman civilization. Gutted walls and fallen columns, and here and there a fragment still erect, are all that remain in this graveyard of antique architecture. Most of the monuments were destroyed by fire in the third century. The sackings by Goths and Vandals (410), upheavals by earthquake, and flagrant misuse throughout the following centuries, have completed the process of destruction. (Facing page.)

a

FORUM ROMANUM

b

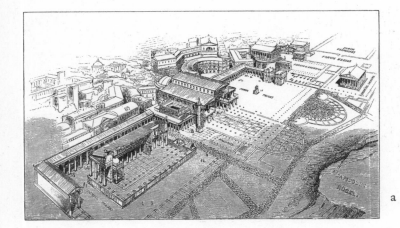

a

b

THE FORUM OF TRAJAN, ROME
Inaugurated, 113.   Restored, Bender.

The series of forums built by Julius Caesar, Augustus, Vespasian, Nerva and Trajan were intended as extensions to the area of the old Forum Romanum, which had become cramped and inadequate by the end of the first century B.C. These forums, as well as monumental temples, porticoes and colonnades, also contained blocks of shops and offices which, as in the Forum of Trajan, were set out in two great semicircular curves. Four or five stories high, these buildings were separated from the forum proper by a wide street and housed some hundreds of different business concerns. They were in effect the precursors of our present-day department stores. The two lower stories of one hemicycle are still extant, showing the typically Roman round arch motif. (Facing page.) The Forum of Trajan was by far the largest and most splendid of the imperial forums. Figure a shows the general layout of the square, entered through a triumphal archway on one side of a court surrounded by porticoes. This area was flanked on the right and left by two immense hemicycles of shops and offices. On the farther side lay the great Basilica Ulpia, each of its short ends closed with huge semicircular apses. Next came a court flanked with libraries, in which stood the Column of Trajan (page 88). Last came the temple of the deified emperor, which stood in a court surrounded by a peristyle.

b) THE FORUM OF NERVA, ROME
Completed c. 98 A.D.
Restored, Buhlemann.

All the imperial forums were planned symmetrically and differ in this respect from the Forum Romanum, which haphazardly developed in the course of the centuries. Every building on the forum was subjected to the rule of symmetry and axiality and subordinated to some central important feature which formed an architectural and spiritual climax. This climax was invariably constituted by the temple (like the Temple of Minerva in the Forum of Nerva), usually situated at the far end of the rectangular site, dominating the whole composition and giving directional emphasis to the longitudinal axis.

THE TEPIDARIUM OF THE THERMAE OF CARACALLA

Rome, after 200 A.D. *Restored, Thiersch and Bäumer.*

The most sumptuous decoration was lavished on the great Roman bathing establishments or thermae. Floors and walls were lined with marble of various colors and the upper parts of the walls were covered (like those of the Thermae of Caracalla) with richly colored paintings. The surfaces of ceilings and vaults were broken by deeply molded coffers with painted or stuccoed decoration. Though it is difficult to imagine these monuments in all their original magnificence, illustrations convey something of their richness and demonstrate the extensive use of colonnades and vaults. Among all the buildings of antiquity, the thermae exhibit the boldest developments in vaulting. The tepidarium of the Baths of Caracalla measured about 79 feet across and was covered by an intersecting barrel vault divided into three great bays, its lateral thrust resisted by barrel vaults at right angles to the main axis of the hall. The central hall rose high above the side aisles, and the spaces between the lower and upper arches could thus be filled with screen walls in which were placed large windows, forming a clerestory. This was in fact a development of the basilican scheme and may well have provided the model for the Basilica of Maxentius (page 79). Nothing now remains of the rich decoration of these baths, but the vast ruins still speak of their former grandeur. (Facing page and Figs. a and b.)

c) THE HOUSE OF THE FAUN, POMPEII

First century A.D. *Restored, Bender.*

In the richer type of Roman house, elaborate decoration again played a large part and was concentrated, like that of the thermae, on the interior. When the building was of more than one story, like the House of the Faun, shops or warehouses might open onto the street, but usually the façades were blank and windowless. Light was admitted from two large courts in the interior — the atrium and the peristyle. The oldest Roman houses consisted of various rooms grouped around a large open court or atrium — a scheme which derives from Etruscan models. Later a second court (*postica*) was added behind the first (*antica*), comprising numerous reception rooms grouped around a Greek peristyle.

d) THE PERISTYLE IN THE HOUSE OF THE VETTII, POMPEII

First century A.D.

Many of the houses of Pompeii, buried under deposits of volcanic ash after the eruption of Vesuvius in 79 A.D., have been preserved almost intact. Flower beds, fountains and statues still adorn the peristyle of the House of the Vettii. These enclosed gardens were the wealthy Roman's means of recapturing something of the countryside in the midst of the city. Opening off the peristyle were libraries and all kinds of rooms for entertaining, banqueting, etc. These were decorated in the most extravagant fashion, with the choicest materials. Floors were laid with costly marble slabs and sometimes, though less frequently, with multicolored mosaics. Walls were covered with delicate fresco paintings (page 84).

a

b

c

d

THE ATRIUM OF A ROMAN HOUSE

The House of the Silver Wedding, Pompeii, first century A.D.
The atrium was the central feature of the Roman house. It was usually rectangular in plan and formed a sort of court. The roof, supported on four columns, had an inward tilt in all directions, leaving a large opening in the center (the compluvium). Under this opening, in the middle of the pavement, was a tank (impluvium) for receiving the precious rain water as it drained off the roof. Around the atrium were grouped the various living rooms; opposite the entrance was the tablinum, a large room containing family archives and works of art; at the sides were passageways leading to the peristyle beyond. (Facing page.)

a) THE WINGS OF A ROMAN PALACE

First century A.D. *Restoration based on descriptions, Vitruvius.*
Imperial villas and palaces were a development of the Roman house in plan and differed only in the greater richness of their architectural and decorative treatment. The ruins of these palaces are hardly sufficient evidence on which to base a reconstruction, but with the help of the excavations at Pompeii, much can be learned of their former magnificence. As the illustration shows, even secondary apartments like the wings were profusely decorated. Every possible means was used to give them grandeur, with painting and sculpture, as well as architecture, contributing to the total effect. One other aspect is worth noticing: glass was certainly not unknown as a material but was still not used for filling in windows. Instead the Romans employed thin transparent sheets of marble, or for large openings, blocks of pierced stone or bronze grilles.

b) MURAL PAINTING OF THE FOURTH STYLE, POMPEII

Detail of a wall in the House of Pinario Ceriale, Pompeii, first century A.D.
From the end of the third century A.D., the walls of Roman houses and palaces were decorated with paintings executed in fresco. As well as being an additional source of decorative richness, these were a means of overcoming the confining character of the walls by *trompe-l'oeil* effects. By the first century, four distinct styles of fresco decoration had emerged. Illusionist painting reached its climax in the fourth and last style. As shown, the whole wall was now transformed into a complex architectural setting treated in perspective and with an illusionist rendering of light and shade. So real is the effect of these paintings, conjuring up new spatial planes and leading the eye into depth, that it is sometimes hard to define the true limits of the room. The scenes were brought to life by figures walking and conversing like characters on a stage. The subject in this case is Iphigenia in Tauris.

c) ARCADE IN THE PALACE OF DIOCLETIAN

Spalato, c. 300 A.D.
Of all Roman imperial palaces, that of Diocletian differs most radically from the usual plan of a Roman villa. Diocletian had been a soldier and remained one when he became emperor. Because of this and because the war-filled years at the turn of the fourth century demanded it, he built his palace in the form of a Roman military camp. Two great streets crossing at right angles divided the vast fortress into four separate quarters. The northern, eastern and western walls were protected by towers, while the south front faced the sea. The streets were flanked by arcades formed by free-standing columns of the Corinthian order with semicircular arches springing from the capitals without the intervention of an entablature — a form with few precedents in Roman architecture.

THE ARCH OF TITUS, ROME
81 A.D.

The original function of the triumphal arch was to provide a monumental gateway to the route taken by the triumphal processions of victorious generals on their way to the Forum. In the Republican period, these arches were built of wood; under the empire, they were made of stone in order to stand forever as testimonies to the glorious deeds of Roman heroes. Those that still survive are therefore purely commemorative monuments, though they retain the gateway form of their wooden prototypes, sometimes having a single archway (as in the case of the Arch of Titus) and sometimes three openings. The triumphal Arch of Titus was erected by the senate and people on the Forum Romanum in memory of the emperor and his victorious campaigns, and thus is not a processional gateway as such. The simplicity of its design is a reflection of the grand style prevalent during the post-Augustan decades. The arch has a barrel vault sunk with deep coffers and is framed by engaged columns. These columns are the earliest known examples of the use of the Composite order. They carry a heavy entablature with a plain frieze. The whole construction is balanced by a small upper story (the attic) bearing the dedicatory inscription and once surmounted by a bronze quadriga. The spandrels are decorated with figures of Victory carved in relief, and below the vault on each side are bas-reliefs representing the victory of Titus over the Jews. (Facing page.)

a) THE ARCH OF SEPTIMIUS SEVERUS, ROME
Forum Romanum, 203 A.D.

This is an example of the popular triple-arch type. Compared with the simplicity of the Arch of Titus, it is baroque in the treatment of its architectural forms and the elaborate decoration of every surface. Detached columns and responds resting on high pedestals frame the arches. Nearly all the flat surfaces are covered with reliefs extolling the fame of the deified emperor, and the dedicatory inscription is spread out across the whole of the attic. Like the Arch of Titus, this is a commemorative monument rather than a triumphal gateway. The victor's chariot could never have passed beneath the central vaulted archway, because its floor was raised with a flight of steps for access. The steps up to the two small passageways are still extant.

b) THE ARCH OF CONSTANTINE, ROME
c. 315 A.D.

The richness and complexity of this arch, latest of the imperial arches, exceeds even that of the Arch of Septimius Severus. Here the attic, too, is decorated with reliefs. The Arch of Constantine is of particular interest to art historians because the sculptures on it date from several different periods. The Victories in the spandrels of the central arch, the reliefs on the column-bases and the sculptured friezes above the small arches, all belong to the time of Constantine, but the remainder is taken from earlier monuments: the statues of Dacian prisoners over the columns date from Trajan's time; the medallions representing hunting scenes were taken from a monument of Hadrian; the reliefs on the attic were from an arch of Marcus Aurelius. The columns themselves once belonged to a monument of the Flavian period. This can only be a reflection of the rapid decline of creative force in antique architecture.

a

b

a

b

c

TRAJAN'S COLUMN, ROME
c. 113 A.D.

The eastern custom of erecting memorial columns was adopted by the Romans, who built them all over the empire to record the triumphs of victorious generals. Columns of Victory had exactly the same significance as triumphal arches: they were symbols of individual greatness and were intended to stand forever as examples to posterity. Trajan's Column, built in the Forum of Trajan, rests on a square pedestal forming a chamber which contained the emperor's cinerary urn. The shaft of the column, composed of 17 enormous blocks of marble, is 97 feet 6 inches high (100 Roman feet) including base and capital. The total height is about 150 feet. The shaft is decorated with a spiral band of bas-reliefs (over 800 feet long) illustrating incidents of Trajan's war with the Dacians. Upon a platform on top of the capital stood a bronze statue of the emperor (replaced in 1587 by a statue of St. Peter). The platform could be reached by a spiral staircase within the column. (Facing page.)

a) THE COLUMN OF MARCUS AURELIUS, ROME
c. 180 A.D.

A close copy of Trajan's Column, this was erected to commemorate the emperor's victory over the Marcomanni and the Sarmatians (171–175) on the Danube. A band of bas-reliefs illustrating this campaign winds around the 28 drums of the shaft, which is about 97 feet high. The whole column, including pedestal and statue, measures about 165 feet. It was once crowned by the bronze statues of Marcus Aurelius and Faustina, but in 1589 these were replaced by the existing figure of St. Paul.

b, c) BAS-RELIEFS FROM TWO PILLARS OF VICTORY
Above: from Trajan's Column; below: from the Column of Marcus Aurelius.

The war against the Dacians is portrayed with unbelievably meticulous workmanship in 124 scenes that make up the 800 feet of bas-reliefs on Trajan's Column. The horses' harnesses, the headdresses and facial expressions of the enemy soldiers and all the warriors' equipment — down to their very water flasks — are faithfully conveyed with an almost photographic exactitude, giving these sculptures a highly important historical significance. Here and in the cruder and much less precise reliefs of the Column of Marcus Aurelius, the emperor himself is always portrayed accompanied by supernatural beings. This may be regarded as an important element in Roman statuary, for the use, as here, of allegorical figures, or elsewhere of political personifications, gave to Roman sculpture a semipolitical, semireligious significance and invested the events themselves with a timeless quality.

THE TOMB OF CAECILIA METELLA, ROME

Via Appia Antica, c. 10 B.C. *(After an engraving by Piranesi, showing the state of the monument in the eighteenth century.)*

Funerary monuments of emperors and great public figures of the empire derived their form from the sepulchral tumuli of the Etruscans (Fig. a) consisting of a circular drum covered with a mound of earth. The tomb of Caecilia Metella (one of the rare instances of a Roman tomb still standing on the Via Appia) shows this form, but the cylindrical drum stands on a high, square podium. In 1299, the Caetani converted it into a fort by adding a castellated super-structure and an adjoining castle, the remains of which are shown in the engraving, though these have since disappeared. Below the cornice is a frieze decorated with ox skulls hung with festoons of fruit and flowers and interspersed with Gallic weapons, all carved in low relief. The weapons are a reference to the relationship between Caecilia Metella and Crassus the triumvir (her father-in-law), one of Caesar's generals during the Gallic War. (Facing page.)

a

a) AN ETRUSCAN TUMULUS

Cervetri, sixth century B.C.

This tomb illustrates the features which the Romans adopted for so many of their own funerary monuments. It consists of a round stone base surmounted by a conical mound of earth. Within the mound was the burial chamber itself, accessible through a passage-way which may be seen at the lower left of the illustration.

b) THE MAUSOLEUM OF AUGUSTUS, ROME

28 B.C.

This cylindrical substructure, with a diameter of over 220 feet, has been excellently preserved. The upper portion consisted of an earth mound laid out in terraces and planted with cypresses and ever-greens. Crowning the whole structure was a colossal statue of the emperor. This mausoleum thus retains the form of Etruscan tumuli, and like these, had an internal burial chamber.

b

c) THE MAUSOLEUM OF HADRIAN, ROME (CASTLE OF S. ANGELO)

Rome, 135–139 A.D.

The tumulus type of tomb was perfected in the mausoleum Hadrian built for himself on the Tiber in 135 A.D. Famous as the Castle of S. Angelo, it now retains little of its original form. From 275, it was used as a fortress. In the following centuries, it was subjected to many alterations. The high podium (300 feet square) and the immense circular tower (240 feet in diameter) have, however, remained unchanged. The composition recalls the tomb of Caecilia Metella. The columns that once surrounded the drum and the white marble facing are completely lost, together with the conical stone mound at the top. The round structure in the form of a temple, which stood at the highest point and was probably crowned with a quadriga of gilt bronze, also disappeared.

c

a

b

c

THE PONT DU GARD, NÎMES
Beginning first century A.D.

While the Romans continued to imitate the Greeks whenever they built temples, theatres and other buildings of mainly architectural significance, their sound practical sense enabled them to create an extremely individual style in the field of engineering works (roads, bridges and aqueducts). Aqueducts supplied water to the large towns. They often stretched for considerable distances (the Aqua Marcia was over 30 miles long) and had to negotiate difficult ground, their arches crossing the valleys in wide spans. The Pont du Gard forms part of an aqueduct, and through sheer proportion its great arches (reaching to a height of about 160 feet) achieve an effect of strength and grandeur. Above the lowest range of arches, whose piers are reinforced with cutwaters, runs a two-way road. A second range of monumental arches carries a third story of smaller arched openings. The water flowed through a channel in the upper part of the last story. (Facing page.)

a) THE RUINS OF THE AQUA CLAUDIA
The Roman Campagna, first century A.D.

Aqueducts were not only built over valleys, but also when the need arose, across wide stretches of plain. It was necessary to maintain a fall sufficient to produce a steady flow of water. The Aqua Claudia, borne on arches for 9½ miles, was erected by Nero (54–68) as an extension to the Aqua Appia, the earliest Roman waterway, and was entirely subterranean (312 B.C.). This aqueduct still dominates the Campagna, exemplifying the simple majesty achieved in such buildings.

b) THE AQUEDUCT AT SEGOVIA
Spain, built in the time of Trajan.

For more than half a mile, this impressive structure is borne on two tiers of arches rising to 182 feet. In contrast to the wide arches of the Pont du Gard (the piers of a bridge cannot be set close together), the piers are closely spaced, giving this aqueduct its fine and massive effect.

c) THE PONS MULVIUS, ROME
109 B.C.

The first bridge known to have been built in Rome was the Pons Sublicius. It was a simple wooden footbridge, so narrow that one man (Horatius Cocles) was able to defend it singlehanded. In 179 B.C., this was replaced by the first stone bridge, the Pons Aemilius, the piers of which, however, originally carried a timber roadway. The arch was adopted in bridge construction only after it had been proved as a structural method in the Aqua Marcia (144–140 B.C.). The Pons Aemilius is thus the prototype of all bridges built in the Roman Empire during succeeding centuries. Only fragments of this bridge remain, buried in the Ponto Rotto, but the Pons Mulvius has survived and provides the basis for our knowledge of early Roman bridge construction. Three of the four arches are antique. Small barrel-vaulted openings are placed on the piers to reduce the weight and to allow the water to flow more smoothly in time of flood.

THE PORTA NIGRA, TRÈVES
Beginning fourth century A.D.

This magnificent gateway was part of the wall that once surrounded the great Roman city, covering an area of more than one square mile. The two passages opened onto a square court which was originally unroofed and flanked by rectangular towers with semicircular projections on the exterior. Ranges of round arches with engaged columns articulate the three upper stories (the top story of the left tower is lost), and the double ramparts that connect the towers have a similar treatment. At ground level on either side of the tall entrance arches, the towers have no openings between the engaged columns, this being the most vulnerable part of the structure. The impressive scale and harmonious proportions of the Porta Nigra make it the finest of all monumental Roman gateways. (Facing page.)

a) REMAINS OF THE AURELIAN WALL, ROME
With the Porta San Sebastiano, 271.

b) THE PORTA MAGGIORE, ROME
c. 280.

Mounting political crisis and uncertainty during the third century resulted in the building of strong defensive walls for the protection of towns all over the empire, including Rome itself. Until 271, Rome had been undefended, but in this year Aurelian and Probus surrounded the city by a powerful wall of which about 8 miles still remain. There were 383 towers, 7,020 lookout posts and 13 monumental gateways (Fig. a). The Aurelian wall was one of the last monumental conceptions of Roman architecture. Their constructive urge by now almost completely exhausted, the Romans concentrated their energies on building defensive towers and gateways. These gates, with their habitual double archways, recapture something of the ancient splendor of Roman architecture. The Porta Maggiore, in front of which stands the Tomb of Eurysaces, recalls the triumphal arches, with its magnificent arched openings and pedimented niches flanked by engaged columns (page 87). This gate is of particular interest because it served as a superstructure for two aqueducts — the Anio Vetus and the Aqua Claudia — which flowed through channels in the three-storied attic. The whole of the face of this attic is covered with inscriptions.

c) THE WALL OF CONSTANTINOPLE
Begun 412.

The last great defensive work of antiquity was this powerful wall built for the protection of Constantinople. About 4 miles long and 15 feet 6 inches thick, it was strengthened by 96 square and polygonal towers. The walls are built of limestone with a concrete core and bonded with brick, the red and white of these materials adding a pleasing note of color to the noble fortification. Until 1453, when it was shattered by Turkish artillery, the wall of Constantinople was proof against all attacks.

a

b

c

IV
EARLY CHRISTIAN
ARCHITECTURE

Historical and Religious Background

The fourth century was of such vital importance for the Roman Empire and for the whole subsequent history of the Western world that modern historians have become more and more inclined to dissociate it from what had gone before. But in fact, events in this period naturally arose from the political and religious situation of earlier centuries. The pace of development was hastened rather than broken.

From the second century onward, the political stability of the empire began to fail, and was precariously maintained during the third century largely by the mobilization of all forces and with the aid of foreign troops. In the British Isles, Gaul, Germania and on the Danube, but chiefly in Asia Minor, subjugated peoples were beginning to rebel against their rulers, and constant defense was needed against barbarian tribes who threatened invasion on the frontiers. The total disruption of the great empire was successfully held at bay and unity maintained, but for some time the situation of Rome had been such that one man alone could no longer bear the crushing burden of responsibility. A tax was levied to finance aid to the provinces and certain concessions became necessary.

In 212, the Emperor Caracalla granted the right of Roman citizenship to all free men of the empire, and in 230, Alexander Severus distributed country estates among the legionaries and the officers of the frontier troops (who had long been recruited from the provinces), with hereditary rights on the condition that they would serve Rome in time of war. Thus the distinction between Romans by birth and Romans by title gradually became less clear cut. More and more names of provincials were added to the line of Roman emperors: Trajan and Hadrian were Spaniards, Antoninus Pius a Gaul, Septimius Severus an African, and Diocletian an Illyrian — to name only a few. This would seem to indicate that from the second century there was already a shift of emphasis from Rome and Italy to the provincial centers, beginning with Spain and Africa. The provinces were now fully assimilated into the empire, and the right of Roman citizenship accorded by Caracalla had merely been the official confirmation of a long-established situation. Its importance was far more moral than political.

Alien modes of thought and conduct imposed themselves on the native Italian traditions when the upper strata of society, and in Rome even those of senatorial rank, mingled with freedmen and the foreign nationals of trading colonies. The infiltration of new ideas led to a transformation of the national character and religious beliefs of the Romans. Their religious cult, which had never had the stability of classical Greek theology, rapidly absorbed the philosophical teachings and mystical beliefs that had grown up in the Hellenistic East. Many new gods took their place among the old. From Cappadocia came Ma-Bellona; from Egypt, Isis and Osiris; from Persia, Mithras; from Palestine, the Jewish God Jehovah. Finally, and of greatest significance, was the arrival of Christianity — a lowly religion that was to spread rapidly throughout the civilized world and to dominate the future of Europe.

Thus the nature of the Roman Empire had become greatly confused and complicated since the Golden Age of Augustus. Demoralization and religious uncertainty went hand in hand with political troubles. It is true that Rome and its senate still stood for the center of power, although the edict of Caracalla meant that the Romans had sacrificed their principal privilege. But the problem of defending the empire on several fronts more and more frequently drew the later emperors away from their tasks of government and to bases near the frontiers. These bases grew into large and important cities where the rulers of the empire held their courts. They were often heavily fortified and were equipped with palaces, villas, theatres and basilicas. Eventually government was divided between various generals who proclaimed themselves Caesars, took on supreme authority, and engaged in frequent combat against one another.

Diocletian, who had himself served in the Roman Army, was proclaimed Emperor of the Eastern provinces in 284. In 285, the West also came under his rule and the administrative system was once more in the hands of one man. But in 286, Diocletian made Maximian his colleague with the intent that the empire should be divided into two parts and governed by two rulers with an equal share of authority. Then in 293, he conferred the title of Caesar on two generals, Constantius-Chlorus and Galerius. These four princes divided the empire and shared imperial power. For some time the harmony of the empire was preserved under this balance of power, called the tetrarchy, which even survived Diocletian's abdication in 305.

One of these men was Constantine, son of Constantius, acknowledged by posterity to be one of the most outstanding rulers of the Byzantine Empire and called Constantine the Great. After having been proclaimed emperor at York in 306, Constantine set out to destroy the supremacy of his rivals in a succession of terrible battles and at last, in 323, he became the sole master of the East and West. He reintroduced many of the ideas of Diocletian, improved upon them, and achieved something that Diocletian had not been able to bring about: the establishment of a strategically placed administrative center, distant from Rome, as a new imperial residence. Diocletian had lived in Nicomedia. Constantine decided on Byzantium, situated on the Bosphorus, about 62 miles farther west. After his final victory, he laid the foundations of the new city that was to bear his name — Constantinople — and in 330 declared it to be the second or new Rome, the capital of his empire and the seat of government.

Whatever the motives for this act, it was to change the course of history. With Rome no longer holding her sacrosanct, inviolable position at the center of world power, the way was prepared for the final division of the empire after the death of Theodosius I (379–395). Constantine died in 337, and his successors once again divided the empire into east and west. Then the political resourcefulness of Theodosius effected a reunification for a time. The Franks, Alamanni and Burgundians were threatening attack on the northern frontiers; on the Danube, there were the Goths and Alans, and Persia presented a continual threat, but still the developing calamity was averted. After the death of their father, Theodosius, Arcadius and Honorius were accepted as the lawful emperors of the East and of the West, and the fate of the Roman Empire was sealed. The break between the two capitals became final and permanent, and slowly but irresistibly the Mediterranean world entered into a new phase of its history.

Rome, in a weakened condition and ruled by ineffectual princes, soon became the victim of the attacks of German tribes. In 410, the city was sacked by Alaric, chief of the Visigoths, and again by the Vandals under Genseric in 455. In 476, Odoacer, the Herulic German ostensibly in the service of Byzantium but taking events into his own hands, deposed the last of the Western Roman emperors, Romulus Augustulus, then a youth of seventeen. Not long afterward, in 493, Theodoric, the Ostrogoth, overthrew Odoacer and founded an Ostrogoth monarchy in Italy. Meanwhile the Eastern empire and its capital Byzantium (Constantinople) steadily increased in independence and power.

The Byzantine rulers had avoided political partition of the empire until the sixth century and had sought to maintain their authority over Italy by military campaigns. Now such a schism was inevitable but there was no corresponding rift in the fabric of Roman culture. As might be expected, Byzantium was subjected to powerful Oriental influences, and since about the middle of the sixth century a markedly characteristic Byzantine style began to develop, but the art of the East, like that of the West, remained deeply rooted in the heritage of ancient Rome. However, the link between East and West was not so much their common inheritance of a great tradition as their mutual acceptance, from the beginning of the fourth century, of the new Christian religion.

Like its founder, the doctrine of Christianity issued from the Jewish people, but it soon became detached from the old Mosaic religion. First of all it spread across the eastern provinces of the empire, gaining many followers in Asia Minor, Syria and Africa. Then the new faith reached Rome, where many Jews lived as slaves or merchants. As early as the year 64, there was a flourishing Christian community in the capital.

The organization of the Roman Empire undoubtedly favored the spread of Christianity, but when — in spite of many setbacks — it was recognized as the official religion of the empire in the fourth century, its victory was largely due to the great persuasive force of its teachings. Humble people were deeply moved by the idea of an omnipotent and benevolent God offering refuge to the poor and oppressed; by the promise of resurrection after death and entry into Heaven; by the doctrine that all men are equal before God without regard to rank or title and that they are to be judged mercifully — not according to their worldly possessions but according to their attitudes and behavior. Above all, they loved the image of Christ, Son of God, who had died to redeem mankind. The overhanging

dread of a Last Judgment, made all the more real by the troubles and dangers of the times and the moral decadence of contemporary life, must also have played its part in turning men toward the new religion, together with the extraordinary fervor of its disciples, who went about preaching the Gospel of Christ and were if necessary prepared to die for Him.

The upper classes of society did not at first take kindly to Christianity, which demanded that worldly existence be regarded only as a preparation for a future life, and questioned the value of those very things — wealth, rank and privilege — that gave meaning to their lives. Moreover, Christianity presented a danger to the empire, and for two reasons. The new teaching implied an absolute allegiance to an ideal which threw its followers into direct conflict with the idea of imperial power and thus forced them to deny the infallibility of the emperor. In addition, Christianity, unlike other religious cults newly introduced in Rome, had not confined itself to a small private community or to any one people, but soon, promoted with missionary zeal, its teaching spread to every level of Roman society.

It is surprising to find that until the third century only rare and inadequate attempts were made to suppress the danger which threatened imperial power. For the most part it was thought sufficient to despise the Christians and to disregard their activities as long as they kept within their own community. When it did occur, persecution served to foment rather than suppress their fervor, for martyrs were regarded as saints and many were eager to follow their example.

The spiritual situation in the Roman Empire during the third century also favored the propagation of Christianity. The ancient pagan deities were viewed with growing skepticism, and, among the sophisticated, philosophical movements such as neo-Platonism (Plotinus 205–270) nourished the idea of an all-pervading god who could be identified with the highest aspirations of the human spirit. A transcendental monotheism was becoming widespread, encouraging men to turn their thoughts in new directions. The status of the emperor underwent a change. No longer a deity himself, he was now only the chosen tool of a higher power. Finally, Christian doctrine itself was somewhat modified, though the old ideals remained unaltered. The early expectation of an impending Last Day was modified by the passage of time. Plans were made for the future, and a missionary Church was instituted with a governing body of clergy organized on the basis of the Roman administrative system.

Yet the decisive question of the relationship of Christianity to the State remained unanswered until the beginning of the fourth century. The two forces stood opposed and irreconcilable. Diocletian, who at first tolerated the Christians, tried to assert the power of the State by publishing an edict against them toward the end of his reign (303). In spite of the atrocious cruelties perpetrated during the ensuing persecution and the unimaginable suffering that it brought about — particularly in the dominions of Galerius in the East — this expedient proved unsuccessful. But ultimately a solution had to be found and it was Constantine the Great who brought about an event that was to change the course of history. In 312, Constantine, whose mother Helena was a devout Christian, had become the sole master of Italy, when according to legend, after seeing the standard of the Cross in a vision, he achieved a decisive victory over one of his rivals, Maxentius, at the Milvian bridge. The following year, by the Edict of Milan, he accorded equal toleration to Christianity and the pagan cults and so paved the way for the adoption of Christianity as the official State religion. Though Constantine thus showed himself to be a true benefactor of the Church, he was not baptized until shortly before his death (337), and there is little doubt that his action had been part of an astute political maneuver rather than the manifestation of a deep religious conviction. Constantine wanted unity, and he must have realized that among all the movements of his time, Christianity was the one through which he could best achieve it.

Christianity and Art

The primitive Christians, like the followers of all Oriental religions, were ill-disposed toward the making of images, defending their hostility by citing the second of the Ten Mosaic Commandments, and quoting from St. John the Evangelist: "God is a Spirit: and they that worship Him must worship Him in spirit and in truth" (4:24). The gods of pagan antiquity were given visible form in sculpture, and temples and altars were set up in their honor, but an Alexandrine theologian writing in the middle of the third

century was able to say that Jews and Christians made no images or likenesses of worldly or heavenly things, having a horror of pagan temples, their altars and statues. And at the beginning of the fourth century, the African rhetorician Arnobius said: "We [the Christians] build no places of worship, we make no idols or images or any god, nor do we set up altars or sacred columns in the name of a deity." In short, their earthly existence had little meaning for the first Christians except inasmuch as it was a preparation for the future life. The pleasures of this world were regarded as the insidious temptations of the Devil and a constant danger to the human soul in search of salvation. So they would gather in one another's homes and hold their celebrations simply, without using any form of image. It is not surprising that art at first played no part in the lives of the early Christians.

But from the second century onward, as their numbers began to increase steadily, the old Christian customs were changed. Ceremony was elaborated and given greater consistency. A whole liturgy developed and a hierarchical order of clergy was established. Consideration was given to the question of using visual representations in the service of religion, as well as the spoken and written word. These were not to be objects of worship in themselves, but merely a means of deepening meditation and helping to establish a closer contact with God. The first examples of Christian painting are to be found in the Catacombs, the oldest dating from the end of the second century or the beginning of the third.

Christian artists adopted the old fresco technique and even borrowed some forms of antique art, but the themes they represented were always symbolic of the abstract ideas of heavenly grace and salvation. The story of Jonah signified the grace of God; the figure of the Good Shepherd symbolized Christ, the Redeemer of human souls — a choice of motifs dictated by the conditions under which the early Christians were living and by their hope of eternal life.

During the third century, the Virgin and the Infant Christ, the Annunciation and several other New Testament subjects began to appear in Christian painting. In the fourth century, churches were decorated with frescoes, and it was not long before these gave way to mosaics, with their effect of greater brilliance. It is important to remember that these sacred pictures were never valued for their own sake as decoration but only for the spiritual significance of their content.

The change in attitude toward the use of images was of immense importance for the history of art, and to understand this development it should be remembered that until the fourth century Christianity was principally the religion of the poor, to whom abstract ideas meant little. Visual images would clearly make a far greater impression on such people, and the acceptance of this method of teaching must owe much to the authority of Pope Gregory the Great (590–604), who said that paintings must be the books of the poor and illiterate, a means of imparting a knowledge of the Holy Scriptures to those who could not read.

Architectural Character

As the early Christians began to find concrete expression for their doctrine in paintings and mosaics they also felt a need to create a more spacious environment for their worship than that afforded by rooms in private houses. Churches were built in all parts of the empire, and in Rome alone (by the middle of the third century) there were more than 40 shrines and halls where Christians would assemble and celebrate the Last Supper. It is probable that these early churches were similar in form to the oldest known Christian shrine (dating from the first half of the third century) in Dura-Europus, Mesopotamia, which was taken by the Sassanids in 256. This shrine, used by the Christian legionaries, consists of a simple chamber for communion and baptism. But there must also have been a number of larger churches, for it is known that the persecution of Christians by Diocletian began with the destruction of a notable church in Nicomedia, and according to the *Ecclesiastical History* of Eusebius of Caesarea (c. 260–340), the same fate overtook many churches in the east and the west. Whether these churches already conformed to either of the types of building which emerged triumphantly after the Edict of Milan (313)—the basilica and centrally planned church—it is impossible to say, for too little evidence is available. Be that as it may, Christianity's hold on the world was strengthening. It was recognized as the official State religion and accepted by the emperor for political reasons in preference to all existing pagan cults. Now was the time to build places of worship that would worthily proclaim this great victory.

The first public churches were built by order of Constantine at Jerusalem, Nicomedia, Constantinople and Rome. In an illuminating letter to Macarius, Bishop of Jerusalem, inviting him to build a church there, the emperor wrote: "I trust to your own wisdom to appreciate how vital it is to build a basilica that will be more splendid than any other and will overshadow the beauty of every other building in the city." Constantine's words echo the old spirit of Roman antiquity when grandeur and magnificence in architecture were regarded as the symbol of power. The early Christian churches were also to be the outward expression of power, but in a new and totally different sense.

From the outset, the conception of the Christian church differed radically from that of the pagan temple. Temples had been sanctuaries for the gods and their sacred images, and entry to them was permitted only to priests. The faithful offered sacrifices at altars in the open air or proceeded solemnly around the outside of the temple. Churches, on the other hand, followed the tradition of the earliest Christian meeting places in private houses. They were places where all believers, regardless of status, could congregate to worship God in tranquil meditation, draw nearer to Him under the spiritual guidance of the clergy, and together prepare for eternal life. The divine service, which in the old religions had been banished from the temple and conducted in the open air as an elaborate spectacle, was now brought inside the church. This was of the utmost importance, for whereas until then the greatest emphasis had been placed on the exterior of the temple for the benefit of those congregated outside, now the architectural as well as the spiritual emphasis was concentrated entirely on the interior. As a result, the exteriors of Early Christian churches have a stark simplicity quite foreign to the temples of antiquity, and decoration is limited to the interiors. Paintings and, more frequently, brilliantly colored mosaics took the place of the old and more complex forms of articulation such as niches, detached columns and statues. Unlike the idolatrous images of the pagans, the sacred pictures on the walls of Christian churches were not the object of worship in themselves but were simple allegorical illustrations telling the Bible stories and helping to bring believers into closer spiritual contact with God. The symbolic images invested with the incorporeality of other-worldly beings lit up the church and transformed the cold flatness of the walls with their glowing colors. Thus the whole meaning of the interior was expressed in the unreal, almost supernatural, quality of its decoration.

The architectural character and the planning of Early Christian churches were strictly dictated by functional requirements. Many that were built in the reign of Constantine and during the succeeding two centuries were placed over the graves of Christian martyrs, on the sites of ancient Christian meeting places, or in particularly holy places like Jerusalem, Bethlehem and Nazareth. They were either rectangular in plan or were given a circular or polygonal form. (The latter type was to be adopted as the theme of Byzantine churches from the fourth century.) Centrally planned buildings were not originally conceived as churches but were used chiefly for baptism (baptisteries) and burial. They sometimes served commemorative purposes, like the two buildings erected by Constantine at Jerusalem — one to mark the place of Christ's Ascension and the other to cover the Holy Sepulchre. The compact, nondirectional character of the circular building composed about a central vertical axis was suited to these purposes, but an alternative plan was needed to meet the requirements of divine service when a large congregation had to face an altar and the officiating priest. It was the basilican plan which was found to be most suitable.

The Basilica

None of the great Early Christian basilicas has come down to us unaltered, and few retain as much of their original character as Sta Sabina in Rome (*c.* 425, page 121 a) and S. Apollinare, Ravenna (beginning of the sixth century, page 120). However, it is possible to form a clear picture of the ideal basilican church and its essential characteristics (Fig. 32). The entrance was marked by a large open forecourt cut off from the outside world by high walls and surrounded by cloisters with roofs sloping inward to the court. A gateway or propylaeum, sometimes with a projecting porch, gave access from the street. In the center of the court was a fountain (kantharos) for purification before entering the church. The architectural character of this square court vividly recalls the peristyle of an ancient Roman house. It was, however, called the atrium, probably because it served a similar purpose to the forepart of a Roman dwelling with its impluvium and proximity to the main entrance.

At the far end of the atrium, opposite the entrance gateway, lay the church itself, an oblong hall as wide as the atrium and almost invariably comprising several aisles. A central aisle — the nave — was divided from the side aisles by rows of columns supporting arches or a horizontal entablature. There was usually one aisle on either side of the nave, though many of the larger basilicas were built with five aisles. The nave roof was raised above those of the aisles, so that windows could be placed in the upper walls between the two levels (the clerestory). The nave, emphasized by its greater height and breadth, was decorated with paintings or magnificent mosaics on the unbroken wall surfaces between the arches or lintels and the roundheaded windows of the clerestory. The ends of the side aisles of the early basilicas were marked on the east by a straight wall, while the nave terminated in a large semicircular apse.

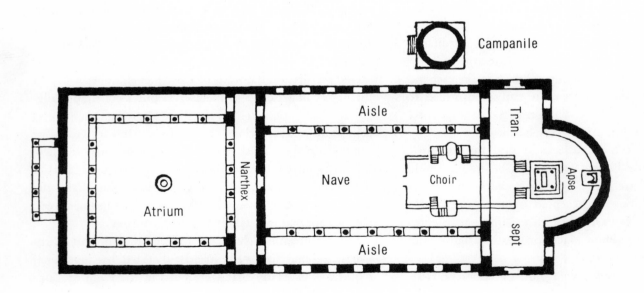

32. Ideal plan of an Early Christian transeptal basilica.

Spiritually, the apse was the most important part of the basilica, for it accommodated the high altar and the clergy. It was covered by a semidome, and the projecting semicircular wall, originally windowless, gave the sanctuary a sense of enclosure. This segregation was further emphasized on the interior by the triumphal arch, which separated the apse from the body of the church. Both triumphal arch and apse were richly decorated with paintings and mosaics. The altar, consisting of a simple stone table (mensa), was usually placed on a stepped platform in the middle of the apse and covered by a canopy (ciborium) supported on four marble columns. Behind the altar, near the wall of the apse, stood the raised throne (cathedra) for the bishop, flanked by seats for the clergy. The floor of the apse was usually set a little higher than that of the nave and was approached by a flight of steps across the end of the nave, thus accentuating the sacred significance of this part of the church. The reason for the elevation of the apse floor was, however, often a technical one, for whenever possible, the altar was placed immediately above the burial place of one of the Christian martyr-saints. This burial place, confessio or crypt, could be reached by side staircases.

From the outset, it was the custom in Roman churches to introduce a transept or open space at right angles to the main axis of the nave, between the triumphal arch and the apse. It was the same height as the nave and approximately as wide, forming very slight lateral projections. The significance of this feature has been the subject of much controversy. To regard it as a means of giving the plan the form of the Cross is certainly mistaken, for this symbolic interpretation of the basilican plan was only to emerge later. Neither can the transept have been intended as an extension to the space reserved for the congregation, for the great nave would have provided ample accommodation. The fact that the transept was principally employed in large episcopal churches, where the liturgy called for an ever-increasing number of priests, would seem to substantiate the theory that its original function was simply to provide extra space for the clergy. If this were the case, however, it remains difficult to understand why it was still found necessary, even in transeptal basilicas, to use cancelli or low screen walls to enclose a portion of the nave and transept for liturgical purposes (page 122 b). The chancel accommodated the lesser clergy and the choir, and hence this part of the church came to be known as the choir. On each side of the chancel was a pulpit (ambo) from which the Gospel and the Epistle were read. There was a short flight of steps to the Epistle ambo, and according to the demands of ritual, two flights to that for the Gospel.

As might be expected, the builders of the Early Christian churches did not always hold to this ideal plan. Even the fact that transeptal and nontranseptal basilicas were being built at the same time indicates that this plan was treated with a certain amount of freedom. In some basilicas (like those in Syria) there was no atrium at all, and the entrance was marked by a simple porch (page 119). In others, a narrow vestibule (narthex) was introduced across the lateral axis of the church, near the entrance. It was isolated from the body of the church by a low parapet, and here the catechumens — under instruction and still not eligible for admission into the church itself — were able to hear portions of the service. In some churches of the East and also in a few rare and early examples in Rome, galleries for women were placed over the aisles. In North Africa, the apse was frequently terminated by a straight wall and did not form a semicircular projection. These were, however, only regional changes and were to have little effect on the general development of basilican churches.

In essence, the character of the basilican plan indicates that in the basilica the Christian saw the path to God and salvation. This path led him from the outside world toward the sanctuary in stages — from the propylaeum to the atrium and thence through the long nave to the altar in the apse; it was a spiritual experience where each stage was more sacred than the last. Every architectural and decorative means was employed to give visible expression to this idea of progression. The worshiper would first purify himself in the fountain of the atrium and make his repentance before entering the church and joining in the divine service. He would then be received into the House of God, where the atmosphere of sanctity and mystery was heightened by dim light filtering through narrow windows and by the unearthly splendor of paintings and rich mosaics. Rows of columns of glowing marble, the continuous line of entablature or the swinging rhythm of arches, the unbroken bands of wall high in the nave and the line of windows above — even the unconcealed trusses of the timber roof — all lead the eye irresistibly down the nave toward the high altar within the apse. The apse and the triumphal arch in front of it form an architectural frame for this point of spiritual climax and as such received the richest and most splendid decoration. The nave walls were adorned with scenes from the Old Testament or from the Life of Christ and the Virgin — events from Christian history that had actually taken place on earth and prepared the way for human salvation. The apse, on the other hand, would usually contain symbolic representations of Paradise, the Heavenly City, Christ with the Evangelists, or the patron saints of the church and themes from the

Apocalypse, among them the twenty-four elders. Above the triumphal arch there would be a figure of Christ as Saviour of the World (page 120), summoning men to the Kingdom of God which was both symbolized and actually present in the sanctuary below. These images were a means of concentrating the attention of the congregation and of directing their thoughts toward God while they joined in prayer with the priest at the altar. Finally, the spiritual significance of the basilica was confirmed in the orientation of the building. The apse faced due east — that is, toward the source of light, symbol of salvation (*ex oriente lux*) and toward the Holy Land.

Origins of the Basilican Church

While the significance of the Early Christian basilican church is clear and uncontested, the origin of this particular form is difficult to determine. The theory that it was invented by the Christian builders of the fourth century is no longer considered tenable. It derives so intimately from antique architecture as to justify the contention that, although Christian in spirit, the basilican form belongs to late antiquity. Methods of wall construction, columns and capitals (which, together with the timber roofs, were often taken from earlier pagan buildings), as well as paintings and mosaics were, initially at least, closely bound to the antique tradition.

The origin of the basilican plan has been the subject of much speculation. Roman temples afford several striking points of comparison, particularly those of the Republican period, which often had an apse or adyton. Moreover, temples, like basilicas, adhered to the trabeated form and were not vaulted. But the typical basilican stepped cross section and the division into nave and aisles have no precedent in Roman temples. These features, however, appear at a very early date in the halls of justice and commercial exchanges (basilicas) which were built in the forums of Rome and other Roman towns. Though these basilicas did not follow a rigid pattern of plan or construction, they invariably comprised a tall, oblong, central nave and lower side aisles divided by rows of columns or piers and covered

with a low pitched roof. Vaulted galleries comparable to those in an Early Christian basilica were occasionally placed above the side aisles, as for example in the Basilica Julia in the Forum Romanum. The praetor would officiate in a tribunal at one end of the hall. The tribunal was on a raised, stepped dais, generally in a semicircular apse at the back of which was the praetor's seat, with seats for the assessors ranged around it to right and left — an arrangement foreshadowing that of the bishop and clergy in the apse of a Christian church. The position of the altar, where sacrifices would be offered before transacting business or pronouncing judgment, was identical with that of the holy table in a Christian sanctuary.

There are thus many similarities between the two types of building, although the Roman basilica lacked one of the essential characteristics of the Christian church: its unequivocal concentration about the longitudinal axis. Though the position of the altar and the official chair in a Roman basilica inevitably gave the interior a directional emphasis, the general arrangement of the building was not wholly subordinated to it. The fact that the nave was enclosed by aisles on all four sides, and not on the long sides only, reduced the importance of the longitudinal axis and gave the plan a more centralized character. Added to this, the entrances were sometimes placed on the long sides. While the general form of Early Christian churches may safely be said to derive from the Roman basilica, the origin of their emphatic axiality must be sought elsewhere. This was clearly not the intention of the first Christians, for it will be remembered that axial planning had been one of the chief characteristics of Roman architecture. Typical examples can be found in Roman dwelling houses, imperial palaces, forums and thermae.

There are also several indications that the basilican plan had been used in conjunction with the idea of directional emphasis long before the first known churches were built. Remarkable evidence of this has been provided by a little pagan temple discovered below the ground near the Porta Maggiore, Rome (Fig. 33 a). It was used as a shrine during the first century A.D. by the devotees of a mystical religious cult. The three avenues are barrel vaulted and divided by massive piers. The nave is slightly wider than the aisles, and the entrance is placed on the central axis opposite the apse, which forms a semicircular projection on the exterior. The basilica of the Flavian Palace on the Palatine (built at the end of the first century A.D.) followed much the same general plan, though here the side aisles are double storied and excessively narrow in comparison with the nave, the basilican section is abandoned, and nave and aisles share the same roof. When giving audiences or administering justice, the emperor sat at the back of a semicircular apse. With different architectural means (cross vaults over the nave and barrel-vaulted aisles), the Romans had combined axiality with a stepped cross section in the last great pagan basilicas, among them that of Maxentius in the Forum Romanum (c. 310, Figs. 23 and 24). Similarly, the Early Christian church is a synthesis of both these ideas.

The problem of the origin of the transept still remains unsolved. One theory is that, like the basilican plan itself, it has some connection with the form of the ancient Roman house. This seems likely, for the early Christians would have used such private houses as places of assembly before special halls had been built for the purpose. The plan of a typical Roman house (Fig. 34 a), with its widening sequence of entrance vestibule, atrium and wings (alae) followed by the tablinum on the central axis opposite the vestibule, does indeed bear a marked resemblance to that of a transeptal basilica. The central nave corresponds with the atrium, the transept with the alae, and the apse with the tablinum. The small chapels built in the Catacombs in the early days of Christianity have also been considered as a possible source. These chapels sometimes show semicircular apses projecting from all three sides of the sanctuary (Fig. 34 b), thus giving the plan a sort of cross axis.

The most acceptable of the many theories concerning the transeptal form seems to be that it was derived from the imperial forums. In spite of obvious constructional differences and the combination of covered and uncovered spaces, the Roman market place, in plan at least, is remarkably similar to a transeptal basilica. Like the basilica, it is elongated in form and is grouped around a dominant central axis terminated at one end by the entrance and at the other by a sanctuary. The position of the temple dedicated to the emperor or to his family gods is the same in relation to the forum as that of the apse in relation to a Christian church. Both apse and temple contained an altar, accommodated the priests, and formed the point of spiritual climax. Moreover, the courts laid out in front of the temple are comparable with the central nave of a basilica, being lined with porticoes which, though less compelling than the serried ranks of pillars in an enclosed church, had the similar effect of leading the eye forward.

Nontranseptal basilicas may be likened to the forums of Julius Caesar and Nerva, while the transeptal type is comparable with those of Augustus and Trajan. In the Forum of Augustus, the farther end of the court was expanded on each side by a magnificent exedra, thus forming an important cross axis. On the Forum of Trajan, the transverse axis is even more strongly emphasized by the Basilica

Ulpia, which lies like a great transept between the porticoed court and the temple precinct. Even the form of the peristyle which surrounds the temple (Fig. 34 c) seems to foreshadow the semicircular apse characteristic of the early churches.

It is not surprising, therefore, that the transeptal basilica has come to be considered as a development of the forum plan, as represented, for example, in the Forum of Trajan. (Many authorities have advanced a similar and equally acceptable theory concerning the origin of the antique

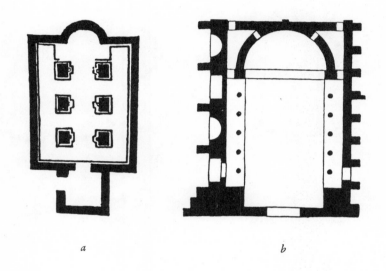

a   *b*

33. *Origins of the basilican church:*
   a) Plan of the pagan temple near the Porta Maggiore, Rome,
      first century A.D.;
   b) Plan of the basilica in the Flavian Palace, Rome,
      first century A.D.

basilica which, they contend, was certainly a roofed-in version of the open forum.) The fact that there are fundamental differences between the two types of construction — one being a completely enclosed space and the other a complex of covered and uncovered spaces — cannot be regarded as a convincing argument against this hypothesis. In each case the same motives had dictated the shape of the plan, which was orientated toward a spiritual centerpoint and then elaborated by the addition of a cross axis. It should also be remembered that as soon as Christianity was recognized by Constantine the deification of emperors ceased and the ultimate significance of the imperial forum was lost. It may well have been regarded as a matter of course to build the churches of the one omnipotent God in a form similar to the forums that had once

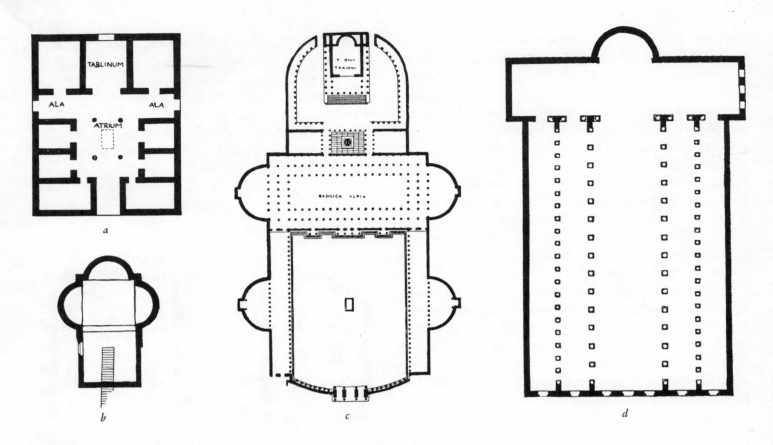

34. *Hypothetical sources of the transeptal basilica: a) Plan of a Roman house with atrium; b) Chapel in the Catacombs of St. Calixtus, Rome, third century; c) Plan of the Forum of Trajan, Rome, dedicated 113; d) Transeptal basilica of S. Giovanni in Laterano, Rome, c. 320.*

glorified an all-powerful emperor. Nor is it a coincidence that the transept first appears in the metropolitan churches built in Rome, Byzantium and the Holy Land by order of Constantine, while never once occurring in the churches of North Africa or Syria, which followed an independent course of development.

The Development of the Basilican Style

It is not easy to speak of development when considering Early Christian architecture. The ideal basilican plan remained almost unchanged until late into the sixth century, by which time the Empire of the West had suffered a long series of disasters following on the great invasions,

and the basilican style of the East was eclipsed by Oriental influences. Until this time, churches continued to be built with 3 or 5 aisles divided lengthwise by rows of columns or piers. On rare occasions, galleries were placed over the side aisles, as in the church of S. Lorenzo fuori le Mura (556) and Sta Agnese (625) in Rome (Fig. 35), or in Syrian basilicas. In some of the later churches, each aisle, as well as the nave, was terminated in an apse, as in Parenzo Cathedral (sixth century). Occasionally the aisles were extended eastward by rectangular compartments—the prothesis, in which gifts were received, and the diaconicon or vestry. The timber roofs were always of low pitch and were usually concealed by flat coffered ceilings, except in districts where wood was scarce, when the roof trusses were left visible. The narrower side aisles were sometimes vaulted, but this was exceedingly rare.

Because the Christians abandoned the vault as a means of covering their buildings, the Roman method of vault construction was forgotten and it was not until the Romanesque period that the old technique was laboriously rediscovered. More than seven centuries were to elapse between the last great vaulted monument of antiquity, the Basilica of Maxentius in Rome (*c.* 310) and the first Romanesque constructions, Speyer Cathedral and the Abbey Church at Cluny (both vaulted *c.* 1080). The absence of the vault in Early Christian architecture cannot have been due to any technical difficulty and may partly be explained by the need for economy and partly on esthetic grounds. Though the basilicas were often of considerable dimensions, they could have been vaulted in stone or concrete, but this would have entailed heavy supporting piers or the concentration of the vault at points, as in the Basilica of Maxentius: effects that were not only beyond the means of the early Christian builders but which would have been irrelevant to their esthetic objectives. These they attained more easily by ranges of pillars contributing to an unbroken perspective. Walls were roughly constructed of brick, tufa or occasionally of stone, and the very pillars and capitals themselves were being salvaged in the first instance from ancient Roman buildings. No value was placed on the ordered principles of column and entablature. If there was not a sufficient number of similarly designed fragments available, others were used. Columns that were too tall were cut down, and those that were too short were given raised bases or heightened capitals. Among the hundred or more columns in Old St. Peter's, Rome, not one was designed and worked for the position it occupied. Entablatures, too, were borrowed extensively. In the church of S. Lorenzo, Rome, various sections of entablature were ranged side by side regardless of dissimilarities.

However, supplies of old material were not inexhaustible, and outside Rome there were far fewer ancient buildings to be ransacked. Thus the time came when new columns and capitals had to be made, and coarse imitations of old Roman types were produced until these were finally replaced by original forms. The two basilicas in Ravenna, S. Apollinare Nuovo (consecrated 504) and S. Apollinare in Classe (534–549), are typical of the marked change in the quality of Early Christian architecture. In 403, the Emperor Honorius, seeking refuge from the attacks of the Visigoths under Alaric, had fixed his residence at Ravenna. In 493, the city was chosen by Theodoric to be the capital of the Ostrogothic kingdom, and from 539 to the year 752, it was an exarchate of the Byzantine Empire. Ravenna had thus for some time been susceptible to the influence of Byzantium, where architecture was rapidly developing an independent style, and it is not surprising to find that the capitals of the two churches of S. Apollinare are markedly Oriental in character. Made specially, for want of old material, they retain the bell-shaped form of Corinthian

35. Basilica with galleries over the aisles, Sta Agnese, Rome, after 625.

capitals, but the characteristic acanthus leaf decoration has been restyled. Particularly remarkable are the deep blocks or dosserets interposed between the capitals and the springing of the arches. These would seem to have no structural purpose but may have been the Byzantine architects' means of recalling the piece of entablature similarly placed in Roman architecture. The first instance of their use occurs in an underground reservoir built about 420 near Eschrefige Sokaghy at Constantinople. Here, as at Ravenna, the columns are no longer of classical form and have no entasis.

Something should also be said of the treatment of windows. These are always quite small and are seldom fitted with glass. It is true that the process of glassmaking was already known to the ancients, and as confirmed by Isidore of Seville (died 636), pure white glass had long been manufactured in Italy, Gaul and Spain. But the old green or yellow tinted glass was a costly material and the white was even more expensive, so windows of early churches were left open and hung with curtains, or following the ancient tradition, filled with thin slabs of translucent alabaster or marble pierced with circles, squares or more complicated patterns (Fig. 36).

The exteriors of Christian basilicas, like their interiors, were subject to few changes. For a long time the walls remained plain and bare, and it was not until around 540 (in S. Apollinare in Classe) that an attempt was made to provide some form of architectural ornamentation. The aisle and clerestory walls are externally decorated with narrow pilaster strips horizontally connected by small arcades under the eaves. The apse, while retaining the semicircular form inside, is externally polygonal. It may well be that this treatment was calculated to increase the strength of the wall, which from now on was frequently pierced with windows and which had to sustain the thrust of the semidome covering the apse. S. Apollinare is important in another respect: as in many of the later basilicas, the atrium has disappeared and the entrance is marked by a simple porch. On the north side, detached from the church, stands one of the earliest known circular towers or campaniles. These towers, circular or square in plan, are a characteristic feature of many later Italian churches — the most famous being the Leaning Tower of Pisa (page 231). Their original purpose still poses a problem. It seems unlikely that they were initially intended as bell towers. Documented proof has yet to be found that bells were made before the Carolingian period (eighth–ninth century), for those that have been discovered do not antedate the eighth century. It may be that plates of metal, serving as gongs, were used instead of bells, but a more probable though as yet inconclusive explanation is that these towers

were modeled on the watchtowers used in fortifications and were simply intended to advertise the location of the church from a distance.

Some basilicas in Syria also have towers, but these are a development of the main building and are not freestanding. At Turmanin (Fig. 37), the nave is preceded by a narthex or porch and above this is an open porch, like a loggia, flanked by low rectangular towers. Thus a new type of external treatment developed whereby the worshiper was prepared for his entrance into the church, not by an atrium — a feature not used in Syria — but by an emphatic façade. This method was later to be adopted in Romanesque churches.

Syrian churches are difficult to date precisely, but almost without exception they belong to the fifth and sixth centuries. In the seventh century, the Mohammedans overran Syria, putting an end to Christian building. Wood was exceedingly scarce in most regions. In the southern part of Syria in what is known as the Hauran, granite was the only available material and everything was of stone, even to the ceilings. Thus massive piers were regularly used, instead of columns, to support the heavy masonry above. At Tafkha, a series of arches was built across the church and the haunches were built up to provide a level seating for the flat granite slabs which formed the ceiling. The Syrian church builders had to be content with naves of limited height. In the north, where soft limestone was in good supply and wood was more easily obtainable, the architecture is much less cumbersome in quality and is often richly detailed. At Qalb-Louzeh and Kalat Siman, for example, there are corbels above the nave arcades supporting colonnettes to carry the roof trusses. Semicircular headed openings are set between the colonnettes (Fig. 38 a). The apse of the church of St. Simeon Stylites at Kalat Siman is externally decorated with two tiers of attached columns (Fig. 38 b). These decorations, joined to the moldings of the doors and windows, anticipate — like the façade of Turmanin — the forms employed in Romanesque buildings. At the same time they reveal a close dependence on Roman work, examples of which could be found near at hand at Baalbek (page 68).

Many churches in Africa confirm that the principles of antiquity had not been forgotten. At Tipasa and Theveste, for instance, columns are applied to the piers of the nave, and at El Hayz, engaged half columns are used. In some Syrian and many African churches (Deir-Seta, Benian, Morsott, Tebessa) the east apse does not form a semicircular projection on the exterior but is built within the thickness of the wall and is flanked by the rectangular diaconicon and prothesis at the ends of the aisles. This type of apse

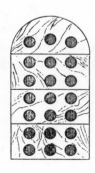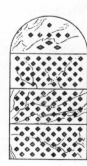

36. Windows with pierced marble infilling.

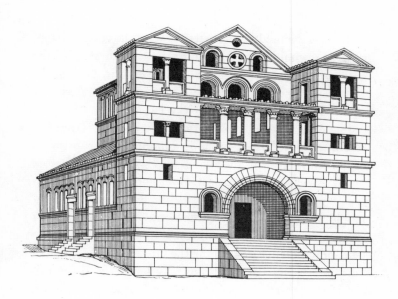

37. *Façade treatment at Turmanin, Syria, fifth century.*

fectory, kitchens and chapter house. Even in the early monasteries like those at Theveste (Egypt), Tebessa (Algeria, fifth–sixth century), Schakka and Kalat Siman (Syria, fifth–sixth century), where the buildings were arranged with much greater freedom, the church was always the most important feature both architecturally and spiritually. The church of St. Simeon Stylites at Kalat Siman is particularly remarkable. It consists of four three-aisled basilicas grouped together in the form of a cross around a central octagonal atrium, with niches in the angles. The eastern arm alone terminates in an apse flanked by two small apses and is thus distinguishable as the principal church. The demands of liturgy or the need for accommodating large numbers of monks may have given rise to this ingenious scheme. Be that as it may, the church provides another example of the interpenetration of the basilican and central plan characteristic of Byzantine architecture since the beginning of the sixth century.

recalls those in ancient temples, which were also built into the wall. Occasionally in North Africa, a second apse was built at the west end and a number of entrances was added at the sides of the church. Such features were probably not simple developments of the basilican plan, for during the fifth and sixth centuries these regions were dependencies of Byzantium (until 534, when dispossessed by the Vandals, Justinian's empire extended to North Africa), where a fusion was taking place between the elements of the basilican and centralized plans. It should also be noted that in Syria and Africa the churches frequently formed part of monastic establishments where side entrances to the church were more convenient.

Enthusiasm for the monastic life and the building of monasteries followed soon after the establishment of Christianity. Ideal monachism demanded that its followers cut themselves off from society, renounce worldly possessions, and devote themselves entirely to the service of God. Monastery buildings were either attached to a church or spread around it in the form of separate dwellings for priests, lay brethren or pilgrims. At first there was no organized pattern, but in the course of centuries the monastic group developed the characteristic plan that has become familiar through medieval examples: a cloister court (possibly derived from the Early Christian atrium) was built on one side of the church, and around this were grouped the monks' cells, common room, dormitories, re-

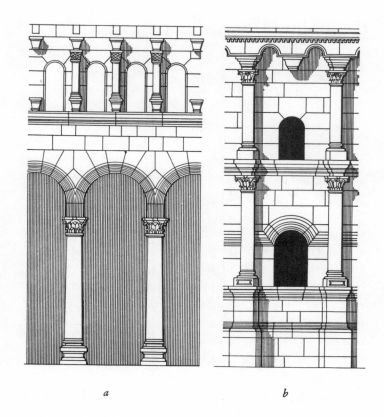

a   *b*

38. *Decoration of nave wall (left) and exterior of apse, St. Simeon Stylites, Kalat Siman, Syria, fifth–sixth century.*

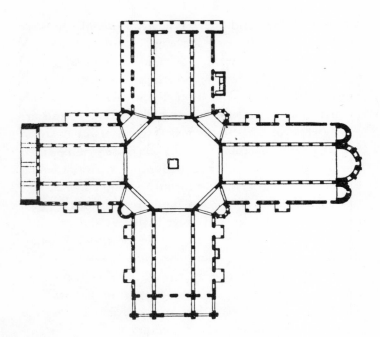

39. Plan of St. Simeon Stylites, Kalat Siman, Syria, sixth century.

Centrally Planned Buildings

1. BAPTISTERIES, FUNERARY CHAPELS AND MEMORIA

Apart from basilicas, the early Christians erected a number of buildings with a centralized plan. These are of several types, being circular, polygonal or later, and particularly in the Byzantine Empire, in the form of a Greek cross. The theme of these structures is very different from that of the basilica. The worshiper entering the building is no longer faced with the perspective of an arcade leading him toward the point of climax in the sanctuary. Instead he finds himself drawn toward the center where, with equal emphasis, the elements are grouped around the vertical axis. The spatial impression characteristic of the centralized buildings was considerably enhanced by the fact that they were generally domed and did not have the flat ceilings of the basilicas. For obvious reasons, buildings of central plan were not originally devised to be used as churches. They could not express (like the basilica) the idea of a path leading toward God, and were used for ceremonies which could take place about a central point. Among these was the ceremony of baptism, and many such

buildings were used as baptisteries. With the congregation, proselytes would gather around a large pool sunk in the center of the floor, with steps leading into it. During the early period new converts to Christianity were usually baptized by immersion, and it was not until the early Middle Ages that fonts of the type used in today's churches were introduced. The custom of administering baptism in the church itself or in the atrium was not instituted before the sixth century. There was never more than one baptistery in any town, even in cities like Rome and Constantinople where churches were numerous, and it was always situated close to the most important church.

Funerary chapels containing the sarcophagi of Christian saints and martyrs were also usually built with a centralized plan. The sarcophagus, or more frequently an altar, took the central position in the chapel. Closely related to this type of building are the memoria — among them the Church of the Holy Sepulchre at Jerusalem — erected in places of particular sanctity.

There can be no doubt as to the origin of the Early Christian, centrally planned building, for several examples of this form had been inherited from the Romans. Baptisteries, for instance, could have found their inspiration in the thermae, where the calidarium was frequently circular and surmounted by a dome and contained a bath corresponding to the baptismal pool (Fig. 27). Funerary chapels were a development of a type of Roman mausoleum, and the numerous tholoi that still survive must also have served as models. The debt to antiquity is confirmed by the fact that many baptisteries of polygonal plan are internally decorated with small rectangular or semicircular niches similar to those in the Pantheon (page 73), the calidarium of the Baths of Caracalla in Rome (Fig. 27) and the mausoleum in the Palace of Diocletian at Spalato (Fig. 40 a). But however closely Christian builders followed ancient prototypes, they also introduced some important changes. The most striking of these is the addition, in many baptisteries and funerary chapels, of one or sometimes two low aisles or ambulatories around the central area — the circular equivalents of the aisles of a basilica. Above these, clerestory windows were pierced through the central drum, which rested on arches, as at Sta Costanza, Rome (c. 330, page 124), or on an entablature, as at S. Stefano Rotondo (472, page 125 d).

During the fifth century a new and effective type of construction appeared — the cruciform building exemplified in the Mausoleum of the Empress Galla Placidia at Ravenna (c. 440, page 125 f). Four barrel-vaulted arms of almost equal length open off the central domed area, the plan resembling a Greek cross.

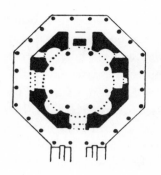 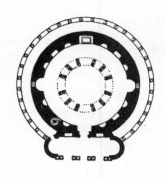 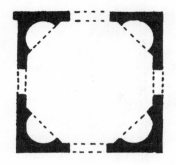 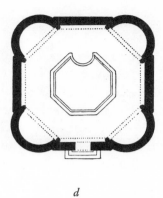

a *b* *c* *d*

40. *Comparison of baptisteries and funerary chapels with antique prototypes:*
    a) Mausoleum in the Palace of Diocletian, Spalato, c. 300;

b) Tomb of Sta Costanza, Rome, under Constantine;
c) Apartment in the Baths of Caracalla, Rome, c. 215;
d) Baptistery of the Orthodox, Ravenna, fifth century.

At first these small buildings remained isolated phenomena, but from the sixth century their plan was to become the standard type of Byzantine churches, and the centralized plan came to be used for constructions on a much larger scale. Because this development took place almost exclusively in regions under Byzantine sovereignty, some authorities consider that a characteristic Byzantine style of architecture had existed as early as the fifth century. It is true that the well-pronounced preference for domed construction, central planning and certain details, would seem to indicate that the stylistic break between East and West had already begun. But at least until the age of Justinian (527–565), there was no conscious opposition between an Early Christian art of the West and an independent art of the Byzantine Empire. The many differences that emerged in the East before this time did not amount to a new and coherent style, and should be classed among the provincial digressions that occur throughout the history of architecture. It must be remembered that in the sixth century the Church was still united, though the first signs of dissent had followed on the division of the empire and in 1054 were to culminate in the great schism between the Roman Catholic Church of the West and the Greek Orthodox Church of the East. It is a measure of the sympathy still existing between East and West at this time that Justinian aspired to extend his supremacy over the whole of the empire by numerous campaigns in Italy and Africa. Thus the architecture of Byzantium before the end of the sixth century must be recognized as a branch of Western architecture and should be called Early Christian. Only after this date can Byzantine art truly be said to have emerged.

2. CHURCHES

It is known that large, centrally planned churches, as well as the smaller baptisteries, funerary chapels and memoria, were occasionally built during the fourth century. Examples are provided in the East by the Cathedral built by Constantine at Antioch and by the Octagon erected at Nazianzus by the father of St. Gregory (died 390). However, these churches, like that described in a letter by St. Gregory of Nyssa (died 394), have now almost completely disappeared. The oldest building of this type is to be found in the West, in one of the regions most susceptible to Byzantine influence. This is the remarkable church of S. Lorenzo Maggiore in Milan.

Opinions about the origin of this building have differed widely. Some authorities contend that it was a part of the thermae of Maximian, who had removed his residence from Trèves to Milan in 293, but recent investigations have shown that S. Lorenzo was built about 360, together with the magnificent colonnade that once stood before the spacious atrium and the cruciform Chapel of St. Hippolytus at the east end, and was used by the Arian Christians. The church was severely damaged by fire several times and the great central dome fell in 1571. Repeated restorations have brought many modifications, but the original plan is preserved. To gallery height, the existing walls are those of the old church and the general character of the shell is unchanged. Since its last rebuilding, the dome is octagonal and the plan is a square with a large segmental exedra on each face projecting into an ambulatory surrounding the central area. Each exedra has two tiers of arcades and is covered with a semidome. These semidomes and the arched angles between them serve to support the central dome. Externally, towerlike features at each corner provide the necessary abutment and articulate the exterior form of the building. This arrangement seems far removed from the Christian ideal of simplicity expressed in the basilicas of the same period and reveals that the architectural concepts of Roman antiquity were by no means forgotten. The bold system of vaulting and counterpoise, and the elaboration of the plan with projecting apses and towers, shows a new approach to church architecture. The simplicity of the basilican church has succeeded to the magnificence of a *castellum dei.*

No immediate precedents have yet been found for the scheme of S. Lorenzo, and it may well have sprung from the inspiration of some architect still steeped in antique traditions who looked back to Roman buildings — perhaps to the thermae — for his example. Similar churches were built in Syria but these are of a much later date. The cathedral at Bozrah was erected in 512 and the Church of St. George at Izra' in 515. Both are square externally. The cathedral is circular inside, while at Izra' the internal shape is octagonal, and in both there is an ambulatory with semicircular angle niches surrounding the central domed area (Fig. 42 a). Though more complex in plan than the old baptisteries, these buildings have neither the double arcades nor the great projecting exedrae of S. Lorenzo. Moreover, the balance of the centralized plan, so completely preserved in S. Lorenzo, is disturbed in both these churches by the addition of a large choir terminated by an apse at the east end. Thus they are given a longitudinal emphasis

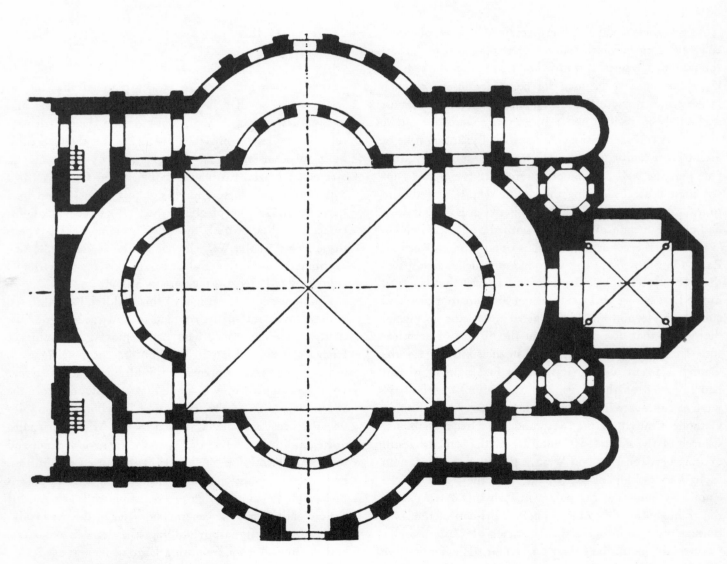

41. Plan of S. Lorenzo Maggiore, Milan, c. 360.

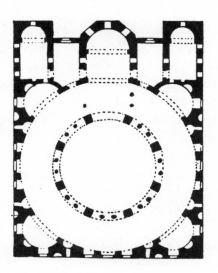
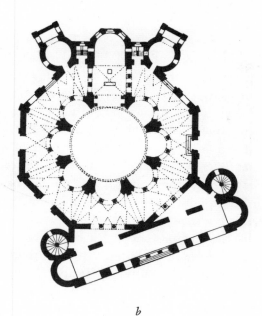
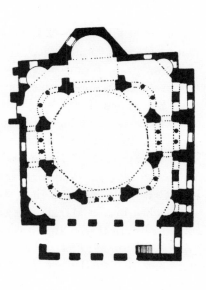

a *b* *c*

42. Centrally planned churches with an elongated choir bay: a) Cathedral at Bozrah, Syria, 512; b) S. Vitale, Ravenna, begun before 526; c) SS. Sergius and Bacchus, Constantinople, from 527.

characteristic of the basilica, and a fusion takes place between the two concepts of the central and basilican plan.

This system was later employed in two important churches—S. Vitale at Ravenna, which was to influence the design of the royal tomb-chapel of Charlemagne at Aix-la-Chapelle, and SS. Sergius and Bacchus in Constantinople, which was to have a vital effect on the development of later Early Christian architecture in the Byzantine Empire (Fig. 42 b/c, page 126). At S. Vitale, the central space is surrounded by an octagonal two-storied ambulatory interrupted on the east by an elongated choir bay, and the whole is contained within an outer octagon. The design of SS. Sergius and Bacchus is remarkably similar, but the exterior forms a square, not an octagon. The corners of the square are filled with semicircular niches, as at Izra' and Bozrah. Such Syrian examples may have had some influence on the design of the church, though in detail the interior arrangement is closer to S. Vitale. Between the pillars that mark the angles of the internal octagon of S. Vitale, semicircular exedrae open toward the ambulatory in two tiers of arches. The same disposition is found at SS. Sergius and Bacchus, although here rectangular recesses alternate with semicircular apses and the columns on the ground floor support lintels instead of arches. Even the

Byzantine cushion capitals resemble those of S. Vitale, with their deep dosseret blocks (page 122 d/e). But all these similarities pose the difficult question as to which of the two buildings is the earlier foundation. Many factors point to the precedence of SS. Sergius and Bacchus: its relation to older Oriental buildings; the fact that it was built, not in a province, but at the very center of contemporary culture; the interesting irregularity and somewhat tentative nature of its plan; and the more primitive character of the carvings on the capitals.

However, recent researches have strengthened the theory that S. Vitale was erected during the lifetime of Theodoric (died 526) and may be identical with the Basilica of Hercules which is mentioned in documents but is believed to have perished. This basilica served the court at Ravenna for state functions and receptions allied with religious ceremony. S. Vitale cannot have been intended as the cathedral church of the city, for that distinction belonged to S. Apollinare Nuovo (493–525). It seems likely, therefore, that at least as regards planning and initial structure, S. Vitale antedates SS. Sergius and Bacchus by a small margin, though it was probably later in its completion. This theory is supported by the fact that only one possible prototype for the characteristic arrangement of recesses around the octagon—S. Lorenzo in Milan—has so far been found. In spite of their structural differences and the long interval of time between them, it is reasonable to suppose that there is some connection between S. Vitale and S. Lorenzo. Both churches were used by the Arians, whose doctrine denying the consubstantiality of Christ had been condemned by the Councils of Nicaea (325) and Constantinople (381). It is true that in 539 Ravenna became a dependent diocese (exarchate) of Byzantium, but the Ostrogoths clung to their Arian beliefs until at least 547, when Bishop Maximianus took rigorous steps to root out the heretical sect. Thus it is probable that the consecration of S. Vitale in 547 marks, not the completion of the building, but the date of its conversion from an Arian to a Catholic church.

Assuming all this, there is one factor which remains puzzling: why should Justinian have had SS. Sergius and Bacchus built on the pattern of the church of his bitter enemy Theodoric? It cannot be that he hoped to outdo S. Vitale in magnificence; any such purpose was achieved in a far more decisive and startling fashion in the great church of Sancta Sophia begun in Constantinople in 532. The problem of the exact relationship between the two churches and the sequence in which they were built remains unsolved, though there is some agreement that on the foregoing grounds the church at Ravenna must, in plan at least, have preceded SS. Sergius and Bacchus.

The similarity of the two buildings raises a fundamental and important question which lies apart from mere dating problems: how did such a close resemblance come about? It could be due to the fact that Byzantine craftsmen were working in Ravenna, as well as in Constantinople, but it may also be seen as an illustration of the rule inherent in the art of the Middle Ages—that of deliberate reference to a model pattern. Creative obedience to traditional forms was not frowned upon as it is today, but actually provided a standard of accomplishment. That this was the case during early medieval times is confirmed in contemporary writings, but the same attitude is revealed long before in the art and architecture of the first Christians.

3. THE DOMED BASILICA

The type of plan used for SS. Sergius and Bacchus reached its culmination in Sancta Sophia at Constantinople, the most important church to be built in the age of Justinian.

The principal church of Byzantium was destroyed by fire during the Nika sedition of 532. Erected by Theodosius II and consecrated in 415, the earlier basilica (like its predecessor built under Constantine) had been dedicated to the Divine Wisdom—hence the name Sancta Sophia. Justinian immediately ordered that a new church be built on the site of the old and entrusted the work to the two Greek architects, Anthemius of Tralles and Isidorus of Miletus. No pains were spared to complete the vast temple in the shortest possible time. Ten thousand workmen were employed on the site and 107 costly marble columns were laboriously transported from pagan temples in Rome and Athens, from the Temple of Artemis in Ephesus and the Temple of Jupiter, Baalbek. Ruthless plundering of ancient buildings was an old custom of the early Christians, reintroduced here because of the need for speed of erection. But once more the use of the spoils of antiquity was also a means of flaunting the triumph of Christianity over paganism, which by this time had fallen into deep disrepute. It is significant that the School of Athens, the last refuge of pagan philosophy, was finally suppressed by Justinian in 529.

In the astonishingly short time of five years, the task of building Sancta Sophia was accomplished and a masterpiece was created. It equaled the finest achievements of antiquity in the grandeur of its conception and surpassed them in the ingenuity and delicacy of its construction. A fitting symbol of the glory of God, the great church was also a glorification of Justinian himself, for in the East the person of the emperor, invested with divine right, had been raised to a supernatural level by an elaborate system of ceremonial.

In plan, Sancta Sophia (pages 128 and 129) is nearly square (220 by 250 feet). At the west end of the main quadrilateral is a double narthex, and adjoining this was once a large atrium, now destroyed (Fig. 43). At the east end there is a projecting apse, polygonal externally and semicircular on the inside. The essential and dominant feature of the whole construction is the great domed central space (107 feet square). At the corners of this space stand four massive towerlike stone piers (25 by 60 feet) supporting four semicircular arches. The spaces between the arches are filled with concave triangular pieces of masonry called pendentives, by means of which the great circular dome is carried over the square space below. The dome is 107 feet in diameter and 180 feet from the floor, having been rebuilt with a slightly higher section after its partial collapse in 557. Like other Early Christian domes, it rises directly from its supports and is not raised on the drum which became customary in later periods (late

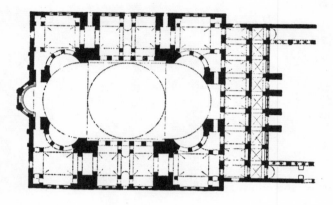

43. Plan and section of Sancta Sophia, Constantinople, 532–537.

again achieved in Sancta Sophia. The two types of plan and the different concepts they represent are thus brought together at the moment when the architectures of East and West were about to take their separate courses. On the one hand began the independent style known as Byzantine, and on the other, emerging from the Dark Ages, the Romanesque and Gothic styles of the West.

4. DOMED CHURCHES OF CRUCIFORM PLAN

The spatial arrangement of Sancta Sophia, combining the basilican and central plans, is found in several other churches, among them St. Irene, Constantinople. Here the longitudinal direction is stressed by an oblong plan with two side aisles and a sequence of two domes above the central nave (Fig. 44). In some churches, on the other hand, this entrance-apse directional emphasis was somewhat reduced by the addition of an important cross axis. The most characteristic example is the Church of the Holy Apostles, Constantinople (built by Justinian, 527–565). It was totally destroyed in 1463, but the plan is known to us and was in fact copied in two remarkable medieval monuments — St. Mark's in Venice (from 1063) and St. Front at Périgueux (from 1122), both of which provide some basis for a reconstruction of the general character of the church. Like St. Front, the Church of the Holy Apostles was a Greek cross in plan (Fig. 45), having arms of equal length on each side of a square central crossing. Thus the plan was again almost completely centralized, although the crossing was given no architectural emphasis other than its position in the center of the plan, and was crowned with a dome equal in height to those over the four arms. The entrance-apse direction is therefore maintained, but is considerably less evident than in the type of domed basilica exemplified in St. Irene.

Domed basilicas and domed churches of cruciform plan were the last architectural creations of the Early Christian period. Both were realized in the eastern part of the Roman Empire. Here alone conditions were ripe for the expansion of new architectural conceptions, for in the West the great invasions had overturned the old Roman rule and there no longer existed a government capable of providing support and patronage for the arts. In 476, the last emperor of the West, the seventeen-year-old youth Romulus Augustulus, was deposed by Odoacer, the East German master of the troops, and sent into exile. Under Theodoric, King of the Ostrogoths (died 526), there was a great re-

Byzantine, medieval and Renaissance). Thus the windows which occur between the forty great ribs are placed immediately above the cornice that defines the base, and the dome seems to float, weightless, above a circle of light. The thrusts of the four arches and the dome resting on them and on the pendentives are ingeniously abutted to the north and south by the immense masses of masonry which stand above the aisle roofs, and to the east and west by lower half domes opening off the transverse arches and themselves resting on two small exedrae also covered with semidomes. These four exedrae open toward the nave in two tiers of arcades and are flanked on one side by the great piers of the central area and on the other by the less important piers marking the entrances to the church and choir.

This building carries to an ultimate perfection the domical composition already explored in S. Vitale and SS. Sergius and Bacchus. The central space, instead of being extended on all four sides, is limited on the north and south by walls pierced with arcades, and the exedrae at either end stress the east-west direction, giving the church a longitudinal emphasis. The interpenetration of basilican and central plan (realized at Bozrah and in SS. Sergius and Bacchus by the addition of an elongated choir) is thus

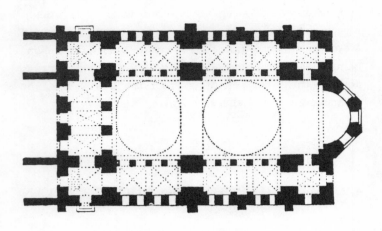

44. *Plan of St. Irene, Constantinople, built c. 535; rebuilt eighth century.*

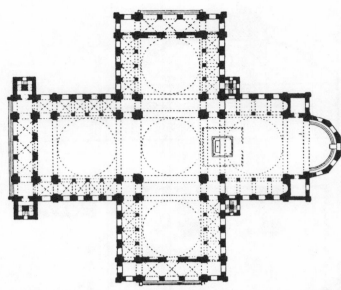

45. *Plan of the Church of the Holy Apostles, Constantinople, 527–565; destroyed 1463.*

vival of architecture at Ravenna, but this age of prosperity and achievement did not last long. It is true that building activity continued in Italy, largely due to the demands of the popes, whose power and influence were rapidly increasing in the absence of any supreme world government. But the churches that were built were unambitious, and for centuries the old basilican plan persisted without any important modifications. In the East, however, following on the churches of Justinian, the rise of Byzantine architecture proper began. It was eventually to become the official style of the whole Greek Orthodox Church and to extend into Russia and the Balkans.

EARLY CHRISTIAN ARCHITECTURE

ILLUSTRATIONS

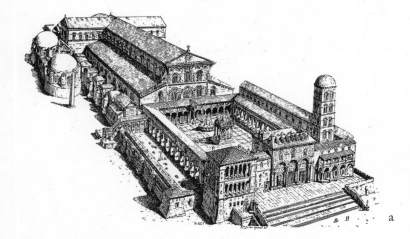

S. APOLLINARE NUOVO, RAVENNA
493–525.

This five-aisled basilica was the imperial church of Theodoric the Great, King of the Ostrogoths. It was originally dedicated to St. Martin and later to S. Apollinare when the relics of this saint were transferred here from the port of Classe. It owes its title of *coelo aureo* to the magnificent mosaic decoration of the interior. The exterior, in contrast, is severely simple, in the tradition of all Early Christian churches. Even the entrance façade is left as a blank wall, though in some basilicas it was given a mosaic decoration. The double window is a later addition. The tall central nave, flanked by lower side aisles, is a characteristic feature. The porch was built during the Renaissance, to replace the old atrium. The campanile which stands detached from the church on the north side is also later in date and is one of the earliest examples of the belfries that became common in Italy from the sixth century. Its fenestration, following a simple numerical progression, increases in richness toward the top with charming effect. (Facing page.)

a) OLD ST. PETER'S, ROME
Erected under Constantine; rebuilt c. 1450.

This basilica was built by Constantine in the circus of Nero where St. Peter was martyred and where his tomb (according to the excavations of 1957) was placed. It was pulled down to make way for the present Cathedral of St. Peter (built 1450–1585), but old measurements and drawings make an exact reconstruction possible (Fig. a). The external features were those of the ideal Christian basilica, consisting of a large atrium with a fountain for purification, preceded by an imposing propylaeum or entrance gateway. The adjoining buildings on the left were added later and the campanile was built in 752. The church had five aisles and a transept the same height as the nave.

b) S. GIOVANNI IN LATERANO, ROME
Built c. 324. After a fresco by G. Dughet in S. Martino ai Monti, Rome, c. 1640.

This five-aisled transeptal basilica was the first Cathedral of Rome and the Mother Church of the Christian world. It was originally known as the Constantinian Basilica, then as the Basilica Salvatoris, and was finally dedicated to St. John and superseded in importance by Old St. Peter's. The church was damaged by fire and earthquake and restored several times, but until the extensive rebuilding undertaken by Borromini in the seventeenth century, the interior retained its original aspect (recorded in Dughet's fresco of *c.* 1640). Columns and their capitals were taken from ancient Roman buildings, accounting for the arbitrary mixture of Ionic and Corinthian details.

c) S. PAOLO FUORI LE MURA, ROME
From 386. Destroyed by fire c. 1823; new building from 1825.

Judging by ancient accounts, this five-aisled transeptal basilica must have been the largest and most magnificent of all the early churches (390 feet long, 200 feet wide, 100 feet high). Piranesi's engraving of about 1750 recaptures the original character of the interior which was considerably modified during the rebuilding of 1825. The description *fuori le mura*, given to S. Paolo as well as to other Roman churches, recalls that it once lay outside the city wall. The tomb associated with St. Paul, over which the church was built, was situated with all other tombs just outside the town gates; Roman law forbade burial *intra muros*.

S. APOLLINARE IN CLASSE, RAVENNA
534–549.

This nontranseptal basilica keeps its original character and provides an almost perfect example of an Early Christian basilican interior. The spiritual and architectural center point is the apse where the altar stands. The monotonous rhythm of the colonnades and arches, the narrow bands with portrait medallions of bishops of Ravenna, the strips of wall high in the nave (now plain but once inlaid with marble), the rows of clerestory windows and even the visible rafters of the roof, all irresistibly lead the eye forward to this climax. The mosaic decoration (dating from the seventh century) is exclusively concentrated on the apse and on the triumphal arch that separates the sanctuary from the body of the church. As in many other churches, the image of the Saviour appears at the summit of the arch, flanked here by the emblems of the four Evangelists. A background of clouds symbolizes Paradise. The earth is represented in a separate zone below, where the souls of the faithful, portrayed as lambs, come to seek salvation in Christ. Lambs also surround the base of the semidome in the apse, where S. Apollinare intercedes for them with God, whose hand raised in benediction emerges from the sky above a huge cross, the symbol of Redemption. (Facing page.)

a

a) STA SABINA, ROME
422–425.

Sta Sabina, a three-aisled basilica, is in an excellent state of preservation, although of the original wall decoration (probably mosaics) only that around the arches is still extant. The arches are carried on magnificent Corinthian columns taken from the ancient temple of Juno Regina. As in S. Apollinare in Classe, there are rows of medallion portraits of bishops and popes. These *imagines clipeatae*, similar to those used previously in S. Paolo, were intended to illustrate the apostolic succession and would thus always begin with portraits of the Apostles and their immediate disciples, followed by successive bishops and popes in chronological order.

b) STA MARIA MAGGIORE, ROME
Original construction 352; rebuilt 432; many subsequent alterations.

Its many alterations have deprived this church of much of its original character. In the sixteenth century, two wider arched openings leading to two large chapels were introduced between the columns at the sanctuary end, thus destroying the rhythm of the colonnade. The pilaster decoration of the clerestory is of the same date. The splendid mosaic paving dates from the twelfth century and is among the finest work of the Cosmati. The richly coffered ceiling was worked by G. da Sangallo (toward the end of the fifteenth century). The apse (built between 1288 and 1292) is decorated with mosaics by J. Torriti (1295) illustrating scenes from the life of the Virgin. (Sta Maria Maggiore was the first church in Rome to be dedicated to the Virgin.) The 44 Ionic columns and their heavy entablature form part of the fifth-century church. The intercolumniation is unusually narrow, giving the nave a much more massive and powerful appearance than that of Sta Sabina. Particularly notable are the original mosaics — those surmounting the entablatures dealing with Old Testament history and those around the triumphal arch representing scenes from the life of Christ.

b

a

b

c

d/e

MOSAIC DECORATION

Early Christian churches preserve a severe external simplicity, but on the interior, the walls of the nave, triumphal arch and apse were elaborately decorated with paintings or mosaic pictures. Mosaic was the most common form of decoration from the fifth century onward. Small squares of colored glass or stones were set in damp mortar, to make up representations of religious themes. This technique, developed in Hellenic times and applied to pavements, was found to produce an effect of brilliance far surpassing that of wall paintings, with their opaque surface. Each piece of glass glows and reflects light, denying the solidity of the wall and investing it with an almost supernatural quality. Mosaic thus lends itself to the representation of sacred scenes that have spiritual, not material, significance.

The interior of the Mausoleum of Galla Placidia at Ravenna (facing page) provides a splendid example of this kind of decoration. The lower walls are lined with marble slabs, and the dome and vaults are completely covered with mosaics. Above the sarcophagus of the empress appears the figure of St. Lawrence, her fellow countryman, his martyrdom symbolized in leaping, rust-colored flames. S. Apollinare Nuovo at Ravenna (493–525, Fig. a) is also remarkable for its mosaics. On the narrow bands of wall above the clerestory is a series of panels illustrating Christological themes: those on the left represent the miracles of Christ; those on the right, episodes of the Passion. These are perhaps the first Passion scenes in the history of art. The Crucifixion, which was to be accepted as a subject in medieval art, is here omitted, as was the rule among the primitive Christians. Solemn saints attired like Roman senators stand between the windows. Below are the mosaics (executed *c*. 540) which replaced the old Arian mosaics of the Goths. On the left, 22 holy virgins march in stately file toward the figure of the Virgin enthroned, with Christ and 12 angels, while on the right (Fig. a), a procession of 26 saints moves eastward to the image of Christ in Majesty with the Evangelists. Nowhere is the theme of the basilica — the progress down the nave toward the altar — more emphatically stressed than in this church.

b) CANCELLI AND AMBOS

In many Early Christian churches, the altar space reserved for clergy was extended by a choir enclosed within low screen walls or cancelli. The cancelli in S. Clemente, Rome (Fig. b), date from 872. They were transported to the present upper church (begun *c*. 1100) from the much earlier lower church which was partially destroyed in 1084. On either side of the chancel is an ambo or raised pulpit.

c, d, e) CAPITALS AND ENTABLATURES

In the first instance, Early Christian builders would frequently use columns, capitals and entablatures from pagan temples and other buildings of antiquity. Apart from its practical advantages, this process of plundering was a means of confirming the triumph of Christianity over paganism. The primitive Christians paid little or no regard to the significance of the classical orders, but usually avoided the worst incongruities such as occur in the entablatures of S. Lorenzo fuori le Mura, Rome (Fig. c). Later, and chiefly at Byzantium where ancient buildings were not so numerous, new forms for columns and capitals were evolved. The acanthus foliage was replaced by flat, sharply outlined patterns carved on the plain convex sides of a new cubiform type of capital (Fig. d) or on the folded capital, as seen in S. Vitale, Ravenna (Fig. e). A characteristic feature of this period is the deep abacus or dosseret block frequently placed over the capitals and which may have been derived from classic entablature.

BAPTISTERIES

The baptismal fonts of today were not introduced until the Middle Ages, and in the first centuries of the Christian Era, baptism was generally by immersion. Originally the sacrament was not administered in the church itself but in small buildings, called baptisteries, erected especially for the purpose. These were always of polygonal or circular plan and centered around the essential feature, a large baptismal pool about which neophytes and congregation would gather for the ceremony. The central area was often surrounded by low aisles or ambulatories which gave the building a stepped cross section like that of a basilica. The Baptistery of S. Giovanni in Laterano (fourth century, Fig. a), perhaps the earliest of the baptisteries still extant, has retained something of its former character despite many later alterations. It is an octagonal building divided into a central portion and a surrounding aisle by a two-storied colonnade with heavy entablatures. The dome is now of timber construction but was originally of stone, and the drum, pierced with windows, rested on the entablature of the lower colonnade, while the aisle, which now has a flat ceiling, was once barrel vaulted. The Baptistery of the Orthodox at Ravenna, also consecrated to St. John the Baptist, is another octagon (rebuilt 449–452, Fig. b). This splendid monument has a rich mosaic decoration. There are no ambulatories, but on four of the eight sides are low vaulted altar niches, and the dome springs directly from the clerestory. A sixteenth-century font now stands within the original baptismal pool.

FUNERARY CHAPELS AND MEMORIA

The churches erected in honor of saints and martyrs followed the same pattern as the baptisteries. Like these, they were centrally planned, the focus of the building being an altar or sarcophagus placed at the central point. The Tomb of Sta Costanza, Rome (facing page), erected by Constantine for his daughter who died in Bithynia, is the oldest and the best preserved of all Early Christian funerary chapels. It is a circular building and the domed central space is divided from the surrounding barrel-vaulted aisle by 24 columns grouped in pairs, each pair surmounted by a heavy entablature. In the windowless walls of the aisle are set alternately semicircular and rectangular niches which still retain some of the old mosaic decoration. A similar scheme was used for the monument of St. Gereon, Cologne (Fig. c). This was built during the second half of the fourth century and no longer exists, though A. von Gerkan has made a convincing reconstruction based on remains found in the Romanesque church which now stands on the same site. It was oval in plan and had a flat ceiling. A ring of semicircular niches opened out of the central space, the intervening piers being decorated with coupled columns. At S. Stefano Rotondo, Rome (472, Fig. d), the central drum is supported by a ring of 22 Ionic columns with polished shafts, bearing a horizontal architrave. The exterior of the building is treated as simply as those of other Early Christian churches (Fig. e). The arches discernible in the wall of the aisle indicate that there was once a double ambulatory with an arched colonnade that was later walled in. Indicating the richer external architectural treatment to come is the arcading on the little Mausoleum of Galla Placidia, a brick cruciform building (c. 450, Fig. f).

a/b

c

d

e

f

a

b

SS. SERGIUS AND BACCHUS, CONSTANTINOPLE
Begun 527.

This church is square externally. Inside, a barrel-vaulted, two-storied ambulatory surrounds a central octagon covered by a dome. Opening into the ambulatory between the piers of the central area are four colonnaded exedrae alternating with rectangular niches also defined by columns. On the east, a large choir and a semicircular projecting apse stress the west-east direction and give the church a longitudinal emphasis that is absent from completely centralized baptisteries and funerary chapels. There is a close resemblance in plan between SS. Sergius and Bacchus and earlier churches in Syria, and these may well have provided a prototype for such a combination of the basilican and centralized schemes. A precedent for the characteristic arrangement of niches cannot, however, be found in Syria, and must be traced to S. Vitale, Ravenna, begun a short time before, and to S. Lorenzo Maggiore, Milan (Fig. a), the oldest of the three churches. Roman buildings of central plan, such as the Pantheon (page 72), may also have served as models. The dull white of the walls and the blue and red arabesques recall the fact that the church was converted into a Muslim mosque by the Turks after 1453. But originally the floors and walls must have had the brilliant mosaic decoration of other churches of the same period. The folded capitals of the ground-floor columns and the deep dosseret blocks above the capitals at gallery level are early instances of the use of the Byzantine forms which developed from the beginning of the fifth century. (Facing page.)

a) S. LORENZO MAGGIORE, MILAN
355–372? Later remodeled.

This church of square plan was built by the Arians. Large double-storied exedrae projecting on each side give the appearance of a round building on the exterior and enrich the spatial effect of the interior with their curving walls, semidomes and columns. The church as it now stands owes much of its character to Martino Bassi's restoration (1576–1619), when the original square of the central area was converted into an octagon and a dome was built in place of a cross vault. However, the foundations and the old structure to the height of the gallery were retained during the rebuilding, and it may safely be said that the arrangement of the interior, with its four great double-storied exedrae, was part of the fourth-century conception.

b) S. VITALE, RAVENNA
Begun before 526; final consecration 547.

Recent research has shown that this church was built during the lifetime of Theodoric the Great (died 526) and does not, as formerly supposed, date from after 530. As S. Apollinare Nuovo (525) was the imperial church, it seems likely that S. Vitale is identical with a certain Basilica of Hercules—mentioned in documents but believed to have perished—which served the court at Ravenna for state ceremonies. The building is octagonal externally as well as internally, and the treatment of the inner octagon, which has an apse on each side, is remarkably similar to that of SS. Sergius and Bacchus. The question as to which of the two buildings is the earlier foundation has been the subject of much controversy.

SANCTA SOPHIA, CONSTANTINOPLE
532–537. Anthemius of Tralles and Isidorus of Miletus.

The imperial church of Byzantium, a five-aisled basilica dedicated to the Divine Wisdom (Sancta Sophia), was totally destroyed by fire in 532. That year Justinian commissioned two Greek architects to build a new church, also to bear the name Sancta Sophia, on the same site, and to erect it with unprecedented speed — within five years. Combining the basilican with the domed centralized plan, the architects created a true domed basilica. This integration of the two types of plan results in an astonishing internal architectural effect. (Facing page. After a lithograph by architect Gasparo Fossati, 1852). The square central space, heightened by a dome on pendentives (with its apex nearly 180 feet from the floor), is the dominant feature of the whole structure. But the fact that two of its sides are closed and the other two open in huge exedrae to east and west results in a modification of the central emphasis, and a great, open longitudinal space is created. The two exedrae which abut the principal dome are themselves abutted by smaller side apses with curved arcading in two tiers — a scheme comparable to that of SS. Sergius and Bacchus (page 127).

Much of the splendid decoration of the interior has been removed as a result of iconoclastic purges or was covered by the Turks, who used the church as a Muslim mosque after 1453. The marble column shafts (all taken from pagan temples) and their beautiful capitals with flat, sharply outlined acanthus patterns, have been preserved (Fig. a). The walls up to first-floor level are faced with marble, but the upper surfaces, vaults and domes (once richly decorated in mosaics), were coated with a thick layer of plaster by the Muslims, who could not bear the sight of Christian images. About 1650, the figure of Christ in Majesty that looked down from the summit of the dome was replaced with an inscription by the calligrapher Tecneki Ibrahim, who was also responsible for the circular medallions on the principal piers. This inscription bore the names of Allah, Mohammed and the first caliphs. Since 1932, American archeologists have been removing some of the plaster, to reveal mosaics that are still in fairly good condition. However, the nobility of the architecture alone is enough to justify the eulogies showered on Sancta Sophia by Justinian's contemporaries and by those who visited the church in succeeding centuries. The central dome, which seems to hover above the circle of light formed by 40 windows around the base, creates a supremely moving impression (Fig. b). In the words of Procopius, Justinian's historian, it rests over the center, "as if suspended by a golden chain from Heaven." It may be imagined how much more magical the effect of the whole building must have been when all the brilliant mosaics were still visible. The exterior of the basilica (Fig. c) is treated with the simplicity characteristic of Early Christian churches, although the architectural effect produced by the great dome, with the semidomes massed around it, is more complex than that of the first basilicas. Later accretions such as the Turkish minarets and additions to the main buttress piers have not seriously affected the original appearance.

a

b

c

V
BYZANTINE ARCHITECTURE

Historical Background

Up to the time of its decline in the sixth century, the development of Early Christian architecture has clearly shown that the political schism in the old Roman Empire (which finally came about in 395) was followed by an ever-widening breach between the cultures of East and West. Conclusive evidence of this is the fact that from the end of the fifth and chiefly during the sixth century (the age of Justinian), religious architecture in the eastern half of the empire broke away from the Roman basilican style to which it had once been closely linked and turned decisively toward the centralized type. That this should have happened at precisely such a time can have been no mere coincidence.

There are many valid reasons for considering the whole of sixth-century religious architecture — whether basilican or centralizing — under the heading of Early Christian. Chief among these reasons, apart from the unifying force of a common faith, was perhaps the fact that the political and spiritual inheritance of the old Roman Empire remained a living and tangible idea until well into the sixth century, at least in Byzantium. There was a short-lived revival of such ideas when Justinian made a vain attempt to recover the lost unity by several victorious campaigns in Italy and North Africa and to bring the West — by now without an emperor and submerged in political anarchy — under the domination of the Byzantine Empire. The architecture of Sancta Sophia reflects the same ambition of Justinian, for it combines the basilican and the domed central plans: the two architectural ideals of West and East. But despite his military successes, Justinian was never to achieve his purpose. The fundamental East-West conflicts, which had made themselves felt even during the early years of the empire, had meanwhile grown too acute to be overcome. The great invasions shook the western empire to its base and changed the course of history by introducing a new, Germanic, element. By the sixth century, no will — however determined, no force — however strong, could have prevented this change of course, so deep was its effect on every aspect of social and intellectual life.

From the fifth century, a powerful Germanic empire began to develop in the northern provinces of the Empire of the West. This was to become a dominant force in Italy. It was only one of the factors instrumental in the collapse of Justinian's plans for reunification, and eventually the eastern part of the empire became an independent Byzantine state, while in the West — laboriously but steadily — the foundations of modern Europe were laid.

Another cause, equally important, lay in the ethnological and religious differences which had always divided the two parts of the empire and which nothing had wholly reconciled. When Byzantium had been proclaimed the second Rome, a great Latin wave swept over the eastern empire, but despite the mingling of populations that accompanied this, the eastern provinces never adopted the racial and social characteristics of the Latins. Though for centuries the Church provided a link between the eastern provinces and between them and the western half of the Roman Empire, it must not be forgotten that in all essentials the spiritual foundations of the Eastern Church were not Latin but Greek, so much so as to justify the title

of the Greek Orient. It is no coincidence that from the time of Justinian, Greek replaced Latin as the official language of the Byzantine court.

Of even greater portent were the political troubles of the eastern empire, which forced the rulers of Constantinople to devote their whole attention to their subject provinces and to neglect their interests in the West. Even the immediate successors of Constantine had to contend with the Persians, who were to constitute a recurrent danger until the seventh century. The Persian menace was more serious than the threat from the Goths on the western frontiers, which Justinian had been able to ward off by the victories of his troops under Narses and Belisarius in Italy and North Africa. The destruction of Jerusalem by the Sassanians took place in 614. Constantinople was besieged in 616 and 626, though each time the Persian troops were repelled at the Great Wall of Theodosius (page 95). By his decisive victory at Nineveh (627), the Emperor Heraclius (610–641) was finally able to defeat and crush the Persians, but to the east lay an enemy still more formidable: the Arabs, adherents of a new faith, Islam, which itself aspired to universal acceptance. The Arabian armies surged across the frontiers under the green banner of the Prophet Mohammed (c. 570–632), making extensive conquests in Asia Minor. They invaded North Africa, and, at the beginning of the eighth century, overwhelmed Spain and wrested it from the Visigoths, crossed the Pyrenees to meet their match at last in 732 at the hands of Charles Martel and his Franks, who ultimately checked their expansion in Europe. Byzantium may be said to have triumphed, although her rulers, many of whom were men of weak character, were not able to avert the final loss of most of the eastern Mediterranean lands or to prevent the Slavs from entering the Balkans. When the Muslim Turks took Constantinople in 1453, the once vast empire comprised little more than this one city.

The pressure of eastern populations hastened the development of an isolated Byzantine Empire and opened the way for Oriental influences at the expense of Western contacts. By the sixth century, this was already evident in the pronounced preference for domed construction — a particularly popular architectural form in the Near East, where it originated. It was in Oriental ideas that the sovereigns of the Eastern Roman Empire, no longer able to rule and dominate by an assumption of divinity, sought, through elaborate and subtle ceremonial, for means to justify the creation of a regal setting in scale with their authority. The old concept of Roman supremacy was forgotten, and even before the time of Justinian, the imperial rule implied religious and political omnipotence and took the form of an absolute despotism. Upheld by a rigid hierarchy of court officials and by the authority of the Church (which suppressed all nonconformist thinking), this system of government stood in direct contrast to that of the West which (from the end of the eighth century), with the Carolingians, had attempted to synthesize the Frankish warrior monarchy and the ancient form of Roman imperialism. Despite many crises, Eastern absolutism lasted until the fall of the Byzantine Empire in the fifteenth century and never had to sustain the dissensions brought about in the Western empire by the struggle between the popes and the rulers during the Middle Ages.

Where the Church was concerned, a schism between East and West was inevitable. Constantinople, founded under the sign of the Cross, soon became a religious center of the first importance and again mirrored the first Rome. Here, or in the immediate vicinity, the first ecumenical councils of the Eastern and Western churches had taken place and the foundations of dogma had been established. It was from Constantinople, too, that the repression of heretics was conducted — heretics implying all those who deviated from the orthodox faith: Arians, Monophysites and others. The Bishop of Constantinople (promoted to the rank of patriarch, 381) rapidly exceeded the patriarchates of Antioch, Jerusalem and Alexandria in importance. His primacy was officially recognized at the Council of Chalcedon (451), and in 518 he took his place beside the Bishop of Rome in the capacity of Ecumenical Patriarch (universal, imperial bishop). Although the latter's status remained uncontested for the time being, this was no longer held to imply the subordination of the Bishop of Constantinople. It was at this moment that the first signs of the coming schism appeared. In proportion as the popes strove to maintain their supremacy over the patriarchs of Constantinople and as they in their turn resisted this pressure, so the rift between the two Churches widened. In 863, Pope Nicholas I and the patriarch Photius hurled at each other the weapons of excommunication, and in 1054 the break already patent in dogmatic controversies was rendered irreparable by the institution of two separate Churches: the Greek Orthodox and the Roman Catholic.

These briefly sketched events, which concerned the progress of ideas and religion as much as the world of politics, resulted in the final opposition of two powers — the Byzantine Empire and the Holy Germano-Roman Empire of the West, each with its own Church. The effect on the development of architecture was decisive, and the individualities of style already perceptible in the sixth century became so pronounced as to produce a distinctive Eastern architectural style that may truly be called Byzantine.

Art and Architecture in the Byzantine Empire

Byzantine architecture, like that of the early Christians, was essentially a religious architecture. It is true that the imperial palaces provided some fine examples of secular building, but few of these are now extant and they constitute a specialized subject that lies outside the scope of this work. Although so many churches survive, it would be a mistake to suppose that they provide adequate architectural witness of the thousand years of the Byzantine Empire. Nor do they in themselves offer the wide range of originality and the rich and varied achievement found in the architecture of the West after the eighth century. The magnificent achievements of the age of Justinian, that had augured so well for the future, were never to be repeated, and no Byzantine building was to approach them in sheer grandeur of conception or in any other respect.

The Church of St. Mark, Venice (built 1063–1085; consecrated 1094) is the only monument that bears comparison with those of the sixth century (pages 148 and 149). How significant it is that this, perhaps the most important example of Byzantine architecture in the Middle Ages, should have been built on territory belonging wholly to the West, though linked with the East by trade. The splendor of St. Mark's was not a natural product of Byzantine art. The design sprang from the ambition of the doges of the Republic of Venice, who aspired to build a gorgeous religious monument worthy of their power and comparable to the buildings of Constantinople and the great cathedrals then being built north of the Alps and in France.

The differences between the architectures of East and West may be explained in a number of ways, but the most profound cause lay in the diametrically opposed political systems and cultures of the two empires. In the West, the breach between the two great powers, the Church and the State, became steadily wider. Rivalry between pope and emperor was frequently heated as each sought to exert his own supreme authority. This rivalry provided new stimulus for architecture and was conducive to variety of style, for it was through buildings erected in their names that pope and emperor hoped to make their own power manifest to the world. Sometimes siding with the Church and sometimes with the State but in the long run following their own policy, the prosperous medieval monasteries also contributed to the great increase in building activity. A further element emerged later in the Middle Ages with the rise of the cities and their independent middle class which — like the Church, the monasteries and the State — was to become an important source of architectural patronage. The distinctive racial characteristics of each country within the Western empire and the gradual tendency of these countries to establish their own national identities finally accounted for the variety in style of Western architecture.

The rivalries between these several powers and the political crises of the West, often devastating in their effects, were as foreign to the Byzantine Empire as Western art was to that of the East. Until its fall in the fifteenth century, Byzantium enjoyed a single and self-sufficient civilization in which the Church was subject to the State and which remained strong enough to overcome all dynastic and ecclesiastical disputes. Dynastic changes (Macedonian dynasty — 867–1081; Comnenian — 1081–1204; Palaeologian — 1261–1453) affected Byzantium as little as did the Latin empire of the Crusaders (1204–1261).

For more than a century (726–842), the arts were seriously threatened by disputes concerning the use of images in the service of religion. Although this question certainly had dynastic implications, it was chiefly the outcome of a series of arguments that had disturbed the Church ever since its foundation. Should man-made images be used in religion, as was the custom in antiquity, or should God be worshiped, as St. John had decreed, "in Truth" alone — that is, as a spirit not made manifest in visible images? The primitive Christians had held to the latter idea, but since the third century and especially since Christianity had become the state religion and churches had been built to serve it, the representation of the divinity in human form had once again become the current practice. The enlightened clergy and the court were against the use of images, but the mass of believers — the common people — felt a need to be guided in their worship by some pictorial means and not simply by the priests. This question was to be taken up by religious orders many times during the Middle Ages, and again by the leaders of the Reformation. Indeed, it has never been resolved.

In Byzantium, the issue was to become vital, for the Arabs — whose religion allowed only abstract representations of God and positively abjured the use of figurative images — were not slow to seize on their presence in Christian churches and their use in worship as material for anti-Christian propaganda. The Emperor Leo III proscribed the existence as well as the worship of religious pictures, and the churches of the Byzantine Empire were cleansed of their images. A bitter struggle then ensued

between the two parties: those in favor of images and their opponents — the Iconoclasts. In the course of this struggle many works of art were destroyed.

The second Nicene Council (787) decreed that the worship of painted or mosaic pictures was permissible, provided they were not regarded as being more than representations of the divine. The contest was maintained until 842 when it ended with the final establishment of images by the Empress Theodora.

These disputes did not directly affect architecture as an essentially nonrepresentational art, except insofar as they tended to paralyze any form of artistic activity. However, architects were forced to abandon the idea of using sculptured figures of saints in their designs. Sculpture — entailing explicit physical representation — remained a forbidden art and was never developed in relation to architecture in the Byzantine Empire. Even relief sculpture, closely related to two-dimensional imagery, was rarely employed.

ARCHITECTURAL CHARACTER:

PLANNING AND CONSTRUCTION

The Justinian era saw no violent change in the direction of architecture, notwithstanding any distinctions that may be drawn between Early Christian and Byzantine building. Though the creative energy and outburst of building activity which characterized the sixth century was soon dissipated and the religious architecture of the succeeding period — manifestly more modest in ambition — never rose to the height of achievement witnessed in Sancta Sophia, the thread of development continued unbroken.

The constructional and decorative themes of the domed basilica (Sancta Sophia) and the domed church (Church of the Holy Apostles at Constantinople) became the subject of many variations on the theme of the Greek cross. But in the thousand years of the empire's history, no really new structural system was to appear. Until the fall of the empire (and even today in the monasteries of Mount Athos), Byzantine architects almost dogmatically adhered to the centrally planned domed scheme, with entrance and apse facing each other on the horizontal axis. Indeed, Byzantine architecture maintained a style so uniform and unchanging that it has sometimes been criticized as monotonous and stereotyped in form. Such a criticism is well justified if certain reservations are made for the period between the tenth and the fifteenth centuries, and this defect is surely to be explained in the light of the nature of the empire itself. It knew nothing of the violent antagonism between Church and State that gave a stimulus to Western art and was favorable to creative activity. Moreover, the Church of the West was more flexible in its doctrine than the Orthodox Church, which remained bound fast to a tradition of doctrine and ritual regarded as final and irrevocable. It is hardly surprising, therefore, that church architecture of the East should express a corresponding dogmatic conservatism.

This is not to say that there is no evidence of change in Byzantine architecture. Between the seventh and the ninth centuries, architects concentrated on the tasks of adapting Early Christian forms to the more modest scale of the new churches and of resolving, in the simplest and most economical manner, the problems of thrust and counterthrust involved in domed construction. Results varied considerably, but there was a general tendency — later to become a standard practice — to group all the elements around a central square surmounted by a dome, and then to enclose the whole within a square or, more frequently, a rectangular shell. As shown in Sancta Sophia, Salonika (Fig. 46 a), the central square could be extended on all four sides to form wide, shallow bays separated from the side aisles by arcades and intersected at choir and entrance by transverse aisles. The domed central area, with its lateral projections, would tend to reduce the importance of the horizontal axis if it were not for the emphasis given to the choir in front of the apse. This has the effect of adding to the length of the nave, so that at Salonika the longitudinal direction is considerably more apparent than in Sancta Sophia, Constantinople. In the Church of St. Nicholas at Myra (Fig. 46 b), the axial tendency of the nave is still more evident, for there are no lateral arms to the domed central area. St. Nicholas differs again from the church at Salonika in the system adopted for buttressing the dome. Four small domes are placed over the square compartments that terminate the side aisles, stabilizing the angle piers and serving to take the thrust of the principal dome. It was this scheme which was to be adopted for most Byzantine churches from the ninth century onward and was to dominate the future of Byzantine architecture.

In later churches, the central area lost the basilican character still evident at Myra, and was given the regular Greek cross plan, foreshadowed in an imperfect form at Salonika. The ideal type consists of a square domed space

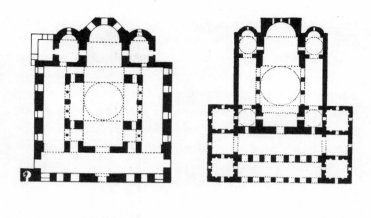

46. *Early domed churches of Greek-cross plan:*
    a) Sancta Sophia, Salonika;
    b) St. Nicholas, Myra.

with bays of equal length on each side — usually barrel vaulted. The two lateral bays are not separated from the central area by arcades but form an uninterrupted space from wall to wall. The corners of the cruciform plan are covered with cross vaults or more frequently with small domes, as at Myra. This arrangement was to be the standard church type of the later Byzantine Empire down to the fifteenth century, and even in countries lying outside the confines of the empire — such as Russia — it received only minor modifications.

The cruciform main structure was not the sole element in the planning of these churches. The plans of those at Salonika and Myra already display two earlier characteristic features found in some Early Christian churches (Fig. 45). There is a porch or narthex in place of an atrium (at Myra the narthex is doubled) in which a gallery for women was sometimes placed. The choir and sanctuary, with its apsidal end, are flanked by side chapels with small apses called pastophoria. These add to the extent of the choir, for they are connected to it by doorways. Like the prothesis (north of the sanctuary) and the diaconicon (south of the sanctuary) in Early Christian churches, one chapel was used as a place for offerings and liturgical accessories, and the other as a vestry.

The ordinance of the east end of Sancta Sophia at Salonika (Fig. 46 a) is an exception to the general rule, for usually the pastophoria were placed in the line of the side aisles, as at Myra. But it does demonstrate the close relationship established between these eastward features — a relationship that was to become still more pronounced when they were later completely separated from the main body of the church. To achieve this isolation, the low chancel walls, used earlier to define the space reserved for clergy, were replaced by tall entablatured colonnades comparable in function to the rood screens of Romanesque churches in the West. Subsequently the sanctuary came to be entirely cut off from the rest of the church by a screen (iconostasis) hung at random with a variety of sacred pictures (icons). These screens, though rare in the Byzantine region, became the rule in Russian churches of the fifteenth and sixteenth centuries. Priests alone were permitted to enter the sanctuary, and the sacred offices were conducted out of the sight of the congregation, which took part only in imagination. The mystery thus surrounding the sacred rites stimulated religious fervor among the people and was characteristic of the Eastern, and particularly the Russian, Church, constituting one of the essential differences from Western practice. It is true that in the West a type of decorated screen — the Gothic winged retable — appeared almost simultaneously with the iconostasis, but this was not intended to screen the ceremonial from the congregation. On the contrary, like the mosaics in the apse of an Early Christian church, its function was to form a background or pictorial accompaniment to the actions of the priest at the altar.

The vital significance of the dome in Byzantine religious architecture may be better appreciated in the cross sections of the churches than in their plans. The central dome governs the effect of the interior as much as that of the exterior where, like a *primus inter pares,* it dominates the smaller domes grouped around it. It is clear that the dome form was welcomed as giving the most favorable opportunity for the display of the preconceived decorative schemes associated with Byzantine art. More important in the present context is the fact that the whole architectural arrangement of the church was inexorably governed by the structural requirements of the dome and its supports. The Early Christian churches of the sixth century (and later buildings like those at Salonika and Myra) had already pointed to a solution of the technical problems. The weight of the principal dome was mainly supported on four heavy piers at the corners of the central square and abutted by a system of arches and vaults varying in complexity, or by a heavy containing wall. This method was adopted in later churches but was considerably systematized and simplified. Owing to the smallness of these buildings (sometimes barely 50 feet long) and their domes (seldom more than 16 feet in diameter), it was no longer necessary to use the powerful, massive supports older monuments had demanded, and the four heavy angle piers were frequently

replaced by columns. Early instances of the use of this system are found in the Church of Theotokos Pammakaristos (the All-Blessed Mother of Christ) in Constantinople (built *c.* 900) and in the smaller of the two churches in the Monastery of St. Luke of Stiris in Phocis, Greece (built *c.* 1000, Fig. 47). In this example, the four columns standing at the corners of the central square first carry the small arches leading to the vaulted compartments in the angles. Above these, the main walls carry the barrel vaults spanning the arms of the Greek cross, and these in turn merge with the pendentives that carry the central dome. Here indeed is a system logically developed from the necessities of structure and expressed in the simplest possible terms.

The old pier system was still employed, though it was the subject of some important changes. One of the most interesting examples is the large Church of St. Luke at Phocis. The relatively large dome is carried on twelve piers. The transition from the square to the round drum is effected by squinch arches across the angles of the square, to form an octagon, and then by small pendentives to form the circle. The grouping of the piers is governed by this method of construction. They are not placed around the central square at regular intervals; instead, four stand at the angles and the others are placed on the sides at the points of the octagon above (Fig. 47). The girdle of piers thus formed clearly defines the central domed quadrilateral. The plan of St. Luke's is more completely centralized than that of the smaller church adjoining it, which represents the classic domed cruciform type where the effect of a central nave running from narthex to altar is modified by the dome and the lateral arms of the cross. The main basilican nave, with its east-west axis, dominates, however, for the arms of the cross toward the entrance and toward the choir are of the same width and nearly the same length as the central square. In the larger church, on the other hand, the piers restrict the arms of the cross, which are of modest dimensions compared with the dominant central space, and this embraces both the central choir and its lateral compartments. The eastern arm is not prolonged in the usual manner but itself forms the choir and is terminated by an apse so that the four arms are almost identical. Thus the plan approaches the complete symmetry which is the basis of the centrally planned building in its purest form.

The coordination of central space and three-part choir which occurs in St. Luke's was copied for many later churches, chiefly those attached to monasteries. In monastery churches, the choir was generally re-established as an extension to the eastern arm, and for smaller buildings,

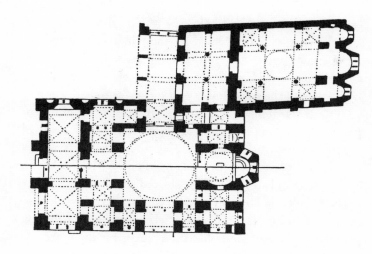

47. Two churches of the Monastery of St. Luke of Stiris, Phocis, Greece. Beginning of the eleventh century.

the supporting piers of St. Luke gave way to a simpler system where the dome was supported by eight columns. Sometimes, as in the Panayia Paregoritissa (end of tenth century) and in the beautiful church of Sta Fosca at Torcello, near Venice (eleventh century), the projection of the arms of the cross was so much reduced that the containing walls themselves took the place of the four angle piers as supports for the dome.

Most Byzantine churches followed one of the foregoing schemes, but some brief mention should also be made of the arrangement which became the standard type for the monasteries of Mount Athos. This differs from those already described in several ways. The transepts, as well as the choir, terminate in apses with semidomes (page 144; Fig. 48), and in the larger examples, a self-contained ante-church is interposed between the narthex and the main building. Of these two main changes, the triapsidal treatment of the east end is the most significant and makes an early appearance in the small church of St. Elias in Salonika (built 1012). This is perhaps the precursor of the trefoil choirs that characterize the great Romanesque churches of the eleventh and twelfth centuries in Cologne, Sta Maria im Capitol, Holy Apostles, etc. (page 235), and which in turn led on to those of Tournai Cathedral (twelfth century) and St. Elisabeth, Marburg (c. 1235). There is indeed a striking resemblance between these Western churches and such Byzantine examples, for in either case a high central dome was surrounded on three sides by semicircular apses with semidomes, while a long nave

opened off the fourth side. However, it is unlikely that Western architects, working under conditions totally different from those in the East, copied these features directly from Byzantine designs, where the idea of a central dome received so much more emphasis.

After the ninth century, the central dome was built upon a cylindrical or many-sided wall or drum by which it was hoisted above the rest of the building to form the dominant feature of the design. Subsidiary domes were also raised on drums, though remaining subordinate to the central element, as may be seen in the beautiful Church of the Holy Apostles, Salonika (tenth century, page 145).

The drum — perhaps the most important of all Byzantine contributions to architecture — had its origins, not in the need for new esthetic effects, but in a practical requirement. The domes of ancient buildings (Pantheon, Rome, pages 72 and 73) and Early Christian churches (Sancta Sophia, Constantinople, pages 128 and 129) started directly from the walls or from the top of the circle formed by pendentives. In centrally planned buildings without side aisles, the problem of lighting was easily solved: windows pierced in the containing wall or — in the case of the Pantheon — a large opening in the top of the dome provided adequate light. Where there were ambulatories, the central space was carried above the adjacent aisle roofs and given clerestory windows. The structural scheme of Sancta Sophia had precluded this solution, and the windows were placed in the dome itself, immediately above the springing. This in turn was not practicable in Byzantine churches, for their principal domes were too restricted in diameter to allow windows to be introduced without

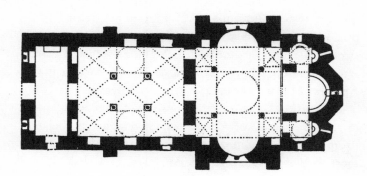

48. Church of the Monastery of Dochiariou, Mount Athos.

clumsiness or risk of weakening the fabric. The other alternatives were equally impossible, for the barrel-vaulted transepts branching off the central area rose to the base of the dome and gave no opportunity for a clerestory. Thus it became necessary to build a drum that could provide a vertical surface for windows.

ORNAMENT

Byzantine architects rejected most of the forms of interior architectural decoration that had been employed in Roman antiquity and were to reappear in Western architecture after the ninth century. Like the early Christians, they preferred to leave the surfaces of walls and vaults unbroken by moldings and other plastic effects. Sometimes narrow cornices articulate the springing line or rudimentary archivolts appear. Door and window jambs are invariably left smooth. When columns are used, their function is primarily structural and they are not entasized: that is to say, they are straight-sided. Carving in relief is limited to the column caps and even these are sometimes left plain. The forms evolved by the early Christians were long retained, and capitals were of the cubiform or basket type, carved with incised acanthus foliage of sharp outline. Later these gave way to a type more similar to the slender bell-shaped Corinthian capital of antiquity. But nowhere in Byzantine capital design is the richness of invention that characterizes its development in Western architecture (pages 238 and 241).

Flat, colored decoration with mosaic or frescoes was, however, elaborate in the extreme. Internal walls were lined with marble, while vaults and upper walls were sheathed with brilliantly colored glass mosaic pictures of a heavenly world inhabited by saints and symbolic figures. These and the incidents of Holy Scripture were the only subjects to be represented in Byzantine art, taking forms that were so strictly prescribed by doctrine that even the twentieth-century paintings in the monasteries of Mount Athos scarcely vary from those of the earliest times. Articles of faith, once instituted, are unalterable.

The spiritual focus of this world of sacred images was always the figure of Christ, which was given the most prominent position in the church — the vault in the apse or most frequently the central dome itself. The dome was regarded as both symbolic of Heaven and an actual part of the Beyond from which the sacred figure looked down,

isolated from the world below by the height of the dome and the ring of light formed by the windows. Christ was represented, not as the Son of God made Man or as the Good Shepherd, but as Pantocrator, the Ruler of the Universe and the stern Judge of the Apocalypse.

Few Byzantine churches still retain their beautiful painted or mosaic surfaces. Much of that which escaped the fury of the iconoclasts in the eighth and ninth centuries was later destroyed by the onslaughts of the Mohammedan Turks. It is only in buildings erected on the outskirts or beyond the boundaries of the old empire that the splendid interior decoration once characteristic of all Orthodox churches has been preserved intact. Among these are the churches of Old Russia, those of Sicily — where Byzantine influences produced a strangely hybrid architectural style — and despite its strong connections with Western Romanesque, St. Mark's in Venice. The monasteries of Mount Athos, too — where the ancient traditions and doctrines of the Byzantine faith have remained unchanged to this day — allow glimpses of that heavenly host that was the inspiration of the Orthodox believer.

The exteriors of Byzantine churches, on the other hand, have survived the vicissitudes of time unaltered. Though Byzantine architects were aware of the esthetic possibilities inherent in that juxtaposition of horizontal wall mass and vertical drum and dome which determined the form of their buildings, they were usually content to allow the external design to grow naturally out of the requirements of internal structure. Whatever could not be justified from this point of view and would only serve as superfluous decoration for the shell — towers flanking façades, for instance — was scrupulously avoided, with the result that the exteriors of Byzantine churches are always the clear expression of internal construction. In spite of this, the Byzantine designers were unwilling to accept the monotonous plainness and total lack of decoration that had distinguished even the latest buildings of the Early Christian period.

A marked preference for a decorative device appeared at an early date and derived from antique models or from Asia Minor; it consisted of bands of light-colored stone alternating with courses of bright red bricks. The mortar joints, which are usually very thick, contribute to the attractive effect produced by these layers of color (page 144). The horizontal lines stress the broad, earth-bound solidity of the lower part of the church and provide a foil for the brief vertical movement of the drums carrying the domes. This effect seems to have been deliberate, for the alternating bands seldom appear in the superstructures. From the tenth and eleventh centuries, much use was made of courses of tiles forming decorative patterns subtly varied in width and disposition, to contribute to the impression of horizontality. This type of decoration was chiefly applied to the east end of the church where the tiles were inserted into the outer face of the projecting polygonal or semicircular apses (page 144) and also to the entrance side, which received no architectural emphasis.

The introduction of multicolored glazed tiles — a technique learned from Mohammedan architecture — added to the richly decorative appearance. These devices were still two-dimensional in their effect, but a more truly architectural type of ornament was being evolved at the same time. The repertoire of forms was limited, however, and blind arcades barely projecting from the surface were almost the only features of this kind to be employed. They relieve the monotony of the walls without destroying the sense of enclosure and with a minimum of modeling. The most pleasing decorative schemes were evolved for the drums. Narrow windows — mere slits in the later period — are set within arches recessed in rings and flanked by slender half colonnettes supporting the heavy eaves. The roof tiling is not carried on rafters but is bedded directly on the outer surfaces of the dome and its haunches, following its curvature and easily and effectively rising over the arched heads of the windows in the drum. The pitched roofs over the lower buildings rise directly from the wall heads. The eaves are usually emphasized by several tiers of roofing tiles rising scallopwise one above the other. In later churches, however, and particularly in Russian examples, the eaves are not level but rise and fall over the blind wall arcades, with a lively and striking result (page 151 b).

The blind arcades had a practical as well as a decorative function, for they helped to reduce the weight of the walls. It is surprising to find that Byzantine architects did not employ large windows to the same end. These were, indeed, always used with excessive restraint, becoming smaller and smaller until they were finally reduced to tall, narrow slit openings. They were usually filled in with pierced slabs of stone instead of glass, which remained costly, and thus let in very little light. This must have been the architects' intention, for even in later churches that exhibit Western influences or were actually built by architects from the West — like the Uspenski Cathedral in Moscow (page 151) — the same slitlike windows were used. The explanation must be that the half-light was a deliberate measure to give the interior an atmosphere of mystery and solemnity appropriate to the church and allow the figure of Christ Pantocrator, floodlit by the windows around the drum, to make a more powerful effect from its commanding position.

THE SPREAD OF THE BYZANTINE STYLE

Though the Byzantine style had contributed little that was new to the repertoire of architectural forms, its influence extended throughout the Greek Orthodox world — into Armenia, Georgia and the north Balkans — eastward far beyond the borders of the empire, and westward into countries linked with the East by trade or other means. The powerful and flourishing Republic of Venice, a depot for merchandise from the East, possesses in St. Mark's (begun 1063; consecrated 1094, page 149) the largest and most beautiful of all churches in the Byzantine style, although it was not modeled directly on the characteristically Byzantine domed cruciform type but on Justinian's Church of the Holy Apostles in Constantinople (Fig. 45). Like this church, St. Mark's is of Greek-cross plan (Fig. 49). There are five great domes, the two larger being placed over the nave and crossing, and the aisles are lined with galleries. Nothing is seen here of the tendency — still hesitant but unmistakable in the Romanesque architecture of the period — toward the sculptural treatment of wall surfaces by the use of buttresses, pilasters, blind arcades and richly modeled piers. On the contrary, the interior decoration of St. Mark's, in the Byzantine manner, relies wholly on the magic of precious materials and their brilliant colors. The ground story has a marble veneer; gilded capitals surmount multicolored marble pillars, and the upper surfaces of the walls, the vaults, pendentives and domes are gorgeous with gold mosaics. All this richness gives the interior something of the mystery and color of an Oriental fairy tale and offsets the heaviness of the architecture with its massive piers and arches supporting the domes.

The church of St. Front at Périgueux (begun 1122, page 217), which also repeats the plan of Justinian's Church of the Holy Apostles, is bare of all mosaic decoration and the wall surfaces preserve a simplicity that emphasizes the grandeur and purity of the architecture. The spirit of Byzantine art no longer dominates, and the church reflects the general Romanesque tendency to stress the quality of the masonry itself. St. Front is in this way closely related to the great Romanesque domed churches built in Aquitaine from the eleventh century, which owe as much to the domed constructions of Roman antiquity as to the architecture of Byzantium.

Byzantine influence was particularly strong in Sicily, where during the reign of the Norman kings (Roger II, William I and William II, 1130–1189), there was a brief but spirited outburst of building activity. The theme of the domed Byzantine church, the architectural forms of the Saracens, who had occupied Sicily and the south of Italy before the Normans, and finally the long-naved basilican scheme then predominant in the West, merged with one another to produce a largely harmonious style. The scheme most frequently employed was the basilican, and the only church which followed the simple Byzantine ground plan was the little Greek Orthodox Church of Sta Maria dell' Ammiraglio (La Martorana) in Palermo (built 1143 by George of Antioch, High Admiral of Roger II, page 148 b). It is rectangular, with three apses at the east end, a narthex at the west, and a central dome supported on four columns. The western arm was later prolonged to form a Latin cross, and smaller domes were erected over the nave, giving the church its present basilican character.

In the church of S. Giovanni degli Eremiti at Palermo (begun 1132), the basilican perspective effect is more evident. There are two domes over the nave and three over choir and transepts. The famous Capella Palatina in the Palace at Palermo (1129–1156) and Monreale Cathedral (1174–1179), generally held to be the finest monument of Sicilian architecture, both have a long basilican nave with two side aisles and a dome at the eastern end. But even these buildings, so close to the Early Christian-Romanesque tradition, exhibit Byzantine features, not in their architecture but in their internal decoration. All the wall areas above the dado of marble slabs, together with arches and vaults, are covered with glittering Byzantine mosaics in which ancient sacred figures stand enshrined in a glowing, golden background, almost outdoing those of St. Mark's itself in richness and sheer brilliance of color.

Countries which had been converted to the Greek Orthodox faith were naturally more susceptible to the influence of Byzantine art than those in the West, for with the new religion they also adopted its traditional church forms. In these regions of eastern Europe (the Balkans, Russia), Asia Minor and the Caucasus (Armenia, Georgia), there was no pre-established architectural tradition to be uprooted, and Byzantine forms readily imposed themselves everywhere. Though local and national characteristics and influences from other cultures occasionally gave an individual flavor to religious buildings, their fundamental structure remained wholly Byzantine.

There are few churches in Bulgaria, and these are of little architectural interest. The buildings in Macedonia, most of which are small (page 147), closely follow the domed cruciform scheme. They date from between the twelfth and the fourteenth centuries and were contemporary with the churches of Serbia (patriarchate of Pec), which are more important stylistically though less depen-

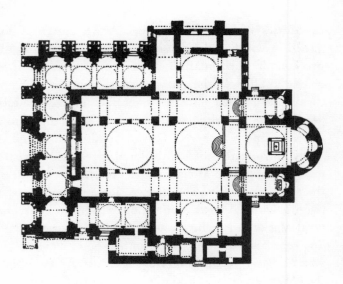

49. St. Mark's, Venice. Begun 1063; consecrated 1093. Plan showing later additions.

dent on Byzantine prototypes. Romanesque influence was strong, owing to the fact that Serbia maintained a large trade with the West and was temporarily reconciled with the Roman Catholic Church. It is manifest, for example, in the church of the monastery of Studenica (page 147), built at the end of the twelfth century. The exterior no longer exhibits the old type of decoration, with alternate layers of brick and stone separated by thick mortar joints, but has the plain ashlar facing typical of Romanesque churches. Even the semicircular arches and the doorway, with its series of receding molded planes, are of Western origin. Nevertheless, this influence was still comparatively superficial and Serbian churches remained Byzantine in their planning and general character.

The buildings of Armenia and Georgia, on the shores of the Black Sea and the Caspian Sea, preserved a certain degree of independence and originality of design. Their plans were cruciform, but the eastern and western arms were often longer than the transepts, forming the so-called Armenian cross. In these churches the unusually high drum rising above the crossing is surmounted by a pointed roof concealing the dome within. As in the Early Christian churches of nearby Syria, the apses seldom form projections on the exterior but are built into the wall of the sanctuary. On the exterior, narrow triangular grooves express the internal divisions between the choir and its lateral compartments. The preponderant use of the barrel-vault roofing system, the accurately cut and jointed ashlar wall facings, and the blind arcades on slender and often coupled attached columns are all features which recall the buildings of Syria and endow these churches with a remarkable Romanesque quality. This is also apparent in the interiors, where structure and mass and the effect of stone may be appreciated undisguised by the familiar profusion of mosaics and frescoes.

Church architecture in Russia is of particular interest, for it represents a singular development of the Byzantine tradition. This vast country, half European, half Asiatic and as enigmatic as the Slavonic people who dwell there, has never possessed a true artistic tradition of its own but has remained dependent on the influence of the art of other countries. Paradoxically, works of art produced in Russia are always typically Russian, and it is one of the essential qualities of this nation to be able to assimilate the widest variety of outside influences and from them form an original and distinctive style. With the exception of the art of the Scythians and the ancient Greek trading towns on the Black Sea, the inhabitants of this area had come into contact with none of the great artistic movements of the West until the end of the first century A. D. In the ninth century, the Varangians, issuing from Scandinavia and moving eastward, took command of the northern regions and established the Russian Empire in 862. They brought with them the northern tradition of timber construction, but no evidence of their architecture now remains. It is known that they built temples with tiered roofs which may have resembled the Norwegian stave churches (page 177) which date from the twelfth and thirteenth centuries and utilized the same principles. In the densely forested regions of Russia, the technique of timber construction — up to the present century — has continued to be applied to secular buildings, although building in stone was introduced after 988 when Vladimir, Grand Duke of Kiev, was baptized into the Greek Orthodox faith and opened the way for the acceptance of the Greek Orthodox Church in Russia. Vladimir favored the use of stone as opposed to wood for religious architecture, although many timber churches were still to be built after his conversion.

The first known Russian building in stone was the Dessiatinnaya church in Kiev (991). It was the work of Greek craftsmen, as were most of the churches of this region, and like St. Irene, Constantinople, took the form of a domed basilica. For Sancta Sophia in Kiev (1017–1037), the cruciform scheme with central and subsidiary domes was used, and though modified many times, this was to be the basis of Russian church architecture until the present day. There is an astonishing proliferation of religious architecture in Russia. At the beginning of the eleventh century, Thietmar of Merseburg was able to count 400 churches in the city of Kiev alone. The passion for church building similarly bore fruit in Novgorod, northern Russia, and from the second half of the twelfth century in Vladimir-Souzdal. Architects from many important centers were invited to undertake the principal building activities in a vast program. Lombards and Caucasians came to work in the region of Vladimir, and there were Germans at Pskov. They brought much that was new from their lands of origin, but the churches continued to follow the traditional Byzantine ground plan. Only in certain details like capitals, cornices or methods of wall construction is it possible to detect the work of foreign artists, as though once on Russian soil, the craftsmen themselves became thoroughly Russianized. At the end of the fifteenth century when the Bolognese architect Ridolfo di (Aristotle) Fioravanti was summoned by the Grand Duke Ivan III to build the Uspenski Cathedral at Moscow (1475–1479, page 151b), he, too — as did his predecessors — followed the Byzantine tradition in his design.

However, the old domed cruciform scheme had by no means remained unaffected by Slavonic taste. As early as the eleventh century, the number of domes had increased and it was not unusual for as many as 7, 9 or 13 to be on any one church. The church of St. Michael at Kiev has 15 domes. They were placed over all parts of the structure, even over the arms of the cross, which had been barrel vaulted in five-domed cruciform Byzantine churches. Double aisles were sometimes added on each side of the nave, providing an opportunity for yet more domes. This development gave rise to an emphatically picturesque effect on the exterior, contrasting with the restrained simplicity of Byzantine prototypes. The wall surfaces, on the other hand, were still decorated with flat, blind arcades, although at an early date the walls were terminated with semicircular tympanums instead of horizontal eaves (page 151 a).

Internally, churches were covered with the traditional mural decoration, painting almost invariably taking the place of mosaics. The sacred images were even carried over the column shafts and onto the lower surfaces of the walls. The spatial unity characteristic of Byzantine examples was not long preserved in Russian churches. Various elements were added to the basic plan or were isolated from the main body of the building to form separate compartments, and in the fifteenth and sixteenth centuries it became customary to cut off the sanctuary from the nave behind an iconostasis reaching to ceiling height.

Under the domination of the Tatars, which began in 1238 and lasted nearly 200 years, several important developments took place in Russian architecture, though not always with good results. The Tatars brought with them from the East the forms of Asiatic art, and during their rule their taste for extravagant decoration and fantastic baroque shapes was to have a profound and decisive effect on Russian architectural style. During the fifteenth and sixteenth centuries the greatest emphasis was placed on exteriors, and it is here that the results of Tatar influence are displayed. The austerity and simplicity that had played a symbolic part in church architecture, even in the earlier many-domed churches of Russia, was now submerged beneath an almost barbaric profusion of bizarre, bulbous and overelaborate forms. The supreme example of this style (which has come to be regarded as typically Russian) is the celebrated church of St. Basil in Moscow (1555–1560) — an extraordinary piece of Oriental magnificence combining every decorative means that was then available to the architect (page 150). Nothing quite like it was ever achieved again.

BYZANTINE ARCHITECTURE

ILLUSTRATIONS

a

b

c

THE CHURCH OF THE HOLY APOSTLES, SALONIKA
Tenth century.

In Byzantine churches, the interior wall surfaces were left unbroken by any form of truly architectural decoration and were lined with a flat, uniform covering of brilliantly colored paintings and mosaics. A different principle governed the treatment of exteriors, as may be seen in the Church of the Holy Apostles, Salonika, one of the finest examples of the Byzantine style.

No attempt is made to disguise the contrast between the main structure, with its broad horizontal lines, and the sharp verticals of the drums and domes. Indeed this contrast is emphasized by the absence of any transitional feature between the two elements. The subordination of smaller subsidiary domes to a high central dome also tends to stress the upward movement of the design. But this is not the soaring, heavenward motion of the spires of Gothic cathedrals; it is so contained and controlled that the whole building gives the impression of compactness and unity characteristic of all Byzantine churches. There is nevertheless a feeling for plastic effects in the Church of the Holy Apostles and this is to be found, though to a lesser degree, in other buildings of this period. The decorative system of arcading relieves the flatness of the walls without disrupting the sense of solidity and enclosure, and extends to the drums, which are also ornamented with attached columns carrying complex arched cornices above tall, narrow windows. The tiled roofs are shaped to the curvature of the domes and continue to the corners of the octagons, their eaves forming a sequence of semicircular curves around the drums — an attractive effect common to most churches of this type.

The entrance side received no particular architectural emphasis, for façades, properly speaking, found no place in Byzantine architecture. The walls are faced with alternate bands of light-colored stones and bright red bricks set off by thick mortar joints. (Facing page.)

a) ST. ELEUTHERIOS, ATHENS
Beginning of the ninth century.

Despite its small size, St. Eleutherios is an excellent specimen of a typical Byzantine building. Its simple external forms are a clear expression of internal structure. An unusual feature is the marble facing and frieze in low relief.

b,c) THE MONASTERY OF LAVRA, MOUNT ATHOS
b) Small church to the west, date unknown;
c) Principal church.

Some twenty monasteries stand, fortresslike, on Mount Athos, to the north of the Aegean Sea — to this day one of the chief centers of Byzantine art and architecture. The monastery churches, dating from the ninth century onward, are notable for the fact that the transepts, as well as the eastern arm of the cross, terminate in apses. The principal church of the monastery of Lavra has a smooth external face which is plastered a uniform reddish brown. The other provides a good example of the decorative use of horizontal courses of masonry and flat, recessed blank arcades.

MACEDONIA

Most of the churches still extant in Macedonia are very small and are interesting chiefly because they show how faithfully the old Byzantine forms were handed down, almost unchanged, from century to century. The little church of St. Panteleimon near Nerezi (built 1164, facing page) could well have been built in the ninth century, so closely is it modeled on the old churches of that time, which were erected at the very center of the Byzantine Empire. It is of cruciform plan, with central and subsidiary domes, an adjoining narthex (to the left in the photograph) and a projecting apse. The walls are externally faced with the characteristic alternating bands of bricks and stones, here somewhat perfunctorily laid. But meticulous workmanship is to be observed in the arcading and the drums, where the windows are framed with the usual recessed arches. The tiled roof over the central dome and its octagonal drum are not shaped to its curvature but are conical, and the eaves, instead of rising and falling over the windows, form a horizontal projection. On the side walls, large blank arches in two orders are so tall that the effect is as though the inner barrel vaults of the transepts have penetrated to the exterior. The fact that the eaves of the roof follow the extrados of these arches gives the design a pleasing lightness.

In the Church of St. Clement, Ohrid (1295, Fig. a), there are pitched roofs over the four arms of the cross and no subsidiary domes. Hence the effect is considerably less picturesque and the design has a certain dry austerity compared with that of St. Panteleimon. Here the groups of narrow semicircular headed windows in the side walls, and their infilling of pierced stone slabs taking the place of glass, are typically Byzantine.

SERBIA

The churches of Serbia are of far greater architectural significance than those of Macedonia, largely due to the Romanesque influence that resulted from a flourishing trade with the West. Some, however, followed the Byzantine tradition closely. The church of the Holy Apostles at Pec (thirteenth century, Fig. b) and its adjoining chapels built a century later are relevant examples. But as early as the close of the twelfth century, in the church of the Holy Virgin at the imperial monastery, Studenica (Fig. c), there is evidence of a link with Italian Romanesque architecture. The dominant theme is still that of the domed centralized church, but Western influence is indicated in the nave preceding the domed area, in the carefully laid courses of squared stones, the series of semicircular arches and the projecting doorway with its recessed portal. The church of the monastery at Gracanica (1321, Fig. d) represents a return to a more strictly Byzantine scheme, although the complexity and sculptural quality of the exterior owes much to Western prototypes.

a

b

c

d

a

b

ST. MARK'S, VENICE

Third reconstruction begun 1063; consecrated 1094.

The most splendid example of late Byzantine architecture is St. Mark's in Venice, where trade with the East brought close associations with Byzantium. For a church on this vast scale, the simple domed cruciform scheme of small Byzantine buildings could not have served as model, and its architects looked to the renowned Church of the Holy Apostles in Constantinople (built in the time of Justinian; destroyed fifteenth century) for inspiration. Hence St. Mark's is a Greek cross on plan and has five domes — one over the square central crossing and one over each arm of the cross. The galleries around the side aisles (poor substitutes, it is true, for their counterparts in Constantinople), the domes that spring directly from the pendentives without the interposition of a drum, and the ring of windows pierced in the dome just above the springing, all find a parallel in the Church of the Holy Apostles. The sumptuous mosaic decoration covering arches and vaults is in the pure Byzantine tradition and gives the interior lightness and luminosity. None the less striking, however, is the sturdy, massive quality of the architecture, which has little to do with Byzantine elegance and belongs rather to the Romanesque style. (Facing page.)

SICILY

In the twelfth century, under Norman kingship, there was a brief flowering of architecture in Sicily, and the buildings of this period are brilliant and original in design. Nowhere was the Byzantine style more happily combined with Muslim forms and Western basilican planning than in Sicily, where Byzantines, Saracens and Normans had followed one another as ruling powers. George of Antioch, High Admiral of Roger II, built the church of La Martorana in Palermo for the Greek Orthodox faith. It is the most Byzantine of all Sicilian churches, almost exactly following the cruciform scheme with central dome supported on four columns, a narthex at the west end, and a three-part choir and apse at the east. The original character of this church has suffered by subsequent alterations — chiefly by the prolongation of the western arm to form a Latin cross (Fig. b). The added nave is distinguishable by its columns, which are raised on high pedestals. The four columns that carry the dome are part of the original conception, but as revealed by the mixture of styles in their shafts and caps, were taken from older buildings. The spirit of Byzantium is reflected in the fine mosaics that decorate the arches and the vault, clothing the stone in a mantle of gold and warm, glowing colors. (The apse mosaics are lost, and the frescoes in the foreground date from the Renaissance.) Their richness is enhanced by decorative bands with geometrical designs and stylized leaf patterns which continue over the marble-lined walls and pavement, contributing to a total effect that is overwhelming in its jewel-like brilliance. This abstract type of decoration, which contrasts with the figurative Byzantine mosaics, comes from Muslim art; the pointed arches have a similar source. Other Sicilian churches of this period, while they sometimes surpass even La Martorana in decorative splendor, remain closer to the Early Christian-Romanesque tradition of the West in that they have a basilican nave to the west of a Byzantine domed central space. The Capella Palatina at Palermo (1129–1159, Fig. a) and the great Cathedral at Monreale (1174–1189, page 233 a) are two such examples.

ST. BASIL, MOSCOW
*Vasilyi Blazennyi, built 1555–1560. Architects, Postnik
and Barma.*

This church was begun by the first Czar, Ivan the Terrible, as an
act of thanksgiving after the conquest of Kazan, the last of the
Tatar strongholds. With its fairy-tale Oriental brilliance and
exotic forms, it is the most singular and important example of the
church architecture of Old Russia. Eight chapels surround the central area, forming a diagonally placed square within an outer
square enclosure. On the exterior, the plan can be recognized by
the two-storied gallery that follows its outline and is actually a
complex development of the Byzantine domed cruciform scheme
(page 144). The chapels are linked by low, narrow passageways,
and in spite of their greater height, admit little light; the interior is
dark and mysterious, though it has a rich fresco decoration. On the
exterior, religious pathos and a love of cheerful decoration and
rich, complex form — both essential facets of the Russian character — are translated into unusual architectural terms. The eight
chapels were crowned with towerlike structures, and in the seventeenth century were completed with bulblike domes, each different — fluted, twisted, scalloped and reticulated. They are gilded
and painted in the most brilliant colors and, like candle flames,
circle the tent-shaped central tower that reaches high above them.
The tent form derives, perhaps, from pagan temples built of wood
or from Persian tombs, which are exactly similar in appearance.
The distinctive arrangement of niches on the towers, formed by
rows of arches in receding stages (kokoschniks), recall the stalactite
forms of Muslim vaults. (Facing page.)

a) CATHEDRAL OF ST. DEMETRIUS, VLADIMIR
1193–1197.

Like all early Russian churches, this follows the Byzantine centralized scheme. Appropriately to such a scheme, with its nondirectional
plan, entrances are placed on three sides, but the three straight-
ended apses at the east end (not visible in the photograph), similar
to those of most Byzantine-Russian churches, restore a longitudinal
emphasis to the interior. The arched eaves projection taking the
place of a horizontal cornice is a characteristic feature. The paintings on the exterior wall surfaces present a fusion of Christian
themes and the forms of Russian folk-art familiar through their
use in textiles.

b) USPENSKI CATHEDRAL MOSCOW
Built 1475–1479. Ridolfo di (Aristotle) Fioravanti.

Summoned to Russia during the fifteenth century with other Italians, Fioravanti here achieved, in a simple plan without galleries,
a harmony of Western and indigenous architectural forms. The
clarity of the design, the columned portal and the blind arcading
on the south side are of Western origin. So, too, are the cross vaults,
round piers and cubiform capitals on the interior. The five domes
on high circular drums, with their familiar bulblike form and slit
windows, symbolize Christ among the four Evangelists and represent Russian tradition.

c) CHURCH AT KOLOMENSKOJE
Consecrated 1532.

The central tower, with its steep tent roof, rises monumentally
from the galleried structure spread out below. The tiers of ogee
arches are typically Russian, though they have their origin in
Western Gothic or Muslim architecture. The great pilasters at the
angles of the tower are Italian in inspiration.

a

b

c

VI
ARCHITECTURE
DURING THE RISE
OF THE WEST

The West

Any reference to the architecture of the Greeks, Romans, early Christians and Byzantines as the architectures of the West has been avoided so far. Before going further, it would perhaps be well to clarify the specific meaning of this term and its significance in relation to subsequent architectural development.

With good reason, it has come to mean that area of civilization in western Europe which developed (following dissolution of the Roman Empire, fifth century) as a result of the fusion of the Germanic element with the Christian world of late antiquity, and which, despite many upheavals, has survived into the present century. Slowly and almost as if by accident, this fusion gave rise to a cultural and spiritual development that, gathering force, produced certain definite characteristics by which the West became clearly distinguishable both from the past and from all that was simultaneously taking place in the Slavic and Byzantine world of eastern Europe.

It is important to explain why this civilization should be called Western and not — as the history of political and spiritual movements would seem to demand — Christian Germanic or simply by the geographical title of European.

The Germanic peoples were genuinely determined to create some new and vigorous system from the ruins of the old world that they themselves had destroyed. To the beginning of modern times, it was they who gave direction and purpose to the development of the arts while drawing on the spiritual heritage of the old Mediterranean world, yet without preventing the heirs of this tradition (the Latin and Latinized peoples) from making a vital contribution to the new civilization. The Latin races never ceased to play a decisive part in the progress of Western culture, and in the fifteenth century and throughout the Renaissance, the initiative was theirs once more. Thus the West was formed from the meeting and interaction of these two elements — the Latin and the Germanic.

The historian who insists upon naming this civilization European will soon meet with an awkward dilemma, for, literally, such a term would exclude western Russia and the Balkans (including Greece and parts of present-day Turkey) from Europe, their civilizations never having been affected — except in a few isolated instances — by events in western Europe. Under no circumstances, it seems, can the political-geographical appellation European be substituted for the term Western when reference is made to this phase of cultural development. Western, then, must be taken to have two meanings: first, the geographical position, as opposed to the East, of the whole of Europe — the sense in which it has been used here so far; and second, a certain aspect of the civilized world and a branch of the development of art and architecture — the meaning that will be given to the term henceforward.

It is a well-known fact that all such labels are open to question, and although this one may be justified in that it best designates our own civilization, it must be remembered that the roots of Western art go much deeper and that without the great classical heritage of Greece and Rome and the intervention of the Germanic peoples there would have been no Western civilization in this sense.

Historical and Religious Background

It was several centuries before the new civilization took on a definite form and found expression in an individual architecture. Nor would this have been possible without an event that was world shattering in its effect: the so-called Völkerwanderung or migration of Germanic peoples which ushered in one of the most dramatic and portentous chapters in Europe's history and brought about in 476 the calamity of the destruction of the Roman Empire in the West.

But to judge the political and spiritual developments that took place between the fifth and the eighth centuries in the western half of the old Roman Empire and the works of art produced in this period, by the standards of late antiquity alone, is wholly to misconstrue their historical significance. Even by comparison with late antiquity, which itself had lost its former grandeur and grown dull and dissipated, these developments appear miserably small and insignificant. So arises the false impression that everything that happened during and after the invasions was nothing more than a sad testimony of the triumph of barbarianism over civilization. It is true that at first the new masters of Gaul and Germania (the Alemanni, Burgundians and Franks), of Spain (the Visigoths) and Italy (the Ostrogoths and Lombards), could offer neither an administrative system nor a cultural background approaching those of antiquity. But for the sake of historical truth, it must be added that in both these respects the ancient world had reached an impasse by the time it broke under the onslaughts of the barbarians. The oppressions and coercions of the government, the iron grip of a bureaucracy that controlled every aspect of life down to the last detail, and all the usual measures of a state verging on collapse had sapped the vitality of the old empire. Freedom was lost, and with it the atmosphere essential to creative activity. Change of some sort was desperately needed.

On the evidence of what was happening in Byzantium, it is doubtful whether the ancient world could have produced the necessary impetus without the intervention of the Germanic tribes. Here lies the true historical significance of the invasions. Their annihilation of the old despotic system removed the great obstacle that stood in the way of progress and artistic development. During the two or three centuries following, the ground thus prepared was by no means to lie fallow but was to be implanted with the seeds of the new Western civilization. This period is called the Dark Ages chiefly because so little is known of its history. The accounts that have survived are rare and are usually biased, for it was only the Roman or Romanized element of the population that was accustomed to recording historical events. Works of high art, which had so nobly signalized the classical civilizations, are almost wholly lacking and what does remain is of little significance.

However, two events of the Dark Ages stand out in importance, for they were to have a profound effect on subsequent history: the foundation of the Frankish kingdom by Clovis (481–511), which was to become a power-ful and united empire under Charlemagne, and the con-version of the Franks to the Catholic form of Christianity, with all its deep implications for the Church and civili-zation.

There is no space here to trace, even in outline, the dramatic history of the Frankish kingdom from its begin-nings. In the present context, one fact alone should be stressed: of the many Germanic tribes that had settled within the Roman Empire from North Africa to Great Britain, the Franks were the only people to seize upon the political inheritance of the Romans and to undertake to restore the arts to western Europe. But these tasks could be undertaken only when the kingdom had established its supremacy and found in Charlemagne a great leader who grasped the significance of his mission in both the political and the cultural fields. Until Charlemagne, the Frankish kings—the Merovingians (from Clovis, died 511) and the Carolingians (from Pepin, crowned 751)—were preoc-cupied with augmenting their power and building up defenses within and outside the kingdom. Some new form of administration had to be substituted for the old, for the needs of the Franks were totally different from those of the people who still clung to the tradition of the Romans. Moreover, the structure of the Roman state in its decline was too far removed from that of the Frankish commu-nities for the Franks to be able to achieve their end merely by adapting it to their purposes.

In the eighth century, the Frankish kingdom extended from the Lower Rhine to the Garonne, and from the Atlantic over much of south and west Germany. From the outset, the political system differed radically from that of the Roman Empire at the time of its collapse. The empire had been a unified and centralized state. A rational and extraordinarily complex bureaucratic system, backed by a superb military machine, had reached out into the farthest and most insignificant corners of the provinces, imposing —through the important key centers—a rigid and relent-less force that eventually amounted to world domination. The Frankish kingdom had nothing at all in common with this centralized and despotic society. Its basis was a loose federation of warrior tribes, and to a great extent its social structure relied on individual loyalty to the demands of the community. A Frankish leader did not hold absolute power; with regard to his companions and followers, his position was that of a *primus inter pares*, founded on his martial abilities, and he was constrained to show as much loyalty to his subjects as they to him. This assembly of peoples had none of the characteristics of a true nation, and since there was no political center (as Rome had been)

to form a rallying point and to operate a legal and exec-utive machine, there was no means of contending with the frequently disastrous results of tribal strife and the short-sighted and selfish maneuvers of the nobility in the interests of their families and their rights of succession. This was a determining factor in the development of the Frankish kingdom, for the efforts of Charlemagne himself to turn his kingdom into a true state, though by no means entirely wasted, did not achieve their goal. The unity of his empire was destroyed under his successors, never to be regained (Partition of Verdun, 843), and the states and nations of Europe gradually emerged from these fragments.

The beginnings of Western political development may thus be traced in the Frankish kingdom, but before the eighth century there is little to indicate that Western culture, too, had its foundations there. Before that time, no evi-dence exists of the building of any monument witnessing to the power of the kingdom or its rulers. The lack of a metropolis and any true form of state organization, and the pressing need to expand and protect the empire, may all be held responsible for this indifference. But in essence, the character of Western civilization had already been formed at the moment of the meeting and fusion of the barbarian and the Roman peoples, of the Germanic and the Christian worlds; in fact, a revival and development of culture was taking place in the shadow of political events, though it was not given official recognition and support until the time of Charlemagne.

The conversion to Christianity of the Germanic races, one of the most decisive events of history, was the signifi-cant factor in the revival of Western art, for it formed a bridge between the ancient and the medieval worlds. Nu-merous contemporary works of literature and art show, however, that the barbarians remained incapable of under-standing some of the most vital aspects of the new religion; the redemption of mankind through the sacrifice of Christ, the remission of sins and brotherly love, were ideas that they could not yet grasp. Above all, they saw in the God of the Christians a champion against the evil spirits that beset them, for had He not demonstrated His power through the miracles of Christ and by His descent into the abyss to overcome Satan himself? It is surely no coinci-dence that until the Romanesque period the Passion and Crucifixion were rarely represented in Western art, while Christ the worker of miracles and Christ the triumphant King figured largely in Christian imagery. The oldest sur-viving Germanic representation of Christ is to be found on a Frankish tombstone in Niederdollendorf (near Bonn), dating from about 700. The figure, bearing the sword of victory, stands within an aureole, pierced with rays of light. In the *Heliand*, written about 830 (probably in the monastery of Verden), Christ is portrayed as a warrior king of miraculous origin, accompanied by a band of disciples (*erlos adalborana*) of noble birth, embodying the Germanic and knightly virtues. It was not the crucified Saviour but the almighty Lord of Heaven and the proud Conqueror of evil who had captured the imagination of the barbaric tribes. And as the Holy Scriptures preached by missionaries assured all believers of heavenly support, it seemed not unnatural that men should enter into a pact of loyalty with God just as they formerly had with temporal powers. Thus the new religion became acceptable only when it had been reappraised in thoroughly materialistic terms. Not until centuries later, in the Gothic era, were the ethical values of Christianity fully assimilated.

This practical and worldly reinterpretation of Christian doctrine (which it invested with a kind of magic) had profound consequences for architecture and the decorative arts during the early stages of Western development. It was precisely this which produced the great rise in the cult of saints among the Germanic peoples, especially after the seventh century. So strong was this cult that men would go to extraordinary lengths, not excluding theft, to gain possession of their relics, and would dedicate the most sacred parts of churches to their safekeeping. The saints were accorded the highest and most honored places among the hosts of Heaven, and contact with their relics was the greatest safeguard against evil influences. Special importance was given to the Archangel Michael, to whom many of the earliest churches were dedicated, because it was he who had fought with the Devil and overthrown the Beast of the Apocalypse (Apoc. 12:7). It will later be seen how this idea came to find concrete expression in architecture.

The event of greatest moment for Western civilization during this period of conversions was the Catholic baptism of King Clovis (496), which was instrumental in preventing the Franks from entering into the federation by which Theodoric (Arian King of the Ostrogoths) hoped to unify the various Germanic powers in the West, and may well have averted from the Frankish kingdom that fate which the Ostrogoths in northern Italy and the Vandals in North Africa were to suffer at the hand of Justinian. Above all, the conversion of Clovis rendered his kingdom especially susceptible to the influence of the civilization of late antiquity, with the result that Christianity slowly but surely strengthened its hold over an ever widening area of northern Europe, though not reaching the Scandinavian races until about the year 1000.

Contrary to what had happened during the first years of Christianity, it was now the leading families and not the mass of the people who were the first to be won over to the new faith, and there were thus no great anti-Christian powers to contend with. But in spite of this, the Church did not act as a stabilizing element in government during the centuries that followed the barbarian invasions. The decline of state administration in the Roman Empire had been accompanied by a corresponding weakening within the Church, and the Frankish ruling class was still too preoccupied with military affairs to give much attention to its reorganization. Whereas formerly, under state protection, the Church had given order and cohesion to the whole Christian community, it now lost contact with the outlying regions, was no longer a national institution, and became more and more divided, even within the confines of the Frankish kingdom. Synods of Frankish clergy had ceased to be held by the end of the seventh century. The turning point for the Church, and also indirectly for art, came at last in the eighth century when the Anglo-Saxon missionaries Willibrord and Wynfrith (St. Boniface), supported by the Carolingian kings, succeeded in establishing papal supremacy over the Frankish Church, thus to a great degree restoring its unity and once again making it part of a vast centralized body controlled from Rome.

Their achievement would scarcely have been possible had the ground not already been prepared by two sixth-century developments that played a vital part in the spread of Christianity: first, the introduction of Frankish ecclesiastics in place of a clergy that had previously almost exclusively been recruited from Roman or Romanized communities; second and more important, the founding in 520 of the first monastic Order (and its monastery on Monte Cassino) by St. Benedict of Nursia, and the institution of a form of religious life in which men would not only fight to subdue bodily desires — as had been the sole aim of the ascetic monks of the East — but would also actively work toward spreading the Christian way of life throughout the world. The Benedictine rule of "work and prayer" strongly appealed to the Germanic populations whose lives centered around their work on the land. It is significant that in sixth- and seventh-century accounts of the lives of the saints, mastery of natural forces, clearing of forests and cultivation of swamps and wasteland were singled out as Christian activities. Increasing numbers of men gave up their military occupations to devote themselves to this kind of active, practical Christian life. With the institution of the new religious orders, Christian missionary work suddenly emerged from stagnation into a period of intense and far-reaching activity. Before the end of the sixth century, there is no evidence of any attempt to start an evangelistic movement on an important scale.

But about 590, pilgrim monks from Ireland and Scotland set out to wander over the Continent with missionary zeal, at first meeting with little support from the Frankish clergy, who were slow to take up the cause. In time the movement gathered force, especially from the action and example of the Anglo-Saxon missionaries in eastern Franconia, led by Willibrord and Boniface, whose work was to have a deep and lasting influence not only on the spiritual but on the cultural development of the West. Sanctioned finally by the Carolingian kings, this mission acted as a civilizing force and advanced Christianity far into the west and north. Through its connections with Rome, it was instrumental in bringing the Frankish Church within the Catholic fold.

The eighth century also witnessed a return to order in the state, seriously weakened in the seventh century by the clash of local interests and the perpetual strife between families of nobles over questions of heredity. This change was signalized by the transference of power from the Merovingians to the Carolingians, an Austrasian family whose first effective political leader was Pepin the Short. In 754, after a judicious appraisal of the situation, Pepin concluded an alliance with the head of the Roman Catholic Church, Pope Stephen II. He thus placed Western Christendom under the power and protection of the Frankish kingdom, gave the kingdom a position analagous to that of the Byzantine Empire in relation to the Eastern Church, and secured for the Carolingian Dynasty the support of ecclesiastics who in the meantime had also consolidated their position and increased their temporal power. It was a crucial moment in the history of the West.

Charles, the eldest son of Pepin, who later became emperor and justly earned the epithet Great, reaped every possible benefit from the alliance between the Papacy and the kingdom. As protector of Christendom, he supported the missionary activities of the Church while giving them a marked political significance. The wars against the Muslims in Spain (778) and against the heathen Saxons (from 772) were ostensibly fought on behalf of Christendom but also served to consolidate his empire. Charlemagne's biographer Einhard tells how the Saxon surrender and the destruction of the Avars meant more than all his other achievements to "the King of the Franks, who reigns over Gaul, Germania, Italy and the countries round about" (*Libri Carolini*, written c. 787).

While Charlemagne thus showed himself to be first and foremost a political leader, he was also a benefactor of the Church, giving the Papacy his firm protection and patronage. On the other hand, he never admitted the Pope as an equal, claiming himself to be the supreme Christian ruler by the grace of God and by consent of the Church and the Frankish nobility. In this capacity, he was equally concerned with the affairs of Church and State, making himself responsible for the nomination of persons of high spiritual and political distinction to the most important Episcopal sees in the kingdom, and in many other respects taking an active part in ecclesiastical affairs. His court was not only the political capital of the kingdom but its spiritual center as well. This subjection of the Church to the interests of the State was to lead to the famous and momentous quarrel between empire and Papacy which was later to shatter the medieval world. Meanwhile it proved favorable to empire and Church, and to the development of Western art.

Pre-Carolingian Architecture

The Germanic tribes, when they triumphantly bore down on the Roman Empire in the West, were confronted with a superior culture and a tradition far removed from their own, where the fine arts had reached an advanced stage of development. The painting, sculpture and architecture that had been brought to their fullest flowering in antiquity must certainly have already been known to the barbarians through their many previous contacts with the Romans, but had remained for them the remote expression of an alien spirit. Before the great invasions, antique art found no echo among the Germanic races. The conditions essential to the creation of an original art were lacking in a society that was both primitive and unformed. Greek and Roman art had emerged only when a primitive community had given way to a politically organized state, accompanied by the development of handwriting and literature. At the time of the invasions, the Germanic races had barely arrived at simple written communication (runes). They were only on the threshold of national unity (tribal confederacies), and their conception of creative art was rudimentary, based on crude animal forms.

But when the structure of the old Roman Empire in the West had crumbled, the spiritual and cultural inheritance of the conquered peoples lingered on, to be assimilated by the new masters and reinterpreted or adapted to their own needs. It has already been seen with what rapidity and lasting effect the Germanic peoples accepted, with certain modifications, the religion of the empire. But the centralized Roman state administered from the cities was not acceptable and was replaced by a system in which every tribe was governed according to its own law and where there was no single center of power. The effects of such a system on architectural development were grave, for there were no public authorities powerful enough to support extensive building schemes and no important cities to provide a field for architecture. Thus it is not surprising that secular architecture disappeared almost completely during the early years of Germanic domination, the barbarians adopting Roman traditions only in the churches that were so important an element of their new-found religion.

The buildings erected during the centuries following the invasions are in no way comparable with those which preceded them. Only once under the reign of a Germanic king did the ancient traditions inspire an architecture that recreated something of the brilliance, grandeur and structural perfection of that of antiquity. This revival took place in Ravenna, the capital of the Ostrogothic kingdom in Italy, where Theodoric built churches of both basilican and centralized plan which are very close to antique prototypes and have for this reason been discussed previously (pages 118, 121 and 126). His architects were not Goths but were either natives of Ravenna or craftsmen trained in Constantinople, who had come to work in the service of the new ruler. Having spent ten years at the imperial court in Constantinople, Theodoric had made himself familiar with Roman customs and traditions. He had overthrown Odoacer in Italy (in 493) and broken away from his overlords in Constantinople, and now, having risen to the position of supreme ruler of the Ostrogothic kingdom, he was determined to recreate the ancient world in the West. By a policy of collaboration, he hoped to unite the various Germanic peoples who had settled all over western Europe, to lead in building up a power equal to that of the eastern empire, and thus to lay the foundations of an enduring state.

But in spite of his many achievements, Theodoric was never to realize his great ambition. The Ostrogothic kingdom came to an end, and not until three centuries later were his ideas finally put into effect by Charlemagne. But the buildings of Ravenna remain as a lasting testimony to the ideals of this self-appointed heir to the Caesars and as a magnificent expression of the idea of imperial power. True, these buildings were possible only because craftsmen were able to avail themselves of the technical skill and experience of Roman builders; the Goths, like all other barbaric races, had no knowledge of monumental architecture in stone. They were only familiar with timber construction, which they had developed to a certain degree of skill in halls and modest hutlike structures, but that hardly could be applied to monumental undertakings. Technical difficulties apart, the barbarians had had no experience of the Roman architectural forms for churches and palaces, and their ability to invent new forms depended as much on the will to discover some individual means of expression as on mastery of technique and knowledge of the formal possibilities inherent in existing buildings. This will was slow to awaken among the Germanic peoples, and before the eighth century, Germanic tendencies are apparent only in isolated instances and do not amount to a clearly defined style.

In this respect, two monuments — the Mausoleum of Theodoric at Ravenna and the Royal Hall at Oviedo — are particularly interesting. Completed before the King's death in 526, the Mausoleum (which is in a good state of preservation) is in two stories, the lower being decagonal in plan and the upper cylindrical (pages 174 and 175). There is a link with centralized Byzantine prototypes, and the masterly handling of the ashlar masonry betrays the presence of Roman craftsmen. But the most remarkable feature of the building — and one which is entirely original, finding no parallel in antiquity — is the roof formed of one huge slab of stone hollowed into a flat dome. Theodoric had this monolith brought to Ravenna especially for the purpose, as if he were taking advantage of the opportunity to express his Germanic origin in a building which did not have to conform to the hard and fast rules of church architecture. Many theories have been advanced to explain the significance of this extraordinary roof covering. The best, if rather romantic, hypothesis may well be that Theodoric was inspired by a memory of the monumental megalithic tombs (dolmens) of his ancestors, still to be found in many places including Spain, Ireland and the regions around the Baltic. In these tombs, the lower part, composed of upright boulders, is also covered by a huge horizontal monolithic slab. Be that as it may, there is little doubt that the Mausoleum at Ravenna displays, for the first time, an architectural conception that is independent of antiquity.

It has long been assumed that Sta Maria de Naranco near Oviedo, in the early Visigothic kingdom of the Asturias, Spain (page 174 a, b), was built to serve as a church. According to the "Chronicle of Abelda," the Visigothic King Ramiro I of Asturias dedicated the building in 848 to Sta Maria, hence the present name. In all probability, however, it was much earlier than this in date, and certain individual features indicate that it was originally designed to serve a secular rather than religious purpose. This is implied by the existence of two baths in the basement below the main hall and by the provision of entrances on both long sides — not a normal procedure in church planning (Fig. 50). Sta Maria de Naranco is now generally accepted as the first known instance of the realization in stone of a traditional timber hall structure, and indeed as the only surviving example of a Germanic royal hall. The earlier stages of the tradition to which it belongs can only be surmised from excavations and from a study of later Germanic poems, but its later manifestations may still be seen in the twelfth- and thirteenth-century castles of northern Europe (page 286) and the halls of the large mansions and universities of England.

Several other aspects of the royal hall at Oviedo are of peculiar interest. Methods of wall construction, the treatment of the architectural elements and unusual decoration, all diverge widely from antique tradition. The highly developed system of ashlar masonry construction inherited from the Romans and exhibited in the Mausoleum of Theodoric has here given way to a much rougher technique, in many places almost amounting to rubble walling. This decline in structural methods is characteristic of architecture in western Europe immediately after the invasions, when carefully laid ashlar was often abandoned completely in favor of rubble construction. How low standards had become among architects of the time is clearly revealed by the "Chronicle of Abelda," which commends the modest barrel vault over the upper story of the royal hall as a magnificent example of the art of vaulted construction — unwarranted praise, in the light of Roman achievement, and only understandable by taking into account the time at which it was written. The system of vaulting that the Romans had brought to perfection had fallen so far into disuse that the vault of Oviedo must indeed have appeared to contemporaries as a work of the greatest daring and skill. The treatment of the clustered colonnettes inside the upper story, which carry the arches of the loggias and the blind arcades, is also foreign to antique tradition. They are carved in the form of twisted ropes and are obviously

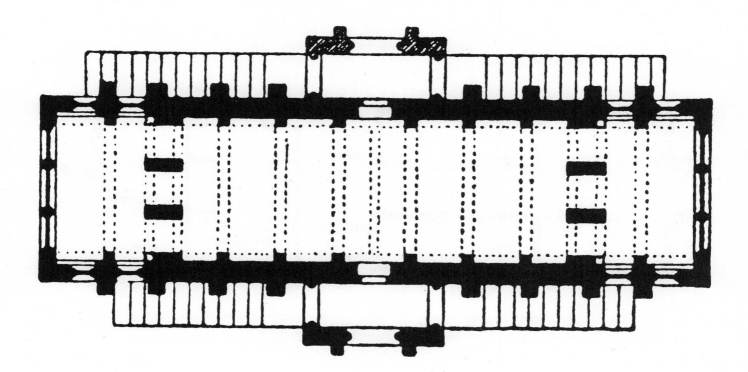

50. *Plan of the Royal Hall of the Visigothic palace near Oviedo, Spain. Consecrated as a church, Sta Maria de Naranco, 848.*

directly derived from wooden prototypes. (Further instances of the influence of Germanic timber construction on buildings in stone will be seen later.) Hanging from the vaulting ribs of the main hall are curious medallions like medals on ribbons, carved with crude human figures within a decorative border. This kind of architectural ornament is never found in Roman buildings, where sculptural decoration — however free and devoid of structural function — is always strictly related to and dependent on the main elements of the construction. No such principle can be applied to these medallions, which even occur on the exterior of the hall (page 174 a). They must be seen rather as a reflection of the Gothic taste for decorating houses — especially the halls of kings and princes — with all kinds of rich ornaments in precious metals and as a transposition into a new medium of the wall decoration formerly employed in wooden buildings.

Pre-Carolingian architecture is distinguished by the fact that enclosing walls were used as fields for applied decoration rather than architectonically, as can be seen in a number of Merovingian churches. At St. Généroux (France, eighth century, page 177 d), for instance, the exterior walls are covered with carpetlike patterns achieved by a lively use of the ancient *opus reticulatum* and *spicatum*.

From the sixth to the end of the eighth century (between the reigns of Theodoric and Charlemagne), architectural activity where the use of stone was concerned was limited almost entirely to the building of churches. Contemporary writers tell of grandiose architectural achievements, of buildings magnificent in execution and design, and it might well be supposed that the high artistic conceptions of the late-antique-Early Christian period had survived the crisis of the invasions and been fully assimilated by the barbarians. In fact there was no smooth continuation of ancient tradition. On the contrary, excavations and the few examples that have come down to us prove beyond any doubt that buildings of this time were both modest in scale and of small architectural significance and that methods of construction were often crude and primitive. The basic cause seems to have been the difficulty encountered by Germanic builders in handling the medium of stone and the painfully slow process by which they acquired something of the technical skill and experience of the Romans. When Trèves Cathedral, which originated during the last years of Roman domination in the city, was due to be rebuilt after its destruction in the early fifth century, Bishop Nicetius (526–566) found it necessary to summon craftsmen from northern Italy to carry out the work. Indeed, the building activity that took place before the seventh century consisted mainly of the reconstruction and renovation of old churches and was almost exclusively entrusted to Roman or Romanized builders.

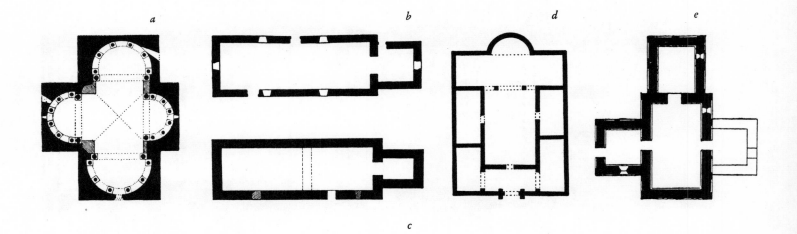

51. a) *Baptistery, Venasque, seventh century;*
   b) *Church at Escomb, Durham, England, eighth century;*
   c) *Church at Westray, Orkney Islands, eighth century;*

   d) *SS. Peter and Paul, Canterbury, England, seventh century;*
   e) *St. Lawrence, Bradford-on-Avon, England, tenth century.*

Their lack of an established tradition led the Germanic peoples to accept Early Christian architecture as they found it, while at the same time making arbitrary and retrogressive stylistic alterations. They cared little whether the models they followed were of Western or Byzantine origin. Basilican and centralized churches were erected side by side, in patent disregard for the peculiar significance of each type. In Spain, for example, some Visigothic churches exhibit the basilican plan, while others (page 174 c) follow the scheme adopted in the eastern Roman Empire, grouping four compartments of equal length around a high square central space, to form a Greek cross plan. In France, there are simple basilicas like St. Pierre, Vienne (fifth century), and also centralized structures of circular or more complicated plan (Poitiers, Aix, Riez, Venasque, seventh and eighth centuries, Fig. 51 a).

These examples — by no means a complete picture of the architecture of the time — are manifest attempts to find a theme worthy of Christianity and capable of future development. Meanwhile in the regions of Europe that had had fewer contacts with Roman tradition and where the population was either purely Germanic or comprised a higher percentage of Germanic elements, local traditions

began to play an important part in the development of church architecture, as may clearly be seen in a number of early English examples. In the fifth century, extensive regions of Britain which had previously been widely colonized by the Celts were conquered by the Angles and Saxons. The churches built by the new masters after their conversion to Christianity were mostly of modest dimensions, like those on the Continent, but were much less dependent on antique prototypes. Their long, narrow naves and generally square-ended choirs with a strongly marked division between the two elements (Fig. 51 b, c) vividly recall the form of Germanic rectangular houses from which they probably derive. The emphatic separation of choir from nave indicates the influence of late Germanic wooden temples, which appear to have consisted similarly of a principal oblong chamber where sacrifices were offered, and a smaller adjoining compartment containing images of the deities (Ansen), but this remains conjectural.

True, in the British Isles there are Celto-Irish stone sanctuaries which show the two elements separated in just this way, built at a time when the Anglo-Saxons were still confined to their native timber construction. The elongated oblong plan is nevertheless a typically Anglo-Saxon feature and reappears constantly in later British architecture. Several churches have secondary rooms of unknown purpose — perhaps large porches — at the sides of their naves, with narrow doorways between (Fig. 51 e). A similar accumulation of compartments is occasionally to be found in churches that broadly follow the Early Christian basilican scheme, among them SS. Peter and Paul in Canterbury (Fig. 51 d). Whether this multiplication of small self-contained rooms derived from timber prototypes is difficult to say, but the feature must be a Germanic one, for it is shared by many Visigothic churches in Spain (page 174 c).

A general survey of Germanic religious architecture from the sixth to the eighth centuries, and in England to the ninth century, presents a great variety of building types, and there is no well-defined thread of development that can be called a style. The revival of building activity — for which the Christian missions and above all the great monastic Order of the Benedictines were largely responsible — had begun to take effect everywhere by the end of the seventh century, reintroducing and further exploring the architectural forms of late antiquity. But the picture would be more complete if the numerous timber churches built during this period had survived; it should also be remembered that only a fraction of the stone examples or their remains has come down to us. The sudden increase in religious building during these centuries was primarily due to the demand for monastic establishments and to the fact

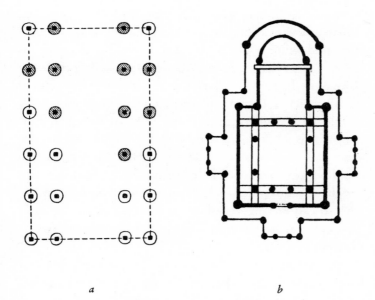

a   *b*

52. *Plans of two Germanic timber churches:*
   a) Church at Breberen, Rhineland, reconstructed from excavations, eighth century?;
   b) Church at Borgund, Norway, eighth century.

that patronage was now provided by a powerful laity, as well as by the ecclesiastics. An important new factor was that (contrary to Roman times when the principal buildings were found only in large cities) churches were now built in the countryside, to serve agricultural communities. A strong incentive was also provided by a Frankish ecclesiastical rule stipulating that the founder or donor was entitled to complete possession (not only of his church or monastery, but of all the gifts and endowments that the establishment would attract) and that all the land belonging to the church or monastery was his by right, to be disposed of according to his wishes. Naturally, wealthy patrons contended for opportunities to establish religious foundations, which were indeed no bad investment.

None of the buildings that resulted from this first wave of enthusiasm was of any true architectural value. Private chapels and the majority of monasteries (which had not yet developed the organized form of their medieval counterparts, but consisted merely of groups of individual monks' cells) were simply and practically built of wood, without ambition toward esthetic effect (Fig. 52a). The Germanic art of timber construction in its richest form seems to have been applied to the palaces of nobles and princes. After a visit to the Rhineland (c. 560), Venantius Fortunatus, poet and Bishop of Poitiers, praised these royal residences in the most glowing terms:

> *Hence with your walls of hewn stone!*
> *Nobler to me is the building of shaped timber,*
> *Which shelters the panelled rooms from wind and weather.*
> *Here the carpenter suffers no gaping vents to mar his craft.*
> *Where once mere stones and mortar gave us protection,*
> *Now the familiar forest bids us welcome,*
> *And elegant galleries encircle the building,*
> *Skillfully carved by the hand of a master and fashioned with marvellous art!*

None of these wooden buildings, which must indeed have been magnificent, has survived, but the so-called stave churches of Norway may provide some clue as to their general character and peculiarities. In Norway (not converted to Christianity until the tenth century), the traditional techniques of Germanic craftsmen were fully maintained until the thirteenth century, and timber churches were not driven out of fashion by stone buildings, as they were in the rest of Europe during the High Middle Ages. The vulnerability and perishable nature of wood has taken its toll of these Norwegian churches, so that of the 750 or

so examples that once existed, only 20 are still extant. They all date from the twelfth and thirteenth centuries and are very similar in arrangement. As in the oldest known Germanic timber churches (among them that at Greenstead in Essex, England, c. 1013), which consist of a single longitudinal hall of small dimensions, the outside walls are constructed of halved trunks or large branches placed side by side vertically. (In the log buildings favored by peoples in the East, these were placed on top of each other horizontally.) But they are more developed, both in planning and construction, than the early one-room structures. A small square-ended or apsidal choir was added to the principal area, which was always square or nearly square on plan. In smaller examples, a single tall post in the center of the floor supported the roof, while the central space in larger churches was surrounded by posts and enclosed within an outer aisle (Fig. 52b, page 177a). Unlike Greenstead and other primitive churches where the whole structure was covered by a simple pitched roof, each compartment received its own shingled covering; the roofs rise from the outer aisles (recognizable as the "galleries" described by Venantius), by diminishing stages, to the central flèche. This effective arrangement gives the exterior a highly unusual and original appearance and a character in striking contrast to that of stone buildings of the same period.

Norwegian stave churches exemplify Germanic architecture in one of its purest and finest forms, but they had no influence on its subsequent development and remained an isolated phenomenon. Such was not the case with the half-timbered building — a form which, according to numerous sources, was known to the western Germanic peoples at least as early as the ninth and tenth centuries. This method of construction became an accepted convention and is still employed in modern times (page 320). At first, half timbering was not applied to monumental architecture in the true sense but was reserved for small undertakings and need only be mentioned here because it may have been the origin of the peculiar form of pilaster-strip decoration and the so-called long-and-short work that occur in early Anglo-Saxon architecture — a kind of half timbering carried out in stone.

The richest example of this type of ornament, peculiar to England, is the tower of the church at Earl's Barton, Northamptonshire (built c. 1000, page 177c). The faces of the stone walls are covered with a network of paneling formed by narrow stone strips, some set vertically and some making lozenge patterns, connecting plain horizontal string courses. At the angles of the tower occurs the long-and-short work consisting of vertical blocks of stone alternating with slabs lying horizontally. Visibly imitating timber prototypes, this ornament still has no structural meaning but is used simply as decoration. It is a demonstration of the Germanic conception of the wall as a field for decorative effects and of the Germanic tendency to break up wall surfaces in an expressive manner. While not entirely without precedent, this tendency is here realized with means that are in themselves original, showing an impulse toward a new language of forms. As a decorative device, this system — with its vertical strips, horizontal courses and latticelike patterning — is to be found again and again in later English architecture. Whether half timbering had a similar stimulating effect on the Continent, and whether it could have influenced the wall treatment of Romanesque stone constructions, have yet to be more fully investigated.

Germanic interpretations of the architecture of antiquity were many and varied. What was achieved between the fifth and the eighth centuries ranged in style from direct imitation of Roman models to complete individuality and led on to the highly significant developments that took place in the Frankish kingdom during the reign of Charlemagne. But of this, as of all architecture before the Romanesque period, it must be said that "it reflected the spirit of an age torn between its own creative urge and the constraint of an alien tradition" (Weigert). It was the product of what might well be called the years of apprenticeship for Western architecture — years that were vital to the formation of a mature, coherent and truly original style.

Carolingian Architecture

During the Carolingian era (which takes its name from the dynasty which preceded and followed Charlemagne) the Frankish kingdom saw a remarkable political and

cultural revival due to the vigorous impulsion of Charlemagne himself, to his political logic and tenacious will. Unlike his predecessors, Charlemagne was not simply content to rule over the Franks, to extend and defend the frontiers of his empire. Although it was he who brought the kingdom to the summit of its power and enlarged it to embrace almost all Latin Christendom by conquering those tribes and kingdoms that had so far retained their independence (the Saxons, Lombards, Bavarians), Charlemagne's highest title to fame is that he used his great authority to promote the renewal of the Roman Empire in the West, under the aegis of the Franks. In realizing his ambition, he succeeded where Theodoric, the first founder of a Germanic kingdom (for whom he had the utmost respect), had failed three centuries earlier.

In 784, having become master of Italy, Charlemagne was acclaimed — at least by the learned men whom he had gathered at his court — as the supreme ruler of western Europe and legitimate successor to the Caesars of the western Roman Empire. He had made himself the protector of the Latin Church and the Papacy and thus represented, like the Byzantine Emperor, both temporal and spiritual power, *regnum sacerdotium*. While he avoided endangering the political status of Byzantium, Charlemagne was determined to rule Christendom as the equal of the Byzantine Emperor, although the latter (as direct heir to the Roman Empire) acknowledged no one but himself to be master of the Christian world. Byzantium and the West would thus once more share control with equal rights, just as they had when the ancient empire was finally divided into eastern and western sections, and the old order would be re-established. In fact, the Byzantine Emperor never recognized Charlemagne's claims, although he was powerless to prevent his rival from gaining the position of equality he demanded. The *Imperium Christianum* (as the Anglo-Saxon Alcuin called Charlemagne's rule) had become a reality, and when at last the Frankish monarch was crowned Emperor of the Romans by the Pope in 800, his ambition to renew the Roman Empire in the West was also realized.

Charlemagne regarded the restoration of the empire as a spiritual as well as a political duty — a fact that was crucial for the development of culture in the Frankish kingdom and for the whole of Western civilization. The political inheritance of the Caesars had been accepted quite deliberately, and a revival of learning and culture could only take place if there was also a conscious return to the traditions of Roman antiquity. It was one of Charlemagne's highest ideals that the Germanic peoples should restore these traditions. The well-known hexameter, written at his court, was no romantic dream but a true expression of the spirit and ideals of the age:

Rursus in antiquos mutataque saecula mores,
Aurea Roma iterum renovata renascitur orbi.
(Through the renewal of the ancient standards
Golden Rome has been reborn upon the earth.)

There can be little doubt that this was a specific reference to the emperor's court and particularly his residence at Aix-la-Chapelle (the empire's center of power and seat of culture from the time of Charlemagne), and that by *aurea Roma* the writer implied not the city itself — and certainly not Imperial Rome — but the Roman world in the wider sense. To Carolingian men, antiquity meant the antiquity of the Christian Era, and it was this aspect of the ancient world alone that they sought to recreate in their art and architecture. Their builders, like those of preceding centuries, indiscriminately borrowed from Eastern and Western prototypes, but they made a conscious effort to create *more Romano* (in the Roman manner), while whatever was previously taken from antiquity had been treated in a more or less arbitrary manner and its original meaning distorted and debased. Regarded in this light, the Age of Charlemagne was truly a Renaissance, finding expression in an architecture based directly on Italian prototypes, maintaining the high artistic conceptions of late antiquity in the West and East, and equaling the achievement of the ancients in grandeur of form. An idea that had grown faint in the course of the three preceding centuries was now brought back into western Europe.

As has already been seen, profound spiritual, economic and racial changes had taken place in the West after the decline of the Roman Empire. It is not surprising that despite such deliberate attachment to antiquity there are some aspects of Carolingian architecture which are new and nonantique in spirit. Even while seeking to recreate antiquity, Carolingian builders were unconsciously laying the foundations of an independent Western architecture.

A crucial influence of the development of Carolingian architecture was the union of Church and State in the person of the emperor. The two great controlling forces formed an indivisible block, while later — when they were once more divided — their rival claims were the cause of much confusion and conflict. As head of Church and State, the emperor's will was paramount. It was he who was responsible for the return to antique sources, he who decreed that churches be built in stone, and he who ultimately molded the character of all Carolingian architecture, both religious and secular. (It will later be seen how the em-

peror's intimate involvement with the Church resulted in the development of a new architectural feature — the westwork.) By wishing to have church services conducted according to Roman liturgical rules, Charlemagne prepared the way for the acceptance of the basilican scheme as the standard type for religious architecture in the West, as it has remained until this day.

At first, Carolingian art (like that of preceding centuries in the Frankish kingdom) had been an eclectic art deriving inspiration from various outside cultures — from Italy, Byzantium, Asia Minor — and the gradual emergence of a uniform imperial style was due to the fact that the emperor's court was not bound to one fixed capital. Although Ingelheim and later Aix-la-Chapelle (Aachen) were Charlemagne's favorite residences, there was never an official seat of government. The emperor and his household were continually on the move, visiting palaces, monasteries and charitable foundations in the course of carrying out their duties. In this way they were able to maintain contact with all the larger building undertakings and could supervise and control the execution of the imperial command. As most of the bishops and abbots were either related to the household or belonged to Charlemagne's circle, there was little to hinder the development of a distinctive architectural technique.

Examples are few and far between; many buildings have been destroyed or later rebuilt on a larger scale, but a fairly reliable impression of Carolingian architecture may still be formed from surviving monuments, excavations and contemporary accounts. Disregarding the differences of planning and construction which inevitably occur from building to building, the following characteristics become apparent:

Churches predominated over other public buildings, both in number and importance.

Stone replaced timber as a building material in the sphere of monumental architecture, timber usually being relegated to smaller undertakings of a domestic nature, such as peasants' dwellings. The Roman technique of ashlar masonry construction now frequently reappeared in place of the primitive methods of rubble walling. In grandeur of form, Carolingian buildings rivaled those of antiquity and surpassed all that had been built in the Frankish kingdom since the fifth century.

Architectural activity began to take place on an important scale in the east of the kingdom.

The Palatine Chapel of Charlemagne at Aix-la-Chapelle or Aachen (pages 178 and 179) is the monument of greatest beauty and significance to have been built during this period. It was erected about 790 as a palace chapel and

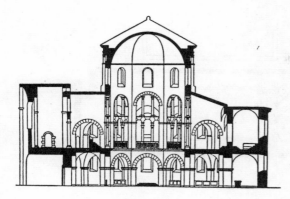

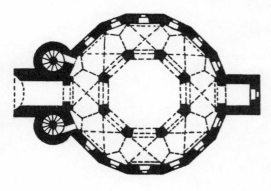

53. Plan and section of the Palatine Chapel, Aix-la-Chapelle, consecrated 805.

royal tomb house and was consecrated in 805. In 814, the emperor was laid to rest within it, in a spot that cannot be identified today. Although the chapel has suffered many alterations since the time of Charlemagne and lost much of its impact by the addition of the long Gothic choir and several chapels which mask the original plan, in all essentials it remains one of the most authentic creations of Carolingian architecture. Built by Odo of Metz, it consists of an internal octagon surrounded by a two-storied vaulted aisle and enclosed within a 16-sided outer wall (Fig. 53). The planning and design and the masterly handling of vault and ashlar construction clearly reveal a close dependence on late Roman-Byzantine models and are a measure of the determination with which the return to ancient tradition was put into effect.

It is of great significance that Charlemagne should have chosen, not the basilican but the Byzantine centralized

plan for his Palatine Chapel. This cannot have been necessitated by the building's function, for the Palatine Chapel of the Palace of Ingelheim (page 181 d) followed the basilican scheme. The founder must have had more positive reasons in mind for adopting one of the schemes associated with the eastern empire. Perhaps he was manifesting a claim to become the equal of the Byzantine Emperor as ruler of the Christian world. Further, the striking resemblance between his chapel and S. Vitale (the royal chapel, Ravenna) can hardly have been coincidental. Although the relationship may be questioned in the absence of documentary evidence and for the reason that in architectural treatment Charlemagne's chapel differs in several respects from S. Vitale, the likeness in plan is unmistakable (page 178). Moreover, they were destined to serve the same purpose, and Charlemagne is known to have held the King of the Ostrogoths in the greatest respect — to the extent of placing an equestrian statue of Theodoric, taken from Ravenna, in the forecourt of his palace. Columns and capitals were also brought from Ravenna, to furnish the new building. In all probability he intended thus to show that he regarded himself as heir to the great Ostrogothic monarch.

A particularly interesting feature of the Palatine Chapel is its adjoining western structure. This consists of a two-storied entrance porch forming a towerlike block and flanked by two staircase turrets. The upper story opens onto the atrium and served as a loggia from which the emperor could show himself to his people assembled below. This was a revival of the ancient custom whereby the conqueror sat enthroned within an apse, elevated above his subjects as the embodiment of supreme power. The placing of the loggia echoes the alignment of apse and nave in the basilicas of Roman emperors and later in Christian basilicas, except that at Aix the apse lies at the west end and outside the body of the structure. The emperor's throne was placed, not in the apse as in a pagan basilica, but within the tribune gallery reserved for the imperial household, where it may still be seen today (page 178 a). From the loggia, the emperor would appear in the eyes of his people as the representative of God, but once inside the chapel, he himself came face to face with his own Lord, for directly opposite the throne on the other side of the gallery lay the altar, and confronting him, too, was the image of Christ in the dome, adored by the twenty-four Elders of the Apocalypse, ranged around the springing. (The original mosaics were executed by Greek craftsmen. The present ones date from the first decade of the twentieth century, but despite a radically altered composition, they preserve the main idea of the originals by placing the figure of Christ enthroned opposite the emperor's chair.)

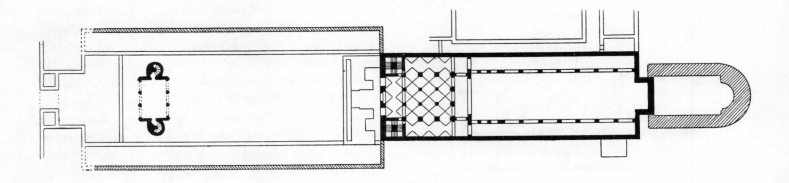

54. *Plan of the abbey church of Lorsch; consecrated 774 (hatching shows later constructions).*

Here, then, the sacred and the secular are found side by side, having been given a particular and symbolic relationship, the secular element (the emperor's loggia) at once forming part of the chapel and yet being clearly differentiated from it.

This interpretation of the structure at the west end of Charlemagne's chapel is the key to the meaning of that feature known in Germany as a *Westwerk* (westwork), the most original and important invention of Carolingian architecture. In several instances before the Palatine Chapel but more especially after it, many important churches — usually basilicas — were provided with large and almost self-contained antechurches at their west ends. These multistoried structures usually comprised a tall central tower flanked by two smaller towers enclosing staircases leading to the upper floors (page 181 a). The precise significance of the westwork has long been in doubt. It could not merely have been a means of giving emphasis and monumentality to the entrance — an effect easily gained without large numbers of rooms and such complexity of design. On the other hand, it was difficult to understand why an antechurch of this kind, opening in arcades toward the nave, should so distinctly be separated from the rest of the church (page 181 a). But by reference to the function of the western block at Aix (structurally simpler but similar in arrangement), it becomes clear that westworks actually were buildings reserved for the use of the emperor and his household, enabling him to participate in divine service on the occasions when he visited cathedrals and monastery churches. That they also had a liturgical significance is shown by the description *castellum* by which they were known and the fact that they frequently contained altars dedicated to St. Michael, whom the Germanic peoples held

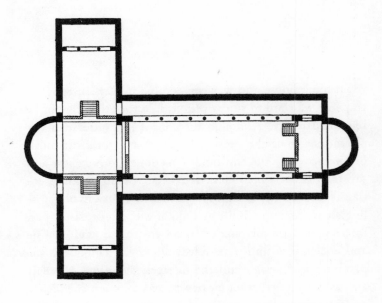

55. *Plan of the abbey church of Fulda. Reconstruction of the new church built between 791 and 819.*

in particular reverence because they believed him to be their chief guardian against evil spirits.

The westwork also has an important esthetic function. Rising proudly between the flanking towers, it not only forms a monumental frontispiece for the building and emphasizes the entrance but provides a vertical foil to the main horizontal of the adjoining church. Although in the Carolingian period this opposition of horizontal and vertical elements was evident only on the exterior and was not reflected in the interior system, it contained the germ of a development away from the longitudinal church scheme, with its monotonous entrance-choir progression, toward the towered church with a stress on the perpendicular—a development that was to reach a climax in the Romanesque architecture of Germany.

Instances of the use of the westwork are confined to the central regions of the Carolingian Empire, which indirectly confirms their function as churches reserved for the visiting emperor. The first surviving example is that of the abbey church of Lorsch (consecrated 774, Fig. 54), followed by those at Centula (St. Riquier) on the Somme (790–799) and Aix-la-Chapelle (before 805). Examples from the period after Charlemagne are more numerous and are almost exclusively concentrated in the region between the Weser and the Elbe (Halberstadt Cathedral, consecrated 859; Hildesheim Cathedral, consecrated 872; Corvey Abbey Church, 873–875; Gandersheim, conventual church, consecrated before 923; Minden Cathedral, consecrated 952)—a reflection of the shift of political emphasis into the eastern section of the Frankish Empire (Germany) after the Partition of Verdun in 843 when the empire was divided into eastern, middle and western kingdoms. They did occasionally occur outside this boundary, as at the ancient Carolingian Cathedrals of Reims (852) and Auxerre (879–887), but in their most developed and monumental form, westworks were essentially a product of Germany, where in some places the tradition was maintained into the Romanesque period (Marmoutiers, pages 208 and 209). These late examples no longer served the purpose for which the feature was first conceived, being employed purely for esthetic effect. Such were the western tower compositions that now prevailed in German churches and that also had their origin in the Carolingian westwork.

Few Carolingian churches adopted the centralized plan found at Aix-la-Chapelle. The small Chapel of St. Michael, Fulda (822, page 178 c), and the church at Germigny-des-Prés (founded 806, page 178 b) are rare examples. The Palatine Chapel of Nijmegen (built c. 830 by Louis the Pious), Essen Minster (end of the tenth century) and even the abbey church of Ottmarsheim in Alsace (as late as the eleventh century), are all to a certain extent modeled on the chapel at Aix, but this out of respect, not so much for the centralized plan as for Charlemagne himself, whose memory was at that time held in the greatest honor. Otherwise the axial basilican scheme predominated, due largely to the emperor's decree that the Roman form of liturgy should be adopted in churches.

It is interesting to observe that after the eighth century the basilican plan itself underwent several changes and was carried so far beyond the ancient construction that its original significance became somewhat obscured. The plan of the abbey church of Fulda (dedicated 819, Fig. 55), which was destroyed in the eighteenth century to make way for the present baroque cathedral by Dientzenhofer, is remarkable in two respects. More than 325 feet long, it illustrated the tendency of the time to build on a monumental scale, and the fully developed transept betrayed direct reference to Roman prototypes. (Other churches, including that built by Einhard, advisor to Charlemagne, at Steinbach in the Odenwald [page 181 c] were also provided with transepts, but these, like the choirs of some Byzantine churches, consisted of a number of separate, self-contained compartments.) It is a fact of great importance that the transept at Fulda was added at the west end and not the east. St. Boniface, who had founded the abbey (744) and used it as a base for his missionary work, was killed by the Frisians (754) and his body, according to his wishes, was transferred to Fulda. Shortly after his death, his fame as a saint and the Apostle of Germany reached such proportions that he was placed on the same plane as St. Peter, the first of the Apostles. Thus, when Abbot Ratgar replaced the abbey church (791) with a larger and more magnificent new building and remembered the saint's wish to be buried on the west side of the church, he consecrated a separate choir to the relics and built a west transept in deliberate allusion to Old St. Peter's, Rome.

A feature which in Rome had been dictated by the practical demands of the site was here given a symbolic meaning by association. The placing of a second chancel at the west end in addition to the traditional eastern apse resulted in the double-apsidal ending—one of the most characteristic traits of the Carolingian period and consequently of Romanesque architecture in Germany. It was the expression of a need to dedicate one church to several saints. Thus where individual churches formerly had been erected side by side when a town had more than one patron saint, their altars now could be combined in a single building. This development deeply affected the character of the basilican plan. The interior lost its single-minded, west-east direction by the opposition of apses that created two focal points or

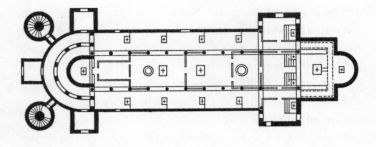

56. *Plan of the Monastery Church of St. Gall, Switzerland. After a plan c. 820, never carried out.*

poles of interest. In some other churches, this balance of elements was carried even further by the addition of a second transept, as in St. Riquier, Centula (after 790) and old Cologne Cathedral (*c.* 830).

The idea, first evident at Fulda, of the double-ended scheme, reappears later in a more developed form in the manuscript plan drawn up about 820 (but never carried out) for the Benedictine church and monastery of St. Gall, Switzerland. The plan of the church itself (Fig. 56) resembles Fulda in that there are two apses, one at each end of the nave, which accommodate altars to St. Peter and St. Paul. At St. Gall, however, there are two additional altars, dedicated to the Saviour and the Baptist, down the center of the nave. These accentuate the even distribution of elements and the lack of a positive orientation, and form a third liturgical center point. True, this has not affected the architectural arrangement of the church, which is divided by two rows of columns into uninterrupted lengths of nave and aisles. Again as at Fulda, the transept is the same width as the nave, and the area of their intersection, the crossing, thus forms a perfect square. But whereas at Fulda the length of nave and crossing was equal to the combined lengths of the transepts—the plan being conceived as a single unity—in St. Gall, the square crossing itself sets the scale of the plan, being repeated in each transept. The transept therefore comprises three units, and the nave four and a half—the half unit perhaps implying a relationship with the width of the aisles, approximately half the width of the nave. The chancel is formed by another square unit between the crossing and the apse. Thus the whole plan is

brought within a simple arithmetical system and at the same time the T-shaped plan of the old transeptal Roman basilicas has become a Latin cross.

The cruciform plan with lengthened chancel was occasionally to be found in churches of late Merovingian date, though resulting here merely from the need to provide extra space for clergy (and perhaps in deliberate reference to the Cross of Christ) and not from the repetition of units. There is no doubt that the idea of the symbolism of the cruciform plan, which had not occurred to the Early Christian builders, was by now a common one, and it is likely that the author of the St. Gall plan was consciously applying it to his design.

In the Latin cross plan, the crossing, surrounded on three sides by arms of equal area, acts as a point of climax and interrupts the longitudinal flow. But in St. Gall, there has been no attempt to exploit this effect by architectural emphasis or to express the units of the nave with structural elements. The pillars are arranged in uninterrupted rows, and the ceiling is flat, while the angles of the crossing are marked only by four columns and no provision is made for a tower that would express the crossing externally as the core of the plan and give it a special symbolic significance. Nevertheless, this tendency to articulate the plan by dividing it into a number of clearly defined spatial compartments grouped around a central point, in the form of a cross, is the first stage in a development from the unarticulated longitudinal building to the structure composed of a series of architectural cells. This development was to culminate in Romanesque architecture of the twelfth century, when each unit was defined by molded wall piers and covered by a vault in place of the flat timber ceiling. The plan of St. Gall only hints at the interior and exterior possibilities of compositions of double apses, transepts and crossing towers explored more fully in such Carolingian examples as Mittelzell (806–816) and Oberzell (*c.* 890), Reichenau, where four arches to carry a tower were thrown over the low screen walls separating the crossing from its adjoining compartments. The towers over the crossings at Fulda and Centula, too, were a cautious forecast of things to come.

The plan of St. Gall poses several other problems that were yet to be resolved in structural terms. One of these was the method of arranging the additional altars occasioned by the growing cult of saints in the Carolingian era and also by the increasing custom of each priest saying Mass every day. Particularly in the case of a monastic establishment where there were large numbers of clergy and monks, a corresponding number of altars was essential. Their incorporation in the plan presented many difficulties, and in most abbey churches they seem to have been placed in the nave and aisles at random, as at St. Gall. Only the high altars—those of the patron saints of the church—had fixed positions. The extension of the eastern chancel had contributed toward solving the problem, and in some churches, under Roman influence, small apses to accommodate altars were introduced along the east wall of each transept. The ideal solution is only to be found in Romanesque architecture, where an ambulatory is carried behind the eastern apse and provided with radiating chapels.

While the cult of saints resulted in the double apsidal ending and in the provision of extra chapels to accommodate their altars, the cult of relics which grew up simultaneously led to the introduction of an element not generally associated with either Early Christian or Byzantine architecture: the crypt. Originating in the small *confessio* of Early Christian basilicas, the crypt was at first a simple underground cave housing a tomb containing the relics of the patron saint of the church. The tomb, always set immediately below the altar, was surrounded by a circular gangway to which staircases led down from the transepts and around which pilgrims would proceed when they came to worship.

By the ninth century, this simple form no longer met the requirements of the rapidly rising cult, and passageways fitted with niches (recalling those first Christian burial places, the Roman Catacombs) were built under the chancel and sometimes under parts of the nave and transepts. Another larger type of crypt comprised several vaulted aisles. The crypts below the chancels of Fulda (Fig. 55) were two of the earliest examples of this type. Not only was this feature to remain an integral part of the church until the late Romanesque period, but it was also to have a considerable effect on the character of the interior. The chancel under which the crypts were built was raised above the floor of the nave and thus structurally emphasized as the liturgical climax of the church, becoming a stepped platform or stage upon which the most sacred parts of divine service could take place in marked isolation from the laity below. From the point of view of the plan as a whole, this development was a further step toward the independent organization of each element and the disruption of a freely flowing interior space.

Carolingian religious architecture may justly be said to have made a vital contribution to the development of a distinctive architecture of the West, for it brought many bold and significant innovations that had advanced far beyond those of late antiquity. But these innovations did not amount to a coherent style, and it was not until the Romanesque period, when Carolingian motifs were combined and resolved into a system, that a true architectural style finally emerged.

Secular building of the eighth and ninth centuries was in no way comparable with religious architecture of the same period. The ancient Roman cities had sunk into obscurity, and no new centers rose up in their place to afford opportunities for building activity on an important scale. Houses and farm dwellings were little more than wooden shelters, and the residences of the nobility were scarcely superior in quality. The only field of activity where architects seem to have displayed their skill outside the Church was in the imperial palaces. Used by the emperor in the course of his travels from one center to another, they were built of stone on a scale of the utmost magnificence. None of these palaces has survived, but some impression of their general character may be gained from excavations and descriptions of the Palace of Ingelheim (page 181 d), favorite residence of the young Charlemagne, and later of Louis the Pious. The palace, with its large range of rooms covering an area of about two acres, was clearly organized on the pattern of the palaces and forums of Roman antiquity—a gesture calculated to draw attention to the parallel between the Germanic and the Roman emperors. The magnificent hemicycle (at left, Fig. d, page 181), with its Corinthian colonnade and central porch, immediately recalls the Forum of Trajan in Rome (Fig. 24). The imperial hall (right, Fig. d, page 181) was a single-aisled basilica not at all resembling the usual Germanic halls built for the same purpose (page 174 a, b) and must have been modeled on the basilicas of Roman imperial palaces. The emperor, as in antiquity, sat enthroned within a semicircular apse. According to ancient descriptions, the walls of the hall were decorated with paintings of great historical figures and their battles—another deliberate attempt to make the Germanic emperor appear as heir to the past and a direct descendant of the heroes of antiquity.

The gatehouse that stands isolated in the atrium of the abbey church of Lorsch (Fig. 54, pages 180 and 181) gives some idea of the originality and elegance that could be attained in Carolingian secular architecture. This small two-storied building may have been erected at the same time as the church itself (consecrated 774), but this is uncertain, and it is more likely to date from the time of Louis the Pious (814–840). (Details of its function and architectural character, page 181.)

To some degree, monastic establishments also qualify as secular buildings. Although none survive from the Carolingian era, the plan for St. Gall (c. 820) clearly demonstrates that the designing of monasteries was an important part of the Carolingian architectural program and that the

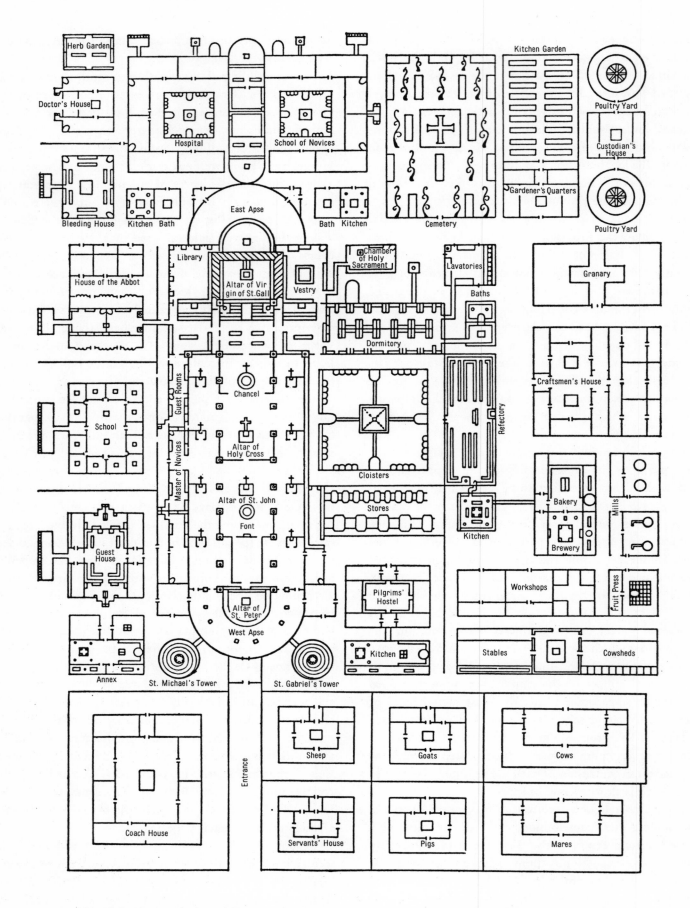

56a. Plan of the Monastery of St. Gall, Switzerland. After the manuscript plan c. 820. After Weigert.

main characteristics which were to recur in monasteries for centuries to come had already been established. St. Benedict of Nursia (who founded the first monastic order, 529, and drew up its rule) had prescribed that a monastery should contain everything necessary to daily life and be a completely self-contained community. Thus in addition to the living quarters of the monks, grouped around the cloister, the St. Gall plan (Fig. 56 a) provides for a wide variety of other buildings including tailors' and shoemakers' workshops, bakehouse and brewery, granary, laundry and stables and sheds for various livestock. There was also to be a school, a guesthouse, a hospital and a cemetery. In short, St. Gall was planned to work with the efficiency of a small town, and it is not impossible that monasteries of this type influenced the organization of the new towns that were to be built in the empire from the tenth and eleventh centuries.

ARCHITECTURE DURING THE RISE OF THE WEST

ILLUSTRATIONS

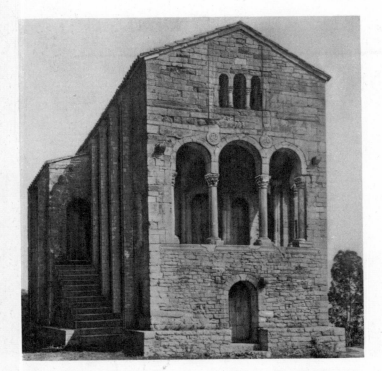

a

b

c

MAUSOLEUM OF THEODORIC, RAVENNA
c. 520.

The churches built in Ravenna by Theodoric, King of the Ostrogoths (who figures in the legends of Germany under the name of Dietrich of Bern as a great hero and leader of the German peoples), are either centralized structures of the Byzantine type (page 126) or Roman basilicas with nave and aisles divided by rows of columns (page 118), and closely follow the late-antique-Early Christian tradition. His tomb, on the other hand (completed before his death, 526), is not so easily classified and presents at least one entirely original feature. True, the two-storied building, with its decagonal lower part and cylindrical upper story, has much in common with the mausoleums of antiquity: the lower part encloses a cruciform barrel-vaulted crypt based on the Tomb of Galla Placidia at Ravenna (page 125 f); the walls, with their beautifully cut masonry, indicate the work of Byzantine craftsmen. But the most remarkable feature of the mausoleum — the roof carved from one huge block of stone — is without precedent in Roman-Byzantine tradition. It weighs 470 tons and is hollowed into a flat dome on which are still to be seen the original stone handles used for hoisting it into position on the drum.

It is tempting to suppose that when Theodoric found himself no longer restricted by the rules of liturgy that had governed the form of his churches, he cast his mind back to his own Germanic origins and remembered the great age-old stone tombs of northern Europe in which the burial chambers had also been covered by gigantic monoliths. Remarkable, too, are the decorative markings around the cornice of the tomb. These are a corruption of the classical leaf-and-dart molding (which has here become an abstract motif typical of Germanic wood carvings) and are open to a symbolic interpretation where the circles would represent the sun and the triangles the earth. (Facing page.)

a,b) ROYAL HALL OF THE VISIGOTHIC PALACE, NEAR OVIEDO
Asturias, Spain, eighth or ninth century.

Ramiro I (842–850) is recorded as having consecrated this building to Sta Maria de Naranco as a church, but in all probability it was designed a century earlier as the royal hall of the Visigothic palace. This is suggested by the provision for baths in the cellar and the position of entrances on both long sides of the hall, accessible by flights of outside steps (of which one flight remains). The tunnel vaulted hall is the oldest surviving stone example of a type of Germanic building formerly constructed only in wood. The strange spiral shafts are evocative of timber prototypes, and the walls are roughly put together, testifying to the decline in antique methods of wall construction characteristic of the period following the barbaric invasions. The "Chronicle of Abelda" betrays the low standards of this age, praising the "wonderful art" of the barrel vaulting displayed in the hall, although these vaults are crude compared with those of antiquity.

c) S. PEDRO DE LA NAVE, NEAR ZAMORA
Spain, seventh century.

In addition to a few small basilicas, Visigothic religious architecture comprises several churches obviously inspired by centralized Byzantine examples. The Greek-cross type with high central area predominates. This form, which probably reached Spain via Ravenna and the Tomb of Galla Placidia (page 125 f), is exemplified in S. Pedro de la Nave, although here the cross is developed into the typically Spanish square plan by the addition of compartments in the four angles.

NORWEGIAN STAVE CHURCHES

The so-called stave churches of Norway provide the best and now almost the only visible evidence of Germanic skill in timber construction. About twenty still exist, all dating from the twelfth and thirteenth centuries and all similar in appearance. The use of timber has resulted in architectural forms that are strikingly different from those of the stone churches being built at the same time in other parts of western Europe. True, the basic elements are the same — a main room for the congregation and a chancel at the far end — but as in the church at Borgund (thirteenth century, facing page), the main area or nave is nearly a square in plan and does not develop along a horizontal center line but is arranged about a vertical axis (Fig. a). This effect is emphasized by the sturdy posts that form the frame of the structure. These are placed around the whole of the central area at more or less regular intervals, separating it from the surrounding aisle and from the chancel — a small, low adjoining compartment of little formal significance. The verticality of these churches is more clearly expressed in the exteriors (facing page), where the steep shingled roofs over the various compartments rise in overlapping stages from the outer aisles to the flèche (stave church of Gol, now in Bygdöy, near Oslo, Fig. b). These pyramidal structures may be compared with the soaring towers of German Gothic cathedrals, for both forms were the expression of an essentially Germanic idea. An interesting feature of stave churches are the dragons' heads on the upper gables. They resemble the figure-heads found on old Norse ships (the ship of Oseberg, Norway), and, like these, were supposed to drive away evil spirits.

c) TOWER, EARL'S BARTON, NORTHAMPTONSHIRE
England, tenth century.

Several Anglo-Saxon buildings indicate that the West Germanic races were also familiar with half-timbered construction where the walls consist of a framework of timber posts and struts filled in with brick or *pisé de terre* (page 320). No early examples of its use have survived, but the strip patterning of wall surfaces produced by this technique was occasionally imitated in stone buildings. The best example of half timbering carried out in stone is the west tower of Earl's Barton. The stone strips, vertically arranged in rows and in zigzag patterns, are structurally meaningless and serve only as a surface decoration. The monotonous regularity with which the same motifs are repeated over the walls and the emphasis on vertical lines are typically Anglo-Saxon. This linear decoration reappears in a more sophisticated form in later English Gothic architecture.

d) ST. GÉNÉROUX, POITIERS
Eighth century.

In many Merovingian churches in the west of the Frankish kingdom (among them St. Généroux), the facing materials of the walls were used decoratively as well as for their structural purpose. Lively effects were achieved with the ancient Roman systems — *opus reticulatum* and *spicatum*. This type of flat two-dimensional ornament is in sharp contrast to the sculptural decorative means employed by the Romans.

a

b/c

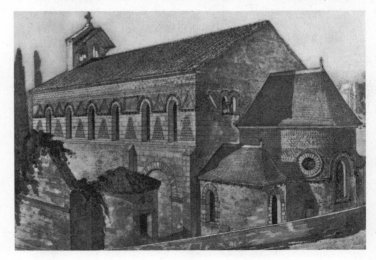

d

a

b

c

PALATINE CHAPEL, AIX-LA-CHAPELLE (AACHEN)

Built by Odo of Metz; consecrated 805.

This was the royal tomb house of Charlemagne and until 1531 the place of coronation of the Germanic emperors. The most impressive monument of early Western architecture, it is convincing evidence of the great emperor's expressed wish to imitate the artistic as well as the political models of antiquity.

There can be little doubt that S. Vitale, the Palatine Church of Theodoric, Ravenna (page 126 b), provided the inspiration for Aix. In architectural conception, the two buildings are strikingly similar; they served the same purpose, and Charlemagne is known to have had the greatest admiration for the King of the Ostrogoths, the first to found a Germanic state. He ordered columns and capitals to be transported from Ravenna for use in his chapel. The central domed space is octagonal and between the angle piers opens onto a two-storied surrounding aisle. In spite of such obvious resemblance to Ravenna, the chapel as a whole remains a typically Carolingian and individual creation. At Ravenna, the central space had been surrounded by curved-out niches and had opened at the east end, to form a high rectangular chancel, but at Aix, the eight sides are treated identically and the central area is thus isolated from the chancel so that the plan is completely centralized. There is also a clear division between central octagon and ambulatory, for the curved niches of S. Vitale (which caused the flow of space from one area to another) are flattened out into simple openings between the corner piers. The massive cornice that separates ground floor from gallery level and the superimposed columns in two orders above (facing page) are features that find no counterparts at Ravenna.

The architecture of Charlemagne's chapel is heavy and austere, while that of S. Vitale is characterized by the elegance and lightness of its forms. The sturdy piers and massive arches and the plain severity of the stone walls (Fig. a) give the monument a nobility worthy of the emperor. Of the two churches, Charlemagne's conveys the deeper impression of religious dignity and grandeur.

b) CHURCH AT GERMIGNY-DES-PRÉS

Founded 806.

This small church was built by Theodulf, Chancellor to Charlemagne and Bishop of Tours, "after the pattern of the basilica that was built at Aix-la-Chapelle." The architectural elements echo those of Aix in their plainness and massiveness. Here, too, there is a mosaic decoration. The plan is centralized, being square externally and cruciform internally where the four arms are grouped around a high central area and terminate in apses.

c) ST. MICHAEL'S CHAPEL, FULDA

c. 820.

This circular structure is directly inspired by late-antique-Early Christian chapels and baptisteries (page 125). It will be noticed with what crudity and clumsiness the columns and their entablatures imitate antique forms.

GATEHOUSE OF THE ABBEY OF LORSCH
c. 770?

The true function of this small and somewhat unorthodox building remains uncertain. The three vaulted passageways of the ground floor and the single hall above (reached by staircases within two round towers on the short sides) would seem to indicate that it served as a gatehouse or porch, but the fact that it stood completely isolated in the atrium of the abbey speaks against this theory. The building may well have been used as an audience chamber by Charlemagne and his descendants—they may have sat enthroned under the vaulting while giving audience or administering justice. The external decoration is particularly interesting because it offers another example of the use of wall facings to produce a decorative effect (page 177 d). Four attached columns with Composite capitals frame the arches of the lower story and support a cornice carved with an antique palmette motif. Above this cornice, nine bays of small fluted pilasters with flat Composite caps carry a triangular arcade (possibly foreshadowing the decoration of Earl's Barton, page 177 c). The attached columns play an integral part in the building's construction, but the pilasters and triangles are structurally ineffectual and serve only a decorative purpose. The facing of red and white stone slabs recalls ancient reticulated masonry and the geometrical motifs of Arab art. (Facing page.)

a, b) THE WESTWORK

The westwork was perhaps the most important innovation of Carolingian religious architecture. These antechurches are self-contained architectural entities generally comprising three towers (Fig. a, model of Carolingian Cathedral of Minden, c. 920; Fig. b, model of westwork of Corvey Abbey Church, 873–875). Giving monumental emphasis to the entrance façade, they may derive their origin from Syrian churches of the sixth century (Turmanin, Fig. 37) and lead in turn to the great towered west fronts of Romanesque cathedrals.

c) EINHARDSBASILIKA,
STEINBACH IN THE ODENWALD
Begun 815.

This three-aisled basilica was built by Einhard (Charlemagne's biographer and advisor) to commemorate the martyr saints, Peter Exorcista and Marcellinus. The nave arcades (later walled in, as seen in the drawing) were carried on the piers that frequently took the place of columns in Carolingian architecture. The transepts formed independent compartments, each with an apse, with doorways from the chancel, like the pastophorion of a Byzantine church.

d) IMPERIAL PALACE AT INGELHEIM
Model, c. 900.

a

b

c

d

VII
ROMANESQUE ARCHITECTURE

Historical and Religious Background

Charlemagne had set himself high political, spiritual and cultural ideals, and by sheer strength of personality had been able to realize many of them. But his son and immediate successor, Louis the Pious (814–840), felt no compulsion to pursue his father's policies or to take responsibility for them. Although he had neither the dominating mind nor the ambition of his great father, Louis was by no means a weak or ineffectual ruler. His decision, sanctioned by the Partition of Verdun (843), to divide his inherited Frankish Empire between his three sons was far-reaching in its effects and decisive for the future of the West. Charles

the Bald was allotted the territory in the west of the empire; Lothar, an intermediate region later known as Lotharingia; the eastern third fell to Louis the German. The breakup of the Carolingian Empire was irreparable and prepared the way for the emergence of the French and German nations.

The partition of Verdun heralded a period of steady decline all over Europe. The internal strife that ensued as a result of disputes over rights of succession in the now independent dominions and the rival claims of their rulers not only prevented any further development of Charlemagne's achievements in the political and cultural spheres but led to the gradual loss of all he had gained. The Frankish peoples, divided and weakened, were unable to put up an effective defense when confronted with attack from outside. The Vikings (or Northmen), the last great wave of Germanic invaders, met with no serious or organized resistance when they swept down from Denmark and Norway into the very heart of the new kingdoms. Coasting the seaboards, they burned and pillaged as they went, raiding Cologne, Paris, Lyon, London and the shores of the Mediterranean, and establishing a reign of terror over Europe. Whereas formerly men had prayed for protection against the forces of Nature: "*De ora leonum, libera nos, Domine*" — now the churches rang with another cry: "*A furore Normanorum, libera nos, Domine*" ("From the fury of the Northmen, deliver us, O Lord"). And in Germany such a prayer must often have been directed against the Hungarians who, with their horsemen, bore down in a concentrated attack on the southern regions. The Saracens — the third danger that beset western Europe — profited by the occasion to spread fear and desolation in southern Italy and along the south coast of France.

For a hundred years (from the middle of the ninth to the middle of the tenth century), Europe lay cast in gloom, and little progress was made. Like everything else, architecture almost came to a standstill, and from an architectural point of view, all that can be said of this period is that as a result of the danger under which men were living, more and more houses and fortresses were built of stone, to provide better protection, and castles were strengthened with outer walls. Here are to be found the origins of the fortified castles of the Middle Ages, and indirectly, of the city walls that appeared with the rebirth of the towns in the eleventh and twelfth centuries.

When at last the Northmen settled in the district around the lower Seine (Normandy, 911) and adopted the Christian faith, and when the Hungarians suffered defeat by Henry I at the battle of the Unstrut (933) and finally by Otto the Great at Lechfeld near Augsburg (955), order began to re-establish itself in Europe. The unexpected turning point that came toward the end of the millennium had two main causes. Most important was the fact that one of the great stabilizing powers in the West, the Church, had survived this period of decadence and disaster almost unscathed. At a time when the State had been rendered incapable of offering protection, men had turned to the Church; and the idea of Christianity which the Church represented had been more deeply than ever before impressed on the minds of the common people. The second contributing factor was the nomination of Henry, Duke

of Saxony, as King of Germany (919), which gave control of the eastern Frankish kingdom to a dynasty that was to produce, in Otto I, one of history's great leaders whose achievement was in many ways comparable with that of Charlemagne. Under Otto, the old concept of imperial power was resurrected, although on a different basis, and limited to Germany and its subject kingdom of Italy.

When in 925 Lotharingia was brought back into the kingdom of the East Franks, the Carolingian idea of unity, never entirely forgotten, was temporarily revived and reasserted itself under Otto, who, like Charlemagne, aspired to renew the Roman Empire in the West. In 962, he was crowned by the Pope in Rome as "Emperor of the Holy Roman Empire of the German nation." In ecclesiastical organization, Otto recognized a convenient means of consolidating the empire and checking the self-interested maneuvers of dukes, counts and tribal leaders. By handing over many of the tasks of government to the episcopate, he acquired — in the solid, hierarchical organization of the Church — an administrative system that reached out to the farthest corners of the empire and was well equipped to uphold the idea of unity and cohesion on the foundation provided by its single-minded purpose of service to God. The interdependence of Church and State was the more real because, as in the time of Charlemagne, prelates were nominated by the emperor or drawn from the royal household or the court.

The effects of the Ottonian system of government, leaning heavily on the help of the clergy, were felt in many quarters, not least in architecture. The system gained the empire a predominant place in Europe, which was maintained for at least a hundred years, and it provided a fund of strength that could be drawn upon in later and less prosperous times. It also began to form a German national consciousness which overrode local allegiances. But there were difficulties and dangers inherent in this system, dangers arising not only from the close interdependence of temporal and spiritual authority, but also from the fact that such a system could succeed only if these two powers had common aims and ambitions and were not in conflict — in short, only while that great political synthesis which was the basis of the *Sacrum Imperium,* the alliance of pope and emperor, could be maintained.

This alliance was broken toward the end of the eleventh century when pope and emperor engaged in a bitter contest over the right of precedence. It lasted, with intermissions, until the thirteenth century and ended in an almost total collapse of the empire's political organization. The revolt of the Church against the intervention of temporal powers in its internal affairs was precipitated by a movement for monastic reform that began in the tenth century. The center of this reform movement was the Benedictine monastery of Cluny in Burgundy. It was here in 910, while terror of the Northmen still held Europe in its grip, that a small group of monks gathered together and started a campaign for greater discipline in the monasteries.

The Cluniac reform spread rapidly, bringing about corresponding changes in architecture, and through the monastery at Hirsau in the Black Forest, it had a lasting influence in Germany. It was no accident that the movement had begun in Burgundy. Although this region (an independent kingdom since 879) came under the jurisdiction of the German Empire under the Salian Conrad II in 1032, it was essentially part of the west Frankish kingdom, where there was not that close interrelation of temporal and spiritual authority which had been effected in the East by the Ottonian system. In Burgundy, Church affairs were independent of political administration.

Conditions in the west Frankish kingdom differed in many respects from those in the German Empire. The Carolingians remained in power until 987, but unlike the Saxon kings of Germany, never regarded themselves bound to fulfill the work their great ancestors had begun. An explanation may lie in the fact that, somewhat toward the east, Charlemagne had already established the cultural and spiritual center of Europe and that the Carolingians themselves were originally an east Frankish family. The Capetians, who succeeded the Carolingians, did not pursue the idea of forming a united empire of the Franks, but concentrated on the single task of consolidating their own domain. There is no space here to follow their history in detail, but it should be emphasized that France was the first country to achieve an administration approaching that of the unified, centralized state of Roman antiquity, and that the French were the first to gain a true national consciousness.

This development was possible only because the French kingdom knew nothing of the local feuds that divided Germany throughout the Middle Ages, preventing the formation of a nation-state. In Germany, bitter struggles for tribal independence caused an endless succession of civil wars, and the Saxons, Swabians, Bavarians and Franconians were each subject to their own laws and preserved a distinct identity — even after their entry into the federation of Frankish tribes, for this had no political basis, but simply depended on feudal ties of allegiance. France, with the exception of Burgundy and Normandy, was subject to the Frankish law alone, and thus had some foundation upon which to build her political unity. That the kingdom of the Franks is called France and the community of Germanic tribes across the Rhine is known as German and not Saxon, Swabian or otherwise, is an eloquent expression of the differences between the two nations. True, such a form of identification tends to conceal the fact that the French population was far less homogeneous than the German, which was purely Germanic. In the West, there was a noticeable dualism arising from the coexistence and fusion of the Germanic and the Gallo-Roman elements. The importance of this for the development of architecture cannot be overestimated and will later be discussed more fully. Here it need only be said that one of the principal reasons for the marked local peculiarities that characterize the development of architecture both in France and Germany must be sought in the various German peoples' consciousness of their own individual identities and in the racial differences that existed between the French people.

Architectural Character

GENERAL

It was only when the forces of order at last triumphed over the chaos that had reigned between the middle of the eighth and the middle of the ninth centuries and political stability was returning in all parts of Europe that the architectural style known as Romanesque was born. At the turn of the tenth century, the Ottonian Empire — the first to regain an internal order and retrieve its strength — saw the beginnings of a building activity more prodigious and more vigorous in its achievements than any seen before, even in antiquity, and comparable only with that of the Gothic and baroque. Given the intimate union of Church and State and the vital part played by the clergy in the government of the empire, it is not surprising that the new artistic energy was concentrated upon the erection of churches and monasteries. Overriding all political considerations was the concept of Christianity. This was one of the reasons why Europe, notwithstanding the fact that each country developed along different lines and despite the lack of political unity, was able to produce the elements of a uniform architectural style.

Another important factor was the emergence of a commonly accepted outlook on life and the relation between the earthly life and the hereafter, which took effect throughout society — politically in the feudal system and socially in the cult of chivalry identified with the Crusades (after 1096) and an adaptation of ancient concepts to the new ideas. Despite local variations, Romanesque buildings are all inspired by the same Christian-chivalric ideals which, as the expression of the new reconciliation of the divine and the human, were not completely lost even when the militant measures of the Church brought about the fatal clash between pope and emperor and architecture came to be a means of representing the freedom of the Church from imperial domination. Until the War of the Investitures (end of the eleventh century), the building of a church symbolized the union of the two great controlling forces — the political and the spiritual — which was never more magnificently represented than in the great cathedrals built by the German emperors — above all that of Speyer. Solemn and monumental in spirit, royal church and tomb house — and at the same time church of the espiscopate and of the people — Speyer is a complete expression of imperial and Christian ideals.

The variety that is to be found in Romanesque architecture, in spite of common spiritual aims, was largely due to the social peculiarities of the German tribes and the racial differences within the French nation. Important also in this respect was the absence of any single unifying, centralized authority like that of Roman antiquity. But the decisive factor, particularly in France, was the internal organization of the Church. The grouping of parishes around the bishoprics, and monasteries around their mother houses, inevitably exercised an influence on architecture, for each religious community strove to express its individuality by creating a distinctive artistic language.

This tendency led to the formation of schools of architecture. The products of each school often bear such a marked family likeness that, conveniently for the historian, they may be named specifically, the variations from one school to another not being confined to generalities but extending to the smallest details, such as column capitals and architectural ornament. Thus it is frequently possible to identify the influence of each school where it occurs and to determine, in any one building, the source of this or that motif, or even to identify the builders and their backgrounds. Identification and comparison of schools is the only means of tracing the development of medieval architecture, for it

is not until later — particularly toward the end of the Gothic era — that architects emerge as distinct personalities and are known by name. The builders of the Middle Ages were craftsmen who worked anonymously, with no ambition to gain personal honor through their skills. The names that have come down to us are exceedingly rare; that they begin to emerge more frequently after the High Middle Ages is a sure sign of the slowly developing cult of the individual and man's awakening consciousness of his own value within the community.

The freeing of the individual artist — whether architect, painter or sculptor — from obscurity is a reflection of the new ideas that had grown up in the West between the early Middle Ages and the beginning of modern times. The Romanesque period marks the first stage in this development, and the anonymity of Romanesque builders is a reminder that until well into the eleventh century the designing and building of churches and monasteries was almost exclusively the concern of clerics, and above all, of monks. In their eyes, architecture was a sacred art dedicated to the service of God and symbolizing His glory. It was inconceivable that monuments built in such a spirit should be a means of satisfying personal ambitions or that man's achievement, so insignificant beside this high ideal, could ever become a source of pride in itself. Nevertheless, the very artistic perfection of the forms that were evolved no doubt contributed to their popularity and widespread use.

By the eleventh century, building activity had reached such proportions that the monks were forced to rely more and more on the help of lay workmen who, in carrying out their masters' orders, gradually acquired something of their knowledge and skill in building construction. When, in the eleventh and twelfth centuries, the rapid development of commercial activity wrought profound changes in Europe's agrarian economy and towns expanded into trading centers, the laity were able to take control of public building schemes without having recourse to the help of the clergy. Thus the sacred art of the monks was in many respects the origin of medieval municipal architecture.

THE MEANING OF ROMANESQUE

The architecture of France and Italy was more closely bound to antique Roman tradition than was that of Germanic or Germanicized countries, and the elements of a new style, free from Roman tradition, are, whenever they occur, the result of Germanic influence. Fundamental to the development of an international architecture was the fact that the same *Zeitgeist* prevailed in both Latin and Germanic countries, motivating a common architectural theme. Racial and political differences only gave rise to superficial variations in form, without affecting the essential elements of style. German historians have attempted to clarify the problem by dividing Romanesque stylistic development into three main phases under headings corresponding with the then-reigning dynasties: Ottonian (Saxons), Salian (Franconians) and Hohenstaufen (Swabians). Obviously, these headings hold good only for Germany and some parts of Italy, and historical truth will hardly allow them to be imposed on the whole of European architecture of the early Middle Ages. There is no doubt that the term Romanesque, first used by a French scholar about 1820 to describe the architecture of this period, finds much in its favor, implying as it does that in spite of regional differences, Western architecture found its origin in the tradition of Roman masonry construction lately revived by Charlemagne.

PLANNING AND CONSTRUCTION

The history of Carolingian religious architecture, especially during the ninth century, has clearly demonstrated that the trans-Alpine renaissance of late-antique-Early Christian forms had by no means involved a slavish repetition and imitation of antique models, but that it had been the first stage in a development toward an independent Western architectural idiom. The most important aspects of Carolingian building — and those that contributed most to the creation of the Romanesque style — had been, first, the new will to monumentalize exterior design (expressed in the westwork and the idea of the crossing tower); second, the preference for clearly defined grouping and articulation (juxtaposition of the perpendicular westwork and the long, low nave, introduction of the transept crossing); and finally, the tendency to systematize the whole church plan on the basis of a single spatial unit, the crossing. Moreover, all these ideas were applied to one type of building alone — the basilica, which significantly became the dominant theme of Romanesque and subsequently of Gothic architecture.

Carolingian variations on this theme all tended in the same direction, their logical outcome being in each case the transformation of the longitudinal church, with uninterrupted entrance-choir development, into a more complex building group with an emphasis on the perpendicular. The addition of high towers was the external expression of this idea, while internally it was best realized by the double apsidal ending found in numerous churches of the period. Romanesque builders, heirs to the Carolingians, took up this theme as their ideal and brought it to a conclusion in the many-towered, fortresslike basilica, the proud *Castellum Dei*. Just as many of the motifs of Romanesque architecture may be traced to Carolingian origins (towers, double apses — found in many German churches), so one of the most important Romanesque developments in church planning stemmed from an element first given significance in Carolingian times: the crossing or the area of intersection of nave and transept.

In some Early Christian basilicas a transept already had been interposed between nave and semicircular apse, and the feature had later reappeared in Carolingian buildings, as for example in the abbey church of Fulda (Fig. 55). But neither these nor Early Christian transeptal basilicas may be said to have had a crossing in the true sense. The crossing in its purest form arises, not merely from the meeting of nave and transept, but from their interpenetration: the nave must extend eastward beyond the point of intersection. In some Carolingian churches, the nave was lengthened by the addition of a short choir in front of the apse, the crossing thus becoming the focal point around which the rest of the plan was grouped in a well-marked Latin-cross form. But the possibilities that this feature offered for the development of both plan and elevation were never fully realized and remained neglected throughout the second half of the tenth century and even during the early Romanesque period (from c. 1000). Only occasionally was an attempt made to express the particular significance of the crossing in architectural terms by marking it out from the adjoining bays with heavy arches on each side or by building a crossing tower to emphasize externally its function as the nucleus of the church plan.

Until well into the eleventh century, the plan of the transeptal basilica was determined by a single dimension (usually the length of the central nave) which also determined the length of the transept (Fig. 57 a). But this elementary form of organization did not yet extend to the other dimensions in the plan, and the widths of nave and transept would seldom correspond — a fact of the utmost importance, for as a result, the crossing was rarely a perfect square and thus lost much of its effect (on plan and in elevation) as a geometrically established center point, seeming to belong as much to the transept as to the nave. Further, crossing arches of unequal spans were unsatisfactory in appearance, for being at this time always semicircular, they rose to varying heights accordingly. By degrees, the idea of a comprehensive internal order led to the equalizing of the widths of nave and transept, the crossing becoming a perfect square and unmistakably appearing as a self-contained, centralized unit — the geometrical center point of the plan as a whole. Romanesque architects were increasingly tending to treat the component parts of the church plan individually and to group and organize the elements of the design. It is therefore not surprising that the possibilities of this development were soon recognized and exploited, the significance of the crossing being emphasized by defining it on all sides with arches, to mark it out clearly from the rest of the church. The effect of the four round arches, now of equal span, was harmonious and pleasing. Here also was a means of satisfying the Romanesque preference for towers, so far limited to the west end — either constituting part of the westwork or taking the form of freestanding elements. It was now possible to build a tower over the crossing, the four arches providing a sufficiently strong weight-bearing structure.

It is characteristic of the new will to organize and articulate space that the crossing was recognized not only as an important element in the construction but also as a starting point for the systematization of the whole church according to a simple arithmetical principle. It became a basic unit in the plan, repeated throughout the building.

This idea had first been applied by the unknown author of the St. Gall plan of about 820. Here the square unit of the crossing had been repeated in the chancel and each transept, and the nave had comprised four and a half square units (Fig. 56). But this plan had never been carried out, and whether it was later adopted for old Cologne Cathedral (c. 830), as has sometimes been supposed, it is now impossible to ascertain. The ideas inherent in St. Gall were not rediscovered and put into effect until the beginning of the Romanesque period, when, together with buildings whose ground plans were still determined by a single dimension (like the cathedrals of Mainz and Strasbourg, begun shortly after the turn of the millennium), there also appeared several churches that were articulated according to the new system.

Although the system was not applied to the whole plan until Romanesque architecture had reached its fullest development in the twelfth century, these early examples of its use decisively went beyond the elementary concept of St. Gall, clearly showing that Early Romanesque architects worked with a new sense of space and rhythm. They regarded the plan not merely as an indication of the shape on the ground that the building would occupy, but also as a starting point for the organization and grouping of each element in elevation. It goes without saying that this had, to some extent, also been the case when plans had been established as single entities, but the decisive factor was that with the adoption of the basic square unit system there now also appeared a tendency to express each unit in structural terms. Nothing of this was yet apparent in the St. Gall plan. The arcades and nave walls were to have been carried on identical supports, in the Early Christian tradition. Many Romanesque churches (especially those in the south of France, northern Italy and southern Germany, and the buildings of the reform orders, the Cluniacs and later the Cistercians) show the same exclusive use of either columns or piers in their arcades, in spite of the fact that their plans are organized on the basic unit system (Fig. 57 d). This was no coincidence, for these regions or schools deliberately clung to the antique basilican plan in the face of new developments, though in elevation their buildings could not remain immune from the spirit of Romanesque arising out of the racial, political and spiritual conditions of the time.

It is easy to understand why the desire to give structural expression to the articulation of the plan was first and most conspicuously manifested in purely or predominantly Germanic regions where antique tradition did not exert a strong influence. The development began in several buildings dating from shortly before or immediately after the year 1000, all situated in and around the old Kingdom of Saxony, just north of the Harz Mountains. Most important of these is the Church of St. Michael at Hildesheim (pages 202 and 203), built between 1001 and 1033 by Bishop Bernward, tutor to the emperor's sons. In this three-aisled basilica with two apses, two chancels and two transepts, the square crossings are not only emphasized by means of lantern towers but serve as a basic unit in the central nave, which consists of a sequence of three such squares. The transepts, with their short rectangular projections, do not yet conform to the new order, but the epoch-making aspect of St. Michael's is that the three squares of the nave are stressed in the arcade by piers at their corners, with columns in between.

An alternation of supports had occurred for the first time in the convent church of St. Cyriakus, Gernrode (begun in 961), but here — where the square unit system did not apply — it had merely been a means of elaborating the design. St. Cyriakus also exhibits the earliest triforium gallery of this period in Germany, and there is good reason to

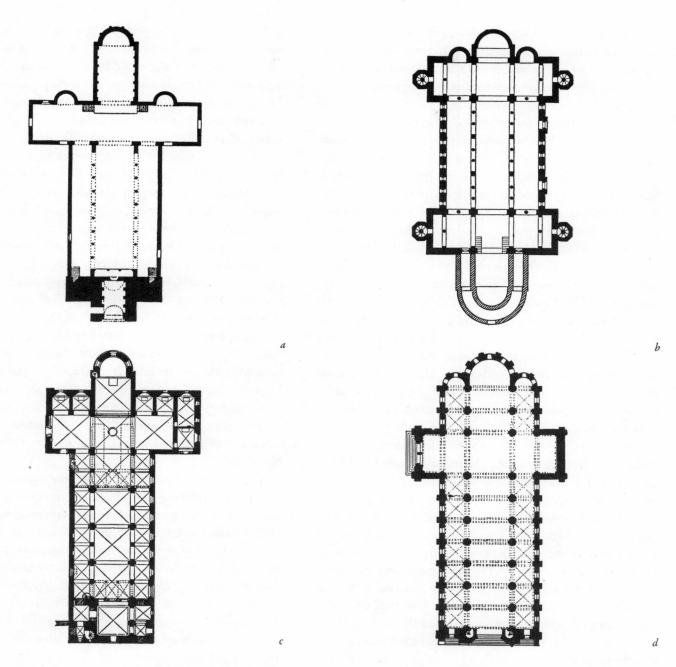

*57. Evolution of the Romanesque church plan: a) Abbey Church, Hersfeld, 1038–1144; b) St. Michael, Hildesheim, 1001–1033; c) Abbey Church,
Steinfeld, Eifel, begun 1142; d) Autun Cathedral, twelfth century.*

suppose that both this and the system of alternating supports were inspired by Byzantine buildings of the type of
St. Demetrius, Salonica (sixth century). Another feature of
the church — the relieving arches that group the gallery
arcades into pairs — has the same origin and contains a hint
of the wall arcades that were to become so important in
Romanesque architecture, lending themselves to the expression of that preference for clearly defined grouping
and articulation which signalized the age. The influence of

Eastern architecture in St. Cyriakus was to be expected,
for the marriage of Otto II to Theophanu, niece of the
Byzantine Emperor, had formed a close connection between the two empires.

It is characteristic that Romanesque builders should
have seized on the idea of alternating piers and columns,
used by the Byzantines for the sake of decorative variety,
as the logical means of making apparent in elevation the
unitary articulation of their plans. In St. Michael's, Hildes-

heim and similar churches, this principle was not, however, carried to a conclusion, and differentiation occurs only in the arcades, where, as at Hildesheim, two columns might alternate with one pier (dactylic alternation) or one column with one pier (iambic alternation). In a typical early Romanesque church, the nave walls between arcade and clerestory are not articulated, retaining an unbroken surface.

The tendency to systematize the ground plan by using a basic unit repeated throughout the building (first evident at Hildesheim) reached a climax in the fully controlled plans of the twelfth-century vaulted churches of France and Germany, exemplified in the abbey church of Steinfeld (Fig. 57 c). Here the square of the crossing is repeated in choir and transept arms, while the nave, as before, comprises several of these squares. The side aisles, with a width equal to half that of the nave, also consist of a sequence of squares, each of which is one-fourth the size of one nave bay. Thus to every square compartment of the nave there are two smaller squares on either side. The last traces of the plan conceived as a single entity have disappeared, to be superseded by a controlled system of articulation extending over the whole church.

This system, usually accompanied by alternating supports, was no more than the clearest and most logical expression of the Romanesque will to build up a plan from a number of independent, clearly defined spatial compartments instead of from the mere juxtaposition of two unities — nave and transept. The new ground plan dominated church architecture in Germany, Lombardy, Normandy and England (then under Norman rule), but the more Latinized regions of France, notably the south, took a different course of development. It is true that here also the crossing of nave and transept formed the nucleus of the plan and was repeated in the nave, but the separation of bay from bay was not made explicit and arcades were carried on identical supports. Thus the nave appears to comprise, not a sequence of squares but a rhythmic succession of narrow oblong compartments (Fig. 57 d). However, it is not difficult to recognize here, too, the articulating, planning spirit of Romanesque: the side aisles are divided into square or rectangular bays, each exactly half the area of one nave compartment. Although no longer dictated by the square, such a plan continues to reflect the tendency to build up a design from a succession of spatial units. It should be pointed out that the division of the nave into narrow oblong bays foreshadows subsequent Gothic developments.

A new system was also devised for the accommodation of altars. It has already been seen how Carolingian build-ers had dealt with this problem, arising from the growing worship of saints and the need for each priest to celebrate a daily Mass. Extra apses had been built at the sides of the main apse, and the double apsidal ending had been introduced, but the plan for St. Gall shows the problem still unsolved. The numerous altars are placed at random in the nave and aisles and are not organically related to the plan as a whole. The double choir was never adopted generally, for it allowed for the accommodation of only two altars and remained a feature peculiar to Germany, where Carolingian traditions exerted their strongest influence. The very fact that until the twelfth century Carolingian architecture was the determining force behind all the larger and most important German churches may explain why the problem of altar accommodation was eventually resolved, not in Germany, but in France. The staggered plan (Fig. 58a) appears for the first time in the abbey church of Cluny, apparently in the second rebuilding (dedicated in 981). The aisles are extended past the transepts to form subsidiary chapels set back from the main apse and parallel with the choir. Apses placed along the east wall of each transept are again set back from these. This type of plan was to exert a profound influence on later Cluniac architecture and was often used in Germany and Normandy.

It was, however, another type — the radiating plan — that was to dominate the future of religious architecture in Europe, and which made a first appearance about the year 1000 in the rebuilt Church of St. Martin at Tours. The main choir and apse were surrounded by a low ambulatory provided with radiating chapels, each containing an altar (Fig. 58 b and page 234 c). In all probability, the inspiration for this form came from those early crypts below the chancels of many churches which likewise comprised a circular passageway around an altar or tomb (confessio). The original Carolingian construction of St. Martin had one such confessio that may well have exhibited niches around the walls comparable to chapels around an ambulatory. It seems reasonable to suppose that the relics of the great patron saint of France were transferred to the chancel of the new church as soon as it was built, so as to be more accessible to thousands of worshiping pilgrims, and that in the process the builders had had the idea of planning the east end in this new way.

The Church of Sta Maria im Capitol, Cologne (consecrated 1065; Fig. 58 c), has a distinctive eastern termination. The choir and the two transept arms are treated in an identical manner, the end motif being in each case a semi-circular apse with ambulatory, thus producing a trefoil shape. The trefoil choir (usually without ambulatory) was

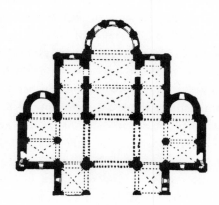

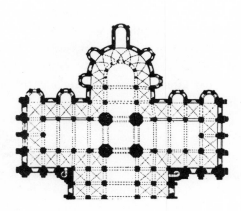

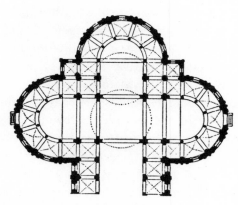

58. *Romanesque eastern terminations:*
    a) *Staggered plan, Cerisy-la-Forêt, Normandy, twelfth century;*
    b) *Radiating plan with ambulatory, St. Sernin, Toulouse, twelfth century;*
    c) *Trefoil choir, Sta Maria im Capitol, Cologne, c. 1040.*

adopted in many churches of Cologne and the Rhineland, including Holy Apostles and St. Martin, Cologne, and Mainz Cathedral. The origin of this form remains obscure, but the east end of Sta Maria im Capitol, which as the name suggests was erected over Roman remains, may well have been inspired by antique centralized buildings. There may also be some connection with Byzantine three-apsed churches. The singular popularity of the trefoil choir during the High Romanesque period in Germany must have been due to the spatial effect it produced on the interior. The markedly centralized character of this eastern termination was bound to find favor with architects whose ideal was the church composed of a number of independent spatial entities. Moreover, the three great projecting apses enhanced the impression of solidity, strength and fortress-like grandeur on the exterior, as is well illustrated by the exterior view of the east end of Holy Apostles, Cologne (pages 234 and 235).

Each development and elaboration of the Romanesque ground plan was governed by a need to create a unified design from a number of separate units determined by a simple yet strict arithmetical system. The same need is found expressed with equal clarity in the building itself in the manner of handling space and elements of structure. In many churches — especially those of Germany built during the twelfth century — the height of the walls is determined by the dimensions of the ground plan, the nave often being exactly twice as high as it is wide. The continuous, even flow of space in an Early Christian, Carolingian or even an early Romanesque church gives way to a rhythmic succession of clearly delimited spatial compartments. This development was indeed foreshadowed during the Carolingian era in the use of towers to punctuate exterior design, in the attempts that were made to isolate the crossing and give it some external emphasis as the nucleus of the plan, and in the accentuation and separation of the chancel by means of raising the floor like a podium above the level of the nave.

But there had never been any attempt to disrupt the spatial unity of the central nave by making it appear to consist of a sequence of separate bays. The walls over continuous arcades carried on identical supports — columns or more frequently piers — were unarticulated except for a row of small clerestory windows. The church was enclosed within its walls and flat wooden ceiling as a single spatial compartment with a compelling entrance-apse directional emphasis. Although this emphasis was diminished with the introduction of double apses, churches retained their single-minded grouping during the early Romanesque period, which is characterized by flat ceilings and unarticulated nave walls. Not until the beginning of the eleventh century do churches begin to show signs of true articulation in their aisles and nave walls. Like so many of the innovations of Romanesque architecture, this development, with all its far-reaching effects, would remain unexplained were it not for one decisive factor in the formation of the Romanesque style: the new conception of the use of stone in building construction.

The history of stone as a building material is as varied as the history of architecture itself. A study of Early Christian basilicas and Byzantine churches has clearly shown that their builders regarded masonry merely as a convenient means of separating one room space from another. The inherent qualities of stone as a carvable, sculpturesque material had been ignored, and even its flat surface effects were disguised by mosaics that covered the walls of churches like veils, denying the solidity of the stone and giving an illusion of other-worldly insubstantiality.

It is not surprising that during these years the Roman technique of ashlar construction, which had so well expressed the natural qualities of stone, fell rapidly into disuse and was superseded by rubble construction. Walls had continued to be built of rubble and mortar until the beginning of the Romanesque period, largely because the Germanic peoples were only accustomed to timber construction. Knowing nothing of the methods of building in stone and slow to learn because of their lack of technical skill, they continued to regard walls rather as a background for applied decoration than as decorative, space-articulating elements in themselves. However, by a slow but inevitable process, stone regained something of the importance that the Greeks, above all, had accorded it. By the eleventh century, not only had the ancient technique of ashlar construction been rediscovered and rubble walling finally abandoned, but builders had come to a new awareness of the intrinsic monumental qualities of stone. So accurate had their stone cutting become and so precise the jointing, that the mortar joints on which even the Romans had relied were hardly necessary. Each stone was given an individual character with drafted edges and fine tooled surface or in some cases (during the Hohenstaufen period) deliberately rock faced.

Thus Romanesque wall construction repeats the same cubic principle and expresses the same preference for clear grouping that characterize Romanesque building as a whole. The feeling for the intrinsic quality of stone that it displays extends throughout the structure, being reflected in the early taste for smooth, undecorated walls, in the increasing use of massive, heavy piers instead of the more slender column, in the plastic treatment of structural elements, and above all in the new emphasis given to the architectural character of the exterior.

The metamorphosis of the central nave from a single spatial compartment to a series of juxtaposed bays covered nearly a century. The first stages of this development are datable around 1000, which has, partly for this reason, been commonly accepted as the true birth date of Romanesque architecture. As has already been said, early attempts to articulate the nave were limited to an alternation of supports (piers and columns) in the arcade, as in St. Cyriakus, Gernrode (c. 961, page 202a), St. Michael, Hildesheim (c. 1001, pages 202 and 203), and many churches in the region around the Harz Mountains. The walls above the arcade still retained a smooth unbroken surface, but an important development took place in the new cathedral at Halberstadt (begun 965), when the arches carried on piers alternating with columns were embraced in pairs by blind arches springing from pier to pier in the nave walls above. In this way, the differentiation so far only expressed in the supports was carried into the wall surface, though not yet in the upper stages. Further, these blind arcades heralded the deep recessing and layering of wall masses that later became a characteristic feature of Romanesque churches.

In the triforium gallery at Gernrode, where they appeared for the first time (probably under the influence of Byzantine architecture), these blind arcades were still closely bound to the wall surface, but at Halberstadt— and subsequently in numerous other churches—they are strongly molded and constitute additional decorative elements. More important were the transverse arches first used in several early Romanesque churches in the Rhineland, not only to separate the crossing from its adjoining compartments, but also to articulate the side aisles. Springing from every second pier or column, they span the aisle, serving both to support the flat timber ceiling and to strengthen the whole structure. The division of the aisles into bays by means of transverse arches prepared the way for a development that was to determine the character of later Romanesque: the reintroduction of vaulting.

In the course of the centuries following the great invasions, the art of vaulting construction and the engineering skill of the Romans had been all but lost. Early Christian builders had already had to resort to timber roofs and simple forms of construction such as king-and-queen post trusses. Although the Byzantines continued to vault their buildings, the flat roof remained predominant in Western architecture until the beginning of the eleventh century. Rare instances of the use of vaulting before this time include several small churches in the south of France where classical traditions lingered on, in crypts, the lower stories of towers and the galleries of Carolingian westworks, and a few centralized structures (such as the Palatine Chapel at Aix) inspired by Byzantium. Use was made of the dome, the barrel vault, and especially in large aisled crypts, the cross vault, but there is no surviving evidence that any of these were employed to cover the whole of a large building.

The small chapel of St. Bartholomew, Paderborn (1017), is outstanding as the first building on German soil to be covered entirely by a vault, but this was built, not by local craftsmen, but *per operarios Graecos* — that is, by Byzantines. Only after the introduction of transverse arches to divide lengths of space into square bays did builders attempt vaulting on a large scale. At first they limited their experiments to side aisles. The east end of Bernay Abbey in Normandy was vaulted after 1013, and about 1030 the aisles were covered with groin vaults. Groin-vaulted aisles appeared at Speyer Cathedral (begun at approximately the same time, under Conrad II) and then in numerous churches — above all those of Normandy and the Rhineland — where this type of vault had been well known since Carolingian times and could be seen in crypts and the lower stories of towers. But builders were still not prepared to face the problem of vaulting the wider nave — a task that was not mastered until the turn of the eleventh century when Romanesque architecture was approaching its fullest development.

The introduction of the vaulting system in side aisles had important consequences for the articulation of wall surfaces. The cross vault (Glossary — under Vault), formed by the intersection of two barrel vaults of identical shape and used over a square compartment, was borne on four arches — the longitudinal arches or wall ribs, and the transverse arches spanning the aisle. These framing arches necessitated corresponding supports and were thus made to spring from pilasters or more frequently from the capitals of attached shafts projecting from the wall face. It was inevitable — in view of that desire for symmetry and balance so characteristic of the age — that the articulation of the aisle should then have been repeated in the nave, the supports of the arcade becoming compound or clustered piers. The need for clarity and consistency of expression led to the elaboration of nave arcades with moldings in recesses or orders. Replacing the early Romanesque arch, generally flat and unmolded, this type of arcade is typical of High Romanesque and is yet another manifestation of the growing tendency toward richer, more complex forms.

There could be no structural justification for compound piers in the nave arcade at first. Flat timber ceilings did not necessitate supports of this kind, and the various instances of the use of clustered piers toward the middle of the eleventh century show them employed purely for decorative effect. In the abbey church of Jumièges in Normandy (consecrated 1067), a galleried basilica with alternating piers and columns in the arcade, shafts attached to each pier were carried up the whole height of the wall to the foot of the roof. Their significance is esthetic; structurally, they would have been superfluous, for the timber ceiling would easily have rested on the nave walls. These shafts were a means of projecting the divisions marked out by the alternating supports of the arcade onto the upper nave walls, which thus lose their old surface unity and become a sequence of well-defined bays (pages 218 and 219, Fig. 59 b). Jumièges was only one of a series of Norman churches of this kind. It was decisive for future developments that the shafts ran straight up to the roof and did not, as in the nave of Speyer Cathedral (Fig. 59 c), meet over the clerestory windows in semicircular blank arches. At Speyer, the arches tend to suppress the upward drive of the shafts and to render each bay static, while in Norman churches this movement continues undiminished throughout the whole height of the wall, each bay rising smoothly from floor to ceiling. This idea was carried to a logical conclusion when flat ceilings like those employed at Jumièges were replaced by vaults in the nave.

The vaulting of the central nave was undertaken at Speyer and in Normandy at approximately the same time. About 1080, under the Emperor Henry IV, the nave of Speyer Cathedral was rebuilt and its original flat roof was replaced with large-scale groin vaults (c. 1090). In order to obtain support for the transverse arches and wall ribs, the shape of the piers at the corners of each square nave bay was modified: on every second pier the tall, slender shafts of the original structure were replaced by broad pilasters reinforced with heavy engaged shafts. These new elements fulfill a double function, carrying the wall ribs and transverse arches and at the same time constituting important decorative features, articulating the nave wall as the previous slender shafts had done. But these had merely served to divide and give rhythm to the wall surfaces, while the new supports, bearing a direct relationship to the arches above, make a vital contribution to the character of the complete interior space. Walls and vaults have become an organic whole for the first time, so that each bay is now a unity in a three-dimensional sense. The nave is no longer a single uninterrupted spatial compartment but the sum of several distinct units of space.

This development, taking place at the end of the eleventh century, was the ultimate fulfillment of that desire for articulation which, in the course of a hundred years, had led Romanesque architects to introduce alternating supports, blind arcades and transverse arches, and subsequently to vault the side aisles of their churches and break up the surface of walls above the arcades with vertical lines of demarcation. What had so far been an experiment with various elements, only rarely bearing any true relationship to each other, was now resolved into a system whereby all parts were strictly interrelated, both optically and structurally, to form a unified whole. But it should be emphasized that a Romanesque church

represents a juxtaposition, not a fusion of parts. Even in this cohesive system, each element is clearly defined and maintains an individuality. The fusion and interpenetration of spatial units was the achievement of Gothic architects of the thirteenth century.

The two central bays of the choir of La Trinité in Caen, Normandy, received cross vaults at the same time as Speyer (c. 1090). The vaulting of the nave was undertaken a little later (c. 1100). Here, instead of the simple cross vault in which the two curved surfaces meet in sharp edges or groins, the rib vault was used, where these edges are accentuated by narrow projecting stone bands or ribs. Undoubtedly suggested by wall ribs and transverse arches,

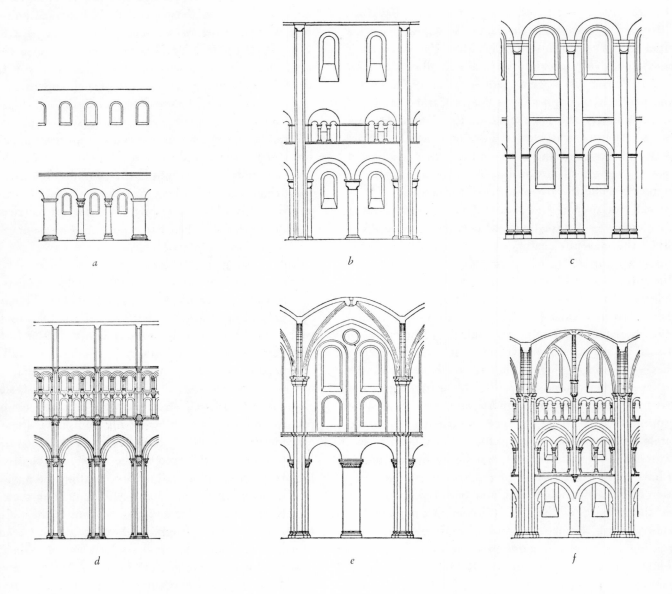

a *b* *c*

d *e* *f*

59. *Development of Romanesque wall articulation: a) St. Michael, Hildesheim, 1001–1033; b) Notre Dame, Jumièges, c. 1060; c) Speyer Cathedral, first construction, c. 1050; d) Cluny III, c. 1181; e) Worms Cathedral, after 1181; f) Limburg-an-der-Lahn Cathedral, before 1235.*

also strongly modeled, these diagonal ribs probably made their first appearance in side aisles, although there is no conclusive evidence of this. The important fact is that the earliest surviving examples of rib vaults occur in the churches of Normandy. They are composed of rubble and large quantities of mortar, and the ribs themselves are purely ornamental, unlike those of Durham Cathedral in northern England (built 1133, page 225 b), and all Gothic ribs, which constitute an independent constructional framework carrying a light infilling or web.

In early Romanesque churches in Normandy (among them Jumièges), the slender shafts of the nave arcades were carried from floor to ceiling without interruption. They had no technical justification but were an expression of a new desire for upward movement in design. As soon as the vault succeeded the flat timber ceiling, the upward forces inherent in the wall shafts were carried on and resolved in the transverse arches and diagonal ribs of the vaults. Indeed, in no Romanesque building before this date is there to be found that vertical impulse which permeates both space and structure in a rib-vaulted church, each element seeming irresistibly to reach upward to the apex of the vault — a development that was to culminate in the pointed rib vaults of the Gothic era.

By the end of the eleventh century, vaulting on a large scale was taking place in those regions of France (central, southern and Burgundy) that had so far remained outside the mainstream of development. Here, where numerous antique Roman buildings had escaped destruction and exerted a powerful influence, the cross vault was not the predominant type, being employed chiefly for side aisles and tribune galleries, while naves — almost without exception — were barrel vaulted. This may have been due not so much to the proximity of antique monuments but to the fact that from the outset the builders of these regions had adopted the basilican, orientated scheme with arcades in unbroken perspective and freely flowing space as their example and ideal.

The activities of the reformed Cluniac Order had had a decisive influence in this respect. The Cluniacs had set out, not only to revive the stricter monastic life, but also to reform religious architecture by advocating a return to Early Christian basilican ideals. Through the monks of Hirsau, the reformatory spirit of the Cluniac movement had a lasting effect in Germany, resulting in the building of large numbers of abbey churches on the pattern of the simple, columned, flat-roofed basilica (page 205), and was largely responsible for the fact that shortly after the onset of the war over the investitures the double-apsidal

ending was abandoned and the old entrance-choir orientation re-established. It is true that in Germany the intended return to the basilican, orientated scheme did not seriously impede the development of a more articulated, complex grouping.

In France, however, it was the determining factor in the general adoption of the barrel vault, which bears a direct relationship to the flat ceilings of Early Christian churches in that it represents spatial continuity as opposed to the separate spatial units created by the cross or rib vault. Here lies the source of that striking difference between the interior effect of a barrel-vaulted French basilica (page 213) and that of a German or Norman church. But it says much for the pervading force of the spirit of these times that French barrel-vaulted churches have the same massive structural grandeur and the vertical divisions of nave walls that signalize Romanesque architecture of other regions during the period. Even the vault is divided into bays by means of transverse arches which span the nave from shaft to shaft (an exception is St. Savin, pages 212 and 213, datable c. 1080, which has the first Western example of a continuous barrel vault — that is, with no transverse arches). Thus here, too, though in a less marked degree, there appears a tendency to articulate and to disrupt the continuity of the interior design. It should be pointed out that the most emphatic division of interior space into separate compartments was achieved in the domed churches of Aquitaine at the beginning of the twelfth century (page 217).

The vaulting of naves involved a serious problem: that of the counteraction of the lateral and vertical thrusts of the vaults. The static forces of a barrel vault, which distributes its weight with equal emphasis along the whole length of the side walls, present certain problems. Thick walls or, in the case of hall churches, heavy Romanesque piers, provided the main support and were reinforced by the vaults of the aisles, and in larger churches, by those of the triforium galleries (cross vaults, barrel vaults or semibarrel vaults). The problems posed by the cross vault and subsequently by ribbed vaulting are conspicuously different. Their weight and thrust are concentrated along the lines made apparent by groins, ribs, wall ribs or transverse arches, and are transferred to the wall and substructure only at the points where these lines converge on their supports. Some examples show that the potentialities of this concentration of thrust were not at first appreciated. At Speyer, the builders seem to have placed their confidence in the support provided by massive nave walls unpierced by triforium galleries. But elsewhere it soon became customary to strengthen the vaulting shafts with shallow buttresses on the exterior. This solution was, however, only effective when the nave wall was sufficiently strong and retained an unbroken surface, as for example in Germany, where Romanesque builders were extremely conservative in this respect, continuing to erect their cross-vaulted churches without triforiums throughout the twelfth century.

Even after 1200, the scheme of the galleried basilica, imitating French precedent, appears only in isolated instances. In Normandy and England (which came under Norman rule after the Conquest of 1066), the triforium had been in common use since early Romanesque times. Here the necessary abutment to the vaulted nave was provided by cross vaults in the aisles, as well as by external buttresses or (as at St. Étienne, Caen) by semibarrel vaults over the triforium gallery, leaning against the nave wall and supporting its whole length — not merely those parts in stress.

It was perhaps in Durham Cathedral in northern England, remarkable for what appear to be the earliest true rib vaults in the history of architecture (page 225 b), that the development first took place which was to be of the utmost significance for the formation of the Gothic system of construction. In the choir, instead of barrel vaults over the aisles, oblique transverse arches were placed against each vaulting pier. In the nave, the vaults of which were erected shortly afterward, appear the first flying buttresses (Glossary). These are quadrant arches rising obliquely against the wall buttresses in the triforium chamber and transmitting the thrusts of the nave vaults down onto the exterior wall. But whereas in Gothic churches the triforium is omitted and the flying buttresses are exposed above the roofs of the aisles, in Romanesque buildings they are habitually covered by the lean-to roofs of the triforium and are thus invisible from the exterior. Though the concealment of these features may have been necessitated by the two-storied aisles, it may also have had an esthetic significance. In some early Gothic monuments, among them Notre Dame in Paris (page 262 b), the buttresses are externally emphasized as a feature of the design despite the fact that the triforium is retained. But their effect is contrary to every Romanesque principle of design; they detract from the simplicity and compactness of the exterior grouping and from the feeling of solidity and unbroken mass that Romanesque architects strove to convey.

The exterior form of Romanesque churches was always subject to the same principles of construction and design that governed interior organization. Indeed, these principles are yet more clearly apparent on the exterior, where building masses alone are in evidence and where spatial relationships do not enter into the problem. That feeling for the natural qualities of stone — for its weight and density and for the peculiar effect produced by the squared block of masonry — may be fully appreciated in Romanesque exteriors characterized by vigorously plastic form and massive, compact grouping. Though each individual part is governed to a certain extent by functional necessity and is a reflection of interior articulation, they are all informed by the innate character of the Romanesque style.

Until the Gothic era, every church is conceived as the sum of various clearly defined, coherent elements, whether or not it be double apsed, transeptal, a hall church or a basilica. A unified design is built up from separate parts, like so many building bricks, each in itself consisting of a number of individual units. Heinrich Wölfflin's descriptive phrase that a Romanesque composition can be dismembered without damage to the parts is, however, valid only within certain limits. This process could hardly be literally applied to the more sophisticated buildings of the period, where the builders were striving to integrate nave and transept and to go beyond the simple relationship between these two elements found in Early Christian, Carolingian and even in some early Romanesque churches. The lantern tower proved to be the most effective means of achieving this fusion. It became the focal point and center of interest on the exterior, as the cross transept was for the interior. Above all, it fulfilled the aspiration to give the church a soaring, heavenward movement, disengaging it from the broad horizontal mass below.

The conception of the House of God as a many-towered fortress found its fullest realization in the double-apsed churches of Germany. The equal importance given to east and west ends, logically expressed on the exterior by corresponding tower groups, tends to detract from the directional character of the long nave, which is now spread out between two emphatically vertical poles of interest (page 206). In France, where the Carolingian tradition of double apses was unknown during the Romanesque period and builders adhered to the orientated basilican scheme, external treatment inevitably developed along different lines. Here, too, however, churches were built with important crossing towers, effectively stressed (as in Germany) by the addition of subordinate towers or turrets, combining to give the whole building a majestic air of verticality. But as these features are concentrated at the east end, they enhance rather than suppress the impression of horizontal west-east development conveyed by the long nave. Both internally and externally, the eastern termination is stressed as the climax of the design and the most important liturgical part of the church. A tendency to give the west end the same importance by means of towers is evident only in isolated instances, and significantly, mainly in Normandy.

French Romanesque architects arrived at several solutions to the problem of how to treat the façades of their basilican, orientated churches. In the south, the richly decorated frontispiece predominates during the twelfth century (page 222). With its profusion of arcades and figure sculpture (heralding the return of monumental sculpture to Western art), this type of façade stresses the importance of the entrance but expresses little of internal structure, in this respect radically differing from Romanesque façades in northern Italy. Nor does it reflect anything of the will to monumentalize the whole building group which is so characteristic of German Romanesque. This inclination was, however, sufficiently strong in France to provoke the architects of Cluny III to build an antechurch with two flanking towers at the entrance to the abbey. Whether in this particular case the old idea of the Carolingian westwork as a fortress of St. Michael and protection against evil spirits for those at prayer played any part in their decision, it is impossible to say with certainty. Ideas of this kind may well have had considerable influence at the time, when esthetic values were never divorced from their spiritual context.

Be that as it may, architectural effect was the prime consideration and this can be seen more clearly in the buildings of Normandy than in those of Burgundy. The two great churches of Caen (St. Étienne and La Trinité, both begun 1064) have true twin-towered façades (page 222 d) —mighty square towers rising on either side of the portaled fronts. This type was to become the rule for cathedrals in northern France and was also adopted in Germany where, by the twelfth century, the far-reaching influence of the Cluniac reform movement had resulted in the disappearance of the double-apsed plan. But buildings like the late Romanesque Cathedral of Limburg-an-der-Lahn (page 210) clearly show that the German preference for compact, close grouping survived undiminished. At Limburg, the nave is so short that the tower groups to east and west almost converge, and the church remains fortresslike, unorientated and majestic in its unequivocal verticality. And yet, like all the monuments of its time, Limburg conveys an impression of ponderous grandeur that is in direct contrast to the soaring, weightless movement expressed in the spires of a Gothic cathedral. The typically Romanesque tower roofs and the horizontal bands of decoration contribute to this effect.

ARCHITECTURAL DETAILS AND DECORATION

The interior and exterior treatment of Romanesque churches everywhere reveals a steady progression toward a greater degree of articulation. Columns and piers, arches, capitals and even walls and vaults, all take parallel courses of development—away from the stark, undecorated, unbroken forms of early years to the more lively, varied and plastic forms of the High and Late Romanesque style. But throughout this evolution, one characteristic remains constant: the individual significance of each form is deliberately preserved; any one element in a design may be said to comprise many separate entities. Constructional necessity and esthetic considerations were accorded equal importance, and it is for this reason that, of all Western architectural styles, the Romanesque is perhaps the most harmonious and the closest to the art of the Greeks.

Even upon so fundamental a theme as the column, Romanesque builders employed variations. Rarely entasized or only slightly tapered, it takes a cylindrical form with a family resemblance to the attached shafts so widely used during the period (page 213). Particularly in later years, the columns of doorways, galleries and cloisters (though seldom those of nave arcades) were often enriched with vertical, zigzag, spiral or lozenge-shaped flutings. In Italy, column shafts are sometimes coupled and "knotted" together by a ribbonlike molding (page 230). In the north, only the columns forming the recessed jambs of door openings were similarly decorated, while those inside the church retained a smooth surface or, during the later period, were halfway interrupted by a molded annulet (page 237). These annulets were first introduced on clustered wall shafts where, both practically and esthetically, they serve to bind the shafts together and link them more closely to the wall or pier. Appearing later on as freestanding columns, they have an esthetic significance only, dividing and articulating the shaft centrally.

Romanesque architects favored the pier rather than the column as a supporting member. Always used in vaulted churches, it is sometimes found in the arcades of flat-roofed buildings. The pier lends itself to manipulation far more than does the column, and its early cylindrical or rectangular form underwent many changes, all tending toward greater complexity. Pilasters and shafts were attached to each side to form the clustered pier which may be seen in its richest and most fully developed form in the Norman churches of England.

The treatment of the arches of nave arcades, triforium galleries and door and window openings, also grew more and more elaborate, the earliest being unmolded, the later composed of a series of concentric rings of varying thicknesses which, in door and window openings, correspond with recessed jambs below. The arch rings were at first square edged but were later molded and enriched. Romanesque arches are predominantly semicircular. The pointed form, at first limited to Burgundy, was much favored later, but its structural possibilities were never fully recognized or exploited.

Methods of wall decoration also reflect the characteristic tendency to enliven and articulate the structure. Walls were vertically divided by attached shafts running from floor to vault, and horizontally by string courses, galleries and triforiums which consisted of either narrow passageways in the wall thickness — with arcading in front on the face of the nave wall — or simply of blind arcades between engaged columns. In Burgundian churches, triforium arcades seem to bear a positive reference to antique precedent. In Normandy, they are often so small as barely to allow passageway. Though the feature was never widely adopted in Germany, an elementary form of triforium story occurs at Worms Cathedral (Fig. 59 e), where the area between arcade and clerestory is articulated with blind arches in the wall surface, but these do not form a continuous arcade. The most developed form of interior wall division is to be found in churches of the transitional style, among them the cathedrals of Laon (pages 220 and 221) and Noyon, and the stylistically dependent Limburg (pages 210 and 211). Here nave arcade, gallery, triforium and clerestory combine to form a quadripartite wall system where each bay between the vaulting shafts is clearly and horizontally divided into four stages (Fig. 59 f).

Exterior wall treatment followed the same evolution as that of the interior. Plain, undivided surfaces gave way to a more open treatment, and walls were vertically divided by thin pilaster strips horizontally connected at different stages by arched corbeled string courses. On towers and apses, semicircular blind arches on attached half columns perform a similar decorative function (pages 234 and 235), giving horizontal emphasis to the design. During the High and Late Romanesque periods, this wall arcading was often superimposed in several stages (page 206). Separated by molded courses that provide a contrasting horizontal articulation, this type of decoration — especially when applied to towers (page 210) — conveys the impression that each building mass is conceived, not as a whole, but as a series of individual structural and decorative units. External dwarf galleries — narrow passageways behind open arcades — are a particularly notable feature of Romanesque architecture, above all in Germany and

northern Italy. Introduced under the eaves of eastern apses, then on towers, and in Italy as a façade decoration (pages 230 and 231), these galleries give the walls a hollowed-out, recessed appearance and represent a further stage in the disruption of surface unity. Together with wall arcades, pilaster strips and string courses, they create that rich and lively interplay of light and shade that is so characteristic of later Romanesque.

Carved ornament attained new peaks of skill and invention during the period. It is mainly to be found on capitals and arch moldings (pages 238 and 241).

THE PHASES OF ROMANESQUE ARCHITECTURE

Romanesque architecture, like all other movements in art, followed a continuous course of development, one form evolving naturally from another to constitute a style. And yet within this development there are certain changes and innovations which are so important and occur so suddenly that this period may conveniently be divided into several distinct stages. It should, however, be remembered that the Romanesque style was by no means uniformly distributed and that such stages cannot strictly be applied to the architecture of every region of Europe during the eleventh, twelfth and early thirteenth centuries. By the second half of the twelfth century, France was already entering into the transitional phase. At the beginning of the thirteenth century, both in France and England, architects were building in the Gothic style, while in Germany the spirit of Romanesque lingered on and Gothic features do not appear until the middle of the thirteenth century. The phases of Romanesque architecture given below are related to developments in Germany but are also relevant to France and England, provided that the last phase — that of late Romanesque — be regarded as a purely German phenomenon.

1. *Pre-Romanesque, tenth century*

Characterized by the continuing use of Carolingian forms. During the second half of the century new elements were introduced in alternating supports and blind arcades, but these had no important effects on interior or exterior structure. The flat-roofed basilican scheme with identical supports (columns or piers) and unarticulated nave walls remained predominant. The clear separation of the crossing from the rest of the church was not yet a common practice.

2. *Early Romanesque, 1000–1100*

There was an increasing use of ashlar masonry in place of rubble construction. During the first decades, alternating supports, transverse arches and blind arcades were widely employed in a conscious attempt to articulate interior space and structure. Vaults over aisles and division of nave walls by means of tall shafts running from floor to ceiling were further stages in this development which culminated about 1090 with the introduction of vaults over the main nave in some churches. It was now a general rule to separate the crossing from the other parts of the plan by means of arches and to build a crossing tower. Clustered piers and molded arches made their first appearance. Germany at first retained the lead in this development, but by the end of the century was joined by Normandy. Burgundy and southern France produced their first major works in the Romanesque style.

3. *High Romanesque, 1100–1180*

The flat-roofed basilica gave way to the vaulted church. The whole structural concept was systematized. Rib vaults, external buttress piers and flying buttresses were introduced. Moldings of columns, piers, shafts and ribs were accentuated. There was a more open treatment of interior and exterior walls and a wide use of triforium and external dwarf gallery. A multiplication of towers occurred and the first monumental façades and sculptured west fronts appeared (south of France). The pointed arch emerged in Burgundy. France now replaced Germany in the forefront of architectural development.

4. *Late Romanesque and the transitional period, 1180–1240*

Large-scale vaulted construction was widely prevalent. The pointed arch began to supersede the semicircular form. There was an accelerating tendency toward elaboration. Moldings became richer and also more delicate. By the end of the twelfth century, French architects were building in the Gothic style.

ROMANESQUE ARCHITECTURE

ILLUSTRATIONS

a

b

c

ST. MICHAEL, HILDESHEIM
Completed 1033; superficial alterations, twelfth century.

Both internally and externally, this church, begun under Bishop Bernward before 1010, is a fine expression of Romanesque structural principles, demonstrating the differences between these principles and those of earlier church architecture. The crossing of nave and transept is clearly singled out from the rest of the plan by means of heavy arches on all sides, to carry a crossing tower. Most important of all, this crossing is used as a basic unit for the central nave, which is divided into three square compartments. The corners of the squares are stressed by piers, with columns in between in the nave arcades (alternation of supports). This disruption of the continuous, even flow of the early basilican scheme — where arcades are carried on identical supports — was the first stage in a development leading to the articulation of nave walls with vertical shafts, echoing the rhythm of the ground floor and culminating in the division of the whole structure into a series of separate vaulted compartments. (Facing page.)

a) ABBEY CHURCH OF ST. CYRIAKUS, GERNRODE
Begun 961; nave dating from c. 975.

The treatment of the central nave made this building one of the most influential of Romanesque churches. The system of alternating supports (piers and columns) appeared here for the first time. This was not, however (as at Hildesheim), a means of expressing a squared grid (at Gernrode the crossing was not originally marked out by arches), but was a decorative motif borrowed from sixth-century Byzantine architecture (St. Demetrius, Salonica). The fact that Otto II had married Theophanu, niece of the Byzantine Emperor, does much to explain this Eastern influence. The triforium gallery — the only one of its time in Germany — is also a Byzantine feature, as are the relieving arches that group the openings of the gallery into pairs. At Gernrode, still flat and part of the wall surface, these were later to become an important element in Romanesque wall articulation.

b) SPEYER CATHEDRAL
Begun c. 1030; vault from c. 1100.

The division of walls and the separation of bays — possibilities only hinted at in St. Michael and at Gernrode — have been fully realized here. Strong attached shafts on the nave piers define the spatial compartments, each of which is covered by a powerful groin vault. The walls are now resolved into various planes by the use of shafts and emphatic blind arcades.

c) MAINZ CATHEDRAL
Main period of construction — second half, twelfth century.

ABBEY CHURCH, PAULINZELLA
Thuringia, begun 1112.

The Benedictine reformatory movement (originating at the end of the tenth century in the abbey church of Cluny, Burgundy) had set out to impose a new discipline, not only on the life of monastic communities, but also on the architectural forms used in churches. The Cluniac ideal — the aisled basilica with flat timber ceiling, transept, no crypt, and west portal — had reached Germany by the end of the eleventh century. The center of the German reform movement was the monastery at Hirsau in the Black Forest (Fig. a), the church of which served as the model for nearly a hundred new abbey churches of the reformed orders. Few of these have survived, but the nave of Paulinzella still stands and bears witness to the strong ascetic spirit of Cluniac builders and to the clarity and simplicity they demanded and achieved in their construction. No recession or division of wall surfaces, no internal spatial compartments, are to be found here as in other churches of the period (page 202 b). In the Early Christian tradition, the arcades run uninterrupted from entrance to choir, and the upper walls of the nave present a smooth face except for a narrow string course, with the checkered patterning characteristic of Hirsau reasserting the horizontal. Cube-shaped capitals of classic simplicity contribute to the building's air of massive dignity, and only the low-relief semicircular designs on the cushions betray the fact that Paulinzella belongs to a period which had developed beyond the smooth undecorated forms of early Romanesque. (Facing page.)

a) MONASTERY CHURCH OF ST. AURELIUS, HIRSAU
First half, eleventh century.

Of this small church built for the first fifteen monks of the monastery of Hirsau (later to become so influential in Germany), only the nave and entrance hall remain. It follows the pattern of the three-aisled basilica with arcades supported on columns that was widely used for the Romanesque churches of southern Germany. (Compare those of Saxony, pages 202 a and 203, and the Rhineland, page 202 b, c.) The columns, capitals and bases are squat and heavy, and the unmolded arcades are characteristic of the early Romanesque style.

b) ABBEY CHURCH, JERICHOW
Saxony, c. 1200.

Although built at a relatively late date, this church — a three-aisled transeptal basilica with flat timber roof — still closely adheres to the Cluniac tradition of Hirsau. The cylindrical pillars, the capitals and walls are of brick — a material seldom used at this period. It will be noted that the cube-shaped capital has given way to a trapezoid form suited to brick construction. Contrary to the Cluniac rule, there is a large crypt below crossing and chancel, the floors of which are consequently raised high above the level of the nave.

c) ABBEY CHURCH, EBERBACH
Odenwald, late twelfth century.

In this three-aisled, piered basilica, one vaulting bay of the nave is made to correspond with two in the aisles. The monastic austerity of the construction complies with the requirements of the Cistercian reform movement. The same discipline is evident in the pilasters that commence at the impost level of the arcade and carry the main transverse arches of the cross vaults.

a

b

c

a

b

c

ABBEY CHURCH, MARIA LAACH
Begun 1093; consecrated 1156. West towers and atrium, end of twelfth century.

Nowhere is the theme of the *Castellum Dei* more splendidly developed than in the many-towered imperial cathedrals of the central Rhineland (notably Speyer, Worms, Mainz, and later Bamberg and Naumburg). All except Speyer display the double apsidal ending, one of the most characteristic features of German church architecture. While naves and transepts retain their traditional disposition, the exteriors of the east and west ends are emphasized as the most important parts of the church. As at Maria Laach, towers flank the structure like so many protecting fortresses, providing a vertical foil to the massive building spread out below. (Facing page.)

a) ST. MICHAEL, HILDESHEIM
Model. c. 1030.

This great monument of early German Romanesque architecture was among the first buildings to be articulated according to the new system (page 202) and also provides the first instance of a true Romanesque exterior, with its strict balance of structural groups (two choirs, two transepts and corresponding towers). The stone walls convey an effect of solidity and mass broken only by unmolded window openings. The simple pilaster strips connected by arcades under the eaves and the double windows of the turrets foreshadow the richly recessed openings and molded string courses dividing the stages of the exterior that were to signalize Romanesque architecture in its fullest development.

b) WORMS CATHEDRAL
Late twelfth – early thirteenth century.

The great three-towered structural groups give east and west ends a monumental, fortresslike appearance. The feeling of mass and weight still predominates, but the wall surfaces have lost their plainness and simplicity (Fig. a) and are divided into several stages by decorative band courses. Tall, flat pilaster strips frame the circular-headed windows whose sides are now formed in a series of receding molded planes. Under the eaves, down the gable verges, and at the various horizontal stages of the design, run ranges of small, round arches on corbels. The octagonal crossing tower and the apse are articulated by small arched colonnades (dwarf galleries) formed in the thickness of the walls (similar treatment of the exterior of Maria Laach, facing page). The twin circular turrets flanking the eastern and western apses illustrate the strong tendency of later German Romanesque designers to produce a composition out of a series of separate elements.

c) BAMBERG CATHEDRAL
Early thirteenth century.

The tower articulation, the canopied treatment at the base of the spires and the pointed arches show the influence of the Early Gothic style of Laon Cathedral, but the various stages of the construction are still clearly divided and the towers are composed of a number of distinct parts.

ABBEY CHURCH, MARMOUTIERS
Alsace, twelfth century.

The plastic sense of Romanesque builders and their desire to achieve a monumental effect led them (in the absence of a western apse) to give importance to the entrances by elaborating the west fronts. In France, this took the form of flanking towers (page 221 b), but in Germany the idea of the Carolingian westwork lingered on, although its function was no longer that of a private antechurch for the emperor. The west front of Marmoutiers exactly repeats the disposition of ninth- and tenth-century westworks (page 181 a, b) with its principal tower set back from smaller towers on either side. The bold and clearly defined grouping of masses is typically Romanesque, though here attaining a rare beauty. The lively plastic effect of the towers and gables is offset by the density of the façade below, which — though articulated by the familiar pilaster strips on two stories — is plain and unrecessed. (Facing page.)

a) WESTWORK, MINDEN CATHEDRAL
Ninth–twelfth century.

The west group of Minden Cathedral evolved from three old towers that had formed the frontispiece of the original Carolingian building (erected *c.* 900, page 181 a). After a fire in 1064, the towers were not developed and the remains of the old structure (traces of which can be seen in the great arch now buried in the wall and in junctions of masonry) were incorporated in the present rectilinear façade with its central portion carried to a higher level. The solemn, ponderous mass of this west front vividly conveys the spirit of early Romanesque.

b) WEST TOWER, PADERBORN CATHEDRAL
Early eleventh century.

A single great tower — its lower walls unbroken by doors or windows — rises over the western choir of this cathedral built by Bishop Meinwerk. Small adjoining turrets containing staircases indicate that this method of stressing the west end of a church — peculiar to Westphalia — also had its origins in the Carolingian westwork. If an impression is to be gained of the original character of the tower, it must be thought of without its spire and with the more compact roof shape typical of the period.

c) WEST TOWER, ST. PATROCLUS, SOEST
Late twelfth century.

In Westphalia, the architectural conception of early Romanesque remained dominant longer than elsewhere. The imposing tower of St. Patroclus in Soest differs from that of Paderborn (built a century and a half earlier) chiefly in the more lively treatment of the upper windows. It is interesting that the church was built, not by clerics, but by the townspeople of Soest, for whom the hall surrounding the base of the square tower served as an arms depot.

a

b/c

a

b

c

CATHEDRAL OF LIMBURG-AN-DER-LAHN
Completed 1235.

Germany was slow to relinquish the Romanesque style, as may be seen in this cathedral erected at a time when Gothic had reached perfection in France, and the great cathedrals of Paris, Rheims, Chartres and Amiens had already been built or were nearing completion. But for inspiration, the builders of Limburg turned to Laon Cathedral (pages 220 and 221) — an older building representing the transition from Romanesque to Gothic. The division of the nave walls into four stories — arcade, gallery, triforium and clerestory — is influenced by Laon, as is the sexpartite vaulting of the bays in nave and transport (facing page). The exterior also owes much to the French cathedral, especially the elegant turrets on the transept arms (Fig. a) which, together with the central tower and the two west towers, give this short, compact building the appearance of a fortress rather than a church. Although important Gothic features — the groin vault and the pointed arch — are employed at Limburg, it still shows a purely Romanesque handling of closely packed yet clearly distinguished towers and masses rising from an essentially simple plan. (Facing page and Fig. a.)

b) TREFOIL CHOIR, ST. QUIRIN, NEUSS
Early thirteenth century.

Characteristic of late German Romanesque architecture, the exterior of the choir of St. Quirin exhibits the rich and almost baroque forms prevalent at this time. Every Romanesque decorative means has been used to enliven the wall surfaces: pilaster strips, arcaded corbel courses, ladderwork, dwarf galleries, and above all a great variety of window shapes. These are not only single and coupled with semicircular heads, but quatrefoil (in the transept gable), cusped (in the aisles), trefoil (in the crossing tower) and keyhole shaped (in the apse) — the somewhat fantastic manifestations of style in its later stages.

c) EAST TOWERS, TOURNAI CATHEDRAL
Belgium, mid-thirteenth century.

Like Limburg, Tournai Cathedral seems to have been inspired by Laon. Again, though with variations in detail, the nave walls are divided into four stories, and four towers flank the ends of the transept arms. These towers have none of the slender elegance of those at Limburg, but are massive square structures rising high above the lantern tower, the five elements constituting what is perhaps the most splendid and impressive tower group of all Romanesque architecture. The stages of the towers are emphatically separated horizontally by heavy string courses, but miniature buttresses at the angles stabilize the lines and form a link between the several parts. This foreshadows the more organic and integrated methods of Gothic architecture.

ST. SAVIN-SUR-GARTEMPE
Vienne, c. 1080.

Barrel-vaulted churchs predominate in the south of France. These are either aisleless or more frequently have two narrow side aisles almost as tall as the nave, which thus has no clerestory. St. Savin represents this type of three-aisled hall church. The continuous tunnel vault (with an interesting fresco decoration) is abutted by cross vaults in the aisles, and the arcade is carried on very tall and closely spaced monolithic columns. The serried ranks of columns and the unbroken perspective of the vault give this interior something of the rigid severity of Early Christian basilicas. But the whole effect, with indirect lighting from the aisles, monumental forms and massive vault, is unmistakably Romanesque. (Facing page.)

a) NOTRE DAME LA GRANDE, POITIERS
c. 1100.

Also a three-aisled church with barrel-vaulted central nave, Notre Dame la Grande is noticeably richer in architectural treatment than St. Savin, which is probably the earlier building by some years. Four half-round shafts are grouped about each square pier, and each shaft in the group supports its own order or rib. Those on the aisle side carry the side vaulting, while those on the nave face run up to the springing line of the vault, to support transverse ribs disposed at regular intervals along the central vault. The lateral shafts carry the arcade. In this way the relationship between supporting and supported parts is clearly expressed and the interior divided into a number of distinctly separated compartments. But the great vault dominates the interior and acts as a unifying element, the quick rhythm of the transverse ribs enhancing rather than suppressing the impression of movement toward the altar. Painted geometrical patterns decorating the shafts and spreading onto all the wall surfaces bear witness to the variety and richness of Romanesque ornamentation.

b) ST. SERNIN, TOULOUSE
Late twelfth century.

St. Sernin is a splendid example of the barrel-vaulted, galleried churches favored in Auvergne. The nave has no clerestory windows, but there are triforium galleries above the arcades. Tall shafts attached to the plain, massive piers run through the string course, dividing the two stories up to the springing line of the vault. They form a skeleton of vertical lines leading the eye upward almost as in a Gothic cathedral. But the ascending movement is checked by the heavy vault, and instead of mounting to a climax (as in the ridge of a pointed Gothic vault), it is thrown across from side to side in semicircular transverse arches. This is not the soaring, leaping space of Gothic, but the controlled, static space typical of Romanesque.

a

b

a

b

ABBEY CHURCH OF STE MADELEINE, VÉZELAY
Consecrated 1132.

This great three-aisled church, with its clustered piers and intersecting vaults, is one of the beautiful creations of French Romanesque architecture. The vaulting differs from the usual Burgundian type established in the pointed barrel vaults of the third reconstruction of the church at Cluny (begun in 1089; consecrated 1130; now destroyed) and which may be seen today in the cathedral at Autun (Fig. a). The Cluniac ideal demanded a roofing system that emphasized the continuous west-east perspective of the interior, while the effect of the intersecting vault was to separate bay from bay — an effect enhanced at Vézelay by transverse arches of alternating pink and gray courses above the central nave. Yet this alternation of color reasserts the perspective, linking the various vaulting compartments and leading the eye to the eastern climax. These relationships between weight and support are expressed with particular clarity. Each element of the compound piers corresponds to an element of the arched construction: the attached columns on the side faces of the piers carry the arcade, and the tall shafts on pilasters on the nave side run up to meet the transverse arches of the vaults. It is characteristic of the Burgundian school that these pilasters and shafts are not carried from floor to ceiling in uninterrupted lines but are broken at two levels by imposts and molded string courses, as if to contradict their inherent vertical movement. (Facing page.)

a) CATHEDRAL OF ST. LAZARE, AUTUN
First half, twelfth century.

This three-aisled basilica has the pointed barrel vault adopted by the Burgundian school as an ideal roofing system. The essential difference between the pointed and the semicircular forms may be appreciated by comparing the transverse arches of St. Lazare with those of St. Sernin, Toulouse (page 213 b). Whereas the semicircular arch smoothly carries the upward movement of the piers from side to side, the opposing curves of the pointed arch bring them together in the center at the apex. The possibilities of the pointed arch were not fully exploited until the Gothic era, and Autun Cathedral — like all Romanesque buildings — remains compact and earthbound, the vertical elements repeatedly interrupted by horizontal lines of emphatic string courses and overpowered by the massive tunnel vault above (*cf.* Fig. b).

b) NOTRE DAME, PARAY-LE-MONIAL
Twelfth century.

The Cathedral of Notre Dame, Paray-le-Monial, was modeled on the third reconstruction of Cluny and on Autun Cathedral. The forms employed in the wall articulation betray an origin in antique Roman gateways (two of which still survive in Autun). The magnificent fluted Corinthian pilasters, the blind arcade between nave arcade and clerestory, and the treatment of the vertical supports as independent elements placed one on top of the other as in Roman buildings, all proclaim a strong attachment to antique precedent.

ST. PIERRE, ANGOULÊME
First half, twelfth century.

The domed churches of Aquitaine are among the most remarkable achievements of French Romanesque architecture. They form an isolated group and their precise origin is unknown, although the inspiration for the most important of these churches (St. Front at Périgueux, Fig. c) seems to have come (through St. Mark's, Venice) from domed Byzantine churches. Except for St. Front, all the larger churches of Aquitaine are aisleless, consisting of several domed bays with transepts. The arches that carry the three domes of the nave of St. Pierre spring from massive piers, and the transition from the square bays to the circular bases of the domes is effected by pendentives between the supporting arches. Behind each lateral arch is a narrow barrel vault which receives the thrust of the central dome, carrying it down to the lower walls and angle piers. The side walls are divided into two stories, the lower parts being decorated with strongly modeled blind arcades. Over the arcade, a small gallery runs around the church below semicircular headed clerestory windows. This interior is the fullest expression of the Romanesque principle of forming a harmonious whole from a number of independent, self-contained parts. Unmistakably Romanesque also are the powerful, plain forms of the piers and arches, the severe and beautifully constructed masonry walls and the clear-cut grouping and definition of each structural member. The view from the crossing into the fourth great dome confirms the impression of grave majesty. (Facing page and Fig. a.)

b, c) ST. FRONT, PÉRIGUEUX
After 1120.

Like St. Mark's, Venice (page 149), and its model, Justinian's Church of the Holy Apostles in Constantinople, St. Front is a Greek cross on plan. The five domes on pendentives, all of the same diameter, rise over each arm and over the crossing, externally showing their smooth silhouettes in the Byzantine manner (Fig. c). As a result, the exterior of the church has a curiously Eastern and un-Romanesque appearance. The interior, on the other hand, bears no resemblance, except in plan, to any Byzantine model (Fig. b). The semicircular arches carrying the domes spring from heavy square piers and are so wide as to form short barrel vaults which differentiate each bay from its adjoining compartments. Here is none of the Byzantine elegance and brilliant decoration that characterize St. Mark's. The sheer stone walls — almost brutal in their austerity — give the building a compact grandeur and an atmosphere of awe-inspiring solemnity unique among buildings of its kind.

a

b

c

a

b

c

ABBEY CHURCH, JUMIÈGES
Consecrated 1067.

This church, now in ruins, was built as a three-aisled galleried basilica with transept and three-aisled choir. The nave arcade has the alternation of supports common to earlier and contemporary German churches, especially those of Saxony (page 202). Whether Jumièges was influenced by such German examples or those of Lombardy — where alternating supports appeared at approximately the same time — is not certain. This church is notable for the fact that the dividing lines between the bays of the arcade are stressed on the upper nave walls by shafts attached to the piers, running through gallery and clerestory to the foot of the roof. The purpose of these shafts was purely decorative, for the church was not vaulted and the flat wooden roof, now destroyed, would not have justified such features. (Facing page.)

a) ABBEY CHURCH, MONT ST. MICHEL
Second half, eleventh century.

Although there is no alternation of supports in the arcade, vertical dividing lines are again provided by shafts attached to the piers, carried from floor to ceiling (the present timber vault, the cross beams of which rest on the shafts, is not the original). These are uninterrupted by imposts or string courses, and the verticality of the design is emphasized by the accompanying upward thrust of the blind arcades linking all three stages.

b) ST. ÉTIENNE, CAEN
1064 – 1077; vault c. 1110.

This galleried basilica, originally built with a flat roof, has the vertical division of the nave walls characteristic of all the larger churches of Normandy. When St. Étienne was vaulted (c. 1110), this wall articulation was logically developed by a corresponding division of the vaulting compartments by means of strongly molded transverse and diagonal ribs continuing the line of the wall shafts. The innovation of ribbed vaulting (an advance on the simple intersecting vaults used about 1000 at Speyer and again at Vézelay in 1120) was of the utmost importance for subsequent Gothic development, but the ribs of St. Étienne do not yet carry the weight of the infilling, as they do in Gothic construction, and were here primarily introduced for esthetic reasons.

c) LA TRINITÉ, CAEN
Second half, eleventh century; vault c. 1110.

The ribbed vaulting of La Trinité was subsequently added to the building's construction, like that of St. Étienne, which may be slightly later in date. The nave vaulting of both churches illustrates the difficulties of spanning oblong compartments without the aid of the pointed arch. The bays marked out by the wall shafts are so narrow in relation to the width of the central nave that they could not each be covered by the usual semicircular intersecting vaults. Thus two bays are included in each vaulting compartment, allowing semicircular diagonal and transverse ribs to be used. Intermediate ribs spring from the shafts in the middle of every bay, lending support to the junction of the diagonal ribs and resulting in the system known as sexpartite vaulting.

LAON CATHEDRAL
Begun c. 1160; completed c. 1210.

All those features that characterize the transitional style may be seen in the articulation of the nave walls of Laon: forms that were to signalize Gothic architecture (pointed arch) appear side by side with others that are still purely Romanesque (round arch). The wall surfaces between the shafts do not yet rise to the sexpartite vaults (another characteristic feature of the transitional style) in a single vertical movement, but are firmly divided horizontally into four stages: arcade (with the cylindrical piers common at this period), gallery, triforium and clerestory (the quadripartite wall system). Their modeling, especially noticeable in the gallery stage, is also Romanesque in spirit. Slender shafts in alternating groups of five and three, resting on the caps of the piers, tend to produce static bays, and because they bear little relation to their supports, to hold in check that soaring movement from ground to vault achieved in Gothic architecture in its highest development by the careful coordination and interpenetration of equally stressed vertical elements. (Facing page.)

a) SENS CATHEDRAL
Built 1140–1160, William of Sens; clerestory, thirteenth century.

As at Laon, the central nave is covered by sexpartite vaulting. The rhythmic division of the nave is marked more strongly here than at Laon, by the use of alternating supports, but the treatment of the wall shafts differs considerably from that of the later church and is to a certain extent more Gothic in character. The clustered piers that mark the angles of each nave bay run uninterrupted from floor to clerestory without the annulet decoration used at Laon. They are the dominant accent in the design, their plastic, massive forms overpowering the effect of the single slender shafts in the center of each wall bay. Their vertical movement is echoed in the articulation of the intervening surfaces. The fourth horizontal division of Laon is omitted, and there are now only three — arcade, triforium and clerestory — the pairs of openings in the triforium being enclosed with pointed relieving arches.

b) WEST FRONT, LAON CATHEDRAL
c. 1210.

Although built at a time when French architects had already achieved a perfected Gothic expression in the façades of their cathedrals (page 262), the magnificent west front of Laon is still wholly Romanesque in character. The twin towers were imitated in several German cathedrals including Bamberg (page 206 c) and Naumburg. Bold and monumental in proportions, the deeply recessed doorways and window openings embody the late Romanesque ideal. The façade is clearly marked out in three horizontal stages (doorways, windows, towers). The towers are not integrated with the rest of the façade (as in a Gothic cathedral where all elements form a single coordinated vertical movement) but are composed of a series of clearly articulated hollow niches piled one on another.

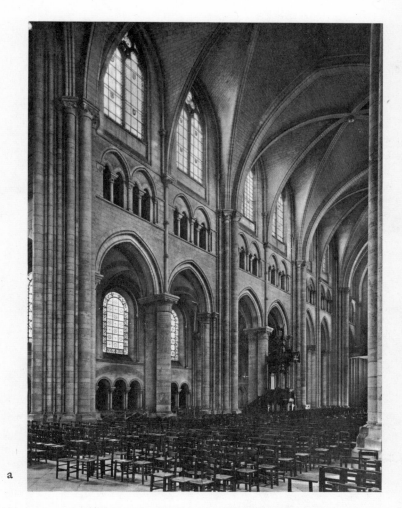

a

b

a

b

c

d

ST. PIERRE, ANGOULÊME
First half, twelfth century.

In France, where the double apsidal ending was unknown and where the simple orientated basilican plan was more commonly used than in Germany, the problem of finding a satisfactory architectural treatment for west fronts was urgent. Responses to this problem differed widely and were often, especially in the south of France, inspired by works of Roman antiquity (town gateways, triumphal arches, Fig. a). The great west towers that constantly occur in northern France (Fig. d) are rare in the south, where the western termination would often consist, as at St. Pierre, of a great decorated frontispiece expressing nothing of the internal structure of the building behind it. (Facing page.)

a) ABBEY CHURCH, ST. GILLES
Provence, c. 1140.

It is not difficult to recognize the prototype for this three-portaled façade. The fluted pilasters, columns with Roman Composite capitals, a wide string course with an antique acanthus-leaf decoration, and the design as a whole, with central arched opening flanked by lower arched portals, are unmistakably inspired by Roman triumphal arches. The figure sculpture also has its counterpart in these monuments, although here—instead of heroes of antiquity and their victories in battle—appear Apostles and scenes taken from Holy Scripture.

b) NOTRE DAME LA GRANDE, POITIERS
After 1143.

This fine sculptured façade masks the internal structure of the church (page 213 a). The lowest stage is divided into three bays (again recalling the disposition of a triumphal arch), but only the central arch contains a doorway, despite the fact that there are three aisles. A strongly molded arched corbel course separates the ground floor from the upper parts in the same way that the passageways of a Roman arch are separated from the attic story by a heavy cornice. The tiers of arcades above also find an origin in antiquity and, with their sculptured figures of saints, may in turn have inspired the galleries of kings on the west fronts of Gothic cathedrals (page 263).

c) CHURCH OF THE PETIT-PALAIS
Twelfth century.

d) LA TRINITÉ, CAEN
Late eleventh century; parapets, seventeenth century.

This façade, with its two square flanking towers, is strikingly different in character from the three sculptured west fronts seen above. Here the three-aisled plan is clearly expressed in the three arched doorways—the taller central portal marking the entrance to the main nave. Each part of the façade is well separated from the next and preserves its individuality. The towers rise fortress-like on either side of a lower central block which is stressed as the nucleus of the design by its richer modeling and deep recessing. Heavy, flat buttresses punctuate the façade and reinforce the vertical lines of the towers.

ELY CATHEDRAL
Begun c. 1090; nave completed, c. 1130.

The forms that characterize Romanesque buildings in Normandy (page 218) and which served as a basis for the Norman style in England are here given a new and peculiarly English interpretation. The walls of the very long, high nave (typical of English Romanesque churches) are divided into three stories and have alternating supports in the nave arcades and galleries. But the differences are unobtrusive, and the narrow bays, marked out by tall, slender shafts rising from floor to ceiling, follow one another down the nave with monotonous regularity. In remarkable contrast to Continental custom, the various stories have received equal emphasis, the tribune being the same height as the nave arcade and the clerestory only slightly less. A typically Norman feature is the gallery passing in front of the clerestory windows in the thickness of the wall. (Facing page.)

a) GLOUCESTER CATHEDRAL
Nave, c. 1120; vault 1245; Late Gothic windows.

Massive cylindrical towerlike piers carry elaborately molded arcades. Above is a miniature triforium, and as at Ely, there is a passageway at the clerestory. Gloucester illustrates another aspect of English Romanesque and was the model for several churches built in the west of England.

b) DURHAM CATHEDRAL
Begun 1093; nave vaulted 1128–1133.

The most remarkable feature of this great cathedral is the rib vaults over the nave bays. No longer sexpartite, as at Caen (page 218 b, c), they again differ from the Norman vaults in that the pointed diagonal arches are not simply applied to the vaults as a decorative motif but form an independent framework supporting the webs between.

c/d) NORWICH CATHEDRAL
Lantern tower, 1121–1145.

The crossing tower achieved a greater significance in English Romanesque and Gothic architecture than on the Continent. Its function as a nucleus around which choir, nave and transepts are grouped is much more apparent, because in England it is rarely an extreme eastern feature of the plan but actually occupies a central position — the choir and nave frequently being of nearly the same length and the transepts proportionately long. The lantern tower of Norwich is surmounted by a spire reaching firmly toward the sky, and has a highly elaborate surface decoration.

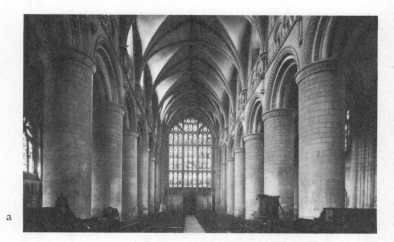

a

b

c

d

a

b

c

MODENA CATHEDRAL
Begun c. 1099.

In the Early Christian tradition and like other Lombard churches, this cathedral was built without a projecting transept. The arcades have the alternation of supports favored in Germany, and the plan is organized according to the system whereby each square nave bay corresponds to two of the aisles on either side, thus having an area four times that of one aisle bay. The heavy transverse masonry arches that spring from the wall shafts originally supported a flat timber roof. The present cross vaults were added in the twelfth century. (Facing page.)

a) S. AMBROGIO, MILAN
Eleventh and twelfth centuries.

This interesting church, with triforium gallery and massive piers of alternating weight, has provoked much discussion, particularly concerning its wide, domical ribbed cross vaults. It was long thought that these were the first vaults in history to have been built with weight-bearing ribs: that is, with ribs built independently of the web or infilling and which are not merely decorative adjuncts to a self-supporting vault. Recent discoveries have, however, led to the belief that they were not installed until the rebuilding of the town in 1176. Thus in all probability it was in Normandy and England (Durham, page 225 b) that the first decisive steps were taken in the development of this type of vault which was to play so vital a part in the formation of the Gothic style.

b) PISA CATHEDRAL
Nave, begun 1063; completed c. 1120.

Pisa Cathedral is a five-aisled cruciform basilica with a three-aisled transept. Galleries run above the aisles of nave and transept. The aisles throughout are cross vaulted, while the rest of the church is covered by flat timber roofs. The treatment of the nave bears witness to the survival of Early Christian traditions in Italy in the face of Romanesque developments elsewhere. The alternating supports, shafts and moldings that separate bay from bay in German and French churches are omitted here. Arcades on identical columns unfold from entrance to apse in continuous perspective, recalling the scheme of early basilicas. True, the upper walls of the nave are broken by the openings of a triforium gallery, but here, too, the succession of openings and supports is uninterrupted, while horizontal bands of light and dark marble casing, carried up to ceiling height, and an emphatic string course dividing arcade from gallery level, reassert the horizontality of this interior. But the design has a firmness and the stonework a grandeur that are unmistakably Romanesque.

c) S. VALENTINO, BITONTO
1175–1200.

The architecture of Bitonto Cathedral reflects the northern influences to which southern Italy and Sicily were subjected during the rule of the Norman kings and Hohenstaufen emperors. It is a galleried basilica with a flat-roofed nave and dactylic alternation of supports in the arcade, with strong shafts at the main piers, rising to the roof. Magnificent Corinthian capitals betray a still powerful attachment to classical tradition, and the low pendentive domes over the aisles show that the forms of Byzantine architecture that predominated in southern Italy until the eleventh century had by no means been forgotten.

FLORENCE

This city has a group of buildings of the eleventh and twelfth centuries that differ in many respects from Romanesque architecture elsewhere — especially in their exterior treatment. Contrasting with the recessions, sculpturesque decoration and rich interplay of light and shade that occur in a typical Romanesque façade, these preserve a smoothness and flatness, but are enlivened with a marble inlay which usually consists of white marble panels outlined with black bands. This two-dimensional ornamentation — so alien to the plastic grandeur of other Romanesque façades — has a certain splendor of its own. Though bearing no true relation to structure, the patterning is set within a framework of architectural forms — columns, arcades, cornices — that are in themselves bound closely to the wall surfaces. In their clarity and simplicity, these forms (common to all the buildings of this group) vigorously point forward to the architecture of the Italian Renaissance which indeed originated in Florence in the fifteenth century. It is for this reason that Florentine architecture during the eleventh and twelfth centuries is known as proto-Renaissance.

(Facing page and a)
  S. MINIATO AL MONTE
  1140–1180.

b) BADIA, FIESOLE, NEAR FLORENCE
  Façade, c. 1130–1140.

c, d) BAPTISTERY
  Begun during the eleventh century, incorporating Roman remains. Main building completed c. 1180; attic story above cornice added later.

a

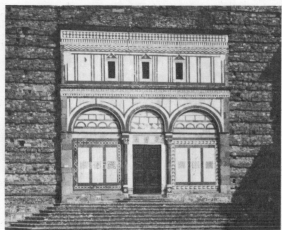

b

c

d

a

b

PISA CATHEDRAL

c. 1250; campanile (leaning tower) begun 1174; completed early fourteenth century.

The architecture of those regions of Tuscany centered around Pisa is characterized by the widespread use of miniature arcading, a motif probably derived from the Romanesque churches of Germany and primarily applied to façades. The richest and most beautiful example of its use is the west front of Pisa Cathedral. The ground story is decorated with blank arcading, but the rest of the façade is entirely covered by a veil of arcaded galleries in four tiers standing away from the wall face. The practical windows are masked by the columns and (contrary to those of a German Romanesque church) play no part in the decorative articulation. Rising one above the other in regular rows, the dwarf galleries accentuate rather than disrupt the flat character of this façade. Clarity and simplicity of outline, recalling the form of an antique temple, reveal a classical spirit similar to that which had informed the Florentine proto-Renaissance (page 229). (Facing page.)

a) S. MICHELE, LUCCA

Twelfth – thirteenth century.

The façade of S. Michele is extremely close in style to that of Pisa Cathedral. A picturesque effect is gained by the curious treatment of the colonnettes: some are carved in the form of twisted ropes; others are covered with a variety of brightly colored stone mosaic patterns. As at Pisa, the façade is so treated that it expresses the internal disposition, although at Lucca the gables are carried beyond the level of the roofs proper, simply to provide space for more arcades.

b) S. MICHELE, PAVIA

Twelfth century.

This flat façade achieves grandeur through the sheer simplicity and clarity of its design. Four groups of shafts running from ground to gable indicate the internal divisions into nave and aisles. The monumental wall face is only broken by three recessed portals (the central portal stressed by its greater height as the most important), a few windows with simple moldings and a raking arcaded gallery under the widespreading gable. Narrow bands of relief carvings — an early and rare instance of the use of sculpture in Italian Romanesque architecture — are set into the wall above and beside the porches, with little detriment to the surface unity.

STA MARÍA LA BLANCA, TOLEDO
Early thirteenth century.

The character of Spanish architecture during the Romanesque period was determined by the country's political development. Much of northern Spain came under the influence of southern French architecture when Moorish rule gave way to the Christian kingdoms of Leon, Castile, Aragon and Navarre in the eleventh century. But in the south, Moorish art predominated until the late fifteenth century. The architecture of those regions recovered by the Christians often shows a remarkable degree of assimilation of Moorish architectural principles. As is shown in Sta María la Blanca, Saracenic forms and methods of organizing space were applied, with few modifications, to Christian churches (Mudejar style). Built in all probability by Moorish craftsmen, the five-aisled, almost square church of Sta. María la Blanca might well be a Muslim mosque with its monotonous rows of identical octagonal piers supporting typically Moorish horseshoe arches. The walls above the arcades have no openings and are articulated only with a low relief decoration directly derived from Moorish prototypes. The remarkable beaded bands on the capitals, transforming Corinthian foliage decoration into flat, tapestry-like motifs, have the same origin. The blind arcades of the upper walls are more Romanesque in spirit, but the general character of this interior, with no precise orientation and no clearly defined grouping or differentiation, remains in all essentials that of a mosque rather than a Christian church. (Facing page.)

a, b) MONREALE CATHEDRAL
Sicily, 1174–1189.

During the reign of the Norman kings (1130–1189), Byzantine, Muslim and Western influences combined to produce a distinctive style of architecture in Sicily (page 148). The most important Sicilian church of this period is the Cathedral of Monreale. The structural composition of the interior is clearly governed by Western Early Christian tradition. The entrance-apse axis dominates, the arcades — carried on identical supports and with no recessed planes — proceed down the nave in smooth, uninterrupted rhythm, while the nave is flat roofed (Fig. a). The walls and pointed Saracenic arches are covered with brilliant paintings and mosaics, both figurative (representing scenes from Biblical history) and abstract (forming bands of geometrical patterns), reflecting the influence of the Byzantine as much as the Mohammedan style. The outside of the church shows the same predilection for highly elaborate decoration: the apses at the east end are ornamented with intersecting pointed arches, roundels and bands filled with brightly colored mosaics — all testifying to the Mohammedan taste for flat, multicolored, intricate pattern in preference to the more sculpturesque articulation of Northern Romanesque.

a

b

a

b

c

THE CHURCH OF THE HOLY APOSTLES, COLOGNE
Trefoil choir, c. 1200.

As in several churches in Cologne and the Rhineland, the east ends of Holy Apostles Church open out into a trefoil pattern. The choir and transepts terminate in great semicircular apses, thus forming a centralized structure around the crossing (Fig. 58). The external treatment of this feature makes this church one of the most impressive and accomplished expressions of German High Romanesque architecture. The horizontal spread of the building masses is beautifully balanced by the vertical lines of two slender towers flanking the main apse; it is indeed the equal emphasis laid upon horizontal and vertical elements that gives harmony and majesty to the design as a whole. The upward movement of the pilaster strips and colonnettes replies to the horizontal accents of the string courses and arcades. The wall surfaces proceed in stages — from unbroken density to a more recessed sculpturesque treatment — to be dissolved completely in the dwarf gallery under the eaves. But although the articulation becomes progressively richer and more plastic and the play of light and shade more accentuated, an optical effect of perfect balance is maintained because as the stages increase in decorative richness they decrease in height. (Facing page.)

a) CHURCH AT AULNAY
Charente-Maritime, twelfth century.

The arrangement of the east end of this small church is common to many others of the Romanesque period. The choir, terminated in an apse, is flanked by two smaller apses opening off the east walls of the transepts.

b) ABBEY CHURCH, MURBACH
Alsace, mid-twelfth century.

This eastern termination — all that now remains of the great Benedictine abbey church — is modeled on the staggered plan of the second church of Cluny, having a three-aisled, square-ended choir. The two towers above the transepts are also a customary feature of churches built by the schools of Cluny and Hirsau. This building group is remarkable for its beautiful wall decoration with tall pilaster strips, ranges of small arches on corbels under the eaves, and stone of varying color (window arches).

c) ST. SERNIN, TOULOUSE
Twelfth century.

The *chevet* of this huge church has its origin in the radiating plan introduced in the Romanesque rebuilding of St. Martin at Tours (*c.* 1000). The extended choir is surrounded by an ambulatory with radiating chapels.

REFECTORY OF THE MONASTERY AT MAULBRONN
Württemberg, c. 1220–1230.

This splendid twin-aisled hall (the refectory of the Cistercian monks of Maulbronn) is one of the first buildings in Germany to exhibit both Romanesque and Gothic features and thus to exemplify the so-called transitional style (page 210). The windows are semicircular headed in the Romanesque manner, and the columns, alternating in diameter, do not rise in one smooth vertical movement to the vault but are interrupted by the annulets that are a familiar motif of late Romanesque. From early French Gothic (page 221) come the sexpartite vaults, their strongly molded red ribs forming a lively and pleasing contrast to the whitewashed webs and the pinkish-yellow walls. The corbels, with their attached truncated shafts from which spring the vaulting ribs, are a characteristic Cistercian motif. Notable also are the squat column bases and the molded abaci over the capitals, both typical of the later period and derived, like the capitals themselves, with their stiff-leaf foliage, from French Cistercian architecture. (Facing page.)

a

a) CLOISTER, ZURICH MINSTER
After 1100.

The various buildings that comprise a monastery are customarily grouped about an open space laid out like a garden, around which runs a covered passageway or cloister. These cloisters, with their arcades opening onto the central court, are among the most beautiful creations of medieval architecture. Simple and coherent in design, the cloister at Zurich well conveys the charm and atmosphere peculiar to this type of building, though it has none of the complex grouping of columns and intricate arcading that appear in later examples. Instead, the imposts of the piers and the bracket dosserets above the cube-shaped capitals have been ornamented elaborately and show a rare richness of invention.

b

b) GALILEE CHAPEL, DURHAM CATHEDRAL
England, c. 1170.

This five-aisled narthex or galilee recalls Muslim mosques, but it would be fanciful to suppose that the design was actually influenced by such Saracenic buidings. The quatrefoil piers, the capitals and the sharp zigzag moldings of the arcades are characteristic of Norman architecture in England.

c) CRYPT, LUND CATHEDRAL
Sweden, 1110–1123.

The crypts so often found in Romanesque churches frequently take the form of large, lofty underground halls. As at Lund, they are usually covered with cross vaults carried on sturdy piers.

c

a/b

c/d

e/f

g/h

i/k

The capital is one of the most valuable guides to the dating of a work of architecture. Architects and stone carvers through the ages have been prompted to find ever-new ways of effecting a transition from column shaft to arch or horizontal architrave, each solution resulting in a new capital form which sums up in itself the style of the period. Thus each new phase of architectural development has its own specific capital form by which it may be identified.

About the year 1000, Romanesque builders in Germany discovered, in the cubiform or cushion capital, an abstract geometrical shape echoing exactly the clear cubic organization of their buildings. A prototype may be found in the similarly shaped Byzantine basket capital (page 122 d), but there is no precedent for the stark simplicity and geometric clarity of the earliest Romanesque block capital and it remains wholly original in conception. The purest form is a cube with its lower angles rounded off so as to effect a smooth junction with the circular shaft (St. Michael, Hildesheim, before 1033, Fig. a). As the style developed and architectural forms became increasingly richer, this austerity was relieved with semicircular patterns in low relief (abbey church of Paulinzella, Thuringia, c. 1120, Fig. b). This type is still purely geometrical but in the same church the faces of some capitals already exhibit a much more elaborate stylized palmette decoration (Fig. c), and an example from the porch of the abbey church of Marmoutiers in Alsace (twelfth century, Fig. d), is entirely covered with an assortment of foliated and geometrical carvings.

At about the same time and probably inspired by the block capital, builders in Normandy evolved the multiple-cushion or scalloped capital (La Trinité, Caen, c. 1060, Fig. e). During the twelfth century the block was elaborated with foliated designs and fabulous and symbolic figures of men and beasts carved in relief (Alpirsbach, early twelfth century, Fig. f) or even painted in bright colors (priory church of Klein-Komburg, near Schwabisch Hall, first half of twelfth century, facing page). Soon the basic form of the capital was obscured beneath its decoration. At Riechenburg (c. 1140, Fig. g), the cube has become a basket form, and at Strasbourg Cathedral (c. 1190, Fig. h), grotesquely carved animals' heads at the angles and small rosettes in the center of each face of the curved abacus are a distant echo of Corinthian moldings. Also Corinthian in shape is the latest type of German Romanesque capital, with its fan-shaped palmette carvings (St. Michael, Hildesheim, c. 1186, Fig. i) or the foliated and corbeled capital (Imperial Palace, Gelnhausen, c. 1195, Fig. k). These are the later stages of a development from the pure geometry of the cubiform capital to a more organic, animated and deeply cut form.

FIGURED CAPITALS

It was in the south of France, where the proximity of antique models encouraged the return of the plastic sense to architecture, that the Romanesque figured capital was first evolved. In this form, the structural role of the column head as the transitional element between arch and support is not expressed in architectural terms. The cubiform capital (page 238), and to an even greater extent the Corinthian (Fig. b), both express the relationship between supporting and supported parts, and their significance as architectural ornament depends on their function. The figured capital, on the other hand, is a sculptural entity in itself and could well be detached from its position with no loss of formal significance. Needless to say, the subject matter of these capitals was preponderantly Christian. An example from the cloister of Tarragona Cathedral in Spain (a building closely dependent on French Romanesque) tells the story of Christ's entry into Jerusalem (facing page), while a magnificent capital from St. Pierre at Chauvigny (eleventh century) shows an angel weighing the soul of a sinner while the Devil endeavors, apparently in vain, to secure the soul's damnation by hanging on the balance (Fig. a).

a

FOLIATED CAPITALS

The Corinthian, and more especially the Roman Composite, capital were frequently imitated by Romanesque stone carvers. The capital from St. Philibert, Tournus (eleventh century, Fig. b), is an eloquent example of such borrowing, though it also shows how arbitrarily the elements of the antique models were treated. The egg-and-dart molding has become a structurally meaningless annulet. A great variety of rich foliage designs were developed from this still markedly antique type. A capital from St. Aubin at Angers (twelfth century, Fig. c) shows how the original significance of the forms was lost in a picturesque profusion of leaf patterns.

b/c

MOLDINGS

The fertile invention of Romanesque artists may be fully appreciated in the moldings that appear on string courses and arcades and around door and window openings. The recessed arches of the west portal of St. Lazare, Avallon (twelfth century, Fig. d), are richly carved with tendrils, rosettes and other decorative motifs. The Greek-key pattern that decorates the extrados, and the spiral rosettes, speak for the continuing influence of classical antiquity. The portal of St. Georges at Boscherville, Normandy (eleventh-twelfth century, Fig. e), is ornamented with the abstract and geometrical moldings characteristic of Norman architecture in northern France and England. These include the chevron, billet and nailhead moldings.

d

e

VIII
GOTHIC ARCHITECTURE

Historical and Religious Background

The emergence of the Gothic style in Europe was not merely the result of a development of Romanesque forms and cannot be explained simply in the light of the steady increase in technical skill and knowledge of stone construction. It is true that many vitally important structural developments did take place — among them the replacement of the round by the pointed arch — and that from the technical point of view, the new system of construction was superior to that of the Romanesque period. But the driving force was undoubtedly the new conception of the relationship between material and spiritual things which was supplanting earlier ideas.

All art, whether painting, sculpture or architecture, is essentially an expression of human aspirations, and techniques and materials are never more than a convenient means of communicating these aspirations in visible form.

Just as Romanesque building cannot be fully understood without taking into account the idea that lies behind it, so the transition from Romanesque to Gothic and the Gothic style itself cannot simply be explained in terms of formal development. A new style is born only when "a new climate of the human spirit demands it" (Dehio), and the features that render it distinct from all other styles are precisely those that reflect a particular way of thought — an individual outlook on life and the world in the widest sense. All styles show an inherent tendency to evolve from plainness and simplicity toward increasing richness and elaboration. Although this tendency may have the appearance of spontaneity, it must not be dissociated from the corresponding pattern of change in the sphere of human ideas.

No aspect of Gothic architecture was the result of mere chance. Its first appearance in France, its spread across the whole of Europe in the course of the thirteenth century, and the emergence in the fourteenth century of marked national characteristics from the architectural uniformity of the early years, were all finally determined by changes in the spiritual, political and social conditions of Europe during these years. The alliance between temporal power and the Church — so brilliantly effected by the Ottonian system of government and theoretically sealed by the founding of the Holy Roman Empire of the German nation — was broken in the course of the bitter investitures struggle between pope and emperor. Germany's political supremacy in Europe, though maintained at least until the beginning of the thirteenth century, was doomed, and the imperial authority crumbled in the struggle, which was finally won by the Papacy; despite the fact that the Hohenstaufen Dynasty produced men of the first quality to lead the empire.

The years following the fall of the Hohenstaufens, when Germany was without an emperor, were dark times of political and economic confusion. The empire disintegrated into many independent states, and by the time political stability was regained with the restoration of imperial authority, it had not only lost Italy and all claim to European supremacy but had also sacrificed its hold over the small states inside Germany. These states were already predisposed toward rivalry by their different tribal origins, and it became wholly impossible to bring them together within a unified state under a centralized government. Only in the fifteenth century did the German people gain some semblance of a national consciousness, and *Germanica Natio* become "the commonly accepted title of the German race" (W. Müller). But even this had no appreciable effect on political events, and rivalry and jealousy between states remained rife until the nineteenth century.

Until the twelfth century, the political development of France (which lay outside the Holy Roman Empire) had been relatively uneventful. It was decisive for the future of France that despite racial upheavals and the resulting coexistence of peoples of differing origin brought about by the invasions, there was never that marked separation of state from state, each subject to its own laws, which determined the fate of Germany. Thus the Capetians (987–1328) met with considerable success in their efforts, sustained over several centuries, to give political unity to the French kingdom. Under Louis IX (St. Louis — 1220–1270), the idea of a unified state had already become a reality, and the French peoples' consciousness of belonging to one nation was further and finally consolidated during the course of the Hundred Years' War against England (1337–1453).

From the fourteenth century on, countries all over Europe — England, Spain, Italy and Flanders — were emerging as individual nations, and this development, in which France took the lead, was to have important consequences for art. But the immediate result of unity in France was to give the country an increasingly important place in Europe, both politically and socially. The spiritual ascendancy that France achieved during the twelfth century was partly due to the fact that the kingdom had not known so close an interdependence of Church and State authority as that established in Germany by the constitution of the Ottonian Empire. It was for this reason that France was scarcely affected by the results of the investitures struggle. The reformatory measures of the Cluniacs, and later the Cistercians (after 1089), are eloquent testimony to the freedom enjoyed by Church and clergy (especially monks) in France at this time. It was no coincidence that France was the first country to respond to the pope's appeal for a crusade and that France provided the Christian army with its most powerful leaders and enthusiastic supporters. Nor is it surprising that this country, where religious concepts were not bound up with political ideas and could develop unhindered, was the first to experience those deep ideological changes that were to lead to the formation of a new architectural style. Given the fundamental part played by religion in everyday life during the Middle Ages, it was inevitable that these changes should have been of a religious nature and thus affect every aspect of medieval civilization.

There is no space here to devote to a detailed study of the rise of the fervent religious attitude that colored the whole of the twelfth century and reached a climax in the thirteenth, but it exerted so deep an influence on architecture during the second half of the Middle Ages that an understanding of Gothic art depends on a knowledge of at least a few of its aspects.

The development of religious thought in the twelfth century, especially toward its close, may be described as a gradual awakening to the fundamental meaning and values of Christianity. Until well into the Romanesque period, the idea of God as a God of grace and love had been the preserve of a very small number of ecclesiastics and thinking laymen. For the common man, Christianity had meant little more than a guarantee of security during life on earth. The concept of God as a loving, not a fear-inspiring, being and of men as partakers in His divinity and grace was as yet unformed. Indeed, men continued to imagine God and His saints as aloof and unattainable, far removed from man and his environment but holding sway over the forces of evil that would otherwise overwhelm the world—a concept that had remained unaltered since the Germanic peoples had been converted to Christianity.

The believer's relation to the deity—the object of his awe and terror—whose grace and protection apparently could be obtained only through sacrifices and gifts of money and land to the Church, was devoid of any human warmth of feeling. Christian imagery of the Romanesque period provides ample evidence of this: the figures of saints found in manuscript illuminations and around the portals of churches, though represented in human form, have such a hieratic aloofness and solemn grandeur that they are unmistakably beings from another world, both lacking in and immune to human emotions. It is a measure of the great importance placed on the saints' power to overcome evil spirits that they are often shown in the sculptured portals of churches standing over monsters symbolizing conquered evil. The church itself was considered largely as a place of refuge from these spirits, a particularly effective stronghold because it was consecrated ground. Before and even for a long time after their conversion, the Germanic peoples trusted in the power of spells and incantations as a means of exorcising devils. They believed that by challenging a devil by name or by making some visible representation of it, they could render it powerless to harm.

Early Germanic images of beasts have their origin in such superstitions, and many of the fairy tales told today still bear distinct traces of these ancient beliefs: in Grimms' fairy tale, the dwarf Rumpelstiltskin lost his magic power and was split in two on hearing the sound of his own name. Old Germanic superstitions have also left their mark on many Romanesque churches where, particularly on the capitals of columns, grotesque heads and strange, monstrous beasts (pages 238 and 241) are carved. But so markedly pagan a conception of Christianity, based as it was on the old superstitions and belief in magic, was to disappear rapidly in the course of the twelfth century. The most obvious and as far as can be ascertained the earliest sign of this changing attitude are the often quoted words of Bernard of Clairvaux, spiritual leader of the Cistercians from the year 1112: "Why must the cloisters house these grotesque monsters? Why these foul apes, these lions and tigers, these centaurs, half-man, half-beast, these warriors and hunters sounding the horn? If the indecency of such images does not give cause for shame, how can their cost at least fail to appal?"

It is possible that the underlying significance of these carvings was not known to St. Bernard or that he deliberately overlooked it. Be that as it may, by the end of the twelfth century, grotesque beasts and other figures were no longer carved on capitals, and from about 1200, only foliated decoration was employed.

In another respect, the spirit of change was reflected in the attitude of St. Bernard and the Cistercians, for it was through their influence that the cult of the Virgin Mary was encouraged. The Mother of God came to be regarded as an intercessor for all believers on the Day of the Last Judgment—a figure of compassion bringing men into a closer relation with the deity.

These and many other factors were instrumental in the decline of the old superstitious form of Christianity, and God and the saints acquired a new humanity and seemed at last to be closer to human experience and understanding. The concept of an all-pervading divine love and the idea of the individual union of each human being with God now reached and began to be accepted by the widest section of the population, and moral law came to be regarded as synonymous with the will of God.

This new relationship of man to God led to a new outlook on Nature itself. The forces of Nature which, until the Romanesque period, had been regarded as the manifestations of evil spirits were now seen as the workings of God, and His presence was felt in every aspect of the visible world. Scholarship, which climbed to new heights during the thirteenth century, was also a powerful influence, for the aim of the scholar was to reconcile Christian doctrine with reason and logic and to bring it within the bounds of a comprehensive philosophy. The scholar saw in Nature the presence of a Divine Order (ordo) and the greatest of all medieval thinkers, Thomas Aquinas (1225–

1274), taught that all beauty is the self-manifestation of God. St. Francis of Assisi (1182–1226) also preached that animals, like men, are God's creatures and not (as Hrabanus Maurus had thought as late as the eighth century) the incarnation of demons and evil spirits.

In view of all these influences, it is not surprising that religious thought should have deepened so considerably from the twelfth century on and that a passionate spiritual idealism began to develop, finding its most extreme expression in the outlook of such fourteenth-century German mystics as Eckhart, Suso and John Tauler. They called for a complete detachment of the spirit from bodily things and for a continual spiritual aspiration toward union with God. This intense longing for an elevation of the spirit beyond the world marks the highest point in the development of that transcendental philosophy which had grown up, parallel with a new understanding of the ethical bases of the Christian religion, since the late twelfth century. The desire for mystic union with Christ gradually spread throughout the medieval world, and the supreme characteristic of Gothic architecture — its vigorous, vertical, aspiring tendency — is the visible expression of the religious aspirations of the age.

As has already been said, by the middle of the twelfth century France had taken the lead both politically and intellectually over other countries of Europe and had been the first to see the emergence of what may be called the spirit of Gothic, which found expression not only in the sphere of religion but in all aspects of life and in every branch of art. Thus it was that France became the artistic center of Europe and the birthplace of Gothic architecture. That the style should then have spread across the whole continent and become truly international is due, above all, to the fact that Europe was spiritually united by the ideals of Christianity. Another important factor was the active zeal of the Cistercians in spreading the new ideas — by the thirteenth century they had established 1,200 monasteries throughout Europe. Nor should it be forgotten that, after the investitures struggle, the clergy had once again become a corporate body and reached the summit of its power. The Crusades, too, had helped to awaken a general religious enthusiasm in the West and had brought Western populations together in defense of a single cause, giving them a new sense of unity which overrode political and national differences. It was, moreover, as a result of the Crusades that the ideal of the Christian knight was first formed and became commonly accepted throughout the Western Christian world.

The regular and secular clergy which represented the hierarchy of the Church and the European nobility — united by the chivalrous ideal and embodying temporal power — were the two great formative influences on the civilization of the Gothic era. With the emergence of a middle class, following the rise of urban populations, a new and increasingly important source of artistic patronage came into being. The towns, which had sunk into obscurity in the period following the great invasions, were now rapidly retrieving their strength, especially those of Italy, Germany and the Netherlands. The replacement of barter by the use of currency and the development of commerce had transformed the townships of small craftsmen into busy, well-populated and flourishing industrial communities with a powerful middle class of artisans and merchants rigidly organized in guilds. During the later Middle Ages the old Roman cities (those that were purely German and those of more recent foundation) had grown so powerful that they became self-governing communities which were virtually independent of the state's jurisdiction. Their increasing wealth and the general feeling of well-being that this and the protection of city walls and fortifications produced was highly conducive to social progress and to the development of interest in the arts, so that by the fifteenth century, the leading role in matters of artistic enterprise had passed from the clergy and nobility to the middle classes.

The effects that this social reorientation had on architecture will be discussed below. Here it need only be said that the cultural advance of the middle class eventually broke up the uniformity of style that had characterized Gothic architecture up to the beginning of the fourteenth century, despite superficial local variations in form. As the unifying ideals of the intelligent aristocracy and those of chivalry and the Church were gradually usurped by the more materialistic values of the bourgeoisie, so local patriotism deepened and the national consciousness of individual countries steadily became more pronounced. The outcome was that by the fourteenth century the national differences between the various populations of Europe were becoming apparent in many aspects of medieval civilization (for example, local dialects were slowly giving way to national languages) — but it was perhaps on architecture that they had their deepest effect. During the fourteenth century stylistic uniformity yielded to a series of national styles, each country of Europe submitting Gothic forms to its own interpretation. The High Gothic (which swept across Europe in the thirteenth and early fourteenth centuries) may to some extent be regarded as the national style of France, where it continued to dominate architecture with no essential modifications until the Renaissance. But in other countries, the late Gothic phase of the end of the fourteenth and the fifteenth centuries was the period when Western art "split into the diverse art of nations" (D. Frey).

Architectural Character

GENERAL

Although architects of the Gothic era were still mainly preoccupied with religious buildings, secular architecture began to take on far more importance than it had in the Romanesque period. The town houses of the nobility, trade halls, town halls and town fortifications afforded as many opportunities for building activity as did military castles and fortresses, and during the later period, castle residences. But all these secular buildings were informed by the spirit of Gothic, their architects deriving the forms they used from the churches in which the Gothic conventions and system of construction had first been evolved.

In the Romanesque period, responsibility for large building undertakings had already begun to pass into the hands of skilled laymen. Architects, stonecutters and masons had at first been lay brothers attached to the monasteries or had temporarily enlisted in the service of ecclesiastical patrons. Now active participation by craftsmen-clerics steadily decreased, and in the thirteenth century lay workmen formed themselves into independent confraternities not always based in one place but moving about from building site to building site. But with the rise of the towns and the demand for religious buildings of greater magnificence, these groups of workmen tended to settle in one area, and the building crafts, like the rest, formed town guilds. One of the reasons for this development was that the towns themselves were now providing many of the most important commissions. In Carolingian

times and even during the early Romanesque period, demands for large architectural undertakings had come in almost every case from the great monastic orders. Subsequently and until the middle of the Gothic era, the bishops provided most of the important patronage: their cathedrals were built within the towns but were not communal churches.

It was not until the fourteenth century, when the towns had reached new heights of prosperity and power, that the citizens themselves felt a need to express their civic pride in the erection of magnificent and conspicuous churches. Though built to the glory of God, these churches were also intended to advertise the importance and prosperity of their municipalities. Freiburg Cathedral (begun at the end of the thirteenth century) was the first true town parish church built by the municipality in conscious rivalry with episcopal churches. At the end of the fourteenth century, the citizens of Ulm rebuilt their parish church on an enormous scale, as if to challenge Strasbourg, the largest and most beautiful episcopal church in South Germany. Many cathedrals financed and begun by the bishops were later carried out by the town populations and thus became parish churches.

Permanent workshops, *fabricae,* were established on the sites of these secular cathedrals, and from the fourteenth century on—in Germany at least—responsibility for cathedral workshops was taken over entirely by the towns. In many respects these workshops were the technical training grounds of the Middle Ages. Around them centered the activities of all the building crafts, organized according to a rigid system of hierarchy. At the top of the scale were the *magister fabricae* (master mason) and the *rector* or *gubernator fabricae* (the clerk or master of the works), an administrative official also in charge of financial arrangements. Then there followed a host of sculptors, glaziers, stonecutters and masons, each with their master craftsmen, assistants and apprentices, each strictly limited as to his tasks and privileges.

An interesting system and one of considerable value in historical research was that for determining the payment of the pieceworkers. Every man, whether master mason or laborer, had a distinctive sign he engraved on each stone that he cut, so that the foreman could pay him accordingly. These pieceworkers' marks (see Glossary) were so complicated that they could not be confused with one another. The implication is that there was a close contact between the various workshops, and this is confirmed by the subsequent formation of large collective guilds. In 1459, at a Regensburg meeting of workshop representatives, it was decided to unite all German-speaking stonecutters in one organization to be divided into four districts with centers at Strasbourg, Cologne, Vienna and Bern (later Zurich), the master at Strasbourg to have preeminence. Once he had been given a sign, a mason would never change it, even when he moved from one place of work to another, as often happened during the late Gothic period. These signs are of the utmost value to the historian, for the movements of a master can sometimes be traced and his work identified, not simply by a hypothetical comparison of forms and styles, but by means of his distinctive sign, which will appear and reappear with the immutability of a coat of arms.

The medieval workshops were vitally important for the development of architecture for two reasons: first, because they encouraged a high degree of workmanship and provided a training ground for the rising generation; second, because they ensured the preservation and transmission of the rules and geometrical secrets of the craft from one generation to another. The fact that each workshop guarded its own discoveries and building experiences with the utmost secrecy does much to explain why Gothic buildings gradually began to show marked differences in form and design from country to country and even from town to town. Distinct schools of architecture become noticeable, particularly during the later phase when the cities had complete control of all building undertakings. That each workshop was not confined to one region but often extended its activity over a wide area (there is evidence that members of the celebrated Parler family from Schwäbisch Gmünd worked at Gmünd, Ulm, Prague, Strasbourg and even as far afield as Milan), resulted from the fact that the towns could not offer unlimited opportunities and architects and builders frequently had to change their fields of activity.

On the other hand, respect for personal achievement was higher than ever before, and cities would often vie with one another to secure the services of the most distinguished master builder of the day. This, too, was largely due to the influence of the medieval workshops, for they stimulated a pride in the work of individual masters whose names and personalities now emerged from the obscurity that had surrounded them in the early Middle Ages and became the object of general interest. Artists would frequently ensure lasting fame for themselves by carving their own portraits or inscribing their work. This positive recognition of the individuality of the master is a marked characteristic of the later Middle Ages. It is symptomatic of the new state of mind that was to replace the traditional idea of works of architecture, sculpture and painting as spontaneous works of communal and almost anonymous craftsmanship — an idea that was finally to produce the self-conscious artist, recognized by himself and the world for his personal achievement. This state of mind was to inform the new era in the history of the West — the Renaissance and modern times.

DEFINITION AND SOURCES OF GOTHIC

To name all architecture between the end of the twelfth and the beginning of the sixteenth century as Gothic is in many respects an unsatisfactory compromise, justifiable only if the term is used in the sense first given to it by the Italians of the fifteenth and sixteenth centuries. In Italy, the Gothic style (which had never taken root there) had already been abandoned by the beginning of the fifteenth century. The presence of antique architecture did not favor the creation of buildings which (like the cathedrals of northern Europe) seemed to deny the inherent quality of stone by making it appear to mount weightless toward the sky. The antique principle that required architectural forms to provide the simplest expression of the fundamental relationship between load and support had never been forgotten entirely, and during the Renaissance, when there was a conscious return to antique methods of construction, this principle was once more to dominate architecture. The restless temperament expressed in the Gothic style was opposed to the calmer spirit of classical Italy and was felt to be alien and un-Italian. As early as 1460, the architect Filarete wrote: "A curse on those who thought of such rubbish! Only barbarians can have brought it into Italy." It was not long before these "barbarians" came to be referred to by name, and the term *stile Gotico* was employed by Vasari (the first great art historian) about 1525. In fact, Gothic has nothing to do with the Goths, this race having disappeared from the European scene six centuries before Gothic architecture succeeded to Romanesque in northern France. But in Italy the Goths were still thought of as the destroyers of the civilization of the old Roman Empire and represented the whole race of "barbarians." Nevertheless, there is an element of truth (though undoubtedly unconscious on the part of Vasari) in the attribution of Gothic architecture to the Goths, for it was indeed an art of northern origin, and an expression of an essentially Germanic spirit.

It was to be expected that the first signs of the coming developments should have appeared in the Norman Romanesque architecture of northern France. Here at Jumièges, at Mont-St.-Michel and other places, engaged shafts running from floor to ceiling were used. With their vertical emphasis, they transformed walls hitherto characterized by their inert horizontality. About 1100, when the vertical lines of the shafts were prolonged by vaulting ribs, the ceiling itself became part of this upward drive. The bays of such Romanesque churches do not have the dynamic quality attained in Gothic architecture in its highest development during the thirteenth century, but there is already a tension between the static calm of round arches, horizontal wall articulation and sequence of square vaulting compartments and the restless thrust of the tall shafts.

The Germanic races were more prone to spiritual intensity than were the rationalizing Latins. It need only be remembered that mysticism, one of the most extreme expressions of religious feeling, found its fullest flowering in Germany, while appearing in Italy only sporadically and then in a considerably modified form. Conversely, the more rational and scholastic theology and philosophy of the Middle Ages issued from the Latin peoples and was expressed in the teachings of such men as St. Thomas Aquinas. It was precisely because France was the scene of the meeting and interpenetration of the Latin and Germanic elements — of the clear, positive and reasoning mind and the more emotional, impetuous and romantic temper of the north — that this country became the cradle of Gothic architecture.

The true Gothic system originated in the Île-de-France, the district around Paris that was the place of coronation of the kings of France and the political heart of the nation. With Bologna and Padua, Paris possessed one of the earliest university foundations (called the Sorbonne after 1255) and was the intellectual center of the Western world — in the words of St. Bonaventura: "The Fountain of Knowledge to refresh the world." Before the mid-twelfth century, the Île-de-France had not taken part in the building activity that had swept over the rest of France. But now, in an outburst of architectural enthusiasm, as though making up for lost time, churches sprang up as if by magic and here for the first time the three basic elements of Gothic architecture — the pointed arch, ribbed vault and flying buttress — were resolved into a system. Each of these features had been used in isolation by the different schools during the Romanesque age. They were now brought together to form the architectural synthesis which is the Gothic style and which reflects, in the precision and logic of its constructional scheme, the rationalism of the Latin mind — and in the other-worldly, soaring beauty of its esthetic effect, the unfettered imagination of the Germanic races.

ARCHITECTURAL IDEALS AND CONCEPTS

As stated above, the three essential elements of Gothic construction are the ribbed vault, the flying buttress and the pointed arch. These had all appeared in Romanesque architecture. The ribbed vault was first used in Norman buildings, where its lateral thrust had been counteracted by semibarrel vaults or (as at Durham Cathedral) with individual flying buttresses concealed beneath the roofs of the triforium chambers — elements out of which the Gothic buttressing system was to be evolved. In the south of France, barrel vaults over naves were similarly supported by semibarrel-vaulted aisles or triforiums. In Burgundy, the pointed arch was frequently employed, perhaps as a result of contact with Saracenic art during the Crusades. But Romanesque architects had never discovered the full constructional or esthetic possibilities of these new elements. It should not be forgotten that their art was governed by a love for the inherent qualities of stone as a solid, ponderous, heavy material, and above all by a desire to give churches a plastic form that would enhance their appearance of massive strength.

It was not until the end of the twelfth century, when the medieval outlook on life began to undergo certain changes and the Christian faith itself was given a more intensely spiritual interpretation — awakening in men a yearning for mystic union with God — that new architectural concepts arose to conform with the spirit of a new age. The effect of massive power for which Romanesque builders had striven could not satisfy the Gothic designers, who wanted taller, lighter and more slender buildings, not disciplined in static compartments but developing unchecked in one heavenward motion. Prime significance was given, not to the building masses, but as in Early Christian basilicas, to the interior space which these masses separated from the outside world. The quiet harmony and the simple relationships between load and support, the impression of weight and power that is conveyed by a Romanesque interior, were rejected for an effect of dynamic energy where stone itself is invested with new life, directing the thoughts of the faithful heavenward with a seemingly weightless vertical motion.

The nature of the Gothic esthetic ideal has been emphasized at this point because the development of the architectural system as a whole depended upon it. In order to create a space suggesting infinity and thus express the religious aspirations of the time, it was necessary to invent some new structural system which would radically differ from that of Romanesque.

The decisive step toward the development of the Gothic system had been taken when builders became aware of the technical importance of the ribs first used for esthetic effect in Norman Romanesque vaults. They had had no other function than to extend the vertical movement of the wall shafts onto the ceiling. They were simply laid under the vault and were in no sense supporting elements. But their structural possibilities were already recognized in the first half of the twelfth century, and vaults were constructed on a new system whereby the ribs formed a supporting framework or skeleton of stone into which were fitted thin curved webs or vaulting panels. Thus the ribs take the whole weight of the vault and direct it down onto the side walls at their springing points in the angles of the vaulting compartments. Consequently these points of concentrated downward and lateral thrust required extra support and abutment. While the walls and nave piers absorbed the direct vertical pressure, the lateral thrust was counteracted by flying buttresses. These were no longer concealed (in the Romanesque manner) beneath the triforium or aisle roofs, but were placed externally above the roofs, taking the oblique thrust of the vault and diverting it to external buttress piers against the aisle walls.

Although essentially a structural feature, the flying buttress was exploited by Gothic architects, not always with happy effect, as an external decoration, and from the middle of the thirteenth century was emphasized with all manner of richly traceried ornamentation and statuary. The external buttress piers, originally given a square or sloping termination, were weighted with pinnacles — small turrets with pointed roofs. These pinnacles, like the flying buttress, arose from structural necessity and were also seen as a means of accentuating the dynamic verticality of the exterior design. They became more and more elongated and tapering, leaping up almost like cathedral towers in Germany. They do nothing, however, to disguise the fact that, externally, Gothic cathedrals do not achieve the perfect equilibrium and ordered beauty of their Romanesque counterparts. But this was a sacrifice willingly made for the sake of that interior effect which was the supreme end of all Gothic ventures.

The confinement of the thrust of the ribbed vault to the areas of support given by the buttresses allowed for an open treatment of the side walls which were merely required to enclose and not to support the structure. Windows became larger and larger and were filled with screens of glass in delicate stone tracery. The handling of weight and thrust was everywhere facilitated by the use of the pointed arch. It could be raised to any required height — that is, over spans of varying width without the stilting necessary to raise all semicircular arches to the same level. The use of the pointed arch in vaulting, for example, frees the architect from the need to build only over square or squarish compartments and allows him to erect a vault over a rectangular space of any required dimensions. Finally, the pointed form is well suited to the expression of that desire for verticality which informs the age. The opposing curves are not (as in a round arch) directed to and fro across the span but are brought together at the apex and made to imply an infinite prolongation of the vertical movement. While the round arch is a static, restful form, the pointed arch is invested with a dynamic, restless energy.

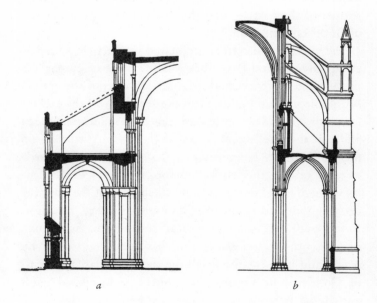

a   *b*

60. *a) The Romanesque buttressing system, Durham Cathedral, vaulted 1133;*
   b) The Gothic buttressing system, Amiens Cathedral, first half of thirteenth century.

The exploitation of the structural advantages of ribs, flying buttresses and pointed arches, and the synthesis of all these features to form a harmonious architectural system, may be ascribed to the medieval architect's increasing command of technique and constructional skill. But Gothic space and internal articulation are much more than the direct results of structural evolution. The new methods of handling wall surfaces—the new emphasis laid upon height and vertical lines—are nothing less than the expression of a specific formal ideal, of the desire to free space from the Romanesque convention of independent bays and to create one spatial unity. A Gothic interior was to reflect that aspiring tendency—that spiritual yearning for union with God—which signalized the religious thought of the age. While the grave, dark majesty of Romanesque churches had compelled the believer to kneel humbly in prayer rather than to lift his thoughts heavenward in spiritual ecstasy, the sky-pointing forms of Gothic would direct men's thoughts toward God and afford a glimpse of a different world.

This new conception of the ideal church lies behind the many important changes and innovations that occurred in the internal organization and general design of churches during the Gothic era. Their planning differed from that of Romanesque examples only superficially. Ritual had remained unaltered and made no specific demands on internal organization. The basilican scheme (with nave and two or four aisles, a transept and a choir with ambulatory and radiating chapels) was still predominant; later, when church building was largely financed by the municipalities, the hall church became popular, particularly in Germany (Fig. 61 c). This type, with its unified spatial composition, answered the need for open churches (in which sermons could be preached to large congregations) that arose during the fourteenth century.

The bishops' cathedrals and large parish churches of the High Gothic period in the meantime adhered to the old basilican plan, and modifications of Romanesque planning tradition occurred only in the choirs of cathedrals. The principal churches of the bishoprics had to have choirs spacious enough to accommodate, not only a particularly large number of clergy, but also the plentiful supply of relics that had been brought back to Europe by the Crusaders. Space also had to be found for the relics of the churches' own patron saints, for crypts were now omitted. This was partly because the bones of the saints and other relics were most easily accessible to large crowds of pilgrims if they were displayed in altar niches or reliquaries within the church itself, and partly because a division into upper and lower church (the crypt) would

not have been compatible with one of the most essential requirements of Gothic religious architecture—the creation of a continuous, unified space. To meet these needs, the choirs were extended well beyond the crossing and provided with a single or double ambulatory and surrounding chapels. A similar type of choir had already been evolved in French Romanesque churches, but here the chapels projected beyond the wall of the ambulatory, as isolated elements with spaces between them (Fig. 58 a). In Gothic examples, the chapels form a continuous ring around the ambulatory, constituting, in effect, an additional aisle. This choir arrangement appeared for the first time in what is acknowledged to be the first truly Gothic construction—the new abbey church at St. Denis, near Paris, the burial place of the kings of France (built by Abbé Suger, 1137–1151, Fig. 62). It represents the new conception of space. Whereas Romanesque interior space is built up from a series of different parts which together form a whole, Gothic space is a unity before it is divided into a number of separate compartments. Against the additive principle of Romanesque is set the dividing principle of Gothic.

This principle determines the character of the Gothic ground plan as a whole and also governs the architectural treatment of the structural envelope. For the sake of brevity, it is necessary to limit this study to the Early and High Gothic cathedral churches that followed the basilican plan, although the Late Gothic aisled hall was perhaps the most satisfying and complete expression of the principle of unity of space and structure, with its integrated and identically treated nave and aisles.

The plan of Notre Dame, Paris (begun 1163, Fig. 61 a), demonstrates with particular clarity the tendency toward a new unity of contained space. The projection of the transept arms has been so much reduced that the transverse movement is hardly apparent against the great leading line of nave and choir. At Bourges Cathedral (first half, thirteenth century), the transept is suppressed altogether so that the interior takes on an enclosed, shut-in character strikingly reminiscent of Early Christian basilicas. It is true that the transepts of most Gothic churches have a stronger projection than that of Notre Dame, but due to the now habitual extension of the choir eastward, the west-east axis dominates the cross axis and the general impression is one of a single, continuous, integrated space. The most elongated of all Gothic ground plans are to be found in England. Here some of the cathedral churches were attached, not to the towns like those on the Continent, but to the great monasteries, and their choirs therefore had to accommodate large numbers of clergy from

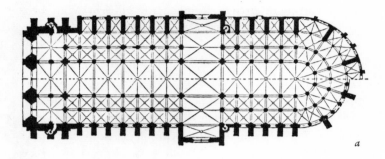

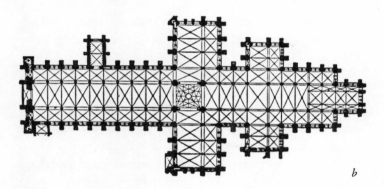

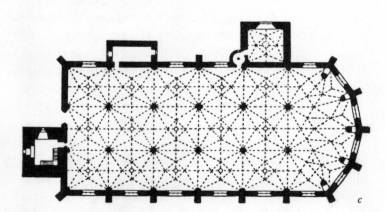

61. a) *Plan of a French cathedral, Notre Dame, Paris, after 1163;*
b) *Plan of an English cathedral, Salisbury, after 1220;*
c) *Plan of a Late Gothic hall church, Marienkirche, Schneeberg, beginning of sixteenth century.*

the monastic community. The length of an English choir often exceeds and sometimes even equals that of the nave, as at Salisbury (Fig. 61 b).

A comparison between French and English church ground plans will reveal several interesting differences. In the French type, with its eastern *chevet*, the streams of energy are concentrated and brought to rest in the semicircles of the choir, its ambulatory and chapels. The square eastern termination of the English plan (resulting from Cistercian influence) brings the longitudinal movement to an abrupt halt and leaves it unresolved. The full significance of this difference becomes evident in the architectural treatment of the respective choir terminations. While the vaulted sweep of the ambulatory in a French church is final and absolute, unifying the whole composition and ruling out all possibility of its further development beyond this firm semicircular boundary, the square-ended English plan could be extended at will without altering the spatial effect. English architects introduced glazed windows at these square east ends, increasing their size until, as at Gloucester (page 266 b), they fill the whole wall.

The introduction of a new choir form was the most important, though not the only, step toward the achievement of an interior unity in longitudinal section. The development of Gothic wall articulation and treatment of ceilings (now almost without exception rib vaulted) reflect the same unifying tendency. In many Early Gothic buildings such as Laon Cathedral (pages 220 and 221), still closely dependent on Romanesque constructional principles, and in nearly all English churches before the fourteenth century (page 265), a tall lantern was erected over the crossing, thus creating an isolated vertical compartment of space amid the adjacent horizontals of nave, choir and transept arms. The demand for unity now led

62. *Gothic choir termination with ambulatory and radiating chapels, St. Denis, after 1137.*

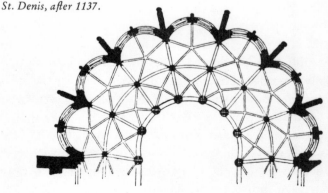

architects to cover the crossing with the same roof and vault it to the same height as its surrounding compartments so that despite structural differences it became an integral part of a unified composition formed by the longitudinal and transverse spaces.

In Early Gothic cathedrals such as Sens (page 221a), Notre Dame (page 258a) and Laon (pages 220 and 221), the vaulting does not yet conform to the unifying principle of High Gothic. Under the influence of the two Romanesque churches at Caen (St. Étienne and La Trinité, page 218b, c), the sexpartite vaulting system is applied; each pair of nave bays forms one square vaulting compartment, thereby avoiding the difficulties incurred by spans of varying width. Accentuated transverse ribs emphasize the fact that the ceiling is still conceived, in the Romanesque manner, as the sum of independent units. When the pointed arch was introduced toward the end of the twelfth century, the problem of vaulting oblong compartments was finally surmounted and the sexpartite system was abandoned in favor of ordinary quadripartite intersecting ribbed vaults covering every oblong nave bay. This innovation changed the whole character of the ceiling, for although each section of the vault is still a unity defined by four diagonal and two transverse ribs, the fact that the bays are no longer square renders these units and the divisions between them considerably less apparent. The compartments now follow one another in rapid succession, like so many bridges thrown across the nave linked together — rather than separated — by the transverse ribs. The general impression, with its emphasis on horizontal movement, is the same as that of a barrel vault.

The progression from sexpartite vaults over square bays to quadripartite vaults over oblong bays had important consequences for the vertical articulation of the nave walls. This may be appreciated by comparing the respective wall treatment of Laon, Notre Dame and Rheims. At Laon, the relation of the supporting shafts to the load of the sexpartite vaults is logically expressed: each rib has its corresponding shaft, so that at the corners of each vaulting bay is a cluster of five such shafts (one for the transverse rib, one for each wall rib and one for each diagonal rib), while the cluster of shafts in the middle of each bay corresponds with two wall ribs and an intermediate rib. The additive principle of the vaults is also expressed on the walls, which are divided into a series of well-marked vertical bays. However, the beginnings of the Gothic desire for unity are nonetheless apparent at Laon, for the vertical wall division is not pushed to its logical conclusion. The alternation between the groups of five and three shafts finds no echo in the arcade (with the

exception of the two last bays before the crossing), for the supports are identical circular piers.

Notre Dame (Fig. 63b) has similar piers and goes beyond Laon in that, although the vaults are again sexpartite, no difference is made in the groups of vaulting shafts which are all exactly alike. Thus at Notre Dame unity is achieved in the vertical wall articulation but does not yet extend to the whole fabric, for the oblong compartments defined by the wall bays are still contradicted by the square compartments of the sexpartite vaults. Finally at Rheims (Fig. 63c), with the introduction of simplified quadripartite rib vaults placed over oblong bays, the system of identical groups of shafts finds a structural as well as an esthetic justification, and the circular piers of the arcades no longer stand in isolation from the shafts above but are visually linked with them by four attached colonnettes — and the whole structure is at last brought within a coherent, unified scheme.

Hand in hand with the process of spatial unification in French and subsequently in German churches went the development of that verticality of design which characterizes the Gothic style. Every element (above all, the pointed arch and clustered vaulting shaft) that could visually contribute to an effect of soaring height was brought into play. While a Gothic plan is longitudinal in emphasis, in elevation the vertical lines predominate over the horizontals. An insurmountable esthetic conflict might have resulted from the tension between these two directional themes, but in effect they were brilliantly reconciled. The object of emphasizing the longitudinal axis, the drive eastward to the altar, was as always to bring congregation and priest into closer spiritual contact during the saying of Mass. But that exclusive concentration on the liturgical center of the church which determines the internal organization of a Romanesque church was not suited to the new requirements of the Gothic age.

It has already been seen how the medieval attitude to religion had undergone profound changes and how men now sought to achieve union with God through a spiritual detachment from the material world. Though continuing to need the help of priests as intermediaries with the deity, the faithful — with their new assurance of being the children of God — believed themselves to have secured an individual, direct access to Him. It is not surprising that mystics should have denied the need for the intervention of a priest in this personal relationship. Master Eckhart's "Wäre aber ich nicht, so wäre auch Gott nicht" ("If I did not exist, God would not exist"), is the extreme expression of a philosophy that disputed the value of the priest as mediator and prepared the way for the theology of

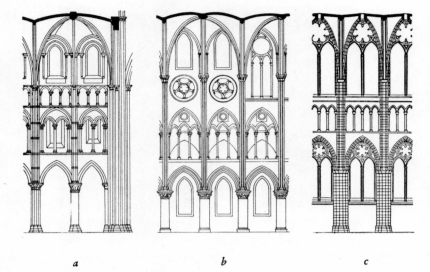

63. Nave elevations:
   a) Laon Cathedral, c. 1200;
   b) Notre Dame, Paris, c. 1180–1190;
   c) Rheims Cathedral, c. 1230.

Martin Luther and the Reformation. Although this individualistic attitude did not take such a strong hold on the Christian world until the Gothic era was well advanced, the celebration of Mass was no longer a collective experience in the old sense, and the act of the priest at the altar was regarded as a symbol of personal intercourse with a personal God.

The form of the Gothic eastern termination may be seen as a reflection of these new aspirations. The choir surrounds the altar with the semicircular sweep of its wall, gathering the longitudinal streams of nave and aisles and concentrating them in the soaring movement of its shafts and vaulting ribs. The same sense of spiritual urgency informs the rest of the church. There is no better example of this than the tendency to increase the height of the nave. In Early Christian basilicas, a relation of 1 to 1.2 had been established between width and height. In Romanesque churches, the relation had at first been 1 to 2, then 1 to 2.5. In the so-called classical cathedrals of the beginning of the thirteenth century (Chartres, Rheims, Amiens), it becomes 1 to 3; at Cologne (begun 1248), 1 to 3.1; and at Beauvais (begun 1225), 1 to 3.3. A parallel development may be seen in the design of the main piers and wall articulation.

At Notre Dame and Laon, the circular piers in the nave arcades are not organically related to the shafts above them. During the thirteenth century the isolation of the piers was overcome by attached shafts, those on the nave

side rising from floor to vault without interruption. The capitals of these shafts become smaller and smaller, losing their character as punctuations, finally (in the later period) to be omitted altogether. Without hindrance, the eye may now travel up the frame of verticals to the vault. Here pointed arches project the soaring impulse onward to their apex, where in implication it is continued beyond the material boundary of the cathedral space, into infinity. So compelling is the combined force of the ascending lines, that the stone loses its effect of mass and heaviness and appears fragile and weightless, as if suspended in air. The impression of upward thrust depends, not only on the piers, shafts and vaults, but on the treatment of the wall surfaces between the shafts, for meanwhile these had undergone a development tending in exactly the same direction.

The wall systems of Laon, Notre Dame and Rheims (Fig. 63) illustrate the main changes that took place between the early years of Gothic and the mid-thirteenth century, when the style had reached its fullest expression. At Laon, the nave wall is divided into four horizontal zones (arcade, gallery, triforium and clerestory) so that almost nothing remains of smooth, inert surfaces (in this respect the effect is exactly comparable to that of mature Gothic wall treatment). But the whole structure retains its enclosing character, solids still predominate over voids, and behind the triforium openings, thick walls reaffirm the general impression of weight and solidity. The vertical thrust is held in check by the obtusely pointed arches and by the round arches in the triforium, and the wall bays are static, dominated by their horizontal divisions.

At Notre Dame originally, the wall was still to have been in four stages, but this treatment was eventually carried out only in the bay adjoining the crossing (Fig. 63 b), where a row of rose windows below the clerestory takes the place of a triforium. These circular windows are omitted in the other bays and the height of the clerestory is nearly doubled — the wall thus being divided into three horizontal zones. In spite of the fact that Notre Dame has a tribune gallery, the wall bays have a distinct upward movement due to the tall, sharply pointed arches. The shafts are identical and not differentiated as at Laon; this also enhances the effect of verticality and quickens the rhythm of the bays.

Rheims goes one step further (Fig. 63 c). The tribune gallery is left out, with the result that the nave arcade is much taller than those of Laon and Notre Dame. The triforium is retained, but with its narrow, tightly packed arcades, it is vertical rather than horizontal in effect. The height of the clerestory windows has been increased strikingly. Now nearly as tall as the arcade, they occupy the whole space between the vaulting shafts and below the wall ribs, transforming the wall into great sheets of glass. The height and slenderness of all openings and the acutely pointed arches conquer the inert stability of the bays that now accompany the shafts in their upward flight. The final achievement of this evolution is represented by the buildings of the thirteenth century where (as in the choir of Amiens) the back wall of the triforium is glazed. At Amiens, the triforium is still separated from the clerestory; at Cologne and Strasbourg, the two stories merge to form one design.

The transformation of nave walls into screens of glass upheld by a skeleton of verticals is to be seen as the expression of one of the deepest esthetic preoccupations of Gothic — as important to the formation of the style as the search for dynamic verticality. In Early Christian times, mosaics and fresco painting had been used to disguise the material reality of solid masonry. Now this idea was pushed to its ultimate conclusion and the density of stone was replaced by the fragile transparency of glass. Yet this expanse of window was not thought of as allowing exterior space to flow into the interior. The light that filters through its brilliantly colored glass is not the light of the outside world but is strange and unearthly, seeming to emanate from the figures of the saints painted on the panes. The whole interior space takes on an atmosphere of sanctity and seems to belong to another world.

That miracle of architecture, the Gothic cathedral church (the creation of French builders, more particularly those of northern France), represents the fulfillment of the Gothic ideal both inside and outside. It is the perfect material expression of the reawakened religious enthusiasm of the time, and is the symbol of a deeply Christian age. The whole of Europe was swept by the wave of church building, and because churches, like all architecture, are the products of human imagination, they underwent constant adaptation. Even at the time when the Gothic style was at its height and most universal, variations in structure and design occur from country to country and from town to town — the manifestations of differing needs and outlooks. No attempt will be made here to describe these stylistic differences. The changing character of Gothic religious architecture and the individual contributions of the countries of Europe to the formation of the style will be best appreciated by reference to illustrations and accompanying text (pages 258 to 285).

GOTHIC ARCHITECTURE

ILLUSTRATIONS

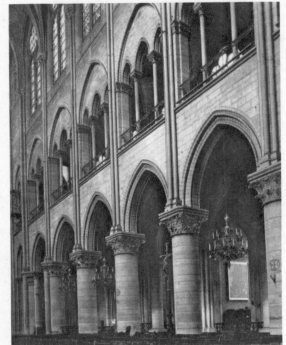

a

b

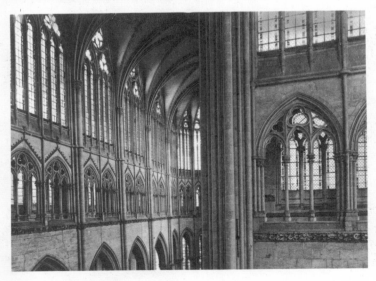

c

RHEIMS CATHEDRAL
Nave, choir begun 1211; completed c. 1250.

At the end of the fifteenth century, Charles VIII called Rheims "the noblest of all churches in the Kingdom of France," and indeed both internally and externally this cathedral seems more nearly than any other to approach to a perfect expression of the Gothic idea. Looking down the nave, the observer is confronted with all those features that characterize Gothic architecture in its fullest development, and comparing his impressions here with those gained in an interior of the transitional style (page 221), will recognize the great changes that had taken place between the twelfth and the thirteenth centuries. The emphasis is now on the vertical instead of the horizontal — on height, not on length. Regularly spaced attached shafts lead the eye upward, and this movement is continued in the pointed arches of triforium and clerestory rising high over the narrow, sharply pointed nave arcades. The galleries, which in Romanesque churches give the strips of wall over the arcades a hollowed-out, deeply recessed appearance and thus emphasize the horizontality of the design, are omitted here, and the triforium openings are so narrow that they echo rather than contradict the upward thrust of the shafts. The crossing of nave and transepts is no longer sharply differentiated from the rest of the church, but is no more than another vaulting compartment leading smoothly from nave to chancel and covered by the same roof. The narrow nave bays are not static (like the square bays of Romanesque) but follow one another in rapid succession, flowing together visually so that the interior is easily grasped as a unity, both in its longitudinal and cross sections. (Facing page.)

a) CATHEDRAL OF NOTRE DAME, PARIS
Nave wall, 1182–1190.

In many respects, Notre Dame belongs to the Early Gothic style. The cylindrical piers of the nave arcades are widely spaced and are not yet integrated with the shafts supporting the vaulting ribs (the two last piers with engaged shafts on the nave side date from the beginning of the thirteenth century). The deep hollowing out of the wall surface with gallery arcades tends to suppress the upward movement of the pointed arches and shafts (the last bay before the crossing, not visible here, is actually in four stages). But Notre Dame goes much further than does Laon (pages 220 and 221) toward the realization of the Gothic ideal, for although there are still sexpartite vaults, the shafts rising from the piers are identical and not (as at Laon) in alternating groups of five and three, nor are they divided by shaft rings.

b) CHARTRES CATHEDRAL
Nave, 1194–1220.

The interior composition is similar to that of Rheims, although not so lofty. Like Rheims, Chartres is a splendid example of the so-called classical phase of Gothic architecture in France — classical, because the vertical lines have not yet been given the exaggerated emphasis typical of the later period (the design still depending on a balanced relationship between height and width) and because the desire for decorative effect has not yet overwhelmed the feeling for structural clarity.

c) AMIENS CATHEDRAL
Choir, completed c. 1247.

Here the triforium stage itself has become a window, and a decisive step is taken toward the transformation of the spaces between the skeleton of vertical shafts into a screen of glass and stone tracery, so that nothing remains of solid wall.

COUTANCES CATHEDRAL, NORMANDY

View from the crossing into the nave, twelfth–thirteenth century.

A comparison between this cathedral and eleventh- and twelfth-century Norman Romanesque churches reveals that the old methods of articulation employed in Normandy still held good during the Gothic period. The various parts of the plan are arranged (in the Romanesque manner) around the crossing. This is vigorously emphasized by four huge clustered piers and pointed arches, with rich, deeply cut moldings, supporting an octagonal lantern. Although the triple vaulting shafts ascend from the floor in un-interrupted lines, the whole design gives an impression of horizontality which is stressed on the walls by carved parapets at triforium and clerestory levels. (Facing page.)

a) LA SAINTE CHAPELLE, PARIS

Upper chapel, 1243–1248; architect, Pierre de Montreuil.

Perhaps the most beautiful creation of thirteenth-century French Gothic, this is a complete realization of the Gothic ideal, the wall surfaces being entirely glazed. The great windows, divided into lights by slender mullions, open above a low arcaded base between the vaulting shafts that form a skeleton of stone. The light filtering through the stained glass gives the chapel an unearthly splendor and a fitting atmosphere of sanctity.

b) BEAUVAIS CATHEDRAL

View into choir, second half, thirteenth century.

The windowed triforium merges with the clerestory to form one design. The nave is of immense height (157 feet 6 inches to the vault — about 3½ times its width) and the building thus sacrifices that beautiful balance of proportion achieved in the classical phase.

c) LA TRINITÉ, VENDÔME

Fourteenth–fifteenth century.

As at Beauvais (Fig. b), the walls above the nave arcade have become windows. The treatment of the piers and arches is characteristic of Late Gothic. The richly plastic definition of the preceding period has here given place to sharp edges and shallow moldings. Capitals, formerly important as transitional members between support and arch, are here reduced to insignificance and have been abandoned altogether in the extreme western bay.

a

b

c

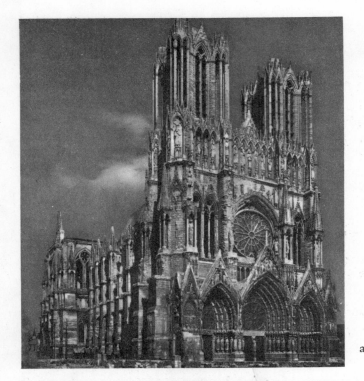

a

b

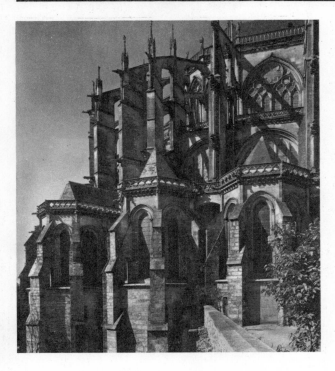

c

CATHEDRAL OF NOTRE DAME, PARIS
West front, c. 1200–1240.

The western façade of Notre Dame, like the interior, does not fully express the soaring, aspiring tendency of later Gothic cathedrals. On the contrary, the horizontality of the design is strongly emphasized, and the division of the façade into rectangular compartments is reminiscent of Romanesque. The main horizontals are formed by a band of statues of the kings of France above the three portals and a pierced arcaded gallery (a derivation of the Romanesque dwarf gallery) in front of the nave roof, connecting the two west towers. They balance the lines of the heavy buttress piers that again divide the façade into three vertical compartments. A magnificently harmonious, balanced and compact effect is achieved by this play of contrasting lines enhanced by the short, square-topped towers. Whether the towers were originally intended to carry spires and owe their present form to a sudden abandonment of work, remains uncertain. But spires would hardly have been in accordance with the general character of the rest of the design, and so perfectly does the great rose resolve the opposing elements in harmony that it would be easy to suppose that the square termination was deliberate. (Facing page.)

a) RHEIMS CATHEDRAL
West front: portals 1200–1260; upper part c. 1290; towers fourteenth century.

In spite of similarities between the two façades, the simplicity and harmony that allows Notre Dame to be compared with a classical temple are no longer apparent at Rheims. This is not only because the height is now greater in proportion to the width — and the two outer zones with the towers considerably narrower than the central bay with main portal and rose window — but because the balance between horizontal and vertical elements is not so strictly maintained. The gallery of kings is now high up at the base of the towers; tall gables over the three portals accentuate the vertical and mask the horizontal divisions between the lower and middle tiers. Tall pinnacled niches containing sculptured figures echo the ascending lines of the buttresses, while much of the centralizing effect of the rose is destroyed by a pointed relieving arch above it. The gallery spread out across the top of the façade is not given the emphatically straight termination of that of Notre Dame, but is drawn into the vertical movement by the gables placed over each arch.

b) EXTERIOR VIEW, NOTRE DAME, PARIS
1163 – late thirteenth century.

The exterior of a French Gothic cathedral shows a simple, uninterrupted west-east development. Just as the interior, in spite of its vertical emphasis, is orientated toward the choir and is a single spatial unity, so the exterior is conceived as a symmetrical body set between a monumental towered west front and an eastern *chevet*.

c) LE MANS CATHEDRAL
Chevet, from 1217.

The treatment of the eastern termination of Le Mans is typically Gothic. The main apse is surrounded by a low ambulatory which is in turn encircled by a ring of closely spaced chapels (*cf.* page 234 c). Notable also at Le Mans are the double flying buttresses, their piers and arches taking the thrust of the vaults over each interior bay.

SALISBURY CATHEDRAL
Nave, 1220–1260.

The Early Gothic architecture of England (known as Early English) differs in many respects from French building of the same period (page 258). Salisbury Cathedral, one of the first and perhaps the most beautiful example of an English Gothic cathedral, displays all the features characteristic of this style. The nave is relatively wide and very long and is remarkable for its lack of vertical emphasis. The long, slender shafts that soar up to carry the vaulting ribs of Gothic churches on the Continent are here reduced to short corbel-like features that appear to be suspended from the ribs and express little of the relationship between supporting and supported parts. The horizontal elements, on the other hand, are vigorously stressed. The suppression of all vertical wall shafts allows the long arcades to unfold toward the choir in continuous perspective, and the openings of the triforium are so closely spaced that this, too, appears to develop without interruption into depth. Strongly marked string courses and colonnettes of Purbeck marble in the galleries contribute to the impression of emphatic horizontality. Comparison with Norman architecture in England (page 225) reveals that the interior of Salisbury actually is not truly Gothic in conception but that Gothic elements (the pointed arch, for instance) have merely been imposed on what is essentially a Romanesque structure. The simple, elegant arch moldings should be compared with their heavy Romanesque prototypes. Unmistakably Gothic in spirit, they are superior to anything of the kind elsewhere in Europe. (Facing page.)

a) LINCOLN CATHEDRAL
Nave, vaulted before 1233.

Both triforium and clerestory are treated as galleries (as at Salisbury) and have triple arched openings. But the continuity of the triforium is not so pronounced here because the shafts descend through it to rest on corbels above the capitals of the piers — descend rather than rise, for they still lack any organic relationship to the piers and are so slender that they seem to hang from the vaulting ribs rather than to rise up to support them. It is true that, although unemphatic, these lines serve to divide the upper walls into vertical compartments, but the interior as a whole retains its unity and the horizontal development into depth is perhaps even more striking here than at Salisbury, due to the great vaults. These are quadripartite, with ridge ribs and extra intermediate ribs, and foreshadow the fan-vault construction peculiar to England. The disposition of the ribs obscures the division into separate bays and the effect is comparable to that of a barrel vault, the ridge rib leading the eye forward to the choir. The eastward drive, however, is interrupted by the crossing, which is marked out as an independent compartment, not integrated with the nave.

b) LICHFIELD CATHEDRAL
Nave, second half, thirteenth century.

The shafts of Lichfield run in continuous verticals from floor to vault, but are too slender to assert themselves in a design that is dominated (as is so often the case in England) by a powerful vault. The arches of each stage reach to the sill course of the stage above, but like the piers themselves, are so amply molded that they reaffirm rather than disrupt the continuity of the wall.

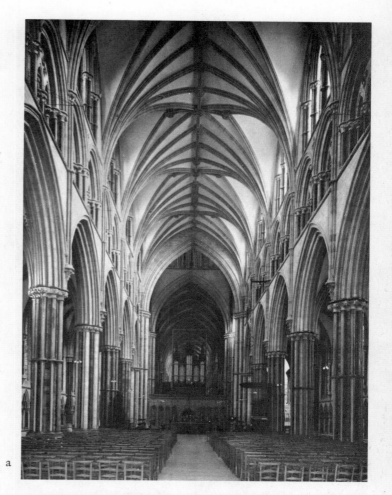

a

b

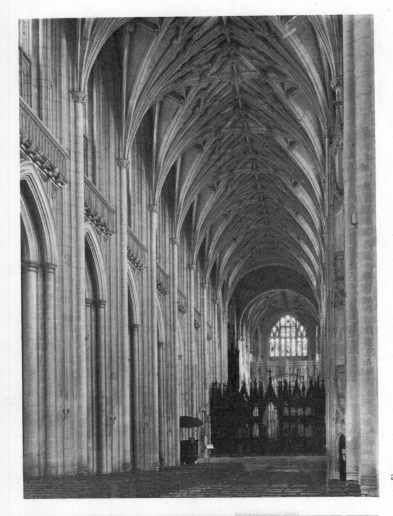

a

b

CHAPEL OF HENRY VII, WESTMINSTER ABBEY, LONDON
1500–1512.

The architecture of this chapel, consisting of a nave surrounded by a low ambulatory, represents the latest phase of English Gothic, known as the perpendicular style. The wall surfaces between the framework of stone shafts and exterior buttresses have become mere screens of glass and stone tracery, although the mullions and strengthening transoms are so closely spaced that they seem to carry the wall surface across the window space. The vault is a masterpiece of decorative art and demonstrates that a taste for excessive elaboration had taken precedence over the need to express the precise structural significance of each element. The ribs that spread out across the whole vault to form a beautiful lacelike tracery serve no structural purpose in themselves, being carved on the surface of the masonry vault as pure decoration. The actual vault is a groin vault divided by transverse arches which disappear into it at points marked by huge fan-shaped pendants. This effect of downward movement is the reverse of that conveyed by earlier fan vaults, where the ribs spring from shafts rising from the ground, the whole vault being part of the upward thrust of the design (pages 270 and 271). Similarly, the pointed arch has undergone a transformation (facing page: heavy transverse arch, foreground). It has lost its inherent ascending movement and is flattened out, as though by some load from above, to form the Tudor arch.

a) WINCHESTER CATHEDRAL
Nave, 1371–1460.

Striking developments have taken place since the thirteenth and early fourteenth centuries (page 265). The strong verticality of vaulting shafts rising from the floor now dominates the horizontal features. Nave arcades occupying half the total height of the unusually tall and narrow nave tend to suppress the horizontal accent of a narrow, blind arcaded gallery above. Nevertheless, the design as a whole has much in common with earlier interiors, for the upward drive is held in check by the powerful vault. The main ribs spring from the shafts at a point far down the clerestory wall, and the complicated lierne vault, with its ridge rib leading the eye forward to the east end, is similar both in form and effect to a barrel vault, providing no climax for the vertical movement but emphasizing the entrance-choir direction.

b) CHOIR, GLOUCESTER CATHEDRAL
1337–1377.

In the fourteenth century, the walls of the Romanesque choir of Gloucester (consecrated 1100) were given a Gothic casing that displays all the characteristics of early perpendicular. The walls are profusely ornamented with stone paneling, the slender verticals of which are repeatedly cut by horizontals that qualify their free development. But the vaulting shafts separating the paneled bays direct the gaze upward with greater force than those at Winchester. As if to counteract this, the vault — actually a solid barrel vault with a closely knit applied decoration — asserts the horizontal with two additional straight ribs running parallel to the main ridge rib, toward the east window.

SALISBURY CATHEDRAL

1220–1266, upper part of tower and spire, late thirteenth century.

The outstanding feature of the exterior view of Salisbury is the great lantern tower, characteristic of many English Gothic cathedrals. The whole building seems to have been conceived in relation to a central tower. This forms the link between the several parts, and moreover is centrally placed, for the choir and nave have approximately the same length, often the case in England, and the transept arms are similarly elongated — whereas in Gothic cathedrals on the Continent, their projection is considerably reduced to give greater unity to the interior space. The double transept, though not a common feature in England, also occurs at Lincoln and Canterbury. (Facing page.)

a) LINCOLN CATHEDRAL

West front: central part Romanesque, c. 1140;
rest of façade, 1200.

English architects derived the type of the twin-towered façade from France, although they rarely followed French precedent as closely as they did at York (Fig. c). When Lincoln Cathedral was rebuilt, the late Romanesque façade, with its flat masses of masonry and giant semicircular niches, was incorporated in a wide screen wall standing away from two west towers rising behind it. The articulation of this frontispiece is distinctive. The harsh verticality of the old Romanesque niches is balanced by a frame of great width. Tiers of blind arcades covering the entire surface emphasize the horizontal, their monotonous regularity illustrating that typically English Gothic preference for a rhythmic repetition of identical elements. The smallness of the actual doorways in relation to the towering mass of the façade also reflects a characteristically English tendency.

b) LICHFIELD CATHEDRAL

West front, c. 1280–1330.

Here the towers are an integral part of the façade design. They do not rise straight from the ground between buttress piers but appear to grow out of the top of the unbroken wall that constitutes the façade proper. The whole of this wall is decorated with blind arcading and figure sculpture arranged with the same stolid regularity observed at Lincoln and executed a hundred years earlier (Fig. a). The three doorways are again reduced to insignificant features of the composition. The sharp separation of the towers from their spires, by means of the same horizontal banding that occurs on the wall surfaces, is typical of tower treatment in England.

c) YORK MINSTER

West front: lower parts, thirteenth century; towers, 1433–1474.

At first glance, this façade appears wholly French in character, apart from the presence of a large and unmistakably English high-pointed window in place of a central rose (page 262 a), but once more the portals are diminutive in relation to the whole and are emphatically separated by strongly projecting buttresses with the usual canopied niches. The three vertical compartments of the façade are clearly marked by the system of buttressing.

a

b

c

a

b

c

CHAPTER HOUSE, SALISBURY CATHEDRAL
After 1263.

Chapter houses are a remarkable and specifically English aspect of Gothic religious architecture. Normally octagonal though sometimes decagonal in plan, they rank among the most beautiful of all architectural achievements, especially in their interior treatment. At Salisbury and Lincoln (Fig. a), the conoidal vault is supported by a central pillar surrounded by slender shafts, the ribs springing from the pillar across the surface of the vault in fan formation, like the fronds of a palm tree. Similar smaller vaults are supported on piers at the eight angles, their ribs meeting those radiating from the center. English Gothic taste for crisp, linear forms has here resulted in a rare refinement and elegance of style. Large windows filling the wall space between the buttress piers enhance the sunny, airy atmosphere of this interior. (Facing page.)

a) CHAPTER HOUSE, LINCOLN CATHEDRAL
1220–1235.

The chapter house at Lincoln, perhaps the earliest of its kind, does not achieve the captivating delicacy and refinement of that at Salisbury, but nonetheless illustrates the beauty of form and composition peculiar to these buildings. The narrow windows are without tracery and have the sharp-pointed lancet shape characteristic of the early English period.

b) OCTAGON, ELY CATHEDRAL
Begun 1322.

The octagon at Ely ranks with the finest and most accomplished achievements of English Gothic. The wooden vaulting, echoing in some respects the pattern of the chapter houses already described, is uniquely adapted to its purpose of covering a lofty central space with lantern cupola above. The crossing is given its full significance as a central, self-contained feature, the meeting place of the adjoining horizontal compartments — choir, nave and transept arms.

c) CLOISTER, GLOUCESTER CATHEDRAL
1351–1377.

This beautiful perpendicular cloister is remarkable for its fan vaults, which may perhaps be traced to the simpler vault form of Gothic chapter houses. The half conoids springing from the slender wall shafts meet in a pattern of semicircles on a horizontal ceiling, the spandrels being decorated with cusped circular tracery. The whole is constructed of large masonry, the ribs being carved in relief and having no structural function (page 267: later fan vaults, Henry VII's Chapel).

COLOGNE CATHEDRAL
View into choir, begun 1248.

Cologne was the first German cathedral to have been inspired directly by French Gothic architecture in its highest development. The model chosen was Amiens (page 258 c). The choir alone dates from the Middle Ages, and the rest of the building was not completed according to the original designs until the nineteenth century. On the interior, the impression of immense height (150 feet — almost as high as Beauvais) is enhanced by the soaring verticals of the vaulting shafts. The nave arcades are almost half the total height, and the glazed triforium merges with the clerestory so that the upper walls become screens of glass, their colored panes lending an unreal, un-earthly quality to the entering light. The piers of the arcade follow one another in rapid succession, and it is the extreme narrowness of the bays that contributes most to the effect of dynamic verticality conveyed by this interior. Nothing is allowed to interrupt the free development of the shafts (at Amiens, their ascending lines were constantly broken by the horizontals of the string courses). Here they rise from ground to springing line in a single, clear movement. (Facing page.)

a) LIEBFRAUENKIRCHE, TRÈVES
c. 1235–1253.

The Liebfrauenkirche at Trèves represents the first stage in the development of the Gothic style in Germany. With St. Elizabeth, Marburg, and the choir of Magdeburg Cathedral (begun c. 1220), it is the earliest German building to show a consistent application of Gothic forms and principles of construction. It does not, however, follow the precedent of the fully developed style of Amiens or Rheims, but is inspired by the Early Gothic of Soissons Cathedral and St. Yved, Braisne. The choir of St. Yved served as a basis for the plan, and the unusual centralized scheme was arrived at by exactly repeating this choir on the west, in place of a nave. The absence of a triforium and the lack of true integration between piers and vaulting shafts are firm indications that this church belongs to an early and formative phase of German Gothic architecture.

b) ST. ELIZABETH, MARBURG
Begun 1235.

This church, built to contain the reliquary of St. Elizabeth, was originally planned as a three-aisled basilica but was altered in the course of construction to a hall church with nave and aisles of equal height. In all probability, the inspiration for this form — un-common during the Early Gothic period — came from Westphalia, where it was sometimes used for churches on a small scale. The trefoil pattern of the east end seems to have been derived, not from Romanesque prototypes in the Rhineland, but — like the two-storied exterior wall articulation — from Soissons Cathedral. (Exterior view of St. Elizabeth, page 276.)

a

b

a

b

FREIBURG IM BREISGAU CATHEDRAL
Nave, c. 1260.

The influence in Germany of thirteenth-century French Gothic architecture, seen in the cathedrals of Cologne and Strasbourg (Fig. a), was not to last. By the end of the thirteenth century, German architects were already turning away from French example, and many cathedrals and parish churches began to exhibit characteristics that are at once pronouncedly German and inconsistent with the pure Gothic style. The most striking differences are the absence of a triforium and the reduced height of the clerestory. Walls above arcades are no longer transformed into screens of glass and tracery, but (as at Freiburg) are left as broad, unarticulated expanses of masonry. The effect is strongly reminiscent of Romanesque treatment and is contrary to the Gothic ideal of verticality, which finds an echo here only in the clustered shafts that rise unbroken from ground to vault. (Facing page.)

a) STRASBOURG CATHEDRAL
View of the nave from the east end, 1235–1275.
Master masons Rudolph.

The treatment of the upper walls, where the glazed triforium becomes a continuation of the clerestory, shows the influence of French Gothic (the first glazed triforium appeared in the nave of St. Denis, Paris, begun 1231). However, the width of this interior and the relative lowness of the ceiling have nothing to do with French examples, although it is possible that the builders were committed to these proportions by the pre-existing eastern portion of the church, dating from the Romanesque period. The clustered piers are set wide apart, and the gaze of an observer standing in the nave is allowed to wander past the arcade into the aisles instead of being irresistibly drawn upward by a closely spaced framework of vertical shafts.

b) ULM CATHEDRAL
Nave from the west, fourteenth–fifteenth century.
Parler, Ulrich von Ensingen and others.

This cathedral, begun in 1377 by members of the celebrated family of Parler from Schwäbisch Gmünd (Heinrich the Elder and his sons Michael and Heinrich), was planned as a three-aisled hall church — a type that was to become a special characteristic of German Gothic from the end of the fourteenth century (page 278). The present arcades reach to a height corresponding approximately to the springing line of the vault that was to have covered the nave. Later the height of the nave was doubled (hence the great wall that so emphatically isolates the choir from the rest of the church) and both aisles were doubled to form a five-aisled basilica. The wall articulation shows the same characteristics as that of Freiburg except that smooth, rectangular pillars typical of the Late Gothic phase take the place of richly clustered piers and the vaulting shafts are much more slender.

ST. ELIZABETH, MARBURG
1235–1300.

This harmonious and unornamented external fabric displays the clarity and severity characteristic of Early Gothic design. There is no element in the composition that is not dictated by structural necessity, and each part retains a plain and massive quality that recalls early Romanesque architecture. The nave and trefoil choir are divided into two window stages of equal height, above a high plinth, and are surrounded by a framework of powerful buttresses identical in form. The roof is clearly differentiated from the rest of the building, its sheer, smooth surface providing an effective foil for the vigorous plasticity and rich play of light and shade below. The two great square towers are heavily buttressed and terminate in octagonal spires. (Facing page.)

a) COLOGNE CATHEDRAL
Choir consecrated 1322; nave and towered west front completed 1842–1880.

In contrast to the austere and massive clarity of Marburg, the exterior of Cologne is a rich and complicated display of many small elements soaring toward the sky and seeming to deny the building's weight and solidity. The chapels around the choir show something of the simplicity of Marburg, but above this lower stage rises a forest of flying buttresses with pinnacles and other features through which the choir is scarcely visible. The transition from walls to roof is masked by the delicately carved pinnacles and by gables over the choir windows. The same teeming detail and dynamic verticalism are evident in the twin western towers that no longer ponderously climb stage by stage but shoot upward like fountains. They are richly ornamented with lacelike detail and are surmounted by spires, the two elements merging in a single heavenward movement.

b) ULM CATHEDRAL
West tower, second stage completed c. 1460; upper part and spire, nineteenth century.

c) ST. STEPHEN, VIENNA
South tower, completed 1433.

The French type of the two-towered façade was seldom imitated in Germany, but a single tower over the west entrance or towers arranged at the sides of the nave (as at Vienna) were often used. They were carried to enormous heights and profusely decorated with stone tracery.

d) STRASBOURG CATHEDRAL
West portal, begun 1277. Erwin von Steinbach.

Perhaps the most beautiful example of paneled and traceried Gothic stonework.

a

b/c

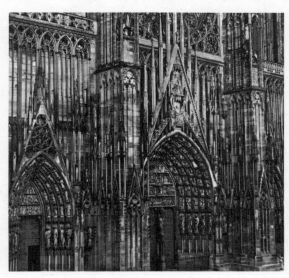

d

a

b

c

ST. LAWRENCE, NUREMBERG
Choir, 1445–1472. Konrad and Matthias Roritzer.

Hall churches and choirs are a characteristic feature of Late Gothic religious architecture in Germany. The basilican interior grouping favored during the High Gothic period was succeeded by a juxtaposition of nave and aisles of equal height and sometimes equal width, while the aisle spaces were no longer clearly separated from the nave by means of walls above the arcade but merged with it to form a single volume. In this choir there are no upper walls at all and the tall piers of slightly differing profiles rise to the springing of the vault — the main arches, to which the side walls have now been reduced, themselves forming part of the vaulting system. Space develops freely in depth and in height: the eye is attracted by both the powerful horizontal of the traceried balustrade around the outer wall and the slender vertical lines of the supports. The ribs, springing from their shafts without the interpolation of capitals, spread out in all directions to form a complicated network across the ceiling. Unlike the simple ribbed cross vaults of High Gothic (page 274), which bring all the vertical forces together to culminate in an apex and constitute well-defined bays, these vaults describe no spatial divisions and reply to the strong upward thrust of the piers with an equally strong horizontal emphasis. (Facing page.)

a) WIESENKIRCHE, SOEST
1331–1376.

In Soest, the hall church, always favored in Westphalia, shows certain characteristics which although unmistakably High Gothic, in many ways foreshadow later developments in South Germany. As in the Wiesenkirche, the spatial interpenetration of nave and aisles, the height of the piers and the absence of capitals between vaulting shafts and ribs, anticipate later ideas. But the most outstanding difference between this and subsequent hall churches appears in the vault, which forms separate bays and thus holds in check that free development of floating space achieved later in St. Lawrence, Nuremberg.

b) ST. GEORGE, DINKELSBÜHL
1448–1499.

Hall churches with very long naves, such as this, cannot convey the same effect of spatial unity that is achieved in hall choirs. Inevitably the entrance-choir longitudinal direction dominates, and in St. George this is emphasized by the magnificent tunnel-like vault, with its spreading network of ribs.

c) ST. BARBARA, KUTTENBERG
Begun mid-fifteenth century.

The churches of the so-called school of Erzgebirge represent the final and logical development of the Late Gothic hall form. The main arches — the last remnants of the old system of divided compartments — now altogether disappear from the vault. This is entirely covered with a curving, intertwining pattern of ribs, eliminating all transitions from nave to aisles and giving the vault the appearance of a single barrel vault covering the whole interior space.

CISTERCIAN ABBEY OF CHORIN
West front, 1273–1334.

In North Germany and regions in the northeast where stone was scarce, brick was commonly used during the Gothic period. Because it is a brittle material that cannot be worked like stone and is unsuited to elaborate carving, Gothic churches built of brick are, with few exceptions, massive, austere and ponderous in appearance. They contrast strangely with buildings in stone of the same period — elegant, complex and richly decorated. The solemn monumentality of the west front of Chorin, with its simple juxtaposition of clearly defined elements, evokes a Romanesque rather than a Gothic style. Even the blank arcades, the small blind rose window with inset cusped circles, and the crowning turrets and gables do little to mitigate the sheer, stark character of this great wall. (Facing page.)

a) ST. NICHOLAS, WISMAR
Early fifteenth century.

Massivity of form is also evident in this church, both in the closely built and in the open areas. Here the arcades are half the height of the whole structure and the walls above are pierced by large window niches of which only the upper parts are glazed. The nave of St. Nicholas, like those of most brick churches, is very tall in proportion to its width, and the aspiring tendency of the whole structure is echoed in the slender vaulting shafts.

b) MARIENKIRCHE, DANZIG
Vault, 1502.

This is a brick hall structure with transept and has the type of vault common at this period. The ribs form a rich and purely decorative stellar pattern over the nave. The aisles have cellular vaults with no molded ribs — the cone-shaped hollows meeting in sharp edges.

c) EXTERIOR, MARIENKIRCHE, DANZIG
Begun 1425.

This church rises over the roof tops of Danzig like a mighty castle, broad and self-contained. The massive square tower should be compared with the soaring spires of stone cathedrals in Germany (page 277, b, c).

a

b

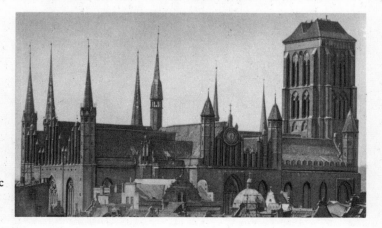

c

a

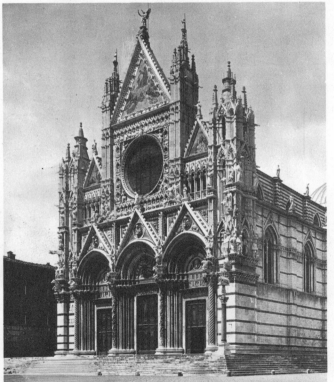

b

c

FLORENCE CATHEDRAL
Nave, fourteenth–fifteenth century.

Elements of Gothic found their way into Italy about 1200 through the Cistercian order but the style never took root there. No church interior in Italy is comparable to those of the High Gothic period in France and Germany, and where they occur, Gothic features are modified by Roman traditions and already infused with a spirit that points forward to the Renaissance. The pointed arches and intersecting rib vaults in the nave of Florence Cathedral are indeed Gothic in themselves, but the vaulting shafts take the form of antique pilasters, and the design as a whole is full of opposing tendencies. The upward thrust of the Gothic arches and vaults is neutralized by a strong horizontal articulation, and the arcades, opening like monumental portals into the aisles, are so widely spaced that the pointed arches lose much of their vertical impulse. Their effect is further diminished by a great corbeled gallery just below the clerestory, which consists of nothing more than the spandrels of the vaults. The round windows are a Renaissance feature. (Facing page.)

a) STA CROCE, FLORENCE
Late thirteenth–fourteenth century.

This interior is similar to that of the cathedral in general character. The reversion to an open timber roof instead of a vault contributes to the harmony of the design and is indeed further proof of the superficial nature of Gothic in Italy and of the underlying presence of late-antique-Early Christian tradition.

b) SIENA CATHEDRAL
Façade, designed and begun 1284. Giovanni Pisano.

Even in this astonishingly elaborate and sculptured façade it is not difficult to discern that feeling for order and proportion, rooted in antiquity, which was eventually to lead to the rejection of the Gothic style. The whole façade has an air of dignity and balance, its basic forms being clear and simple: the rose window is set within a square and the false gables are echoed in the triangular canopies over the semicircular recessed portals.

c) MILAN CATHEDRAL
Façade, fifteenth century.

In spite of close links with northern Gothic — many of the architects employed on the cathedral were Germans (including Heinrich Parler and Ensinger) — the façade of Milan expresses the same feeling for geometrical clarity and simplicity that has been observed at Siena. Interior divisions into nave and four aisles are marked by flat buttresses.

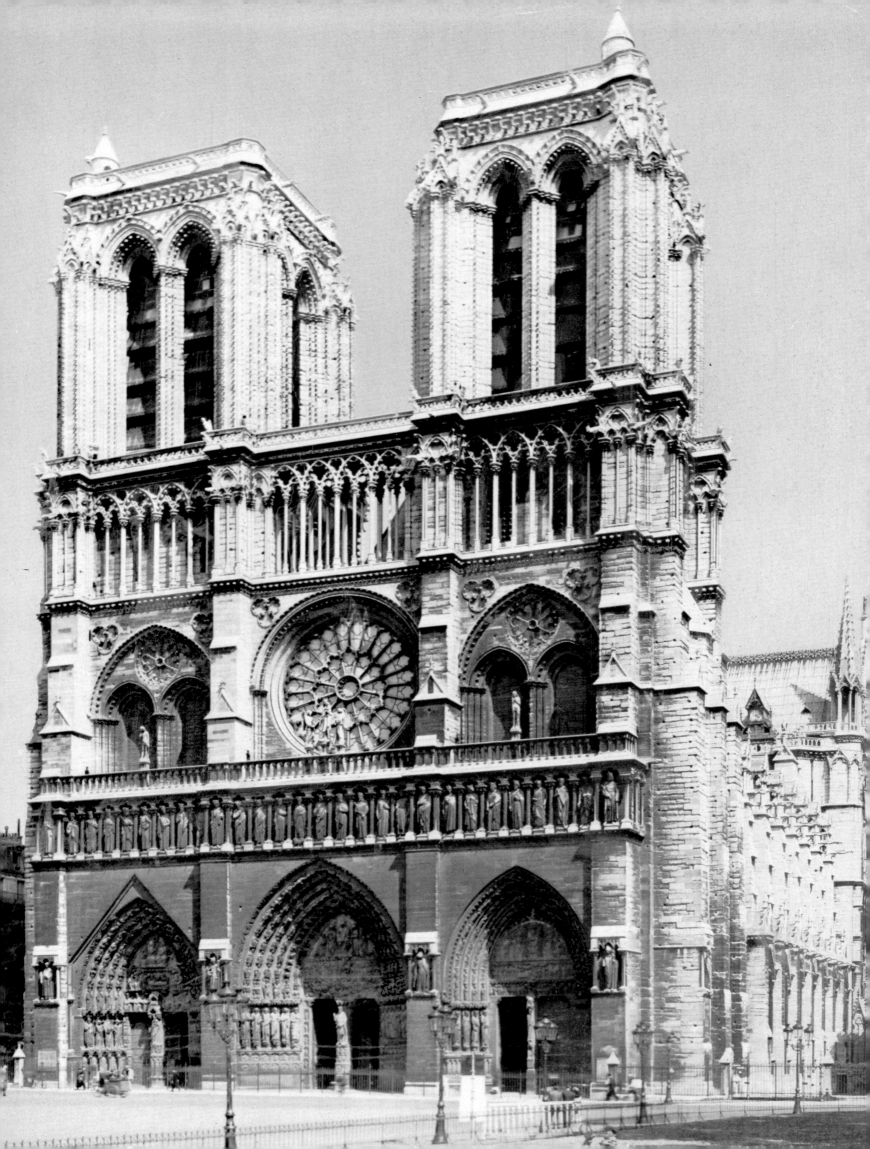

BURGOS CATHEDRAL
Begun 1221; west towers 1442–1458, Hans of Cologne;
central lantern 1539–1567, Juan de Vallejo.

The exterior of this cathedral, one of the most splendid and important achievements of Spanish Gothic architecture, shows a rich variety of forms through which may be traced the development of Gothic in Spain from the thirteenth to the middle of the fifteenth century. The twin-towered façade is colored by the influence of French architecture — the determining factor in Spain during the greater part of this period. The clarity of the whole composition (surmounted, in the spirit of German Gothic, by Hans of Cologne's magnificent openwork spires), the quality of the paneling and tracery and the great central rose window, all betray northern influence. The richly treated central lantern (ciborium) has the curiously characteristic forms of later Spanish Gothic, the so-called *Estilo Plateresco* or silversmith's style (mid-fifteenth–mid-sixteenth century). Plateresque work, as its name implies, is essentially decorative and lacks true architectonic quality. It is a combination of Moorish intricacy and exuberance of detail, French Flamboyant and Italian Renaissance forms, as shown in this cimborio — where Renaissance roundheaded windows are framed in the ogee arches typical of the Late Gothic style, and balustraded walking ways are also Renaissance in character. There is the same picturesque juxtaposition of Plateresque and northern Gothic forms inside the cathedral. Intersecting rib vaults, with ridge ribs perhaps derived from English examples (page 265 b), are placed side by side with vaults decorated with intertwining rib patterns found in Late Gothic churches in Germany (page 278 c). (Facing page and Fig. a.)

b) ABBEY CHURCH, BELEM, PORTUGAL
1500–1522. João de Castilho.

The Plateresque style spread to Portugal, where it was further enriched by borrowings from Indian art (Vasco da Gama returned from India in 1499) and from Italian and Flemish Renaissance architecture. After the art-loving King Emanuel I (1495–1521), the style came to be called *arte Emanuele* and may be seen at its finest in the work of João de Castilho, who was largely responsible for the design of the monastery church at Belem. This is a lofty, three-aisled hall structure — a type also common in Spain during the late period and perhaps influenced by Moorish architecture. The slender, richly ornamented pillars and the stellar vault, with its ribs growing palmlike out of the shafts, are hallmarks of this late style.

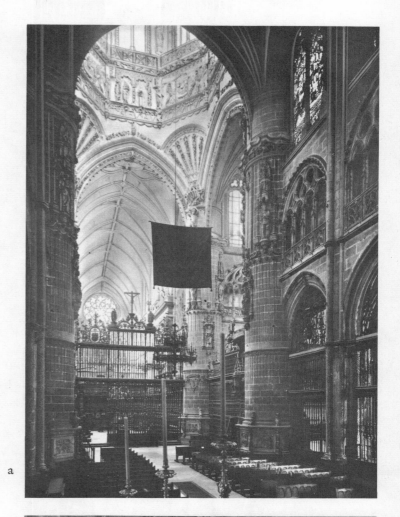

a

b

a

b

c

d

Castles and palaces are the most important aspect of secular architecture during the early Middle Ages. They were used as temporary residences by kings and emperors during their travels from one place to another rather than as permanent homes, and were not always heavily fortified. The military castles erected by nobles and princes during the eleventh century were monumental stone structures that served both as permanent dwelling houses and for defense. At first the external fortifications — powerful walls and gateways — were given an architectural importance far exceeding that of the living quarters within. In the course of the High Middle Ages, the defensive purpose declined and castles took on the character of residences (*cf.* page 289).

ROYAL RESIDENCE, GELNHAUSEN
Great Hall, first half, thirteenth century.
This type of hall, usually in two stories with an entrance on one of the long sides, finds its origin in ancient Germanic royal halls and was the most important feature of the medieval feudal residence, especially the German burg. From the evidence of Gelnhausen, it is clear that the secular architecture of the Middle Ages was deeply influenced by the conventions evolved for religious buildings. (Facing page.)

a) DONJON, CHÂTEAU DE LOCHES
Twelfth century.
Many castles in France and England took the form of a strongly built rectangular keep or donjon. These donjons were at first severely utilitarian, although the rounded buttresses of Loches (derived from church architecture) may be considered decorative in intention to some degree. While those in France served as convenient permanent dwelling houses and were indeed the first stage in the development of the Renaissance château (page 311), their similar though usually less massive counterparts in German fortresses were only lived in during times of attack. The entrance doorway of a keep is normally on the second story and was thus accessible only by ladder.

b) CONWAY CASTLE
Wales, twelfth–thirteenth century.
Conway Castle is strongly defended by eight towers projecting boldly from the outer wall, to allow for a complete command of the panels of wall between them during an attack.

c) CASTELLO D'ESTE, FERRARA
Fourteenth century.
Whereas northern European castles were asymmetrically planned to suit the siting and the needs of defense, in Italy they followed the pattern of ancient Roman military camps and were symmetrically built around an internal courtyard. As at Ferrara, they usually have a tower at each corner, with bare walls between.

d) MONASTERY OF MONT-ST.-MICHEL
Normandy, twelfth–fourteenth century.
For strategic reasons, elevated sites were generally chosen for citadels in northern Europe. Mont-St.-Michel is a typical example. The fortified monastery is surrounded by a second defensive wall enclosing the town below.

Town houses began to acquire significance as architecture with the new growth of urban life during the twelfth and thirteenth centuries. They are a clearer reflection of the individual and national tastes and characteristics of their builders than are churches and monastic buildings, which in spite of marked differences from country to country, had to conform to a general pattern of construction and design. The house has its roots in local traditions alone. A comparison between an Italian and a German example (facing page and Fig. a) will reveal their main differences but will not permit any general conception of the character of the medieval house as an architectural form. It becomes apparent however that, like fortified castles and castle residences, the dwelling house shares the characteristics of the style primarily evolved for religious buildings. The first town houses to achieve true artistic significance were those belonging to the merchant princes and, in Italy, to the ancient families. Later, in the fourteenth and especially during the fifteenth century, important town residences were built by the nobility in addition to their country homes (page 320).

THE DOGE'S PALACE, VENICE
1309–1424.

This great palace is a three-winged structure arranged around an inner court, with its long façade facing the piazza, and represents — though on a monumental scale — the scheme adopted for large town houses in Italy. The delicacy and elegance of the architectural treatment reflects Venetian taste for decorative richness. The upper story, faced with white and rose-colored marble patterning and pierced with few windows, seems to float above the tiers of pointed and traceried open arcades which form the substructure. (Facing page.)

a) HOUSE OF THE TEMPLARS, COLOGNE
Early thirteenth century.

In northern Europe, it was the custom to build town houses with their long axis at right angles to the street, behind a tall, narrow façade. All architectural ornament was concentrated on this frontispiece, which was richly and elegantly articulated and later entirely covered with paneled and traceried decoration (Fig. b). The stepped gable of the House of the Templars is characteristic of the Romanesque period.

b) THE SKIPPER'S HOUSE, GHENT
1531.

Guild houses are similar to ordinary dwelling houses, both in structure and general appearance. They served as meeting places for the powerful trade guilds of the Middle Ages and of the Renaissance. This house repeats the basic design of the House of the Templars, but the stepped gable is now less regular in outline and has lost its battlemented character, while the still Romanesque forms of the earlier buildings have here given way to a Gothic decoration. The depressed arches over the windows herald the Renaissance.

c) THE HOUSE OF JACQUES CŒUR, BOURGES
Façade onto court, fifteenth century.

The town residences of the nobility and of many of the wealthier citizens and merchant princes often comprise several blocks of buildings grouped around an interior courtyard, with an elaborate façade to the street. The House of Jacques Cœur in Bourges is a particularly fine example of a French medieval residence of this type.

a/b

c

a

b

c

d

TOWN HALL, LOUVAIN
1447–1463.

Special importance was accorded municipal buildings during the late Middle Ages. Town halls and guild houses were symbols of civic pride and were built on a magnificent scale, though following the general pattern of the town house in architectural character. Most of the town halls of the prosperous trading towns of Flanders date from the Late Gothic period (that of Louvain has the exuberant decoration typical of its time) and are usually several stories high, with a spacious main hall and the entrance on the long side facing the street. (Facing page.)

a) TOWN HALL, MÜNSTER
Fifteenth century.

The link with German domestic architecture is immediately apparent (page 289 a, b). Characteristically, a splendid façade emphasizes the building's importance. The stepped gable (a development of the Romanesque form) is effectively enriched with finials at the corners and a surmounting traceried screen wall. The large hall on the ground floor, opening through arcades onto the street, is particularly common in Westphalia (though it is also found elsewhere) and housed market stalls and the public scales.

b) TOWN HALL, SIENA
1289.

Town halls in Italy were also modeled on domestic buildings and were monumental in scale. The tall, slender tower at Siena recalls the private watch towers erected by the Italian nobility during the early Middle Ages (page 293 a).

c) CLOTH HALL, YPRES
Completed 1380.

The cloth halls and *boucheries* that have survived in some Flemish towns (including Bruges, Louvain, Ghent and Ypres) reflect the prosperity and artistic enterprise of the burghers of the Netherlands during the Middle Ages. The majestic façade of the Cloth Hall at Ypres is 440 feet long and is surmounted by a great central tower which architecturally is closely related to the towers of medieval cathedrals, which served as town arsenals and belfries.

d) PALAIS DE JUSTICE, ROUEN
Early sixteenth century.

The arrangement of the building group around an interior court recalls that of the House of Jacques Cœur in Bourges and similar domestic buildings (page 289 c). The magnificent architectural decoration makes this one of the most outstanding achievements of Late Gothic municipal architecture in France.

Towns, as large communities of people living by choice under one jurisdiction, had constituted a vital aspect of civilization during antiquity but had rapidly lost their importance during the dark centuries following the invasions. Their regrowth in the eleventh and twelfth centuries was an outward sign of the new prosperity in western Europe. It is true that at first they were merely trading centers — placed where people could come to buy and sell the produce of the land. Organized administration, division of labor, the monetary system, a more highly developed trading and not least the citizens' consciousness of belonging to an independent community — indeed all those aspects of community life that were to give the towns a strong political significance — gradually developed over a long period of time.

The erection of municipal buildings — town halls, guild halls and fortifications (to say nothing of religious architecture) — to serve the needs of the community is an eloquent testimony to this great revival. Town fortifications, which apart from their defensive purpose were the visible expression of the urban community, did not become general until the twelfth century. There is evidence that before this time there was not sufficient communal feeling to impel citizens to unite in so important a task as the building of communal fortifications. At Regensburg, Trèves, Bologna and Siena — to mention only the most important examples — private watch towers resembling belfries were built by the nobility and the wealthier citizens as additions to their houses, indicating that personal safety was still put before the general security of the town as a whole (Fig. a).

Most of the early fortified towns date from the thirteenth century. Some have both inner and outer walls with towers and fortified gateways, and many are also provided with a surrounding moat. The appearance of these walls is somewhat enlivened by crenelated parapets (usual in the south) or roofed ramparts (in the north). The gates (Figs. c, d) are often elaborate, and many achieve considerable artistic significance. They served the double purpose of providing defense and impressing visitors with the town's prosperity and enterprise.

Facing page:
CARCASSONNE
Double curtain wall, twelfth–thirteenth century, with remains of ancient Roman fortifications.

a) SAN GIMIGNANO
Private towers, twelfth century (13 of the original 48 survive).

b) AIGUES-MORTES
Rectangular town wall, c. 1270.

c) HOLSTEN GATE, LÜBECK
Brick, fifteenth century.

d) TOWER AT THE OLD BRIDGE OF PRAGUE
Fifteenth century.

a

b

c

d

IX
RENAISSANCE ARCHITECTURE

General Background

The transition from the Gothic era to the Renaissance represented a far more radical change in the intellectual, social and artistic conditions of the West than did the transition from Romanesque to Gothic, and in architecture it manifested itself as a complete revolt against an established European tradition. The new movement, beginning in the thirteenth century, had gained so firm a hold by the fifteenth century that the period around 1500 may be considered the end of the Middle Ages and the beginning of modern times. It is true that no precise incident may be singled out to mark the boundary of transition between the two eras. The new intellectual climate did not descend on the entire West at the same moment but first made itself felt in Italy and then gradually spread to northern Europe during the course of the fifteenth and sixteenth centuries. But the difference between the medieval and the Renaissance outlook on life is so fundamental that this alone is sufficient to justify the idea of a new beginning in the evolution of the West.

During the two great periods of Western medieval history — the Romanesque and the Gothic — the highest spiritual aim of mankind had been to achieve, through Christianity, a state of detachment from the material world, in order to come nearer to a mystical participation in the cult of Christ, His saints and the world beyond. The stages in the evolution of this way of thought had found symbolic expression in architecture, and the Gothic cathedral church of the thirteenth century was the perfect reflection of the world-renouncing spirit of the Middle Ages at the moment of its highest development. With their drive eastward to the altar and their seemingly weightless upward flight, these great works of architecture symbolically pointed to Heaven and owed their whole dynamic character to the fervent spiritual aspirations of the age. But the architectural ideal of the High Renaissance was to be the unorientated, centrally planned structure where no forward or upward drive dominates the thoughts of the believer; where space is self-contained and held in perfect balance and tranquillity.

This new interpretation of the meaning of the church corresponds to a new and original attitude to life and to the relationship between material and spiritual things. Although Christian concepts were by no means abandoned, the other-worldly mysticism and the fearfulness of medieval thought gave way to a joyful acceptance of life on earth and to the idea that this acceptance and self-realization was itself pleasing to the Deity. The development of religious ideas from the Romanesque to the Gothic era might be described as the gradual discovery of God. The Renaissance movement was the discovery of man, revealing man to himself and firing him with a new awareness of his call by God to "replenish the earth and subdue it; and have dominion over the fish of the sea, and over the fowl of the air, and over every living thing that moveth upon the earth" (Genesis 1:28).

The part played by religious doctrine in the formation of this modern philosophy was relatively slight. By the end of the thirteenth century, the idea of the religious authority of the Church as the measure of all things, unassailable and omnipotent, was already being called in question and the Church began to lose its pre-eminent position in society to a merchant class that steadily gained in power and in prestige. Those three formative influences on medieval thought and culture — the clergy, the nobility and chivalry — had mainly been guided by spiritual rather than by material ideals. The new ruling class, too, was idealistic, but in a totally different sense. The ordinary citizen of a trading or manufacturing town did not center his life around a transcendental ideal; on the contrary, he took diligence, technical skill, thrift and other tangible virtues as the standards by which he lived. Rooted in reality, materialistic in outlook, it is not surprising that the middle classes should have been the driving force behind the spiritual upheaval from which the Renaissance movement emerged.

The materialistic values of middle-class society had profoundly important consequences for the arts. A study of the religious and social background of Gothic art has shown that one of the principal characteristics of the Late Gothic period, when most of the important commissions came, not from the clergy but from the municipalities, was the emergence of the individual artist from the anonymity of the early Middle Ages. Self-portraiture, signed works and even pieceworkers' marks, all provided evidence of the artist's awakening consciousness of his personal achievement, of a newly felt desire for self-identification with the work of art, for fame among contemporaries, and above all, for immortality. It has also been seen how this developing cult of the individual made itself felt in the sphere of religion, when each man believed himself to have secured a direct access to God, to be able to approach Him, not simply as one of a vast community, but as an individual soul. The new self-knowledge of the bourgeoisie tended only to strengthen such beliefs, and it was inevitable that men should grow more and more intolerant of the restraints imposed upon them by the profound religiosity of the Middle Ages. The freedom of the individual in the political as well as the spiritual sense became the battle cry of the new era — the accepted standard of the widest section of the population of the Western world. Ideas of pronouncedly democratic, materialistic tendencies took an increasingly strong hold on men, and the influence and power of the Church declined in proportion. This development was ultimately to lead to the Lutheran Reformation in Germany.

Freed from the shackles of a too tyrannical religious authority and filled with self-awareness, Renaissance man pursued earthly glory and fulfillment as passionately as medieval man had sought spiritual, other-worldly perfection. Not content merely to study his own nature and personality, he yearned to extend his knowledge and power to everything around him. It is no coincidence that the Renaissance stands alone in the history of civilization as the age of the universal genius. Neither before nor since has any age produced a company of men of such brilliant versatility, such all-embracing curiosity and creative genius. The classic examples of this wide competence are Michelangelo — painter, sculptor, architect, poet and man of affairs — and Leonardo — not only painter, sculptor and architect but scientist, engineer and inventor, making designs for flying machines and engines of war that are astonishing in their ingenuity, and concerning himself with the problems of anatomy, geology and linear perspective. The contemporaries of these great masters — although men of less exalted gifts — strove to conform as nearly as possible to the ideal of the age — the *uomo universalis*, the accomplished human being versed in all arts and sciences. This ideal was to become increasingly difficult to attain, for the new philosophy had opened fields of knowledge and thought too vast for one man to explore in a lifetime.

Since the end of the thirteenth century, man's relationship with nature had undergone fundamental changes and by the Renaissance little remained of the old uneasy, superstitious beliefs. True, the Christian outlook of the Early and High Gothic periods had already rejected the idea of the workings of nature as inherently evil, and men had increasingly come to regard nature as the gift of God and as the revelation of divine will and power. But the concept of nature subjected to the mastery of mankind as set forth in the Story of the Creation was not yet formed. When a stronger element of realism had entered into Christian thought; when trade on land and sea was widening horizons; when more was learned of the true causes of natural phenomena and at the same time means discovered for mastering them and putting them to practical use, men acquired a new conception of the world around them and learned to value and enjoy the wonders and beauties of nature. Enthusiastic descriptions were written of these newly found delights, by Petrarch, for example (1304–1374), and man was fired with the spirit of adventure, with a desire to explore the mysteries of nature and to discover the secrets of the world. He stood on the threshold of a development that continues through modern times. It was during the Renaissance that the foundations of modern science — of our own knowledge of the world and the universe — were laid.

Thus after the discovery of man came the discovery of the world, and men eagerly began to grapple with the vast fields of knowledge laid before them. Dissection of the bodies of humans and animals for the purpose of anatomical studies was practiced for the first time. Leonardo's notebooks contain the earliest known scientific drawings of the human body. As far as we know, he was also the first to climb mountains and thus penetrate the hitherto unknown. Interest in distant lands is reflected in the passion among kings and princes of the time for collecting exotic beasts in private menageries. The invention of the compass and the telescope symbolizes the same urgent curiosity and enthusiasm for travel and exploration. Painters began to look at nature with new eyes and strove to reproduce reality as faithfully as possible. The discovery of linear perspective (perhaps by Brunelleschi, early fifteenth century) made possible a complete illusion of three-dimensional form in depth. Geographical knowledge was vastly increased with the voyages of discovery made under the Spanish and Portuguese flags (Christopher Columbus, Vasco da Gama etc.) which forced a complete reassessment of ideas of the extent of the earth's surface and its position in the universe. This spirit of inquiry is most typically represented by the demonstration of Copernicus (1473–1543) that the earth is no more than one of a number of planets revolving around the sun.

The spirit of curiosity and interrogation spread rapidly as a result of these discoveries, and even the unlettered masses were no longer content to accept the world around them at face value or simply as the manifestation of divine will. All men longed to experience the happier, fuller life that deeper understanding seemed to offer. This universal hunger for learning and education may well have given impetus to the invention of printing, due in part to Johann Gutenberg of Mainz (died 1468), which enabled the written word to reach a wide public and increased the intellectual opportunities of mankind beyond all expectation.

It is natural that the Renaissance movement should have begun, developed, and reached its effulgence in Italy, for the Italian towns and Italian middle class were the first to achieve an extent of power sufficient for the formation of a new philosophy of life. Venice and Pisa had risen to be rich and flourishing republics as early as the Romanesque period, and Milan, Ferrara, Mantua, and above all, Florence — the very cradle of Renaissance painting, sculpture and architecture — had not been far behind. Moreover, the Italians had never been so deeply affected by the intense mystical tendencies of Christian thought that grew up in France and more especially in Germany during the Gothic era. A practical people, they had remained as essentially materialistic, as rooted in reality, as their great forefathers. That the rediscovery of antiquity should have happened at precisely this moment in time was not least because the Italians of the early fifteenth century found that the life and letters of pagan antiquity (which they now studied with passionate concern) reflected an ideal and an outlook on life that corresponded closely with their own. The classical inheritance seemed to breathe the same free, outward-looking spirit, the same *joie de vivre*, that informed the new age. The ancients, too, it was discovered, had looked for fulfillment in the earthly life, had enjoyed its beauties, and had striven to achieve perfection of mind and body.

Both intellectually and morally, classical language and literature provided mankind with inexhaustible sources of education — an education for which the way had already been prepared by the speculations of medieval scholars and philosophers. Thus, paradoxically, antiquity itself was not the starting point for the Renaissance movement; it emerged from the dust of centuries only when the spirit of the new age was already ripe for its reacceptance and rebirth. Though Wölfflin has gone so far as to declare that: "The great river of Italian art flowed its course and the cinquecento would have been what it was even without the tribute of antiquity," Italian Renaissance buildings are surely a visible evidence that Renaissance architects took their inspiration from the architectural style and forms of ancient Rome.

Architectural Character

In considering the architecture of the Renaissance, especially that of Italy, its birthplace, it would be wrong to take it for granted that the return to the forms and principles of antiquity was the whole basis and *raison d'être* of the new style. The conscious aim of Italian architects was to recreate their classical past. The writings of Vitruvius (the Roman authority on architecture), rediscovered in 1414, were studied with devotion; antique monuments or their ruins which he had mentioned were identified and measured; his canon of proportions for the classical orders and rules for the use of decoration served as a general guide in the rediscovery of the system behind the styles of Roman antiquity. Yet in spite of this — and here lies the essential difference between the classicism of the fifteenth and that of the early nineteenth century — Renaissance architecture was no mere imitation of antique models. Antiquity could provide a repertoire of forms but could not supply the answers to all of the problems with which architects were now faced. No direct precedent or terms of reference existed for the churches, middle-class town residences, town halls and palaces which constituted the main architectural tasks of the age. (A comparison between the illustrations on pages 300–309 and those on pages 64–85 will show that Renaissance architecture outdid the Roman in the versatility and resources of its handling of space. The vocabulary of antiquity was employed in the service of an entirely original style of spatial organization.)

The growing cult of the individual, inevitably gaining the artist a position of increasing importance in society and encouraging personal expression in art, must be held responsible for the fact that architecture no longer consistently developed in a single direction (as in antiquity or through the Middle Ages) but became the product of individuals, each of whom placed his own interpretation on the commonly held principles, ideas and forms, creating a personal style, and with his pupils, formed a separate school of design sometimes traceable over long periods of time. Palladianism is a particularly characteristic example of the power of the individual to influence the course of architectural history. The style of Andrea Palladio (1518–1580), the greatest master of the later Italian Renaissance, who evolved an architecture of pure classical forms, became the inspiration of architects in France and particularly in England, where, through Inigo Jones (1573–1652) and later Sir Christopher Wren (1632–1723), it was the driving force behind the whole of the English Renaissance and baroque movements. Indeed it may be said that from the Renaissance on, the history of art becomes the history of artists and their individual styles.

During the Middle Ages churches had been the main concern of the builders. It was in their service that the Gothic style and system of construction had been evolved, and secular buildings had derived their forms directly from religious architecture. But during and after the Renaissance, secular architecture achieved a position of equal importance and was the testing ground for many of the forms and motifs of the new style. The wealthy patrician families of Italy demanded houses and palaces on a scale without precedence, to serve for receptions and lavish entertainments as well as to provide comfortable and elegant living conditions. These demands reflect — as does every other aspect of the times — the reawakened consciousness of the material world and its delights. Not until the Renaissance did the interiors of secular buildings receive a true architectural treatment.

(This brief glance at several of the most important aspects of Renaissance architectural activity is supplemented by the more detailed accounts of the buildings themselves and their salient characteristics — pages 300–323.)

RENAISSANCE ARCHITECTURE

ILLUSTRATIONS

a

b

c

d

PALAZZO RUCELLAI, FLORENCE
Façade, 1446. Leon Battista Alberti.

One of the most important works of the early Florentine Renaissance, the Rucellai Palace shows how deep was Alberti's determination to recreate the spirit of classical antiquity. He was perhaps the first to make a conscious return to the architecture of ancient Rome, and his inspiration for this façade seems to have come from that system of superimposed orders of columns used for Roman amphitheatres, notably the Colosseum (pages 76 and 77). The façade, which has the horizontal division into three parts characteristic of Early Renaissance palaces (Fig. a), is articulated with three superimposed orders of pilasters (free Doric on the ground floor; free Ionic on the first floor; Corinthian at the top). These vertical divisions balance the horizontals of the entablatures and give the façade a clear-cut symmetry and ordered harmony in which every part has its fixed position and is dictated by strict rules of proportion. (Facing page.)

a) PALAZZO MEDICI-RICCARDI, FLORENCE
Façade, c. 1435–1440. Michelozzo.

It is clear that the Renaissance palazzo has its architectural roots in the houses and palaces of the preceding era (page 289), but the confusing details and abundant decoration have vanished and the Gothic pointed arch has given way to the round arch of antiquity. Clarity, precision, massive scale and an almost melancholy austerity are the qualities that distinguish the early palace residences of Renaissance Italy. The Riccardi Palace, like the Rucellai, is in three horizontal stages, the divisions reinforced by the use of string courses. Arched portals and evenly spaced semicircular windows with a restrained decoration break the wall surfaces, which show the effective use of graduated rustication. The ground story is heavily rusticated, the middle story is channeled smooth, and the upper story has plain ashlar masonry.

b) PALAZZO FARNESE, ROME
Façade, from 1534, designed, Antonio da San Gallo the Younger; top floor and cornice added 1547, Michelangelo.

The grandeur of this High Renaissance façade is the grandeur of austere simplicity and massive scale. The rustication seen in the Palazzo Riccardi is limited here to the quoins and the entrance portal, and for its effect this front solely depends on the contrast between smooth wall surfaces and the plastic treatment of the windows, which have straight cornices on the ground floor and alternating triangular and segmental pediments supported by columns on the middle story. The single entrance is emphasized by its central position but is not yet made to dominate the composition, as in baroque architecture.

c) PALAZZO CHIERICATI, VICENZA
Façade, 1550–1557. Palladio.

This Late Renaissance palace shows the colonnaded treatment favored by Palladio. Only the five central bays of the upper story contain solid walling. The columns and frieze are strictly classical. The rich modeling of the central block anticipates baroque taste for compact grouping, and the statues and vases above the upper parapet terminating the vertical movement of the columns below also look forward to the baroque.

d) PALAZZO VALMARANA, VICENZA
Façade, 1566. Palladio.

The strong central accent, the projecting cornices, the use of a giant order of pilasters (embracing ground floor, mezzanine and upper story) and the small attic story above the cornice, all foreshadow baroque treatment.

PALAZZO GONDI, FLORENCE
Internal courtyard, 1490–1498. Giuliano da San Gallo.

Like Pompeian houses, Renaissance palaces are arranged around a square or rectangular courtyard. In Florentine examples these courtyards, following the precedent of the antique peristyle, are surrounded by open colonnades carrying, not a horizontal architrave but semicircular arches. The court of the Palazzo Gondi, with the simplicity and clarity of its forms, is a particularly beautiful example. The delicately carved staircase is, as usual at this period, placed outside the building under the arcade. During the High and Late Renaissance large and ornate staircases were to become an integral and important part of houses and palaces. (Facing page.)

a

a) PALAZZO DEL CANCELLARIA, ROME
Courtyard, before 1496. Built, Bramante, perhaps after designs by Alberti.

This great courtyard has two tiers of open arcades and finds its origin in Florentine buildings of the Palazzo Gondi type. The top tier is closed and has a pilaster decoration recalling that first used in the Rucellai Palace (pages 300 and 301). Above the windows are small semicircular headed openings — an early instance of the mezzanine story so often to be used during the baroque era. They do not correspond to any internal floor divisions but merely provide an extra half story of windows.

b) PALAZZO FARNESE, ROME
Courtyard, c. 1540. Michelangelo.

In this, the most beautiful of Roman High Renaissance palace courtyards, the antique system of superimposed orders revived by Alberti is taken up once more and the model of the Roman amphitheatre is followed exactly. The cloistered ground floor, with engaged Tuscan Doric columns framing the arcades, appears to have been derived directly from the Colosseum, Rome (*cf.* Fig. 18). The first floor has blank arcades and an Ionic order, while the upper story again recalls the Colosseum, with its Corinthian pilasters instead of half columns. The small rectangular recesses beneath the windows also have their counterparts in the amphitheatre, where they occur in an identical position around the base of the top story (*cf.* page 77). The architectural details, the proportions and use of the classical orders, all denote the architect's deep attachment to antique example.

b

c) OSPEDALE DEGLI INNOCENTI, FLORENCE
Façade, begun 1421. Brunelleschi.

The open loggia — one of the themes of the Early Renaissance in Florence — was used by Brunelleschi, pioneer of the new architectural style, in the façade of the Foundling Hospital, which has been called the first truly Renaissance building. A disciplined classicism is apparent in this design, with its arches, Corinthian columns and entablature, its tranquillity and harmony.

c

d) STA MARIA DELLA GRAZIE, AREZZO
Loggia, c. 1470. Benedetto da Majano.

Airy and graceful, this is a delightful example of Early Renaissance design. The architect's respect for antique forms has not prevented him from exaggerating the scale of the sections of entablature that form impost or dosseret blocks.

d

a

b

c

PAZZI CHAPEL, STA CROCE, FLORENCE
Façade, 1430–1443. Brunelleschi.

This narthex-like vestibule, inspired by Early Christian precedent, forms the frontispiece to a small domed chapel that was one of the first centrally planned buildings of the Renaissance (page 307 b). Despite the general clarity and symmetry of its arrangement, the façade—echoing the triumphal arch theme—shows several unresolved problems and should be compared with later and more sophisticated compositions. Pure, classical Corinthian columns carry a delicate entablature with a frieze bearing the circular medallions so often employed by Brunelleschi and here decorated with cherubs' heads. The upper structure of the façade, pierced by the round arch that emphasizes the central entrance, is reminiscent of the attic story of Roman triumphal arches and is decorated with double fluted pilasters and paneling. This type of wall decoration is scarcely antique in spirit, but recalls the surface patterning found on buildings of the Florentine proto-Renaissance (page 229), by which it may well have been inspired. (Facing page.)

a) S. ANDREA, MANTUA
Façade, after 1472. Alberti.

In contrast to the flat and typically Early Renaissance treatment of the Pazzi Chapel façade, this front is modeled in several planes. As in the Rucellai Palace (pages 300 and 301), Alberti imposed a layer of decoration on the flat wall surface, the dominant elements being the great Corinthian pilasters (an early example of the giant order much used during the later period). These pilasters and the crowning triangular pediment reveal that the idea of the classical temple front lies behind Alberti's façade.

b) IL REDENTORE, VENICE
Façade, begun 1577. Palladio.

The layered treatment already seen in S. Andrea has here attained a rich plasticity typical of Late Renaissance architecture. A classical temple front corresponds with the main nave. Its great triangular pediment is repeated in the entrance bay filled with a columned tabernacle framing the door and is re-echoed in the parts of pediments over the side bays, set slightly back and at a lower level. The high basement, with a wide staircase leading to the level of the columns, imitates that of ancient Roman temples.

c) IL GESÙ, ROME
Façade, 1573. Giacomo della Porta.

The façade, like the interior design of Il Gesù (pages 308 and 309), served as the starting point for innumerable churches of the baroque era. This two-storied front is vertically divided by superimposed orders of smooth coupled pilasters framing pedimented niches. The problem of reconciling the difference in width and height between upper and lower stories in the stepped façade of a basilican church is here resolved by scrolls rising against the pedimented top floor from the entablature over the aisle roofs, so that the two parts are linked firmly together. The central vertical axis and the importance of the centerpiece on the ground floor are stressed by the projecting entablature, by attached half columns flanking the door, and by the double pediment.

FLORENCE CATHEDRAL
Dome and choir, 1420–1436. Brunelleschi.

The three immense apses around the octagon and the great dome were built in the Renaissance as additions to the Gothic cathedral; the dome by Brunelleschi was the result of a competition. This is the first building group in which the spatial ideal of Renaissance architects — the centralized structure — was realized. Although the dome is not hemispherical but rises steeply to the crowning lantern, the building complex conveys an impression of self-contained mass, enhanced by the emphasis placed on the horizontal lines. (Facing page.)

a) ST. PETER'S, ROME
View into dome, 1588–1590. Completed, Giacomo della Porta, after designs, Michelangelo.

The most important building of this period, St. Peter's owes the greater part of its design to the genius of Michelangelo. The drum of the dome was completed before his death (1564) and he left models from which it was finally realized. Unlike the ideal dome of the High Renaissance, which was a perfect hemisphere, Michelangelo's is elongated; the ascending lines of the coupled pilasters in the drum are continued in the soaring movement of the ribs to the apex and on into the light-filled lantern. The vertical movement beginning in the piers is not resolved and brought to rest by a self-contained hemisphere (as in a High Renaissance conception), but reaches a stupendous climax above, and calm gives way to a controlled restlessness that points forward to the baroque.

b) PAZZI CHAPEL, STA CROCE, FLORENCE
Interior, begun 1430. Brunelleschi.

The body of the chapel is square and covered by a dome on pendentives. A second smaller dome covers the altar niche, and coffered barrel-vaulted transepts are added on either side. The simple mathematical relationships, the purity and clarity of all the forms, are characteristic of Early Renaissance architecture.

c) THE TEMPIETTO IN S. PIETRO MONTORIO, ROME
1500–1502. Bramante.

Based on the design of a Roman circular temple, this small domed centralized building is the purest and most beautiful expression of a Renaissance ideal. In the words of Burckhardt, it was: "The first recreation after an interval of 1,200 years of a building completely in the spirit and style of antiquity."

d) STA MARIA DELLA CONSOLAZIONE, NEAR TODI
Begun 1508.

The simplicity of its geometrical pattern (probably based on a design by Bramante) makes this church one of the most beautiful achievements of the High Renaissance. Four identical apsidal arms with semidomes open off the central square, surmounted by a dome on a high drum. The entrance portal is understated, as though the architect wished to disturb as little as possible the perfect symmetry and detachment of the design.

a

b

c/d

a

b

c

IL GESÙ, ROME
Interior, begun 1568; consecrated 1584. Vignola and Giacomo della Porta.

The ideal High Renaissance expression of space and volume had been the self-contained, perfectly symmetrical, domed centralized structure. Later (at the time of the Counter-Reformation), architects deliberately reverted to the basilican, longitudinal scheme, and this form predominated once more. But the new churches are not modeled on the Early Christian basilica type, with rows of columns in unbroken perspective (Fig. a). They are a fusion of the domed centralized plan and the longitudinal barrel-vaulted hall interior with isolated side chapels in place of continuous aisles developed by Alberti and Palladio.

The interior of Il Gesù in Rome exemplifies this type and was to be imitated throughout the world. Indeed, the baroque style has its roots in the architecture of the Counter-Reformation during the last years of the Renaissance. The motif of the barrel-vaulted hall flanked by side chapels and combined with a domed centralized composition had already been used by Alberti for S. Andrea in Mantua (after 1472). But here Vignola was the first to achieve that arrangement of such significance for future development, whereby the domed area is not merely a centerpiece but gathers up the whole design to a climax. The projection of the transept arms is reduced to almost nothing, and the windows are so placed that the tunnel of the nave remains dark while the area beneath the dome is flooded with light, thus dramatically emphasizing the region around the altar. Here for the first time, light (which was to be of major importance in baroque architecture) is a positive factor in the composition. The articulation of the nave walls, the spatially insignificant accompanying chapel niches, the low gallery (*coretti*) over the chapels and the small clerestory windows, all find an echo in churches of the baroque. (Facing page.)

a) S. LORENZO, FLORENCE
Nave, begun 1421. Brunelleschi.

Clearly the origin of this type of three-aisled Latin-cross basilica is to be found in such Italian churches of the Gothic era as S. Croce, Florence (page 282 a). Here, however, Gothic forms are replaced by forms derived from antique architecture, and the chapels opening off the aisle bays point forward to Il Gesù.

b) STA GIUSTINA, PADUA
Interior, from 1521. On plans, A. Leopardi.

The Greek-cross form of the eastern part of this church was perhaps inspired by St. Mark's, Venice (pages 148 and 149). The crossing and three of the arms of the cross have identical domes on pendentives, while the fourth arm, constituting the nave, is a sequence of independent bays covered by saucer domes. The aisles, too, under barrel vaults at right angles to the nave, are conceived as a series of well-defined compartments.

c) S. GIORGIO MAGGIORE, VENICE
Interior, begun 1565. Palladio.

S. Georgio may be likened to Il Gesù in the prominence given to the dome and in the reduced height of the upper story in the nave. But here the domed area is not (as at Il Gesù) the point of climax at the end of a single dark tunnel, but the central feature of a cross-shaped plan, the transverse arms boldly projecting as apses. The treatment of the nave, with arcades carried on piers faced with Corinthian columns, follows antique tradition.

CHÂTEAU D'AZAY-LE-RIDEAU
On the Loire, c. 1520.

This small château is clearly a development of earlier fortified castles. The characteristic defensive angle towers have here become graceful turrets corbeled out from the building and with tall, steeply tapering roofs; the rampart running below the eaves is now a kind of attic story carried on corbels. Tall gabled dormers break the horizontal of this attic, and like the larger dormer in the center of the long side, continue the perpendicular accent of the windows in the wall surfaces. (Facing page.)

a) CHÂTEAU DE BLOIS
On the Loire, staircase of Francis I, c. 1520.

The wing built by Francis I is only one of many buildings grouped around an irregular quadrangle and dating from various periods, the earliest being thirteenth century. This wing is one of the masterpieces of the early French Renaissance. The great spiral staircase in its open tower dominates the courtyard. There is a combination of Renaissance motifs — pilaster paneling, capitals etc. — and Gothic elements — gargoyles, statues in niches and ornate decoration.

a

b) CHÂTEAU DE BLOIS
Francis I wing, main façade, 1515–1524.

The arrangement of columns and pilasters and the two-storied open arcades recall the façades of Italian Renaissance palaces, but the lack of geometrical clarity — and above all the asymmetrical arrangement of the oriel windows — are typically French. The spirit of Late Gothic is still apparent in these oriels, in the magnificent gargoyled cornice below the crowning attic loggia, and in the display of richly detailed decoration.

b

c) CHÂTEAU DE CHAMBORD
On the Loire, 1519–1533.

Chambord, with its four hundred rooms, is the largest of all the châteaux on the Loire and dates from the time of Francis I. The central square block has a great circular tower at each corner, and its façade is in the same line with that of the outer court which surrounds it on three sides. This outer court is also provided with round towers, so that together the two elements form one imposing four-towered front. At the center of the inner block is a double spiral staircase leading to the roof and ending in an extravagant turret 104 feet high. Around this feature are grouped hundreds of dormers, turrets and chimneys, the whole composition giving the appearance of a miniature city.

c

d) CHÂTEAU DE CHENONCEAUX
On the Cher, 1513–1550.

The oldest part of the château, the square block with corner turrets (1513–1521), displays the essential characteristics of the Early Renaissance already seen at Azay-le-Rideau. About 1547, Diane de Poitiers, mistress of Henry II, had a bridge built across the Cher on which Philibert de l'Orme erected the long two-storied wing. This wing, with its lucid articulation and calm horizontal emphasis, is an example of French Renaissance classicism in its fullest development.

d

ST. PIERRE, CAEN
Apsidal chapels, 1518–1547.

This church is a wholly characteristic example of how, north of the Alps, Renaissance detail was appreciated in a purely decorative sense and used to clothe Gothic forms. The ring of chapels and flying buttresses around the choir are essentially Gothic in conception, with superimposed Renaissance decoration. The lower windows have round arches without tracery. The buttress piers, although still carrying Gothic gargoyles, are treated as pilasters, the pinnacles as Renaissance candelabra. Vases with curling foliage take the place of the old cusped circle decoration, while on the balustrades double-tailed mermaids borrowed from grotesque Italian ornament replace flamboyant Gothic tracery. (Facing page.)

a) ST. EUSTACHE, PARIS
Interior, begun 1532. Pierre Lemercier.

Like the choir of St. Pierre at Caen, the interior of St. Eustache preserves forms that are basically Gothic yet clothed in modern details. The nave walls have the traditional divisions into arcade, triforium and clerestory. The vaults, with their pendant bosses and stellar rib patterns, belong to Late Gothic in spirit, and the whole interior space, with its framework of verticals, still has the soaring quality of an early cathedral. But the arcades, except those in the polygonal choir and triforium openings, are semicircular. The shafts are treated as pilasters, with Corinthian capitals.

b) ST. MICHEL, DIJON
Façade, first half, sixteenth century.

This twin-towered façade also offers remarkable evidence that early French Renaissance ecclesiastical architecture compromised with a mixture of Gothic conceptions and Italian decorative detail.

c) ST. GERVAIS, PARIS
Façade, 1616–1621. Salomon de Brosse or Clement Métezeau.

There are few Renaissance churches in France. So many had been built during the Romanesque and Gothic periods that there was no real need for new foundations. On rare occasions, existing buildings were redesigned in the new style, as for example at the Gothic church of St. Gervais, where an important screen façade was added during the early seventeenth century. Taking over the scheme of the Gesù façade (page 304 c), the architect has if possible surpassed his prototype in the classicism of this design. The paired columns — Doric on the ground floor, Ionic on the first, and Corinthian at the top — are detached from the wall on high pedestals. This and the strong projection of the entablature produce an effect of rich plasticity that heralds the baroque.

HEIDELBERG CASTLE
The Otto Heinrichsbau, 1556–1559. Dutch architects.

Despite its breadth and emphatic division into horizontal zones, this three-storied façade radically differs from Italian palaces of the same period, such as the Palazzo Farnese completed some ten years earlier (page 300 b). The balanced contrast between smooth wall and sculptural window treatment, the economy and geometrical lucidity of the Roman palace, are not to be found here. Though Italianate in the sense that the forms employed are classical in conception, this façade is so encrusted with complex detail that clarity is sacrificed and almost nothing of the flat surface remains. The Ionic pilasters supporting an entablature on the ground floor are rusticated; those above are Corinthian and richly carved with grotesque ornament. Shell niches containing symbolic statues alternate with pilasters between windows having sculptural frames of columns and entablatures, and on the ground floor, triangular pediments. The central mullions are also carved with figures, and the pediments are filled with medallions supported by putti, while on the upper stories, fantastic half-figurative, half-abstract ornamental carvings replace the pediments. Compared with the classical simplicity and restraint of Italian Renaissance achievement, the design of Heidelberg shows a grossness of taste that treats the wall less as building than as a field for decoration. (Facing page.)

a

a) CASTLE AT HARTENFELS, NEAR TORGAU
Spiral staircase, 1535. Conrad Krebs.

This structure is entirely Gothic in conception, but Renaissance characteristics are apparent in the individual forms and grotesque carvings covering every available surface of the staircase tower.

b) CASTLE AT ASCHAFFENBURG
1605–1614. Riedlinger.

The four identical wings of this great castle are grouped along the sides of a square courtyard, the corners punctuated with massive towers — an arrangement that may have been influenced by French châteaux (page 311). The steep gabled dormers at the center of each side are typical features of the German Renaissance.

c) TRAUSNITZ CASTLE, LANDSHUT
c. 1580.

Many buildings in southern Germany bear witness to the proximity of Italy and to the activity of north Italian architects. Here, for example, the arcades carried on piers, with attached pilasters on the two upper stories of the L-shaped block, are obviously of antique origin.

b

c

RATHAUS, ROTHENBURG OB DER TAUBER
From 1571. Jakob Wolff.

The lavish decoration which characterized German architecture until after the middle of the sixteenth century and was due in part to Dutch influence here gives way to greater clarity and simplicity, although there are still several disturbing features. True, the stair tower is centrally placed and rises in front of the roof to provide an effective foil to the horizontality of the broad façade. But the three-storied angle oriel echoes Late Gothic taste for asymmetrical, picturesque arrangements. The rusticated portico, with round arches on piers in the antique manner, is a later addition. (Facing page.)

a) RATHAUS AND STADTWEINHAUS, MÜNSTER
Rathaus, fourteenth century; Weinhaus, sixteenth century.

Standing side by side, these two buildings provide striking evidence that the type of stepped gable façade so popular during the Gothic era was taken up by Renaissance architects and adapted to the new conventions. The earlier front bears no organic relationship to the interior structure and has a free traceried and sculptural decoration, while the portico takes the place of a single entrance. In the later façade, on the other hand, the internal divisions into stories are marked by the clear horizontals of string courses; all purely decorative detail (typical of the Renaissance) is limited to the gable steps, and the entrance is vigorously emphasized by a projecting porch.

b) PELLERHAUS, NUREMBERG
1605. J. Wolff. Now destroyed.

With its ornamented gable in stepped stages, this building appears to have its long axis at right angles to the street but actually lies parallel with it, one long side forming the façade. Despite a rich decoration, this front is coherent and harmonious in design.

c) ARSENAL, AUGSBURG
1602–1607. Elias Holl.

From the outside, this building might be taken for a church rather than an arsenal. Holl was certainly inspired by the façades of Italian churches, and with happy effect applied what he learned from them to this front. The design is clear and simple and a harmonious balance is achieved between vertical supports and horizontal cornice bands. The vertical axis predominates and is stressed by the broken pediments of the gable and windows. This tendency toward dramatization—to use forms disrupted as if by some invisible inner force—is a bold anticipation of the baroque. Prophetic also is the exploitation of light and shade by the employment of superimposed pilasters and strongly modeled entablature.

d) RATHAUS PORTICO, COLOGNE
1569–1573. Vernucken.

The end and middle bays of this fine two-storied structure are emphasized by their projecting entablature. The column pedestals are richly carved and the roof is concealed by a riot of ornament.

THE OLD COURT HOUSE, BRUGES

Façade, 1535–1537. Executed, Chr. Sixdeniers, after designs by Joh. Wallot.

This is a particularly characteristic example of Early Renaissance architecture in the southern part of the Low Countries (modern Belgium), where French influence was more deeply felt than elsewhere. Superimposed orders of columns and wide, carved friezes form a coherent grid of horizontals and verticals which is an evidence of a strong classicizing tendency. Nevertheless, the entrance is pushed to one side in a typically Gothic manner, and the classical entablature is wholly misunderstood, being treated here as a flat molding carved with classical acanthus and grotesque ornament. The exuberant scrolled gables are also Gothic in spirit, although they are clothed with early Renaissance forms — volutes (lined, it will be noticed, with Gothic crockets), medallions and grotesque decoration. (Facing page.)

a) HOUSES, ANTWERP

Sixteenth–early seventeenth century.

This row of houses affords a good opportunity for a comparison of Late Gothic and Renaissance façade treatment. The two buildings on the right belong to the Gothic period. The one in the center, erected by the Guild of Archers, dates from the beginning of the seventeenth century and marks the end of the evolution represented here.

b) THE OLD MEAT MARKET, HAARLEM

1602–1603. Lieven de Key.

During the whole of the sixteenth century the northern part of the Low Countries (Holland) clung to old traditions. Its municipal buildings are Gothic in conception with superimposed Renaissance detail. At the Old Meat Market of Haarlem, for example, nothing is to be seen of the classical orders; the dormers, with their magnificent gables and the rustication on the façade, belong to the new style.

c) WOLLATON HALL, NOTTINGHAM

England, 1580–1588.

The influence of Early Renaissance architecture in England gave the elements of the new style an essentially decorative interpretation. Superimposed orders of pilasters occur for the first time at Wollaton Hall. However, they are conceived, not as part of the structural framework of the building, but as a means of breaking up wall surfaces to convey a paneled effect. It will also be noticed that the massive central block retains the form of the medieval keep or donjon, and that the façade is not a flat, closed surface but is given movement and spatial openness by the wings which project forward in stepped stages, anticipating the baroque palace façade.

d) BANQUETING HOUSE, WHITEHALL

London, 1619–1622. Inigo Jones.

A typical example of early English Palladianism — that is, of the adoption in England of the precepts and style of Palladio, architect of the Late Renaissance in Italy. The Palladian Renaissance was introduced into England by Inigo Jones, starting an architectural revolution following on the Gothic style of the sixteenth century and later leading to the baroque. The Banqueting House (the only executed part of Jones' Whitehall Palace in London), with its rusticated lower story and two upper stories each with an order, echoes the finely adjusted proportions and severely classical treatment of the works of the great Italian (page 300 d).

a/b

c/d

e

Half-timbering has its origins in Germanic wooden constructions, the earliest surviving examples of which are the stave churches of Norway (page 177). It was used above all in countries where the stone architecture of the Romans was little known and where the people were mainly of Germanic stock, as for example in Germany, northern France and England. Half-timbered buildings dating from before the fifteenth century are rare, and due to alterations and additions, difficult to date precisely.

In Germany, the best examples — both from the point of view of preservation and architectural value — belong to the second half of the fifteenth century and the sixteenth century, that is, to the Late Gothic and Renaissance periods. There are many regional variations in the handling of the essential elements of half-timbering construction — horizontal sills and ledges, vertical posts and diagonal braces. Among peoples of Frankish origin, the timbers were relatively widely spaced, as in the Town Hall at Michelstadt (1454, facing page), while in Saxon examples they are set very close together and sometimes, as in the magnificent Knochenhaueramtshaus, Hildesheim (sixteenth century; destroyed in World War II; Fig. a), each one is placed over a row of beautifully carved wooden corbels supporting the overhanging stories. In Alsace and Swabia, the windows are emphasized by frames jutting forward above the corbels (Kammerzellschen Haus, Strasbourg, 1580, Fig. b). In simpler buildings, decorative effect is limited to the picturesque patterns formed by dark timbers and lighter-colored infilling. Some more ambitious examples are ornamented with painted wooden carvings with a stucco (Hildesheim) or painted (Kammerzell) decoration in between. The ground story is usually built of stone.

In northern France, the compactness of the posts and beams is a striking feature of half-timbered buildings. Occasionally (as at the Maison Quatrans in Caen, sixteenth century, Fig. c) the intermediate spaces are filled with diagonal members halved together to form a series of crosses.

Half-timbered buildings are particularly numerous in England, where the ancient tradition of timber construction is still continued. In the west of England, it is usual to find all the outer surfaces divided up into rectangular compartments (Feather Inn, Ludlow, Shropshire, Fig. d) which are given a different patterning on each story. In the eastern counties, the tradition was to place the upright posts so close together that the vertical strips of wall between were scarcely wider than the posts themselves. Horizontal beams and struts were avoided wherever possible. This narrow spacing is also evident at the house in Caen (Fig. c), and in both cases there may well be a debt to Norman tradition. The ground story of Bramall Hall, Cheshire (fifteenth century and later, Fig. e), illustrates this style, while the upper stages and gables belong to the tradition established in western counties.

An extraordinary exuberance in interior decoration is found in Renaissance architecture, especially north of the Alps. Great halls and galleries, generally with flat coffered or beamed ceilings, provided — within the simple classical shapes of the Renaissance style — the setting for the combined arts of painters, cabinetmakers, wood carvers, sculptors and many others. The examples given here will provide some idea of the splendor and variety of Renaissance internal fittings.

Facing page:
GREAT CHAMBER, CHÂTEAU DE BLOIS
Early sixteenth century.

a) GALLERY OF FRANCIS I, FONTAINEBLEAU
Sixteenth century.

b) GALLERY OF HENRY II, FONTAINEBLEAU
Sixteenth century.

c) GOLDEN ROOM, RATHAUS, AUGSBURG
Early seventeenth century.

a

b

c

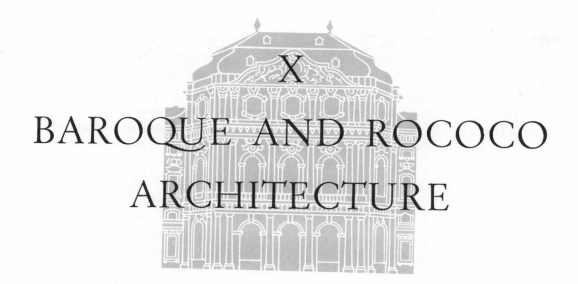

X
BAROQUE AND ROCOCO ARCHITECTURE

General Background

The cultural basis of the so-called baroque era (c. 1580 to 1780) was laid during the half century known as the age of mannerism or as the Late Renaissance. This period (1530–1540 to around 1580) brought profound changes and developments in the spiritual atmosphere of the Western world. The preceding decades (the years of the High Renaissance, 1500–1530) had, in Italy above all, recon-

ciled man with himself and liberated him from a too exclusive devotion to the Church and to the transcendent philosophy of the Middle Ages. He had discovered the world and all its beauties and had acquired a new self-knowledge and awareness.

This conception of life found symbolic expression in the ideal type of religious building at the beginning of the

Renaissance — the centralized church (page 307). Here the worshipers are sheltered on all sides and brought into a harmonious relation with the architecture. No one direction compels attention. The interior space revolves around the central cupola space, and even here its vertical impulse is limited and contained by the curve of the dome. But the basilican, orientated scheme had never been entirely abandoned in favor of the centralized plan, and when (from c. 1550) it regained its preeminence as a building form, this was no more than the inevitable reflection of a new spiritual attitude.

Humanist thought during the High Renaissance, universalist and worldly as it was, had not only tended to estrange men from God and the Church, but had encouraged a supreme self-confidence which affected even the clergy and the Papacy. But such a philosophy depended on spiritual unity, and this unity was shattered when Martin Luther (1483–1546) rose up against the infallibility of Roman Catholic doctrine, against the beliefs professed by the clergy and the whole aura of omnipotence that surrounded the Roman Church. His rebellion announced the Reformation that finally led to schism in the Western Church. Now the very existence of the Universal Church was threatened and with it the whole fabric of its teaching. In the name of God and in the cause of self-preservation, the Papacy began the counteroffensive, and a new ardor fired the supporters of Roman Catholicism, who were to fight for their beliefs not only in the pulpit with theological argument but on the battlefield in the Wars of Religion. The Council of Trent (1545–1563) launched the Counter-Reformation to combat the Protestantism which by this time had spread over much of northern Europe. The bitter strife and devastation of these long years of crisis culminated in the Thirty Years' War, and many people, especially in Germany, were brought back into the Roman Catholic fold. But although the Roman Church consolidated its authority in these areas, its highest aim — to reunite the Church — was never attained. The greater part of northern Europe remained Protestant.

The religious wars deeply undermined man's so recently won self-assurance and pride, and in their place there grew up a sense of spiritual insecurity and doubt. It is therefore not surprising that during this period the Church, especially the Roman Church, should have vastly increased its hold over men and regained much of the power it had held in the Middle Ages. The clergy and the Church, as arbiters of the newly invigorated religious thought, retrieved their right — lost to the middle classes during the Renaissance — to give art direction and content.

It is true that their patronage was confined to sacred art, for the Renaissance had seen the final disruption of the great synthesis formed at the beginning of the Middle Ages between temporal and spiritual power. It was, moreover, in the Roman Catholic Church that religious art found an active and understanding patron, for Protestantism fundamentally rejected the arts as a form of religious expression and as a means of directing the thoughts of the faithful toward God. This is why all the decisive impulses in the formation of baroque ecclesiastical architecture came from the Roman Catholic countries of Europe. Thus baroque church architecture is essentially Roman, and it is only to be expected that the finest and most characteristic achievements should have appeared in those countries that remained faithful to the Papacy — that is, Italy and southern Germany.

That secular building should have equaled, and in the palaces of the high and late baroque even surpassed, religious architecture in magnificence, was largely due to the continuing influence of Renaissance ideas. Even the renewed ascendancy over its people of the Roman Catholic Church could not destroy that consciousness of human dignity and individuality the Renaissance had implanted in man. The collectivism and the commonly held ideals of the Middle Ages were irretrievably lost. Nevertheless the renewal of faith was so strong that the forces of individuality were considerably diminished and finally came to be limited to the ruling classes. This development was determined by the fact that the princes were rapidly recovering the power they had relinquished (in the fifteenth century) to the municipalities and the middle classes.

In Spain and France, temporal rule was concentrated in the hands of the kings to a more marked degree than in Germany and Italy, subdivided into numerous small principalities. The sovereigns constituted the highest power in their countries and their significance increased even further when, appealed to for help by the Church in the Counter-Reformation movement, they reassumed the aura of divine right as protectors of the orthodox religion: Roman Catholicism. This idea that they ruled by the grace of God was the basis of the secular absolutism of the baroque era. The monarch, enthroned in unapproachable majesty, acknowledged no man as his equal or God as his superior, and his will was paramount. The fateful article of the Peace of Augsburg (1555), which obliged subjects to adopt the religion of their sovereign ("*Cuius regio, eius religio*"), was the first sign of the absolutism to come. Louis XIV (1643–1715) was the embodiment of absolutism at its height. The Sun King became the model for all the rulers of the period, great and small, secular and ecclesiastical. He is said to have proclaimed: "*L'état, c'est moi!*" ("*I am the State!*") and in 1682, the French clergy declared that: "Monarchs are not only chosen by God, they have in themselves a quality of divinity."

This boundless pride and self-adulation gave rise to a need for some extravagant display of magnificence that would lend visible support to the legend of the godlike sovereign. A solemn and elaborate court ceremonial was developed and every resource of art—painting, sculpture and architecture—contributed to the glorification of absolutism in royal palaces of unprecedented splendor and arrogant luxury. Hangings of shining silk were offset by the glorious colors on walls and ceilings, by the rich glow of marble and the sparkle of crystal and gold. The superhuman status of the sovereign was also symbolized in the colossal scale of the palaces and their apartments.

Secular absolutism and the triumphant Church of the Counter-Reformation were the two great patrons of architecture in the age of the baroque.

Architectural Character

(The following general observations are intended to complement the more detailed explanatory notes and illustrations on pages 330–361.)

The term baroque was used for the first time by nineteenth-century historians, to refer to the period covering the seventeenth and the first half of the eighteenth century. The word comes from the Spanish *barucca*, meaning an unusual pearl of irregular shape, and was employed to denote the original style of the period immediately following the Renaissance—an exultant, exaggerated style, turbulent, passionate and bold in its most characteristic manifestations and with a strong tendency toward overornamentation. Although originally used in a derogatory sense to describe what was then considered a degeneration of Renaissance forms and a contradiction of the strict classical principles to which the neoclassicists of the early nineteenth century were returning, it captures the very essence of this period and its artistic achievements.

The transition from Renaissance to baroque architecture may indeed be considered as a degeneration insofar

as serenity, restraint, order and harmony are understood to be the essential qualities of a perfected style. These qualities characterized Renaissance architecture in its highest development (1500–1530). Economy of form and a tranquil, harmonious balance signalized the design of interiors and exteriors alike, so that the relationships between one form and another were at once apparent to the eye. Baroque architects destroyed this classical tranquillity with dramatic effects and agitated movement. They defied the rules of clarity and economy by covering wall surfaces with a profusion of detail, gave their buildings colossal scale, and invested forms with a tempestuous inner force. The evolution from simplicity to complexity is to be observed in every aspect of architecture from the Renaissance to the baroque and may be illustrated with particular clarity in the ground plans of churches.

Bramante's plan for St. Peter's, Rome (Fig. 64 a), projects the characteristic scheme of the High Renaissance—coherent, centralized and composed of simple geometrical shapes. With complete symmetry, the plan is developed around the central domed area and is a perfect square externally. The smaller domed compartments adjoining the central space are conceived as identical elements and are symmetrical in themselves. The position of each element in the plan is governed by this principle of symmetry: the whole is conceived as a series of three superimposed squares—the central domed area, the square described by the outer sides of the four secondary domed compartments, and finally that of the outer wall.

The plan of Il Gesù, Rome (1568–1584, Fig. 64 b) exemplifies the basilican type that returned to favor during the Counter-Reformation and which here incorporates the ideal domed centralized scheme of the High Renaissance at the east end. This Late Renaissance plan still has something of the old clarity and geometrical simplicity; a circular dome is raised over a square compartment.

The plans of the abbey church of Banz (Fig. 64 c) and the pilgrimage churches of Vierzehnheiligen (Fig. 64 d) and Wies (Fig 64 e)—all works of the German late baroque or rococo—no longer employ the square and the circle but are based on the ellipse, the favorite form of the high baroque phase. With its two focal points, the ellipse is not a centralizing force but has the fluidity and ambiguity necessary to the creation of that spatial complexity for which baroque architects strove. This tendency to enrich spatial effects and to exploit the possibilities of spatial relationships is one of the most striking aspects of the development from the Renaissance to the baroque conception of architecture.

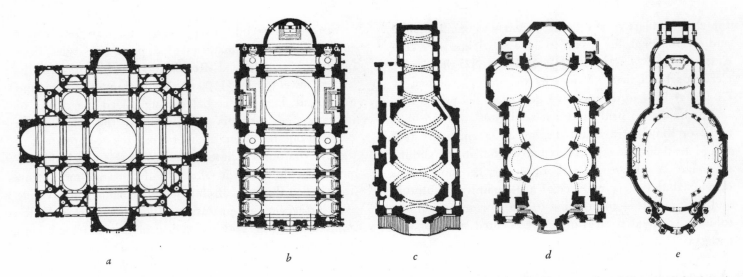

a   *b*   *c*   *d*   *e*

64. *The development of the church plan from Renaissance to late baroque: a) St. Peter's, Rome. Bramante's plan, c. 1506, never executed; b) Il Gesù, Rome, 1568–1584. Vignola and Giacomo della Porta; c) Benedictine Church of Banz, Upper Franconia, 1710–1718; d) Pilgrimage Church of the Vierzehnheiligen, 1743–1772. After plans, T. Balthasar Neumann; e) Pilgrimage Church of Wies, 1746–1754. Dominikus Zimmermann.*

It should be added that the term baroque is sometimes extended beyond the seventeenth and eighteenth centuries, to embrace the late manifestations of any stylistic phase if — as is usually the case — these are characterized by agitated, voluptuous forms and rich detail. Thus later Gothic might be considered as a baroque development in that forms once severe, static and self-contained became detailed, flamboyant and interdependent. The baroque style itself underwent this inevitable formal progression.

Early baroque (first appearing in Italy and Spain *c.* 1600) was characterized by a solemn and austere monumentality. By 1650, classical restraint was left behind and in its place came richness and profusion of form and decoration and complexity of spatial impressions. Late baroque (after 1700) and rococo (1720–1730) brought the extravagance of the style to its logical conclusion in an effervescing, brilliant display of ornament beyond which no development was possible.

BAROQUE AND ROCOCO ARCHITECTURE

ILLUSTRATIONS

a

b/c

d/e

The evolution of Italian church façades reveals two things. First (and equally true of the treatment of interiors up to the middle of the seventeenth century), that the basic principles employed were those already laid down at the end of the Renaissance in the work of Palladio and Vignola. In form as in structure, Renaissance and baroque were not as essentially different as Gothic and Renaissance had been. Second, that baroque architects — after having at first continued this development — eventually created a new and original style. The simple imitation and reinterpretation of antique forms characterizing so much Late Renaissance work was abandoned and architects began to make use of available forms, without regard to the canons laid down by antiquity. Whereas the Renaissance had sought classical simplicity, timeless tranquillity of design and a harmonious and even distribution of masses, the baroque looked for lively contrasts, for dramatic effects, restless rhythm and colossal scale.

The façades of those churches which derived their inspiration from Il Gesù, Rome (page 304 c), perhaps best demonstrate the growing tendency to translate baroque ideals into architecture. This is seen (Figs. a, b, c) in the greater plasticity of moldings, in the lack of flat surfaces, in the complexity of the entablature projections, in the framing of pediments and the richness of the resulting play of light and shade. The baroque impulse to build on a colossal scale is illustrated in the great façade of St. Peter's, Rome (facing page), where giant columns and pilasters embrace the lower stories, their upward thrust carried beyond the entablature through to the attic and terminated in statues. The search for surprise and excitement in design is evident in the façade of Sta Agnese, Rome (Fig. d), where two graceful corner towers flank the central concave block; and in the front elevation of S. Carlo alle Quattro Fontane, Rome (Fig. e), which is dominated by the dynamic rhythm of alternate concavities and convexities.

Facing page:
BASILICA OF ST. PETER, ROME
Façade, 1612. Carlo Maderna.

a) STA SUSANNA, ROME
Façade, 1605. Carlo Maderna.

b) S. ANDREA DELLA VALLE, ROME
Façade, c. 1665. Carlo Rainaldi.

c) STA MARIA IM CAMPITELLI, ROME
Façade, c. 1670. Carlo Rainaldi.

d) STA AGNESE, ROME
Façade, c. 1650. Rainaldi and Borromini.

e) S. CARLO ALLE QUATTRO FONTANE, ROME
Façade, c. 1650. Francesco Borromini.

STA MARIA DELLA SALUTE, VENICE
1631–1687. Baldassare Longhena.

This domed church is octagonal on plan, with an aisle surrounding the central space. For effect, it relies on the richness and exuberance of its baroque forms rather than on its architectural conception. The lateral thrusts of the dome are transferred to the outer wall by scrolled buttresses coiled like immense snails, and supporting statues that seem curiously unintegrated with the rest of the design. This charming though somewhat overelaborate central group forms a striking contrast to the chapels projecting from the outer wall, whose simple articulation is almost Renaissance in spirit. It contrasts, too, with the central portal, which exactly repeats the theme of the Roman triumphal arch and where the only baroque features are the deeply hollowed niches, the strong projection of the entablature and the crowning statues. (Facing page.)

a) LA SUPERGA, NEAR TURIN
1717–1731. Filippo Juvara.

Late Italian baroque and its first great exponent, Juvara, turned away from the turbulent and often tectonic style of the preceding period and once more looked for the serenity, ordered symmetry and restrained monumentality of the works of Palladio and his contemporaries. In this, his finest work, Juvara made a deliberate return to the principles of the High Renaissance. The great dome is directly inspired by that of St. Peter's. But despite its classicism — especially evident in the chaste simplicity of the portico — this imposing building, with its lateral projections and elaborate campanile flanking the soaring dome, basically remains a baroque conception.

b) S. IGNAZIO, ROME
Ceiling frescoes, 1685. Andrea del Pozzo.

During the Renaissance the ceilings of churches were still conceived as true space-enclosing elements. In the baroque era they became the means of suggesting an infinite extension of space. At S. Ignazio, dramatically foreshortened painted figures and architecture are made to give an illusion of another world opening above the actual interior. The handling of the perspective and the juncture with the building itself are so skillful that it is almost impossible to tell where reality ends and illusion begins.

c) S. MARTINO, NAPLES
c. 1650. Cosimo Fansaga.

This church, an example of the baroque architecture of southern Italy, is modeled on Il Gesù. Only the ostentation and exuberance of the decoration betray its late date.

a

b

c

a

b

c

d

THE CAPITOLINE MUSEUM, ROME
1534. After designs by Michelangelo.

Michelangelo's right to be called the Father of Baroque extends to architecture, for in the buildings he constructed and projected he introduced features that go beyond the Renaissance context to which they chronologically belong. In the Capitoline appeared — possibly for the first time — the giant pilasters embracing two stories that were to become one of the leitmotifs of baroque architecture. Their ascending movement is, however, contained by the heavy cornice in a way that is alien to baroque. It is interesting to note that the Capitoline Museum (unlike other palaces built at this period) is not isolated but is conceived as an integral part of a building group surrounding the Piazza Capitolina. The three other sides of the piazza are formed by the Palazzo del Senatore, the Palazzo dei Conservatori and a balustraded approach stairway. Here Michelangelo anticipates the baroque conception of building masses as a means of defining and limiting an open space. (Facing page.)

a) PALAZZO ODESCALCHI, ROME
Completed 1665. Bernini.

Bernini, the master of Roman baroque in its fullest development, here created the model for late seventeenth-century palaces. That balance of the various elements still evident in the storied treatment of the Capitoline Museum is now sacrificed. The ground story is dominated by the two upper stages, bound together by giant pilasters. Whereas Renaissance façades had been composed of a number of independent and well-balanced elements, the separate parts here lose their independence and are subordinated to certain emphasized features, to form a single unity. This unifying tendency is evident in the treatment of the cornice with its heavy consoles that carry the vertical lines of the pilasters up to the pedestals on the crowning balustrade.

b) PALAZZO BARBERINI, ROME
1629. Maderna, Borromini and Bernini.

A fine example of baroque palace layout. The building masses are not (as in the Renaissance) grouped around an interior courtyard but open freely onto an expansive court or garden. Here the front has short wings projecting forward on either side and acting as space-containing elements.

c) PALAZZO CARIGNANO, TURIN
Façade, 1680. Guarino Guarini.

This is a characteristic work of the Theatine monk Guarini, "The most baroque of all Italian architects" (Gurlitt). The central mass of the façade is emphasized by its tall crowning feature and by its rich, undulating rhythm of concave-convex-concave curves contrasting with straight wings. The elaborate curling window surrounds are remarkable for their affinity to German rococo.

d) VILLA ALBANI, ROME
Garden front, c. 1757. Carlo Marchioni.

This noble façade is an evidence of the classicizing tendency that entered into later baroque architecture.

THE DOME OF THE INVALIDES, PARIS
1680 – 1706. J. H. Mansard.

French baroque is characterized by a cold and restrained clarity. It has many classical features, while sharing with the baroque of other countries a taste for the colossal and for sculpturesque decoration. It represents a striving for the triumph of rationalism over emotional freedom and for purity of style over turbulent complexity. This type of architecture has much in common with that of Palladio and Juvara (page 333 a), which also displayed a strict regularity and calm grandeur of design. The Dome of the Invalides perhaps best illustrates these characteristics. The exterior of the structure — a Greek cross on plan — offers a contrast between the horizontals of the square two-storied substructure, with its Doric and Ionic orders, and the soaring cylinder of the drum — a contrast sharpened by the compactness and clear definition of these two main elements. A perfect balance between horizontals and verticals is maintained throughout the design. The interior (Fig. a), in the center of which Napoleon's tomb was placed in 1840, shows a severity of form and composition that far surpasses any Italian baroque achievement in classicism. (Facing page and Fig. a.)

b) CHAPEL OF THE PALACE OF VERSAILLES
Begun, J. H. Mansard; completed (1710), Robert de Cotte.

This two-storied interior follows the tradition of earlier palace chapels and has the same majestic classicism that signalizes the Dome of the Invalides.

c) VAL-DE-GRACE, PARIS
1645 – 1665. François Mansard, Lemercier and Le Duc.

Like the Dome of the Invalides for which it provided the inspiration, this is a domed centralized building with angled chapels and short arms forming a cross. Its prototype was S. Andrea della Valle in Rome, and the façade is an almost exact copy of the earlier front (page 330 b). A comparison between the architectural treatment of this drum and that of the Dome of the Invalides reveals that the principles of Italian baroque had not yet been abandoned for the more classical manner of the Invalides.

a

b

c

a

b

c

d

PALACE OF VERSAILLES
Garden front, 1661–1682, Le Vau and J. H. Mansard; gardens begun 1663, André le Nôtre.

A symbol of secular absolutism and the model for many other palaces (notably in Germany), Versailles was designed around the old hunting château erected for Louis XIII (from 1631) and now preserved within the architectural scheme of the *cour d'honneur* of the new palace (Fig. a). Vast wings were added to this nucleus in order to form a building over a quarter of a mile long. On the garden side opposite the *cour d'honneur*, Le Vau and Mansard built an imposing façade that clearly reveals its origin in Italian *palazzi*. The vigorously emphasized central block which dominates and unites the various elements of the design is characteristically baroque. Typical, too, is the manner in which the gardens are integrated with the main building and are conceived in relation to it. With their walks laid out in a simple geometrical pattern, their avenues, ornamental lakes and fountains and hosts of marble statues, they echo the reckless extravagance of the great palace. (Facing page and Fig. a.)

b) MAISONS-LAFFITTE
Courtyard, 1642–1651. François Mansard.

In many respects this symmetrically E-planned building is still close to Renaissance châteaux, particularly in the importance given to the roof and in the individual treatment of the different elements, especially at roof level. The clear separation of the stories, the absence of mezzanines and the use of superimposed orders instead of the single giant order (*cf.* Fig. c), also reflect the earlier style. On the other hand, the forward extension of the wings and the emphasis placed on the central projecting bays are baroque in spirit.

c) CHÂTEAU VAUX-LE-VICOMTE, NEAR MELUN
Garden front, 1643–1661. Louis Le Vau.

The general organization of its masses rather than its architectural detail makes this one of the most important of French mid-seventeenth-century buildings. The central pavilion is occupied by an oval chamber with a dome that dominates the exterior view. In the courtyard, a rectangular vestibule with staircases along the sides emphasizes the longitudinal axis of the building. The oval form of the principal room helps to delineate this axis, which here for the first time imposes itself on the succession of secondary rooms in a way that was later much imitated. The rooms are *en suite*, with the communicating doors in line on the axis of the principal room. The punctuation of the ends with pavilions is a motif frequently found in German baroque; at Vaux-le-Vicomte it has its origin in the corner towers of Renaissance châteaux.

d) THE LOUVRE, PARIS
East façade 1667, begun, Charles Perrault, after plans by Claude Perrault; completed, Napoleonic times.

This is perhaps the finest and purest example of classicizing French baroque architecture. The main story, with coupled giant Corinthian columns, is raised on a massive, smooth, podium-like ground floor. The central part and the two end motifs project slightly and with their solid walling provide a striking contrast to the freestanding columns between. The effect of the building as a whole is one of grandeur and studied elegance.

LE PETIT TRIANON, VERSAILLES
1762 – 1764. Jacques-Ange Gabriel.

From an architectural point of view, this little château (erected by Louis XV as a *maison de plaisance* for his mistress Madame du Barry) falls between two periods, being baroque in date but having much in common with the later Empire style. The taste for the picturesque and the decorative that prevailed in France during the late baroque or rococo period is no longer evident here, and the design is severe and clear cut, with a few restrained enrichments. Economy and clarity of form and firm, straight lines are the outstanding characteristics of this cube-shaped building. Even the giant order of attached Corinthian columns does little to disturb its compact, self-contained quality. (Facing page.)

INTERIORS

The interior ornamentation of baroque palaces is of an overwhelming splendor. Walls and ceilings are the background for a seemingly inexhaustible wealth of inventiveness of decoration and color. In early baroque, wall decoration comprises an equal balance of architectural articulation and free ornament (Fig. a). More and more emphasis is given to this applied decoration (Fig. b), which finally flows unhindered across walls and ceilings, and in the later (rococo) period completely triumphs over architectural detail (Fig. c). In the gradual development of interior decoration, the movement from baroque to rococo may thus be traced from a somewhat heavy and solemn magnificence toward an increasingly animated, playful profusion of detail. The three halls of mirrors shown here represent a type of palace apartment beloved by baroque designers. The large mirrors on the walls and doors serve the same purpose as the frescoes on the ceilings — to create an illusion of space continuing into infinity, so that the real and fictitious worlds become one.

a) PALACE OF VERSAILLES
   Gallerie des Glaces, 1678.

b) HÔTEL LA VRILLIÈRE, PARIS
   Gallery, 1719.

c) HÔTEL SOUBISE, PARIS
   Salon de la Princesse, c. 1730.

a

b

c

a

b

c

PLACE DE LA CONCORDE, PARIS
Begun 1753, J.-A. Gabriel; completed 1836.

The great elongated quadrilateral of the Place de la Concorde links the Champs Élysées and Tuileries Gardens. It is one of the finest baroque squares in Europe. The design as a whole is restrained and coherent and bears witness to eighteenth-century French rationalism and sober purity of style. Until 1753, the square was used as a store place for the material intended for the royal buildings of Paris. Then Louis XV expressed a desire to have his equestrian statue erected there and given a monumental setting (which the city was to build in his honor). Some twenty distinguished architects offered their services for this great enterprise. Finally the king commissioned Jacques-Ange Gabriel to undertake the work. Gabriel made use of the various projects that had been submitted in competition in his first designs for the square. Limited on its short sides to the south by the Seine and to the north by the Hôtel Crillon (left, illustration) and the Ministry of the Marine (the façades of which recall the east front of the Louvre), the Place de la Concorde is surrounded by balustrades (the original moats were later filled in) and enriched with allegorical statues on high pedestals and magnificent fountains along its main axis. It is famous as the scene of the execution of Louis XVI, Marie Antoinette, Madame du Barry and many others, and here, too, the Revolutionaries celebrated their bloody victories. The square is dominated by an obelisk 78 feet high, brought from the Temple of Luxor in Egypt and erected (in 1836 by order of Louis-Philippe) on the spot chosen by Gabriel for the equestrian statue of Louis XV, which was destroyed during the Revolution. (Facing page.)   *(Photo Jeanine Niepce)*

a) HÔTEL MATIGNON, PARIS
1721. Courtonne.

This is one of the relatively rare examples of French baroque where the light and graceful articulation (foreshadowing rococo), usually reserved for interior decoration, has been applied to the exterior structure.   *(Photo Payes de France)*

b) ÉCOLE MILITAIRE, PARIS
Cour d'honneur and central pavilion, 1725–1769. J.-A. Gabriel.

This strictly classical manner — particularly noticeable in the temple-like design of the central pavilion — anticipates the historicism of the late eighteenth and early nineteenth centuries.
                    (Photo Hachette)

c) HÔTEL DE LA MONNAIE, PARIS
1768–1775. Jacques Denis Antoine.

Vast, austere and coherent in design, this building is a magnificent example of the first phase of French neoclassicism and inspired many works of this period. Clarity and simple grandeur now take the place of the picturesque effects sought by baroque architects through a profusion of rich detail.   *(Photo Hachette)*

ABBEY CHURCH OF OTTOBEUREN
1737–1766. J. M. Fischer.

Ottobeuren is one of a group of churches (Upper Swabia and Switzerland) that adopted what is known as the Vorarlberg scheme — so called because all the architects, many of whom were related, came from Bregenz, the capital of this region. The type of interior they created is not entirely new but derives from Il Gesù or from St. Michael in Munich. The containing walls are reduced to a series of massive piers with engaged columns and pilasters between which are galleried chapel recesses rising to the full height so that the entablature follows the outline of the plan. Thus, as in a hall church, the barriers between the spatial compartments are broken down and the main nave and the side niches meet and interpenetrate. This spatial complexity is typical of baroque architecture in its highest development. The riot of stuccoed and painted decoration plays a vital part in the composition, serving to soften the transitions between the compartments. (Facing page.)

a) MONASTERY CHURCH OF ST. GALL
Switzerland, 1755–1767. Bagnato, J. M. Thumb and Fr. Beer.

This is a variant of the Vorarlberg type. The piers are no longer closely bound to the outer wall and there are no galleries. The choir (Fig. a) and the nave, each with three bays, form — with the aisles — an undulating sequence of spatial elements grouped around a central area surmounted by a magnificent saucer dome.

b) PILGRIMAGE CHURCH OF THE VIERZEHNHEILIGEN
Franconia, 1743–1772. J. Balthasar Neumann.

This church illustrates to perfection the rococo concept of interior space as a complicated, undulating, interpenetrating sequence of spatial shapes. The nave consists of two ellipses: the first, immediately beyond the entrance façade, is the same size as the choir, which is also an ellipse; the second, considerably larger, is occupied by the great shrine of the fourteen saints. These ellipses are not isolated elements but interact and are welded together by other ellipses with long axes lying transversely so as to allow the longitudinal vaults to meet in the center and the small transverse vaults to remain visible. The wall piers carrying the vaults enclose the nave in a series of undulating curves beyond which is an ambulatory.

c) ABBEY CHURCH OF WIBLINGEN
1772–1781. Specht and J. Zick.

This interior shows an unmistakable tendency toward classical severity. Late baroque profusion of details and decoration and rich color effects have given way to a somewhat stark and soulless design with an unsatisfactory mixture of classical detail and late baroque features.

a

b

c

a

b

c

PILGRIMAGE CHURCH OF WIES
Choir tribune, 1746–1754. Dominikus Zimmermann.

In this church, as in the Frauenkirche at Günzburg (1735–1740), Zimmermann has given an extended choir a two-storied ambulatory, thus creating a curtain of light behind the arcades around the altar, which now lose their enclosing, space-defining character and take on the appearance of a baldachino. As in all German architecture of the late baroque or rococo period, the light has become an essential element in the composition. It plays on the scagliola columns and enhances their pastel shades; it sparkles and glistens on the gold of the trelliswork, on the capitals and the fantastic *rocaille* ornament; and flows through the undulating window openings onto the white figures of the saints in postures of ecstasy and rapture and onto the hovering *putti* and angels, so that they emerge from the shadows of their columns and seem to approach the altar. The turbulent forms and effervescing decoration, enhanced by light, transform the choir into a magic world where nothing is at rest. (Facing page.)

a) PILGRIMAGE CHURCH OF WIES
1746–1754. Dominikus Zimmermann.

Eight pairs of freestanding pillars with richly modeled entablatures are set in the large central ellipse of the interior. They rise, luminous in their blinding whiteness, to support the timber-framed saucer dome above spacious arcades. Together with this vault (on which the architect's brother, J. B. Zimmermann, painted the splendors of the heavenly regions in iridescent colors), they convey—like the arcades in the choir—the effect of a great baldachino. They help to elaborate the spatial impression, as does the ornamentation running riot over the moldings, cornices, wall surfaces and arches, and the openings—with their undulating contours—which constantly break the surface of the outer wall.

b) ABBEY CHURCH OF WELTENBURG
1717–1721. Cosmas Damian and Egid Quirin Asam.

Here architecture, sculpture, color and light combine to produce an interior of sensational effect. The nave, an ellipse with altar niches, is covered by a dome open toward the top to reveal a second dome decorated with frescoes. Because its support is hidden, this second dome seems to float in mid-air and—with its frescoes lit by windows invisible from below—to be part of another world. The choir repeats this idea; into the darkness of its oval rides a silver St. George on horseback against a background of dazzling light coming from concealed windows, while high above the altar, saints stand silhouetted against the same golden, unearthly light.

c) CHAPEL OF ST. JOHN NEPOMUK, MUNICH
1732–1733. The Brothers Asam.

Once more, in this tiny chapel—unusually narrow in relation to its height—every imaginable device has been used to create an unreal and marvelous effect. Everything is in motion. The gallery curves forward and back, the cornice rises and falls, the columns around the gallery altar twist and writhe and seem to deny their own solidity. Ornament froths and sparkles everywhere, and angels hover weightlessly, as though in mid-flight. As at Weltenburg, the ceiling is transformed into a heavenly world against which the Trinity appears in a magical flood of light from a concealed source.

The external richness and magnificence of baroque churches are concentrated on their façades, which may be divided into two main types: first, those modeled on Il Gesù in Rome (page 304 c) and the buildings that immediately followed it, where an important central block is flanked by two smaller side pieces; second, the twin-towered type that kept closer to national tradition. The examples shown here demonstrate that the characteristics already observed in baroque church interiors equally apply to the exteriors. Here, too, architects strove for complexity and elaboration with rich modeling and complicated spatial and structural relationships. Here, too, an effect of dynamic rhythm is achieved with the curves and counter-curves of pediments, cornices and hollowed-out surfaces. Most baroque churches of the twin-towered type are attached to large monasteries where they form a majestic culminating feature (Fig. e).

Facing page:
ABBEY CHURCH OF OTTOBEUREN
Before 1766. J. M. Fischer.

a) NEUMÜNSTER, WÜRZBURG
   After 1725. J. Balthasar Neumann.

b) ST. NIKOLAUS, PRAGUE
   Before 1751. Chr. and K. I. Dientzenhofer.

c) PILGRIMAGE CHURCH OF THE
   VIERZEHNHEILIGEN
   Before 1772. J. Balthasar Neumann.

d) ABBEY CHURCH OF GRÜSSAU
   Silesia. Façade, 1728–1735. School of Dientzenhofer.

e) BENEDICTINE ABBEY OF MELK
   Austria, 1702–1736. Jakob Prandtauer.

a

b

c/d

e

a

b

c

RESIDENZ, WÜRZBURG
Garden front, 1720–1744. J. Balthasar Neumann.

The Würzburg Residenz rivals the Palace of Versailles in magnificence and is comparable to it in style if not in scale. The various blocks that comprise the great scheme are arranged around five courts, with the principal court (like the *cour d'honneur* at Versailles) open on one side. The rooms on the garden front are *en suite,* and the façade is punctuated with a powerful projecting central block and delicate end pavilions. (Facing page.)

a) UPPER BELVEDERE, VIENNA
Garden front, 1714–1749. Lucas von Hildebrandt.

The special charm of this palace, surrounded by gardens and built for Prince Eugene of Savoy, lies in the original handling of the roof line which descends in stepped stages from the tall central block to the octagonal angle pavilions. The articulation of the façade recalls that of Würzburg (facing page), although the end motifs now project as towerlike pavilions. The gardens, laid out in terraces and ornamented with fountains, form a magnificent prelude to the palace itself.

b) DAUN-KINSKY PALACE, VIENNA
Façade, 1713–1716. Lucas von Hildebrandt.

The three central bays of this façade are remarkable for the dramatic emphasis placed on the supporting function of the verticals. The two inner columns flanking the portal have become atlantes, their heads bent and arms raised to receive the weight of the entablature. The giant pilasters broaden toward the top, and their upward thrust is continued through the consoles, ornamented with masks under the cornice, to the statues on the roof balustrade. Despite its stylistic caprice, this façade betrays its origin in Italian prototypes (page 334 a).

c) PALACE AT MÜNSTER (WESTPHALIA)
Central pavilion, town front, c. 1756. Schlaun.

The three central bays, with their great pediment, swell out between narrow concave bays on either side. The plastic effect of the giant order embracing the two upper stories is accentuated by the use of attached half columns superimposed on pilasters. Effective, too, is the color contrast between the light, free stone used for the architectural details and the red brick of the intervening wall surfaces.

PAVILION, DRESDEN ZWINGER
1711–1722, M. Daniel Pöppelmann; sculptured decoration,
B. Permoser.

Built for Augustus the Strong, Elector of Saxony, this pavilion was originally intended to form part of a vast palace that was to have equaled Versailles and surpassed the extravagance of Würzburg. The Zwinger itself was conceived as a court surrounded by an orangery and grandstand for tournaments and pageants, and was no more than a permanent version of the wooden grandstands often erected for the duration of some important festivity. The short sides of the rectangular court open out in semicircles, and the surrounding flat-roofed, single-storied galleries — comparatively restrained in design — are dominated by two-storied pavilions lavish with decoration. The pavilion is the finest of the group and is perhaps the most characteristic achievement of all German late baroque architecture. The ground-floor room of the oval structure presents a fantastic complex of openings, piers and curving staircases. The upper story served the royal party as a retiring room. The exterior effect is of an astonishing exuberance and variety, and the very stone is brought to joyous life with coats of arms, masks, statues, scrolls and vases. The pilasters of the ground floor are transformed into hermae, and the cornices spring forward and back as the broken pediments rise and fall in a turbulent rhythm. (Facing page.)

a) AMALIENBURG, PARK OF NYMPHENBURG PALACE, NEAR MUNICH
1734 – 1739. François Cuvillies.

Maisons de plaisance were a favorite luxury during the baroque era. They were usually built (like this one) in some remote corner of the great palace parks, to serve kings and princes as places of relaxation and private enjoyment. Although such buildings lack the architectural nobility of the palaces, they often provide evidence of an acute artistic sensibility.

b) SCHLOSS SOLITUDE, NEAR STUTTGART
1763 – 1767. De la Guepière.

This single-storied building is raised on a high arcaded basement that served as a stable and coach house. On each of the long sides of the palace, curving double staircases lead up to the surrounding terrace. The large oval domed central pavilion projects on both sides, giving power and pleasing variety to the composition. The striking severity and masculinity of this design furnish the clue to the architect's nationality. De la Guepière represents the later phase of French baroque, which was returning to strict regularity and clarity of design, heralding the neoclassicism of the late eighteenth century.

c) SANS SOUCI PALACE, NEAR POTSDAM
1745 – 1747. W. von Knobelsdorff.

This architecture is simple and coherent, although the magnificent hermae place this palace nearer to the baroque in spirit than to the classicism of the previous example.

a

b

c

a

b

c

Staircases are among the finest achievements of baroque palace architecture, often surpassing the great state rooms in richness and architectural splendor. The fullest advantage was taken of their spatial possibilities. The simplest solution — that of filling the space between the floors with a straight, uninterrupted flight, like a vaulted corridor set at an angle — could not satisfy baroque architects, who saw the staircase as a means of allowing the prince and his court to make a splendid and triumphant entry into the palace. Various systems and enrichments were brought into play. Balthasar Neumann, whose staircases are among the finest and most grandiose, begins those at Würzburg and Brühl with a short straight flight followed by a landing, then turns the staircase 180 degrees and continues the ascending movement in two parallel, flanking flights, enriching the scheme with a gallery around the wall above. The staircase is thus allowed to develop freely in space. (Facing page and Fig. a.) In other types of baroque staircase, lavish decoration also echoes the magnificence of the conception (Figs b, c).

Facing page:
AUGUSTUSBURG, BRÜHL
Staircase, 1744–1748. J. Balthasar Neumann.

a) BISHOP'S PALACE, WÜRZBURG
Staircase, 1737–1744, J. Balthasar Neumann; statues and decoration, 1752–1765.

b) SCHLOSS WEISSENSTEIN, POMMERSFELDEN
Staircase, 1713–1714. Johann Dientzenhofer.

c) SCHLOSS MIRABELL, SALZBURG
Staircase, 1724–1725. Lucas von Hildebrandt.

German architects of the late baroque or rococo phase developed a type of interior decoration that is unique in richness of invention. True, the kind of ornament they used was dependent on motifs invented by French artists (namely the *rocaille* that gives rococo its name), but the relative severity and restraint of French ornament is rarely found in Germany (*cf.* page 341 c). Although symmetry is not abandoned altogether, it is disguised by so complicated a profusion of forms that no clear pattern is visible to the eye assaulted by the giddy rhythm of curling, swaying, sinking detail. This effect is best appreciated in the small mirrored chambers (facing page and Figs. b, c) where the complexity of the ornament is reproduced into infinity in reflecting surfaces. As is to be expected, such exuberance is less apparent in the great state rooms, where the composition is governed by a framework of architectural forms that control, though by no means overwhelm, the decorative detail.

Facing page:
AMALIENBURG, PARK OF THE NYMPHENBURG PALACE, NEAR MUNICH
Hall of mirrors c. 1739. Stuccowork, J. B. Zimmermann; wood carving, J. Dietrich.

a) RESIDENZ, WÜRZBURG
Salon, 1744, J. Balthasar Neumann; frescoes, 1752, J. B. Tiepolo.

b) RESIDENZ, MUNICH
Chamber, c. 1736, F. Cuvillies; decoration, French and German artists.

c) SANS SOUCI PALACE, NEAR POTSDAM
Library decoration, 1746. After designs by J. Aug. Nahl.

a

b

c

a

b

c

CHARTERHOUSE, GRANADA
Sacristy, 1727–1764. F. Manuel Vasquez.

Spanish baroque, which had cultivated a severe classicism during the first half of the seventeenth century, developed with marked originality during the later period. From a fusion of the late Gothic *estilo plateresco* (page 285) and Italian high baroque, was created a style comparable with German rococo in ornamental display and called Churrigueresque (after its chief exponent, José Churriguera, 1650–1723). The sacristy of the charterhouse at Granada is a characteristic example of this style. The walls are piled with complex moldings, scrolls and cornices that roll across the surfaces, independent of the basic structural details — clear evidence that Churrigueresque is essentially a decorative and not an architectural style. (Facing page.)

a) MAURITSHUIS, THE HAGUE
1633–1644. Pieter Post.

Holland was slow to adopt the early baroque style and contributed little to its development. The Mauritshuis is of a simple classicism and owes much of its charm to the contrast between the stone of the architectural details and the plain brick of the intervening wall surfaces.

b) MANSION HOUSE, LONDON
1739–1753. George Dance the Elder.

c) BLENHEIM PALACE, OXFORDSHIRE
Begun 1715. Sir John Vanbrugh.

A classical manner similar to that of France and dependent on the strict principles of Palladio was maintained in England during the baroque period (Figs. b, c). The façade of Blenheim typifies English taste for compact massing. The close spacing of the vertical elements is also characteristically English.

One of the most important preoccupations of the baroque age was with the spaces in which buildings were set. Palaces overlooked wide piazzas; churches were often designed as the central culminating point of vast monastic projects or (instead of being hemmed in on all sides by other buildings, as in the Middle Ages) were conceived as the dominant feature of large squares designed to offset their splendor and defined with colonnades (facing page and Fig. a) or flights of steps (Fig. b). Sometimes, particularly in Italy, the piazza itself received an architectural enrichment with elaborate fountains of which the magnificent Trevi Fountain in Rome (Fig. c) is an outstanding example.

Facing page:
ST. PETER'S PIAZZA, ROME
Colonnade, 1656–1663. Bernini.

a) PLACE STANISLAUS, NANCY
   1753–1755. Here de Corny.

b) SPANISH STEPS, ROME
   Seventeenth century.

c) TREVI FOUNTAIN, ROME
   1735–1762. Niccolò Salvi.

a

b

c

XI

ARCHITECTURE DURING THE LATE EIGHTEENTH AND NINETEENTH CENTURIES

General Background

The French Revolution, which marked the beginning of a new era in the history of the West, was the political manifestation of a spirit of change that had made itself felt several decades earlier. The driving forces behind this reorientation had been the bourgeoisie, who were gradually replacing the two great powers of the baroque period—the Church and the nobility—in the forefront of moral and social development. The period leading up to the revolution had been one of great social, ethical and religious upheavals, of radical changes in man's conception of life and of religion.

During the early eighteenth century, secular absolutism had degenerated into a total disregard for human dignity and had brought with it a corresponding decline in moral behavior. In the eyes of the ruling class, burghers and peasants were mere chattels. Augustus the Strong, Duke of Saxony, gave whole regiments in exchange for a service of porcelain; Karl Eugen, Duke of Württemberg, sold legions of his fellow countrymen to England in order to maintain his court of 1,800 persons and to indulge his ostentation and passion for building on a colossal scale. Self-indulgence and reckless extravagance brought in their wake an indescribable extreme of moral decadence among court and official circles. Diplomacy was often founded on the whims and self-interested demands of powerful mistresses (of whom Madame Pompadour was only one of the most famous), and court intrigues were rife. It is scarcely surprising that social relations rapidly deteriorated in every country. The misery endured by the masses, increased year by year by a succession of futile wars, fanned the flames of bitterness and hatred against the ruling class.

The people were to rise up, not only against the profligacy and tyranny of the court, but against the art and architecture that was being created in its service and that mirrored its decadence. The royal palaces, symbols of arrogance and luxury, seemed to be the quintessence of all that was most intolerable — the scenes of the shameless squandering of taxes extorted from the people by the most questionable and merciless of means. Designed in the late baroque and rococo styles, these palaces could only be seen as the reflection of court life, and these styles themselves became the object of scorn and disgust. The Louis XV or rococo style mirrored the spirit of the age with patent truth, though using the same forms that had served to evoke a spiritual response in churches. The playful elegance of *rocaille* ornament — the lightness and sensuous abandon with which it curls and froths over walls and ceilings, glittering and sparkling like a fireworks display — was taken to be a flagrant symbol of the gay abandon and unbridled voluptuousness of the lives of the aristocracy — a symbol that found an exact musical counterpart in the minuet and the gavotte.

It was inevitable that this age of license and outmoded conventions should have been cast aside as soon as the third estate was able to sweep away the privileges of the aristocracy. The rise to power of the bourgeoisie first took effect in France, and in the following decades the machinery of revolution was set in motion in other countries of Europe still in the grip of absolutist regimes. In the words of Frederick the Great, kings became no more than the first servants and citizens of the State.

The outburst of the third estate was directed against the Church as well as the nobility. Here it was not so much political power that was challenged, but the restrictions on thought imposed by medieval theology. The weapons taken up against the narrowness and restraints of dogma and the arguments in favor of freedom of religious thought were those of the intellectual movement of the Enlightenment. This might be described as the struggle, based on rationalist thought, to establish the right of human reason "to follow its own path, regardless of the separate teachings of the various Churches, and to regulate life according to rational judgment" (Koch). The Christian faith was submitted to the harsh light of criticism founded on new scientific knowledge and on the principles of the English empirical philosophy which had been publicized in the 35-volume *Encyclopédie* of Diderot and Alembert, a collection of lucid and learned articles on all aspects of knowledge. God was still acknowledged as Creator of the world, but the idea that men's lives and thoughts were directly governed by Him was no longer acceptable. Works of art created for the glorification of the Christian faith were seen as products of superstition. Many churches were destroyed in the course of the French Revolution, and statues of saints were cast down from the portals and façades of Gothic cathedrals. At Notre Dame, a figure of the Virgin was replaced with a statue of Reason, goddess of the enlightened iconoclasts.

In view of the political and social happenings of the nineteenth and twentieth centuries, it is hardly necessary to show that the bourgeois revolution and its aftermath (which continues into modern times) brought neither universal peace nor ushered in a golden age. True, belief in progress found ample justification in the rapid strides made in the sciences, commerce and technology during this period. Political revolution was followed, in the nineteenth century, by the first industrial revolution, which transformed the conditions of economic life in Europe. The forces of Nature were mastered by the forces of Reason, and their innermost secrets laid bare by science. Technologists invented machines to harness first steam and then electricity to the practical needs of mankind. Undreamed of possibilities lay waiting to be explored. The advances of medicine revolutionized hygiene, and this — together with triumphs in technology and agriculture — was to contribute to a vast increase in the population of Europe. But these successes, brilliant as they were, were dearly bought and engendered new problems, chief among which were those that arose with the emergence of a new element in society — the industrial worker — problems that today still await a satisfactory solution.

The gravest consequence of the new development was the loss of a basis of common understanding out of which all intellectual activity could grow. Throughout the Middle Ages and even to a lesser degree during the Renaissance and baroque periods, Christianity had provided this basis. But the Enlightenment had undermined its doctrines, and all the substitute philosophies such as nationalism, communism and other isms subsequently offered, were to prove unconvincing.

During the turbulent decades of the last half of the eighteenth century, men looked back to ancient Greece and Rome and discovered the source of the doctrine of the rights of man. Antiquity was seen as an intellectual, artistic and social ideal that again had to be attained if the despised conventions of the modern age were ever to be overthrown. The words of the French painter David, spoken in 1784 — five years before the outbreak of the Revolution: "Morals, literature and art must be transformed by the study of antiquity," are a measure of the deep conviction with which men pursued the new-found goal.

Architectural Character

NEOCLASSICISM

The upsurge of idealism based on the antique way of life and thought was to have a profound effect on architecture. The buildings of antiquity began to attract the interest of all cultured men and awakened a passion for literal imitation no less enthusiastic but more slavish in spirit than that of the Renaissance. While the excavation (1711) of Herculaneum, buried beneath the volcanic ash of Vesuvius in 79 A. D., awoke little enthusiasm at the time, the discovery of the nearby town of Pompeii (1748) became the object of world-wide interest. Artists and scholars from all countries made pilgrimages to see the excavations. The ruins of ancient buildings in Italy, Greece and even Syria, were sought out, measured and described with passionate zeal, and their manifest simplicity and dignity were held up in damning contrast to the outrageous affectations and meaningless extravagance of much of late baroque architecture.

Innumerable books and folios made the new discoveries available to a wide public. Foremost among them were Piranesi's *Vedute di Roma,* published in 1748, followed by his *Antichità Romane* in 1756 — two comprehensive collections of plates of Roman buildings; in 1750, the Englishmen James Dawkins and Robert Wood brought out *Illustrations of Palmyra and Baalbek;* in 1757, Robert Adam published the results of his research at the remains of Diocletian's Palace at Spalato; and in 1762 followed the most important work of all, James Stuart and Nicholas Revett's *Antiquities of Athens.* The illustrations and texts of such publications, while adding greatly to the general interest and knowledge, did not approach the degree of authenticity and objective evaluation expected in modern research. But in an age preoccupied with the past as much as with the future, they mark the beginning

of the development of two new fields of study — archeology and the history of art.

The true originator of modern art criticism was Johann Joachim Winckelmann (1717–1768), whose first book, *Thoughts on the Imitation of Greek Works of Art in Painting and Sculpture,* appeared in 1755 and was enthusiastically received. His classic work, *The History of Ancient Art,* was published in 1764. Here for the first time Greek art was considered apart from its archeological aspect and was subjected to esthetic and historical analysis. In this book, Winckelmann laid the foundations of a totally new concept of art that was to color the whole nineteenth century and remains valid today. At any period before the eighteenth century, whatever had been the prevailing architectural style and esthetic principles of the time were accepted without question as absolute – as the only true form of expression. Whenever (as in the Carolingian or Renaissance eras) there had been a return to antique principles, it was precisely because these principles were believed to have an absolute and timeless value. But the art of antiquity no longer represented absolute perfection, nor was it seen as the only expression worthy of imitation, but as one style among many that had developed out of certain prevailing conditions and that — like all other styles — was the inevitable expression of those conditions. Judgment and appreciation of different styles no longer depended on a standard of values common to all men but varied according to the tastes and preferences of the individual. Each man was free to interpret a work of art, to praise or condemn according to his own inclination.

Until the beginning of the nineteenth century, the belief in the absolute value of a chosen ideal was still widely held, and this ideal — in art as in everyday life — was antiquity. The return to the classical past was not always achieved by literal copying of prototypes. It should be described rather as a return to the classicism of Late Renaissance architecture, as exemplified by the style of Palladio. From the mid-eighteenth century on, enthusiasm quickened as more and more was learned of the classical heritage. A desire for order, tranquillity and greater clarity of design to replace the fantasies of rococo was manifest everywhere. The classical revival (led by Robert Adam, 1728–1792) began in England which throughout the sixteenth and seventeenth centuries had remained closer to Palladian standards than had France, Germany (especially the Roman Catholic south) and Spain. From Britain, the movement spread to Germany, and in France — where strong classicizing tendencies had been perceptible throughout the baroque period — architects also rediscovered the strict principles of Vitruvius and Palladio—as shown in St. Sulpice (page 370a) and the Pantheon (page 370b, c). The Petit Trianon (pages 340 and 341) reveals that even court architecture did not remain immune from the new developments.

Austere and simple as these buildings were, several architects rejected such classicizing columnar architecture as being still too ostentatious in character, and strove for even greater severity and gravity of design. For example, Ledoux (1736–1806) and Boullée (1728—1799) in France, and later Friedrich Gilly (1772–1800) in Germany, took the simplest geometrical shapes—the cube, the sphere, the pyramid—as the basis for their work, seeming to anticipate many of the ideas of twentieth-century architects who (like Corbusier) once again base their designs on the most elementary of forms. But the grandeur and monumentality of their projects—their conception of their work as something enduring, as a concrete and eternally valid expression of the golden age that was to come or was believed to have already arrived—was to find no response among their successors. None of their major projects was ever carried out, although the few smaller works that were realized illustrate the tendency to return to simple geometrical forms.

Why architects such as Ledoux, Boullée and Gilly were forgotten during the nineteenth century is to be explained by the fact that the bourgeoisie, so recently risen to power, were intellectually incapable of fostering a new philosophy which (like Christianity in the Middle Ages) could find expression in an original architectural style. The first and essentially materialistic preoccupation of the bourgeoisie was with the reorientation of society. Men no longer sought in art a unique symbol of their own society or felt bound by one accepted rule of taste. The associational values of the individual were the only remaining guides by which to judge architecture, and styles were borrowed from the past whenever they seemed to correspond to the ideals of the revolutionary age. Hence the eclecticism of the nineteenth century—preventing an original interpretation of the old styles and resulting in the literal imitation of their forms and principles.

ECLECTICISM

At first, the dominant theme of the eclectic movement of the nineteenth century was the architecture of classical antiquity. In France, after the revolution, it was recognized as: "The voice of reason and virtue, expressing the austere and noble spirit of the ancient Romans" (Pauli). During the reign of Napoleon the classical revival came to mean

—in the so-called Empire style—the literal copying of antiquity approached from the viewpoint of archeology. This new classicism—characterized by historical exactitude rather than by genuine creativity—spread across the whole of Europe and even reached America. To an increasing extent, it was a return to the Greek antiquity in which historians had discovered the origins of Roman architecture. As Winckelmann wrote: "The springs of art are tapped and to find them means going to Athens."

Neo-Gothic came into being in England at about the same time, and buildings in the medieval manner sprang up beside others in the classical idiom. The Gothic revival in architecture was one of the consequences of the romantic movement, which also had its beginnings in England and which was characterized by the substitution of the cult of sensibility and emotions for the rationalism of the Enlightenment. The romantics aimed to achieve a reawakening of the medieval world by going back to native sources and architectural styles. The movement lasted for the whole of the nineteenth century, although by mid-century its vigor already was declining. Castles, associated closely with romantic ideas of medieval chivalry, were enthusiastically restored; uncompleted Gothic cathedrals (Cologne and Ulm, for instance) were finished with an astonishing degree of archeological exactitude, either with the aid of rediscovered original plans or simply by means of precise historical research; and as more and more municipal buildings and churches were needed to meet the demands of the sudden and immense development of cities, they, too, were built in imitation of the past.

Gothic was not the only style to be used as a model. It was not long before architects also turned to the Early Christian basilica (Church of St. Boniface, Munich, page 374a), to Romanesque (Gnadenkirche, Berlin, page 374b) and even to Byzantine forms (Sacré-Coeur, Paris). That these styles were preferred for churches was precisely because research had shown them to have originally been conceived for ecclesiastical purposes and to be thus best suited to suggest a building's function as a church.

Secular buildings commissioned by private citizens, states or municipalities, continued to be designed in the Greek style for some time, and several distinct stages are perceptible in the development of this type of architecture through the nineteenth century. The earliest Neo-Greek works (among them Schinkel's Theatre in Berlin, 1818–1821) show the use of the oldest and most severe Greek architectural style—the Doric (page 373b). At the Old Museum, Berlin (built 1824–1828 by the same architect), the more graceful, slender Ionic order is employed (page 373a). Later on, Corinthian columns make an occasional appearance and many examples of about 1850 show the richer forms of the Renaissance architecture of Palladio superseding the antique as a model. Finally, at the end of the century, the splendor and extravagance of baroque forms became the inspiration for buildings like the Opéra, Paris (Garnier, page 376), and the Bourse, Brussels (Suys, page 377 b).

This pseudo-evolution may well be due to the spontaneous tendency of all art forms to progress from clarity, severity and simplicity toward complication, richness and variety. Be that as it may, it is true that nineteenth-century architecture as a whole was an architecture of eclecticism and that no true style emerged during this period. None of the resurrected idioms ever took root or was the starting point for an original and creative development. In this respect, the nineteenth century may be contrasted with the Carolingian and Renaissance periods, when architects had also turned to antiquity but had recognized in their borrowings a spiritual affinity with their own values and the underlying presence of an esthetic sensibility that had grown out of a conception of life and art similar to their own. Not only the superficial forms but the whole outlook of antiquity had been regarded as worthy of imitation and as having an absolute value. Imitation of past styles during the age of eclecticism was merely a question of good taste, a means of clothing certain sentiments and esthetic conceptions in a mantle of received forms for which history had already provided the necessary justification. This is not to say that the works of Schinkel, Semper, Kleuze, Sir George Gilbert Scott, Barry, Chalgrin and other masters of the period are not in themselves distinguished and scholarly achievements and of lasting value, but the fact remains that they lack true originality and liveliness. The borrowed forms were not organically related to structure, whereas in former times each architectural type had been given its own characteristic form. Now museums and churches, banks and theatres, railway stations and factories, might resemble one another so closely as to be indistinguishable from the outside.

The architectural confusion caused by such reckless borrowing was soon to become apparent. In 1834, Gottfried Semper wrote: "The young architect travels across the world, stuffs his folder with sketches of every kind, and goes confidently home again in the happy expectation that there will soon be orders for a memorial hall à la Parthenon, a basilica à la Monreale, a boudoir à la Pompeii, a palace à la Pitti, a Byzantine church or a bazaar in the Turkish style." Heinrich Hübsch denounced neoclassicism as the "style of lies," and called for "truth" as the fundamental requirement in architectural design. In 1850, Théophile Gautier was expressing an opinion shared by many men of his time and one which was eventually to lead architecture out of the bondage of historicism when he wrote: "At that instant, when man makes use of the new materials that modern industry can supply, a new architecture will be born."

But these new materials—iron and steel, reinforced concrete and plate glass—were little used by architects before the twentieth century. The needs of commerce and industry—two of the driving forces behind architectural development today—were mainly served by engineers whose standards were strictly utilitarian, while architects would design buildings such as banks and shops in one or another of the period styles. The great patrons of the nineteenth century came from the bourgeoisie, self-made men of the new aristocracy of wealth, living by and for commerce and industry. Their sole requirement of art was that it should suitably express their power and social status. Thus architects continued to produce buildings in period styles for a society which lacked the underlying idealism necessary for the creation of an original artistic idiom. Artists themselves were conscious of this failing, and Semper wrote: "Let mankind first formulate a new philosophy: we shall soon find the means of recording it in our architecture. Meanwhile let us rest content with the past."

At the end of the nineteenth century, architecture was thus divided into two camps. In one was the recognized, fashionable architecture of an eclecticism, now grown flat and soulless and for the most part only reluctantly maintained by the architects themselves in answer to popular demand. Iron and reinforced concrete were already being employed in construction but were masked externally by a conventional shell. Architectural ornament based on ancient precedent was mass produced by machine in shameless imitation of true handicraft. On the other side was the industrial building of the engineers, starkly simple, utilitarian and without esthetic pretensions but having the inestimable advantage of structural truth. Ignored by architects, the engineers worked on unhampered, discovering new possibilities and unexpected sources of beauty, acquiring, too, that feeling for the peculiar qualities and characteristics of building materials which was to play so important a part in the architecture of the future.

Only when architects came to study the ideas of engineers and to work on similar lines and when a reconciliation had been achieved between craftsman and machine, was this dilemma resolved and did a true architectural style responsive to the modern age evolve.

ARCHITECTURE DURING THE LATE EIGHTEENTH AND NINETEENTH CENTURIES

ILLUSTRATIONS

a

b

c

d

The word classicism does not, like Renaissance or Gothic, denote a specific phase of architectural development. It means, rather, a confidence in the power of the classical principles as laid down by Vitruvius and Palladio, expressed through a strict application of supposedly authentic antique forms. That classicism in architecture need not mean mere copyism is shown by the Renaissance movement and by baroque in France and England, which were eminently classical if by this is understood clarity, ordered proportions and economy of form. It was not until toward the end of the eighteenth century and more especially at the beginning of the nineteenth that the word classicism took on another meaning when architects began to by-pass the Renaissance and to approach Greek and Roman antiquities directly, copying them literally whenever the occasion allowed. Thus the classicism of the examples shown here may be described as an exercise in historical re-creation rather than as part of an organic development. It was the deliberate transplantation of classical forms and principles in their purest state — an expression of a new and academic veneration for the classical past. This enthusiasm for buildings in the antique manner led to plagiarism and was responsible for the lack of vitality in many neoclassical works which are "more contrived than inspired" (Viollet-le-Duc). When buildings that are nonclassical in plan and mass are dressed in classical forms, a dryness and dullness of effect may too easily result.

MONASTERY CHURCH OF ST. BLASIEN
1768 – 1783. Ixnard.

This French architect took the Pantheon in Rome as his model for this impressive domed church. The drum conceals the fact that internally the dome rests directly on the circular entablature of the substructure, just as it does in the Roman prototype (pages 72 and 73). Two towers, austere and somewhat lifeless in design, flank a strictly classical Doric portico. (Facing page.)

a) ST. SULPICE, PARIS
Façade, 1733. Servandoni.

This famous façade is a measure of the extent to which strict classicism had already taken hold in France during the first half of the eighteenth century.

b,c) THE PANTHEON, PARIS
1764 – 1781. J. G. Soufflot.

This is the masterpiece of the early French classical revival. A temple front leads into the main building, which is a Greek cross on plan and has a geometrical clarity of design that embraces the ornamental detail as well as the general form.

d) LA MADELEINE, PARIS
Completed 1824. Barthélemy Vignon.

This neoclassical monument was begun by order of Napoleon as a Hall of Fame and later converted into a church consecrated to St. Mary Magdalen. It is designed in imitation of a Greek peripteral temple. The podium follows Roman precedent.

By the early nineteenth century, churches and palaces no longer provided the main opportunities for architectural activity, the religious faith and political absolutism that they symbolized having lost their former importance in society. Now museums and galleries (the characteristic institutions of the nineteenth century) to house collections of works of art for the benefit of the public, theatres, memorial halls, triumphal arches and other public buildings, were the new subjects for the architect.

Facing page:
BRITISH MUSEUM, LONDON
Begun 1823. Sir Robert Smirke.

a) ALTES MUSEUM, BERLIN
   1824–1828. Karl Friedrich Schinkel.

b) SCHAUSPIELHAUS, BERLIN
   1818–1821. Karl Friedrich Schinkel.

c) THE PROPYLAEA, MUNICH
   1846–1863. Leo von Klenze.

d) ARC DE TRIOMPHE DE L'ÉTOILE, PARIS
   1806–1836. J. F. T. Chalgrin.

a

b

c

d

a

b

c

d

The architecture of the nineteenth century produced no new and original style but followed the neoclassicism of the preceding years with a revival of most of the styles of the past. Early Christian, Romanesque, Gothic and even Renaissance buildings (page 377) were often copied as assiduously and as unimaginatively as the buildings of classical antiquity had been imitated by the neoclassicists of the late eighteenth century. Baroque alone went almost unnoticed, and few buildings worthy of note were designed in that style. The Gothic revival (part of the romantic movement which originated in England and Germany and was the expression of a longing for the medieval past) was first manifest in England where the Gothic style had never been entirely forgotten. Germany soon followed suit and in turn rediscovered and attempted to recreate other past styles. The whole of Europe participated in the movement, though never to such an intense degree as did England and Germany. Later in the same period, side by side with the prevailing eclecticism, appeared the first signs of a new style that was finally to triumph over backward-looking attitudes and gradually lead to modern architecture.

Facing page:
HOUSES OF PARLIAMENT, LONDON
1840–1852. Sir Charles Barry and A.W.N. Pugin.

a) BASILICA OF ST. BONIFACE, MUNICH
1835–1850. G.F. Ziebland.

b) GNADENKIRCHE, BERLIN
1891–1895. Spitta.

c) VOTIVE CHURCH, VIENNA
1856–1879. Heinrich von Ferstel.

d) RIJKSMUSEUM, AMSTERDAM
1877–1885. P.J.H. Cuypers.

Toward 1850, the grand style of the Renaissance replaced the severity of the Neo-Greek of earlier years, Italianate forms becoming more and more elaborated and exuberant until, by the end of the century, architects had reached an ostentatious neobaroque. Buildings on the scale of the great Munich Residenz (Fig. a), modeled on the Pitti Palace in Florence, are rare and for the most part belong to the first half of the century, when there was still a close attachment to classical antiquity.

Facing page:
L'OPÉRA, PARIS
Staircase, 1861–1874. Charles Garnier.

a) RESIDENZ, MUNICH
   1826–1830. Leo von Klenze.

b) THE BOURSE, BRUSSELS
   1868–1875. Leon Suys.

c) LAW COURTS, BRUSSELS
   Grand staircase, 1866–1883. Joseph Poelaert.

a

b

c

XII
TWENTIETH-CENTURY ARCHITECTURE

This chapter, dealing with the architecture of our own time, makes no pretense to be — and indeed could not be — an account of everything that has been built in the past sixty years. Rather, it is the author's intention to give some indication of the events that have most contributed to the birth of the style that characterizes our age and is unbound by tradition — the style that we call "modern." Therefore we shall not be concerned with the architecture of Nazi Germany, Fascist Italy or Communist Russia.

In an attempt to maintain tradition and the eternal values, architects in the dictatorships designed public buildings that were reiterations of every eclectic theme, or made a great display of neoclassicism with colossal proportions; or as during the last twenty years in the U.S.S.R., lapsed into a completely frigid "governmental" style drawn from historical sources. Such architecture has little to do with the modern way of life and cannot express the spirit of the age.

Of all the arts, architecture is the most directly exposed to the influences of the environment in which it is created.

Geography, climate, religion, politics and the structure of society all play a part in determining both the character and appearance of buildings. Some of these factors have declined in importance in our period; regional differences have become less marked as man's capacity to combat the elements has increased and as better systems of communication have facilitated a more rapid dissemination of ideas. There are, however, equally important emotional and esthetic factors connected with the constantly changing "image" of itself which every society seeks to project. The story of architecture in the late nineteenth century and in our own century reflects the problems of a society very gradually and reluctantly coming to terms with the technological era.

In the nineteenth century, increasing material wealth was accompanied by a desire for ostentatious buildings, the façades of which reflected the glories of great civilizations of the past. It was after all a century conscious of history, and period revivals in traditional materials served to display the erudition and "good taste" expected of the somewhat dilettante figure its fashionable architect had become. Because architecture had thus come to be thought of as mere decoration rather than an integral part of modern life, the potentialities of the new materials and techniques of the Industrial Age either went unrecognized or were dismissed as alien to prevailing notions of beauty and "good taste."

In reality, the "new" materials were improved old materials. Glass, for example, was new only in the sense that large panes could now be easily produced. Iron was used more daringly than ever before, but its brittleness led to its replacement by steel, made more easily obtainable by the Bessemer process of 1856.

Concrete was of course used by the Romans, whose enduring monuments eloquently speak of its immense strength in compression. By the 1890's, a method of compensating for its weakness in tension by reinforcing it with hooked steel rods running in the direction of the stresses had been worked out and applied to building in France.

Reinforced concrete greatly increased the strength of the supporting members, enabling functional construction elements to be reduced to a minimum. The structure itself could simply consist of a framework of slender pillars and beams with a thin infilling of concrete, brick, glass or other fabricated material. Roofs, too, could be made comparatively light — hitherto an impossibility — and as soon as their volume and weight were reduced, it became easy to span greater distances. Schumacher calculated that the Pantheon in Rome, with a diameter of 142.4 feet, might have been spanned by a reinforced concrete dome only 2.36 inches thick, creating no lateral thrust.

Architects neglected the new techniques of mass production for a long time. As early as 1852, Gottfried Semper (1803–1879) had said that the machine was capable of outdoing human craftsmanship, and now its almost unlimited possibilities were exploited at last. With unprecedented speed and precision, machines produced the various building parts preplanned on the engineer's drawing board.

It became possible to carry out enormous undertakings with a speed that would have been inconceivable in the past. It was a horticulturist, Joseph Paxton, who demonstrated the principle of building with prefabricated elements assembled on the site in his famous Crystal Palace designed for the London Exhibition of 1851. Engineers were responsible for the fine series of machine halls for the exhibitions in Paris. The most impressive was that of 1889, which employed the principle of the three-hinged arch in spanning the then record distance of 385 feet, and Alexandre Gustave Eiffel's tower at the same exhibition was a forceful example of the possibilities of skeletal frame construction in steel.

In buildings such as these and in the others characteristic of the new era — bridges, railway stations, factories, mills, water towers and grain sites — the new methods were pioneered, not by architects but by engineers. They had fewer preconceptions as to how a building should look, a more exact knowledge of the behavior of load-bearing structures, and with their more direct and un-self-conscious approach, they created some of the most impressive buildings of the nineteenth century. Perhaps the greatest of these were the Englishmen, Thomas Telford and Isambard Brunel, and the Frenchman, Eiffel.

Engineers, in their factories and power stations, their bridges of iron, steel or concrete, had discovered a new kind of beauty that stemmed from a scrupulous use of only those elements that were absolutely necessary, from the perfect adaptation of structure to function, and from the esthetic qualities of the materials themselves. But at first this new beauty went unnoticed, and architects, when they did use the engineers' techniques of iron and concrete construction, lapsed into a style with forms conspicuously derived from construction in stone. Thus the architecture of the end of the century seems false and derivative, the more so because it was embroidered with machine-made ornament intended to look like handicraft. Decoration, until then the product of creative artists, was to an increasing extent fabricated mechanically and copied from the old designs of craftsmen. It is sufficient to recall the pillars of early railway stations which were given cast-iron Corinthian capitals, or the street lamps posing as Renaissance candelabra, to realize the absurdity of these industrial replicas. Ornamentation produced by machine was at once a mockery of handicraft and a steadily more emphatic denial of its very right to exist. Inversely, inasmuch as it continued to imitate hand-made works of art, this decoration was a betrayal of the machine itself, which had to produce forms for which it was not suited. Industrialization also involved the violation of materials, which were forced to take on forms foreign to their natures.

During the latter part of the nineteenth century, however, an undercurrent of discontent with Ruskin's concept of architecture as the adornment of structure made itself felt.

Some who were not afraid of innovation came to revolt against meaningless eclecticism, realizing that this kind of architecture could not meet the requirements of the vast program of work necessitated by living conditions revolutionized by industrialization and by technical and economic advances. Any attempt to resurrect past styles would be inherently weak because it lacked integrity of necessity. Forms conceived in another spiritual climate could never take root; to wish them to do so was futile. Moreover, it was realized that borrowing from the past was sufficient to prevent the development of an architecture that would be both closely related to its own time and capable of giving inspiration in the future. Form and structure as a whole should be the natural result of a specific architectural program and a determined purpose. Semper expressed the need for an architecture "of the age" when he said that: "The contemporary architectural problem must be sought unswervingly in the conditions of our time." This state of mind was not exclusive to Semper; it was shared by many contemporary architects in France, Germany and England. Viollet-le-Duc extolled the logic and honesty of Gothic buildings and urged his contemporaries to make use of iron in their architecture. Neither he nor Semper, however, was so revolutionary in approach when seated before his drawing board. The pen, it seems, spoke another language from the pencil!

In England, the arts-and-crafts movement inspired by William Morris proclaimed a gospel of honest craftsmanship and truth to materials. Philip Webb exemplified these virtues in architecture, particularly in his earliest building (the Red House at Bexley in Kent, built for his friend Morris in 1859). Webb's disciple, W. R. Lethaby, became the propagandist of what he called "our English Free Building." This was an attempt to speak the direct language of the native English tradition with simple eloquence rather than with the fashionably garbled classical forms so popular at the time. Richard Norman Shaw, C. F. A. Voysey, and for a time Sir Edwin Lutyens, were among those who approached building in this way. Voysey especially deserves mention for his austere and precise expression of planes and volumes. This was already a new architecture in the sense that function and site were carefully considered, and the plans and elevations reflected this although the style of the buildings still used a traditional vocabulary.

In the face of this unhappy state of affairs, it was inevitable that hitherto unspoken protests against architectural "dishonesty" should, by the turn of the century, have been given tangible expression. The first signs of an innovating movement appeared in France with *art nouveau*, and in Germany with its equivalent, the *Jugendstil*.

A reaction against the disasters of the previous period, this new style was "an attempt in the midst of the bedlam of out-dated styles which covered the whole of Europe to a degree unprecedented in the history of civilization, to discover forms that would be inherently new to the entire human race" (Ahlers-Hestermann). *Art nouveau* was an attempt to bring about an esthetic revival and was directed solely at artistic and esthetic values. This may explain why such a style, so modern in inspiration and rejecting all academicism, left its deepest impression in the field of decorative design.

The importance of *art nouveau* stems not so much from the few buildings directly influenced by it but from its ability to act as a catalyst bringing the tradition of the arts-and-crafts movement into contact with the new structural concepts of the engineers. Gaudi, the Spanish architect, applied the new engineering skills to traditional materials in creating his bizarre and intensely personal fantasies in buildings such as the Casa Mila and the Church of Sagrada Familia, both in Barcelona. The Belgian, Horta, was able to use boldly exposed steel beams in association with his sinuously flowing ironwork. Scottish architect Charles Mackintosh, in his Glasgow School of Art (1897–1909), showed a new feeling for and awareness of space — inherent in the architecture of our century — and a delicate and restrained handling of the new materials. A new purity of style also was discovered in Austria and Germany.

Several buildings by Endell, Joseph Olbrich and Otto Wagner stand out as entirely original creations amidst an architecture still blind to the requirements of modern life and fostering an eclecticism totally unadapted to the age. But in the sphere of domestic building, on the outskirts of fine art, architects working in the new style achieved some pioneering advances that were not slow to bear fruit. As a result of the patronage of the modern-spirited Ernst Ludwig, Grand Duke of Hesse, many artists of the new school gathered on the Mathildenhöhe at Darmstadt, under the direction of Olbrich, and were able to give substance to their ideas. The houses of the artists' colony built on the Mathildenhöhe and opened to the public in 1901 reveal a character that is quite different from anything that had gone before.

It is in books like those of Otto Wagner, more than in actual buildings, that one notices the change in ideas which was decisive in the birth of modern architecture. In 1906, Wagner, one of the most influential architects of this period, laid down a program for the new architecture: "Modern architecture seeks to create forms and motifs that are the direct result of constructional necessity and the materials employed. These forms must be kept as simple as possible if they are to express what we feel. They must be harmoniously coordinated so as to produce elegant proportions, for the effect of modern design depends almost exclusively upon these." He also states that the general appearance as well as the details of a building must be functional if the whole is to have a true esthetic value in itself. Beauty must derive from the internal truth of the building's structure, in which each part, taken separately, serves a clearly defined purpose. Reading Wagner, one realizes how closely the ideas of the architect are linked with those of the engineer; first and foremost, he deals with problems of construction — to him the most important aspect of his art. Wagner, however, was primarily an architect when he concerned himself with those problems which scarcely affect engineers — for example, the question of handicraft and machine production. Basing his opinion on the example of nineteenth-century architetcure, when the desire to imitate past motifs led to a corruption of materials and they were mechanically molded into unnatural forms, Wagner proposed that the form given to any material should take account of its inherent character. Therefore handicraft, which had so recently fallen into disrepute, should once again be favored because it had the advantage over the machine that every problem could be treated individually. The machine should only be used when there was no doubt that it could produce forms compatible with the inherent nature of the material. Finally, Wagner advised that the esthetic potentialities of the new materials, notably their color, should be exploited as a means of arriving at new visual effects.

Viennese architect Adolf Loos (1870–1933) went as far as to reject everything that remotely resembled a familiar style (to him all style and all ornament were nothing but lies) and denounced architects as criminals. To provide the first example of what he considered the only form of sincere architecture, Loos built a house in the shape of a cube, with a flat roof and completely bereft of decoration. His choice of a flat roof may have been due to the fact that he regarded traditional roof forms as insincere because they were not strictly indispensable on a purely constructional level.

The *Deutscher Werkbund* was founded in 1907. Its prime mover was Hermann Muthesius, who from 1896 to 1903 had been attached to the German Embassy in London for the purpose of studying English Free Building. With these ideas fresh in his mind, he brought together architects and designers who wanted to give a previously neglected "quality" to the objects of everyday life and to work toward the creation of a more harmonious culture. Within this culture, even industry would achieve nobility, and a final reconciliation would take place between man and the ever-problematic machine. The success of this venture was only partial, for frequently machines were still to imitate hand-made forms; in the work of Hans

Poelzig, Tessenow or the great Peter Behrens (1868–1940), there is an evident desire to achieve esthetic or artistic effects which are not always strictly justified by the functional program. In his industrial buildings, especially those built in Berlin between 1907 and 1909 for the A.E.G. (General Electric Company of Germany), Behrens came very near to the kind of functionalism that distinguishes later architecture. Like Frank Lloyd Wright (1869–1959) in America, who followed in the steps of Louis H. Sullivan (1856–1924, the building-engineer and the true father of reinforced concrete construction and the skyscraper) or like Auguste Perret (1874–1954) in France, Behrens derived much from the formal language of the engineers. The clean lines and almost mechanical exactitude of his industrial buildings are a result of this influence, and their sober architecture perfectly answers to the demands of objective necessity: they were to open the way for future enterprises. Behrens was the founder of the Bauhaus school through which he transmitted his experience and ideas to a rising generation of architects from all over Europe. Walter Gropius, Mies van der Rohe and Le Corbusier (Charles Édouard Jeanneret), who after World War I became the leaders of the new movement, worked together in his studio and all were stimulated by his influence.

In 1911, Gropius went still further toward the engineers' esthetic in the workshop block of the Fagus shoe factory at Alfeld-am-Leine. In glazing even the corners of the building, he achieved a new feeling of lightness in architecture by expressing the skeletal construction in the simplest and most direct manner.

It was about this time that the ideas and buildings of Frank Lloyd Wright first became known in Europe through lectures and the German publication of two volumes on his work.

America was by now one of the great industrial powers; in certain parts of the country, notably in Chicago, her architects had more readily responded to the change of conditions than had their counterparts in Europe. The invention of the electric elevator and the use of steel frame construction (after 1889) made possible the skyscraper, a new building type characteristic of modern commercial society. The greatest of the many fine architects concerned with its evolution was Louis Sullivan, Wright's *lieber Meister*. Despite the flowery *art nouveau* decoration around its base, his masterpiece, the Carson Pirie Scott store in Chicago (1899–1904) — with its strongly stressed verticals and horizontals and long bands of tripartite "Chicago windows" — is a bold exposition of his famous (though plagiarized) dictum: "Form follows function."

With a poet's fervor, Wright believed in an "organic architecture" which grew spontaneously out of the nature of sites and clients' requirements. In his famous Prairie Houses, of which the Willetts House was the first masterpiece (1902), he pioneered the open plan in which the interior space is not broken up into small rooms but is essentially one large room modeled into zones by means of partitions. In this and in his use of oversailing roofs, he was influenced by Japanese architecture, although some features are already foreshadowed in the American tradition. Living space which extends upward into the second story in a kind of spatial explosion and the use of long bands of casement windows are entirely original and personal ideas. Wright's delight in the honest expression of materials used as far as possible in their raw, natural state, he owed to Morris, whom he acknowledged in an important paper, "On the Art and Craft of the Machine," delivered in 1901. However, more clearly than Morris, he saw that "tools today are processes and machines where they were once a hammer and a gauge," and that the artist's salvation lay in handling them with skill and simplicity.

The subtle arrangement of simple planes in space (seen perhaps at its best in the Robie house of 1909 in Chicago) which is the essence of Wright's architecture was also a preoccupation of the most vital movement in the art of that time — cubism. Cubist space was essentially for the painter, of course, but it contained the principle of combining several views of the same object at once — the space-time concept which was already inherent in open skeletal constructions and where glazed "curtain walling" was used over a structural framework.

The derivatives of cubism were also influential in helping to nourish and form a new esthetic. The Italian futurist movement, with its violent rejection of the past and joyous acceptance of mechanization and the dynamic tempo of modern life, was particularly important. The manifesto of futurist architecture and the projects left in sketch form by Sant'Elia — the architect most closely associated with the group — contained many important concepts which still hold some validity. The Russian suprematists, who sought a return to first principles in using only the simplest possible abstract elements, the constructivists, who flourished after World War I, and the Dutch de Stijl group (with its restrained use of geometrical elements and bold primary colors), with which Mondriaan was associated, all played a part.

Germany and France are the main centers of interest, although many buildings and housing schemes by J. J. P. Oud, Rietveld and others are of considerable interest.

The Bauhaus, opened by Gropius in 1919 at Weimar and subsequently transferred to Dessau, became a center of creative energy for Germany and soon for the whole world, encouraging and promoting the movement which we may consider as the second stage in the history of twentieth-century art. Art nouveau had marked the first stage, which culminated about 1920, and the Bauhaus was a summary of all the most logical and significant aspects of architecture up to that time. "This school," as H. Hoffmann wrote, "which deliberately set itself apart from the purely theoretical teaching offered by the academies, sought to bridge the gulf between art and life. It accepted the preponderant role of the machine and recognized the machine as a tool worthy of the artist. It worked actively on problems concerned with the suitability of certain forms for mass production, and with the bond that should exist between industry and the creative artist. Painting and sculpture were subordinate to building, which took central place in the new system of teaching, and practical work within the community of the studio became the essential part of the training."

Architects and designers, working in fruitful collaboration with painters and sculptors of widely differing origins and outlook (Feininger, Klee, Kandinsky, Moholy-Nagy, Schlemmer and many others), sought self-discipline and tried to establish an order in every aspect of the world of form. Discipline, sincerity and simplicity became supreme ideals. The Bauhaus building at Dessau, which was designed by Gropius and built in 1925 and 1926, is symbolic of the new forms. As in the shoe factory for the Faguswerke, Gropius clearly differentiated between wall and supporting member. The walls are constituted by a framework of metal filled with glass panels, and are cantilevered out from concrete posts which support the structure as a whole. The building, with its flat roof, is a composition of rectangular shapes shorn of all irrelevant detail; the right angle reigns supreme and is the essential element in the plan. Associated with the principal block are various other buildings such as the staircase towers, all with equally clear-cut cubelike forms. There is a perceptible influence of the Dutch de Stijl movement — indeed, Gropius' building seemed like a manifestation of the ideas expressed by its undisputed leader, Theo van Doesburg, who wanted to rationalize architecture: "On the practical level seek functional efficiency; on the artistic level seek harmony of proportion." The Bauhaus buildings do in fact answer, both to functional requirements and to this demand for esthetic effects derived from scrupulously considered proportion. These two precepts were to be the basis of all future architecture and were as important to its development as the deployment of the inherent esthetic qualities of materials.

Meanwhile, Ludwig Mies van der Rohe, who as the last director of the Bauhaus was to close this famous institution under Nazi pressure, was working on projects for office blocks of "skin-and-bone" construction, with glass as the skin and steel or concrete skeletons. His designs and theories were published in the magazine *G*, which he ran in Berlin. In 1927, he organized the famous Weissenhof Siedlung Exhibition at Stuttgart for the *Deutscher Werkbund*, of which he was a vice-president. The unity of style and purpose that existed among *avant-garde* European architects (afterward dubbed the "international style") was at once apparent. Its common features were flat, undecorated and unmodulated surfaces; geometrically exact planes arranged at right angles; flat roofs; large windows for living rooms; other windows arranged in long horizontal bands; and considerable freedom in internal planning, the whole decked out in the most puritanical black and white.

There was nothing puritanical, though, about Mies' *Werkbund* Pavilion at the Barcelona Exhibition of 1929. An Aladdin's cave of freely disposed partitions under an oversailing roof slab, it displayed a hitherto unknown fluidity of space, its rich marbles and tinted glass saved from vulgarity by Mies' almost Mozartian sense of proportion. Similarly luxurious was the Tugendhat Haus at Brno in Czechoslovakia in 1930; the living space, almost surrounded by glass walls, offered magnificent vistas of the landscape.

Among the contributors to the Stuttgart Exhibition was the Paris-based Swiss architect Le Corbusier. His influential manifesto *Vers une Architecture* was published in 1923 at a time when he had in fact built very little; the text, which reveals the influence of the futurists, is strongly worded and idealistic. He compares the healthy state of engineering with the sickness of architecture and those who have "eyes which do not see." The famous statement: "A house is a machine for living in," which gained for him a reputation as a functionalist (which he specifically denied later on in the text), also appeared in the book.

In his early buildings, the vocabulary of Perret, of the Paris studio-house style, and elements such as the two-storied living room (which presumably come from Wright) are merged within an apparently severe geometric discipline. The beautiful Villa Savoye at Poissy (1928) is basically a tunneled-out cube set down on, rather than integrated with, the landscape. The complex series of vistas from the ramps and patios of the interior belies the simplic-

ity of the exterior. In the Pavillon Suisse (1932) in Paris, an amazingly subtle relationship is worked out between the low common room with its random rubble wall and the stilted dormitory slab beneath which it fits.

By the mid-1930's, the international style inspired by the ideals of the pioneers, and sporting the Weissenhof uniform, had taken root but was still having to struggle for survival in almost every country in the Western world. In America, the work of the Austrians, Schindler and Neutra, had obvious affinities with the European trend, and even their teacher Frank Lloyd Wright, who as always followed a very individual path, briefly came within the orbit of the international style with his famous house "Falling Water" at Bear Run, Pennsylvania, in 1936. Huge cantilevers of reinforced concrete boldly leap out over a tumbling waterfall balanced by rearing walls of stone which blend with the wooded surroundings in what is surely the most poetic and imaginative of modern dwellings.

Apart from this and Wright's own Johnson Wax Administration Building (also begun in 1936), the most exciting work of the period was done in Scandinavia, where Asplund's noble forest Crematorium near Stockholm, and a number of buildings by Finnish architect Alvar Aalto, must be mentioned. The sanatorium at Paimo (1929–1933), so lucid in its expression of structure, in its free and sensitive site plan already reveals the flexibility which he expressed so dramatically in his undulating pavilion for the 1939 World's Fair in New York.

Since the end of World War II, the major developments have been the evolution of a widely accepted esthetic for glass and skeleton constructions, the exploitation of "surface structures" (mainly in ferroconcrete), the gradual and painful realization that design is lagging too far behind technology, and a belated awareness of the necessity for properly coordinated town planning.

Concerning the latter, it must be recorded with sorrow that, with a few exceptions such as Rotterdam, the opportunities for large-scale reconstruction after the most destructive of wars were frittered away. The problems of dealing with the rapid and chaotic growth of large cities, the paralysis caused by traffic congestion and the mindless wastes of no-man's land between town and country, which have been dubbed "Subtopia," have not been solved. The English concept of resettlement in self-contained new towns ringing the great cities was a bold, though not entirely successful, attempt at a solution. The need for effective and coordinated planning on a nation-wide, perhaps even a world-wide, scale is apparent, but even if powerful resistance to this is overcome, planners sufficiently imaginative and, above all, flexible in outlook, may be hard to find.

Lever House in New York (1952), by Gordon Bunshaft of Skidmore, Owings & Merrill, took up the Miesian idea of "skin-and-bone" construction, and through its success and the wartime advances in technology, initiated the era of large-scale curtain walling. A tall, elegant slab poised on a low podium, it makes an urbane and sophisticated composition which has been imitated with varying degrees of success the world over. Mies (who, along with Gropius and many other leading German architects, had found a new home in America) replied by creating his own masterpiece in the genre—the Seagram Building of 1956–1957 directly across the street. The cool dignity and restrained opulence of its bronze-and-tinted-glass façade offer a mild reproof to its more worldly neighbor.

In the interwar years, engineers such as Freyssinet, Maillart, Torrojo and Nervi had created exciting new structures in reinforced concrete, using the inherent rigidity of curved surfaces to span large spaces. Nervi's great exhibition hall at Turin (1948–1949) directly and dramatically expresses the flow of stresses and strains in ferroconcrete structures. The striking barrel vault of the main hall was composed of channels of precast, lightweight vertebrae glazed at the sides to flood the building with light. Nervi is chiefly famous for his graceful dome structures, which also employ precast elements but are partly constructed *in situ;* his impressive conference hall for Unesco in Paris (1960), is a pioneer use of folded-slab construction. He was also a structural consultant for Ponti's elegant Pirelli Building in Milan (1955–1958).

The Spanish-born Candela, who now lives in Mexico, is another engineer-architect who creates daring and moving structures in ferroconcrete but feels monolithic construction to be better suited to the material.

To the American Richard Buckminster Fuller (b. 1895), individual *tours de force* are not enough. His dream is a building industry geared to mass production in the same sense as the automobile or aircraft industries, tackling the problem of providing shelter and environmental control on a world-wide scale. His right to denounce the international style as an esthetic aberration is established by the Dymaxion House Project, contemporaneously developed with the *Weissenhof Siedlung* Exhibition. This domed hexagonal chamber suspended from a mast—the service core of the building—was the first really serious attempt at a mass-produced *machine à habiter* and involved radical rethinking of the problem from first principles. It is interesting to note that Le Corbusier, who has recently tended to become increasingly personal and enigmatic (witness the profoundly moving chapel at Ronchamp of 1950–1955), anticipated Fuller in his enthusiasm for mass-produced housing developed from aircraft technology at the end of World War I. In their attempts to discover a "cosmic significance" underlying form, their different characters are revealed: Le Corbusier falls back on the traditional shapes of solids and the mystique of the Golden Section (which eventually produced his modular system based on human proportions); Fuller justifies his use of the polyhedron framework by reference to the closest packing of spheres around the central nucleus and his use of dome structures by reference to the curvilinear tendency of lines of force. The strict expression of these principles is inherent in his demand for "maximum gain of advantage from minimal energy input." His experiments with many materials, including plastics and even specially prepared paper, as infilling for domes, and the speed and ease of construction of fairly large undertakings such as the Kaiser Aluminum Dome in Honolulu (1957—one of his most beautiful structures) amply demonstrate the effectiveness of his methods.

With space frames like these and surface structures in ferroconcrete, the problem of spanning large areas of space has virtually disappeared. The technological skills at the engineer's command have made possible a plasticity of form which is almost without limits. At the same time, the rectangular discipline of early twentieth-century architecture now appears as a product of an emotional rather than an entirely rational reaction to the Machine Age. Its virtues cannot be denied or dismissed. It produced great architecture, and in many of its fundamentals it retains its validity today. The major problem facing the arts today—possibly more acute in our time than it was in the past—is that of making the right use of hard-won freedom. Perhaps it is from the apparent breaking down of the compartments into which we divide our thinking about our environment, from the union between the rational and the irrational—the scientific and intuitive sides of man's nature—that the forms and disciplines of a whole new architecture will be born.

TWENTIETH-CENTURY ARCHITECTURE

ILLUSTRATIONS

a

b

c

GROSSES SCHAUSPIELHAUS, BERLIN
Interior, 1918–1919. Hans Poelzig.

The extravagant design of the interior of the Grosses Schauspielhaus in Berlin is a product of *art nouveau* which, at the turn of the century, had openly revolted against the eclecticism hitherto prevalent. It is also an expression of the desire to exploit the possibilities of new static forces inherent in new materials (iron and reinforced concrete). As in Moorish "stalactite" domes, festoons of concrete arches arranged in tiers hang from the ceiling which is constructed of horizontal concrete slabs without apparent support. The strength of reinforced concrete enabled the architect to give the whole structure an air of lightness: the slender, tapering pillars look like continuations of a stalactite rather than supporting members. The design is governed by a taste for the strange and striking and is at the same time free of all reference to past styles. This element of fantasy may still be traced in the modern demand for matter-of-factness, clarity and truthful handling of materials in architecture. (Facing page.)

a) THÉÂTRE DES CHAMPS-ÉLYSÉES, PARIS
Façade, 1912. Perret brothers.

The Perret brothers played an important part in the development of modern architecture in France. In the Théâtre des Champs-Élysées, perhaps for the first time in a public building, they made use of the qualities of reinforced concrete first put to the test in industrial building. The clarity of line and geometric harmony of this entrance façade explicitly demonstrate a new trend in architecture and a new feeling for material. However, the use of reliefs, cornices and a type of pilaster to articulate flat surfaces, and the emphasized roof, are features which testify to the continued presence of conceptions belonging to the past. They reveal a concern with visual effects and pronounced classicizing tendencies.

b) MUSÉE D'ART MODERNE, PARIS
Court, 1937. Dondel, Aubert, Viard and Destugue.

The court, on a raised plinth, is surrounded by pillars on three sides and links the two wings of the museum. Although the simple lines and flat roof are enough to give the design a modern look, a desire for grandiose effect produced the distinctly neoclassical character shown.

c) PALAIS DE CHAILLOT, PARIS
General view, 1937. Carlu, Boileau and Azéma.

Both buildings and gardens are designed with a view to magnificence, and the whole enterprise directly recalls the best examples of French baroque architecture. Two emphatic quadrant wings enclose the gardens which are arranged on either side of a spacious avenue on the central axis. The columnar architecture of the wings reveals a sense of construction which, like that of the Musée d'Art Moderne, owes many elements to the past.

Public buildings of the first decades of the century reveal a classicizing tendency and an inclination to contrived effects, and their part in the evolution of modern architecture was not as important as that played by industrial buildings. In this field, where the functional aspect was the most vital of all, the conceptions of the engineer were allied with those of the architect; this gave rise to the idea that design should follow from constructional necessity, taking into account the esthetic and structural qualities of materials. One of the chief works of the period before World War I is the turbine factory built by Peter Behrens in 1909 for the A.E.G. in Berlin: this stands at the beginning of modern architecture (Fig. a). The great hall has walls of glass between reinforced concrete corners and more slender steel supports. There is no applied ornament. The building derives its effect from the horizontals and verticals of the constructional frame, from the simplicity and force of compact geometrical volumes, and from the play of one material against another.

a

But while here one still feels the link with tradition in the method of composing masses, Walter Gropius' Bauhaus Building at Dessau breaks with the past completely and decisively (1926, Fig. b). Unity, simplicity and clarity had reached their most extreme expression, but here — with the separation of wall and supporting members and the treatment of the walls themselves (which have become transparent, insubstantial sheets of glass) — a fundamentally different kind of architecture has been created.

b

The Bauhaus Building paved the way for the future and directly influenced many other enterprises, including stores and offices. Significant examples are Frank Lloyd Wright's administration building for the Johnson Wax Company in Racine, Wisconsin (1939, Fig. c), and the controversial United Nations Building in New York (1950, Fig. d).

Now and then, glass walling was used in domestic building and particularly in private houses, though modern man's urge to let nature penetrate his most intimate surroundings — the home itself — only rarely permitted architects to build walls entirely of glass, as Mies van der Rohe had done in a house at Brno (Fig. e). The need to preserve some intimacy and privacy limited the extent to which these methods could be applied. None the less, private houses provided architects with ample scope, for here the creative spirit was not hampered by the necessary restrictions involved in other forms of architecture such as administrative buildings and flats. It was perhaps in this domain that modern architecture found its finest and most rewarding manifestation. The discipline of providing for the occupants' individual needs, of submitting to various conditions of landscape, climate and life itself, was conducive to designs of great variety, according to the country in which the houses were built, while this rarely happened in larger buildings. Though there is a stylistic relationship, it would be impossible to confuse an American house (facing page, Frank Lloyd Wright, 1952, Phoenix, Arizona) with one from central or southern Europe or from Scandinavia, for each possesses distinctive characteristics.

c/d

e

a

b

c

NOTRE-DAME-DU-HAUT, RONCHAMP
1955. Le Corbusier.

Contemporary architecture, prosaic because it is practical and functional, has not found it easy to create churches that truly seem worthy of housing and symbolizing religious experience. The architectural and decorative style of Gothic and baroque churches, on the other hand, succeeded in directing men's thoughts onto a spiritual plane. The problem of church construction may always be resolved on the formal level, insofar as the church fulfills practical demands and is pleasing esthetically, but it would be difficult to cite a single typical example of modern church architecture. Without the cross and tower of the exterior and the altar and pulpit inside, many churches could well be made to serve some function quite other than that of a place of worship. Thus it is no accident that many architects, when faced with this problem, have attempted to escape it by turning to the past and adapting the basilical type, for example, to modern requirements. Only rarely has a contemporary architect succeeded in so completely breaking with tradition as to build a church like Notre-Dame-du-Haut at Ronchamp (facing page). Different from anything seen before, this church may be considered an authentic manifestation of modern religious architecture. Inside the building, where the asymmetrical design is bold and striking, one experiences a true sense of awe: the light that filters in through tiny, deep-sunk windows or comes indirectly from the towers of the adjoining chapel lends an air of mystery and spirituality to the interior and gives it the solemnity of a place set apart from the world.

a) EXHIBITION HALL (CNIT), PARIS
1957–1959. Zehrfuss, Camelot and de Mailly.

The reinforced concrete shell roof, which has a clear span with no intermediate supports, and the great glass walls in their slender metal frames, give this striking building its distinctive character.

b) UNESCO BUILDING, PARIS
1955–1957. Breuer, U.S.A.; Nervi, Italy; Zehrfuss, France.

Concrete frame and walls treated as a transparent glass membrane are characteristic features of this building, and thus it may be classed among the many others representing that modern style first realized by Gropius, who had logically exploited its potentialities.

c) HANSA-VIERTEL, BERLIN
Part of model for Interbau Exhibition, 1957.

Town architecture and town planning are among the most important of the tasks which face contemporary architects. Like individual buildings, towns — which Le Corbusier called "machines for working in" — must be built with regard to future purpose and function. This photograph clearly demonstrates that nature has an important part to play in the realization of such a many-sided project. Trees and lawns are introduced, not only in the residential areas but also among the offices and administrative buildings of the industrial quarter.

TELECOMMUNICATIONS OFFICES, FRANKFURT AM MAIN
1952–1955. Heinrich Ebert.

After the destruction of whole sections of one town during the course of World War II, the town planner was faced with the delicate task of preserving what remained of historic buildings and incorporating them within new constructions. When destruction had been complete, it was possible for planning to be conceived on a grand scale, without regard to any form of compromise (as at Rotterdam), but this was not the case when existing buildings had to be taken into account. The modern telecommunications building in Frankfurt, constructed on the basis of a metal frame, harmonizes in form and proportion with the remaining parts of the baroque palace which surround the front courtyard. The tower block, fourteen stories high, gives the dominant accent to the whole architectural scheme without overpowering the effect of the old palace. (Facing page.)

a) TERMINI STATION, ROME
1950. Calini, Castellazi, Fadigati, Montuori, Pintonello and Vitellozzi.

The roof of this vast hall is carried on slender, elegant supports conceived in relation to the functional demands of the construction. The glass walls and ceiling have a skillful and varied treatment.

b) HALL OF CONGRESS, BERLIN
1954–1956. Stubbins, Duttmann and Mocken.

In their pavilion, built at Raleigh, North Carolina, in 1954, architects Nowicki, Severud and Dietrick had already exploited the constructional idea of two intersecting parabolic arches holding steel cables from which a roof was suspended. The Hall of Congress in Berlin — America's contribution to the International Exhibition of Architecture — takes up this theme while boldly exaggerating the overhang of the roof.

c) ALHAMBRA CINEMA, MANNHEIM
1951. Paul Bode.

Contrary to theatre architecture, an original style has been evolved for cinema design, issuing from the close interrelation of form and function in such buildings. This, however, applies only to the interior, for cinema exteriors are not subject to the same discipline. The cinemas built by Paul Bode are good examples. In addition to the Alhambra at Mannheim, we may cite the Capitol at Cassel (1950) and the Atlantic at Nuremberg (1954).

d) MUNICIPAL THEATRE, MÜNSTER
1954–1956. Deilmann, von Hausen, Rave and Rhunau.

From an architectural point of view, modern theatres frequently either tend toward the conventional or the experimental, despite numerous attempts to find new forms relevant to the changes that have taken place in our society. Theatre interiors, which call for a certain splendor and magnificence, are often left sober and austere, while the treatment of the exterior will be calculated to give the building a functional appearance.

This theatre's foyer, a broad semicircle, is raised on a rectangular podium with denticulated ornament. From the outside, the foyer is most expressively picked out by alternating panes of glass and their supports, vertical slats.

a

b

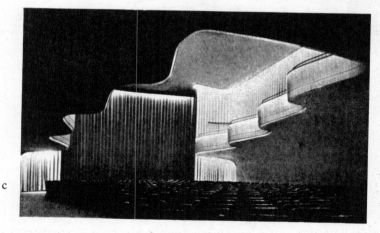

c

d

a/b

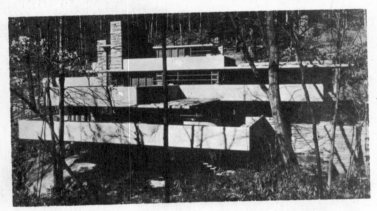

c

d

Two of the most elegant and original of modern curtain-wall buildings are the Pirelli Building in Milan (Gio. Ponti and others, 1955–1958, Fig. a), and the Phönix Rheinrohr Building in Düsseldorf. Floating loftily above the neighboring buildings, the Pirelli headquarters is characterized by a sleek sophistication in harmony with its role as a commercial status symbol. Internal services are housed in the stem and stern of the boat-shaped plan, and the uncluttered floor slabs are cantilevered out from two tapering concrete piers. (Photo, Pirelli Ltd., London.)

The Phönix Rheinrohr Building (Hentrich and Petschnigg, 1960, Fig. b) divides the working space into three slabs. The two main office blocks are asymmetrically placed against the central one which contains the services, to form a noble and aspiring composition. (Photo, Arno Wrubel.)

Frank Lloyd Wright and Le Corbusier probably must be regarded as the leading domestic architects of this century, but despite the apparent similarities of the two buildings shown here, they could not have been more different in approach. Falling Water (Bear Run, Pennsylvania, 1936, Fig. c) is as close as Wright came to the international style, but its position astride the waterfall and the prominent use of rough stone show his sensitivity to the site and his feeling for an ideal harmony between the works of man and nature. (Photo, U.S. Information Service.)

Even in its present ruined state, Le Corbusier's Villa Savoye (at Poissy, near Paris, 1928–1930, Fig. d) is a statement of a very different kind. The exterior, far from flowing into the contours of the landscape, is raised on stilts and given the precise geometric form of a perfect cube. The interiors reveal no stark use of materials in their raw state, as Wright's so often do. Details such as the handrails and the build-up toward the curved windshield on the upper terrace recall the architecture of passenger liners which Le Corbusier praised in his early writings. The architect here is stressing the independence and alien character of man's contribution to the landscape.

a) EXHIBITION HALL, TURIN
1949. Nervi.

Though less dramatic than the earlier Exhibition Hall in Turin, this pavilion shows the uncluttered expression of structure and thoughtful detailing characteristic of Nervi's straightforward approach to the problems of design. Sixteen mushroom columns supporting steel roof slabs give the building its broad sweep of uninterrupted space. (Photo, G. E. Kidder Smith.)

b) KAISER ALUMINUM DOME, HONOLULU
1957. R. Buckminster Fuller.

In a world confronted with a rapidly expanding population and a shortage of skilled labor, current building methods seem slow and inadequate. Fuller's dream of "turning the energies of the universe to human advantage" in a way dictated by a comprehensive science of design holds the possibility of averting a nightmare situation. The Kaiser Aluminum Dome was erected from parts flown from the United States. Within twenty-four hours, the entire 145-foot-span concert hall had been erected and the inaugural concert had been given. The implications of this feat, and the smaller and less costly structures designed by Fuller on similar principles, are obvious. (Photo, R. Buckminster Fuller.)

a

b

GLOSSARY

▶**Abacus** Slab forming upper member of a capital, effecting the transition between the support (column or pier) and the load (arch or architrave). Used by the Egyptians and in Mesopotamia, the abacus was employed by the Greeks in the Doric capital, taking the form of a plain, square block. Appears in capitals of the Ionic, Corinthian and Roman Composite orders.

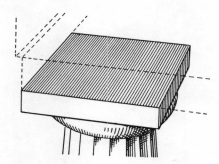

ABACUS *of a Doric capital*

Abbey A monastery ruled over by an abbot. As with all monastic establishments, the buildings which comprise an abbey — chapter house, refectory, dormitory, library etc. — are grouped around the cloister, limited on one side by the abbey church. The first abbey was founded by St. Benedict in 529 on Monte Cassino, near Naples.

Abbey church Church attached to an abbey.

▶**Abutting wall** A cross wall built on the back of an early flying buttress, to give added weight.

ABUTTING WALL *above the aisles at Durham Cathedral, twelfth century*

▶**Acanthus** A plant with large, jagged-edged leaves. From the fifth century B.C., this leaf form was adapted for use as architectural ornament and became one of the characteristic features of the Corinthian style. Occurs on capitals, decorative borders etc. throughout the subsequent history of architecture.

Acropolis Citadel or elevated part of a Greek city, usually a temple precinct. Best-known example is the Acropolis of Athens.

ACANTHUS *foliage on a Corinthian capital*

▶**Acroteria** Ornaments on the apex and above the lower angles of a classical pediment.

Adyton Greek: not to be entered. The inner sanctuary or holy of holies of a Greek temple, forbidden to all but the priests.

Aedicule Latin: *aedicula,* a small temple. Term used by the Romans to describe a recess for a statue with an architectural surround consisting of a pediment supported on two columns.

Agora An open space serving as a market place or public meeting place in a Greek town. The forum is the Roman equivalent.

ACROTERION, *palmette design*

Alabaster A soft, translucent limestone resembling marble in appearance.

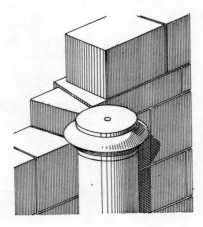

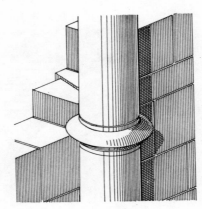

ANNULETS

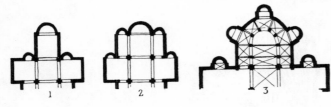

TYPES OF APSES

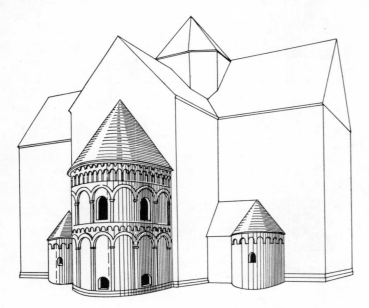

Apse flanked by small apsidal chapels

Alcazar Arabic. A term used in Spain to describe castles, originally with four fortified angle towers.

Alcove Recess in room wall, especially a recess for a bed.

Alternation of supports The alternation of columns with piers, in a rhythmic sequence in a nave arcade. Iambic alternation — one column to one pier; dactylic alternation — two columns to one pier.

Ambos Small raised pulpits to left and right of the chancel in Early Christian basilicas. That on the right, with one short flight of steps, was used for the reading of the Epistle; that on the left, with two flights, for the Gospel.

Ambulatory An aisle, frequently with radiating chapels, surrounding an apse. The ambulatory may be doubled in large, five-aisled churches.

Amphiprostyle A Greek temple with a portico at both ends.

Amphitheatre Oval or circular building with tiers of seats arranged around a sand-strewn central open space called the arena. The oldest surviving example is that at Pompeii (*c.* 70 B.C.); the best known is the Colosseum, Rome (completed 80 A.D.). The Roman amphitheatre is the prototype of the modern stadium.

► **Annulets** Rings — the deep grooves around the lower part of the Doric capital, between the echinus and the shaft. Also the molded bands encircling the shaft of a column or connecting a group of vaulting shafts in Gothic architecture. Sometimes purely decorative, they occasionally are tailed into the wall to strengthen the shafts.

Anta A rectangular pilaster that terminates the side wall of the pronaos (porch) of a temple. The moldings of its base and capital (called anta-capital) usually differ from those of the adjacent columns and vary in richness according to the order employed.

Antefixes Upright ornaments placed at regular intervals on the cornice along the sides of a temple, to mask the ends of the covering tiles over the joints between the rows of flat roof tiles.

► **Apse** The vaulted semicircular or polygonal termination of a church sanctuary. The apse was first applied to antique Roman basilicas where it was built into the thickness of the wall, making no external projection. Often flanked by smaller apsidal chapels opening off the transept arms. These may be of varying length (staggered plan, 2). Subsidiary apses may radiate from the main apse (radiating plan, 3).

Aqueduct Roman system for the conveyance of water to cities. When spanning valleys, it took the form of a succession of monumental arches carrying the channel through which the water flowed. Ruined aqueducts are still to be seen in most of the regions once part of the old Roman Empire.

Arabesque Painted or low-relief decoration composed of flowing, intertwining scrollwork, tendrils and stylized flower patterns, usually symmetrically arranged about an axis. Much used by Florentine Renaissance designers and during the early French Renaissance. *See Grotesque.*

▶ **Arcade** Range of arches supported on piers or columns, either open or attached to a wall (blind arcade).

▶ **Arch** A curved structure consisting of a number of wedge-shaped stones or bricks (voussoirs) so arranged as to be supported over a void by their mutual pressure. The principal arch forms are: 1. Round; 2. Horseshoe; 3. Trefoil; 4. Segmental; 5. (Pointed) Equilateral; 6. (Pointed) Lancet; 7. Ogee; 8. Curtain; 9. Tudor.

Archaic Term mainly applied to the beginnings of Greek art (eighth–sixth century B.C.) but also used to qualify the early stages of any style.

Archaistic Describes an art which deliberately uses archaic features.

Architrave The horizontal beam or lowest part of the entablature of an order, resting directly on the capitals. The term is also used of the moldings around the openings of doors and windows.

▶ **Archivolt** The group of moldings on the face of an arch. In its most elaborate form — on the recessed portals of Romanesque and Gothic doorways — carved with geometrical and naturalistic patterns or decorated with figure sculpture.

▶ **Ashlar** Masonry of large rectangular blocks accurately worked and laid in continuous regular courses. Sometimes rock faced.

Atlantes Sculptured male figures used in place of columns or piers, to support an entablature. (Not to be confused with hermae, which are busts on square pedestals.) The female equivalent is the caryatid. The term comes from Greek mythology in which the giant Atlas is said to have held up the pillars of the universe. The first atlantes appear in Greek architecture — those at the Olympieum, Agrigentum, were some 25 feet high. They frequently occur in baroque architecture.

ARCADE, *nave, Fountains Abbey, England, c. 1140*

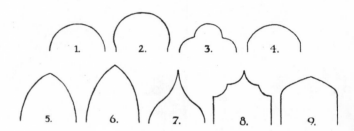

ARCHES

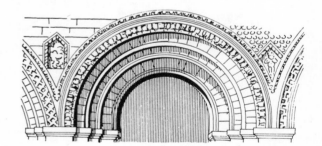

ARCHIVOLT, *Bayeux Cathedral, eleventh century*

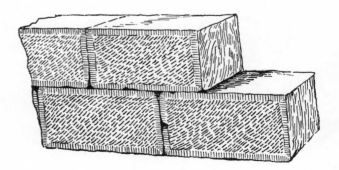

ASHLAR CONSTRUCTION

Atrium 1. The central court of a Roman house, around which the various rooms were grouped. It had an opening in the center of the roof under which was a tank to catch rain water.
2. The open court, surrounded by arcades, before the entrance of an Early Christian basilica. A fountain in the center was for ritual ablutions.

Attic A small story above the main entablature in classical and Renaissance architecture.

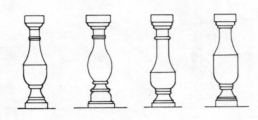

BALUSTERS

Baldachino In Renaissance and baroque architecture, a fixed canopy supported on columns over a high altar or tomb. The bronze baldachino in St. Peter's, Rome (1633, Bernini), is a celebrated example. *See Ciborium.*

▶ **Balusters** Miniature columns, swelling out at the center or toward the base.

Balustrade A row of balusters supporting a handrail or coping on staircases, around the roofs of buildings, on balconies etc. Much used in baroque architecture.

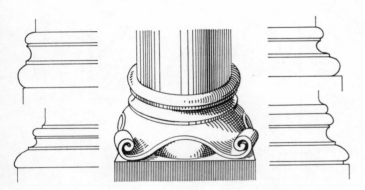

BASE. *Above and central, Romanesque; below, Gothic*

Baptistery A building set aside for the sacrament of baptism. Circular or polygonal in plan and containing a font at the central point. The Baptistery of Florence is a celebrated example.

Baroque A term applied to the predominant stylistic tendency in art during the late sixteenth, seventeenth and eighteenth centuries. Baroque design is characterized by over-elaboration, animated forms, dramatic effects.

Barrel vault *See Vault*

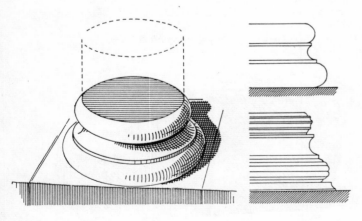

ATTIC BASE

▶ **Base** In architecture, the lowest member of a column between the shaft and the pavement or pedestal. Consists of a combination of moldings and fillets, with profile varying according to the different orders. The commonest form for Ionic and Corinthian is the so-called Attic base with one scotia (hollow) between two torus (roll) moldings. This base was adopted by the Romans, appears in Early Christian architecture, and was to assume many varieties of form during the Romanesque and Gothic periods.

► **Basilica** Greek: *basileios,* a king — hence *royal hall:* 1. A large hall built on the forum of a Roman town as a commercial exchange and law court. Usually rectangular in plan, divided into 3 or sometimes 5 aisles by 2 or 4 rows of columns or piers. The central aisle was carried to a greater height than the side aisles and was provided with clerestory windows. Roman basilicas included the Basilica of Maxentius and the Basilica Julia on the Forum Romanum.

2. Basilican church: the name given to the characteristic form of Early Christian church, derived from the Roman basilica. An atrium or forecourt led into a covered narthex for penitents, and this in turn opened into the nave, lighted by clerestory windows and divided from 2 or sometimes 4 lower side aisles by rows of columns carrying arches or architraves. The nave was terminated by a semicircular apse or sanctuary, usually at the east end, and this was often separated from the body of the church by a transept. The basilican plan, with numerous variations, has recurred throughout the history of church architecture.

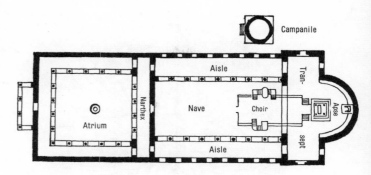

1. BASILICA, *ideal plan*

Bas-relief *See Relief.*

Bays The internal compartments of a building, marked by divisions on the side walls — columns, piers etc.; or on the ceiling — transverse arches, beams etc., and repeated down the nave from entrance to apse. Also the external divisions of a building by fenestration.

Biedermeier Style of the 1814–1848 period in Germany, corresponding with early Victorian in England.

2. BASILICA, *S. Paolo Fuori le mura, Rome. Constructed to give the effect of tiers of naves*

Blind window Recess in a wall, with or without an architectural surround, simulating a window for decorative purposes or for the sake of symmetry.

► **Boasting** The rough cutting of a stone by the carver, in preparation for architectural or sculptural decoration. In the illustration, the figure on the left is fully finished but the others are only roughed out.

► **Boss** A knob or projection placed at the intersection of the ribs of a vault. In Gothic architecture, often carved with flowers and foliage or heraldic ornaments; in Late Gothic, made to hang from the ceiling, like stalactites, and profusely decorated.

Brick Molded clay baked by sun or fire. Much used by the Romans. Brick architecture flourished during the Romanesque and particularly the Gothic period in northern Germany. Brick was also used in southern Italy at this time.

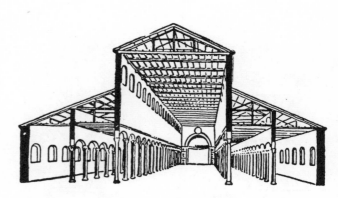

BOASTING

Buttress A pier of masonry projecting from a wall, to resist the thrust of a vault or roof and to give additional strength. Usually the projection at the base is reduced in stages by sloping offsets and the buttress is weighted by a pinnacle. *See Flying buttress.*

BOSS

CARYATID, *Erechtheum, Acropolis, Athens*

CANOPY *over statue of Adam, Bamberg Cathedral, thirteenth century*

CARTOUCHES

Byzantine art The art of Byzantium (the ancient Constantinople, capital of the eastern Roman Empire) which developed during the fifth century A.D. and may be said to have continued until the conquest of Constantinople by the Turks in the fifteenth century. The Byzantine style spread across the whole of the Balkans and Russia and was the predominant influence on Italian art until about 1300. In architecture, the basilican church gave way to the domed structure with a plan based on the Greek cross — a type that flourished in the Balkans and Russia and of which a magnificent example is Sancta Sophia, Constantinople, sixth century.

Calathos The bell or basket shape supporting the acanthi of the Corinthian capital. A similar feature sometimes forms the capital on the head of a caryatid figure.

Campanile Isolated bell tower, common in Italy. Probably first developed as a feature of Early Christian basilicas in the fifth or sixth century. The campanile of S. Apollinare in Classe, Ravenna, is one of the oldest surviving examples (sixth century); the Leaning Tower of Pisa (twelfth century) is the most celebrated.

Cancelli Low screens of wood or stone which, in an Early Christian basilica, enclosed the choir or space reserved for the clergy (hence chancel). Origin of the rood screen.

▶ **Canopy** In Gothic architecture, a small sculptured covering over a statue, tomb or other object.

▶ **Capital** The crowning feature of a column, pier or pilaster, effecting the transition from the shaft to the arch or architrave. The principal types of capitals are: *classical:* 1. Doric, 2. Ionic, 3. Corinthian, 4. Roman Composite; *Romanesque:* 5. Cushion or cubiform, 6. With stylized animal and vegetable forms, 7. More elaborate type with narrative figure sculpture, 8. Scalloped or multiple cushion, 9. With stiff palmette decoration, 10. Corinthianizing, with small corbel volutes and stiff foliage; *Gothic:* 11. Stiff-leaf or crocket capital, typical of Early Gothic, 12. With naturalistic foliage, typical of Middle Gothic, 13. Molded, typical of Late Gothic; *Renaissance:* 14. and 15. Playful variations of the Corinthian motif.

Carolingian art Art during the time of Charlemagne and his immediate successors (late eighth–ninth century).

▶ **Cartouche** A tablet with an ornate frame, resembling a sheet of paper with the edges rolled up, usually bearing a coat of arms or an inscription.

▶ **Caryatid** Whole sculptured female figure supporting an entablature, as in the porch of the Erechtheum, Athens.

Catacombs A system of subterranean passages used as burial places, the sides of the passages containing tiers of niches or graves. The Catacombs in the neighborhood of Rome — some extending over an area of several acres — were used by the early Christians during the time of persecution as places of worship, as well as for burial, and their walls are rich in paintings and inscriptions. Others are known to exist in southern Italy and the Near East.

Cathedral The principal church of a diocese, in which the bishop's cathedra (or throne) is placed.

Cella The principal room of an antique temple, containing the ritual image.

Cenotaph Commemorative sepulchral monument to a person whose body is buried elsewhere.

Chamfer The surface formed by cutting off, at an angle of 45 degrees, the edge made by two surfaces of a block of stone, wood etc., meeting at right angles.

Chevet A term applied to the apsidal east end of a church when it is surrounded by an ambulatory with radiating chapels.

Choir Strictly, that part of a church occupied by choir and clergy, separated by a screen from the body of the church. Usually applied to the whole space east of the crossing.

Churrigueresque Denotes early Spanish baroque, named after its chief exponent, José de Churriguera. Characterized by a wild profusion of ornamental detail.

Ciborium A canopy supported on four columns, generally over an altar or tomb. The Early Christian or medieval equivalent of the baldachino.

Cinquefoil *See Foil.*

Classic or Classical 1. Term used for Greek and Roman art and their derivatives — the art of "calm simplicity and noble grandeur" (Winckelmann). The classical spirit in painting and sculpture is expressed in the representation of the perfected human form without abstraction or excessive naturalism, the forms being generalized rather than individualized and divested of all accidental features, serene and harmoniously proportioned. Classic architecture is characterized by clarity and simplicity in construction and design and rejects superfluous detail.
2. Term used to denote the perfected phase of any style. Thus Notre Dame, Paris, might be called the classic expression of Gothic. The classic phase of Greek architecture was the fifth century B.C. (the Parthenon); that of Roman art, the age of Augustus; that of the Renaissance, the period around 1500.

 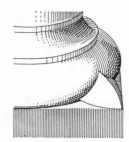

CLAW FEET

► **Claw foot** Carved boss, often in the shape of an animal's claw, filling the triangular space between the circular and square members of a column base.

Clerestory The upper story of the nave walls of a church, rising above the aisles and pierced with windows, hence clerestory windows.

Cloister A covered passage around four sides of an open quadrangular court, with an arcade or colonnade opening onto the court. The cloister, a medieval derivation of the antique atrium, forms the central part of a monastic establishment around which the different buildings are grouped. The arches or lintels carried a lean-to roof in early examples. Later, cloisters were vaulted and the arches were sometimes wholly glazed.

► **Coffers** Sunken square or polygonal panels formed in ceilings, vaults and domes, hence coffered ceiling etc. Used by the Romans and in Early Christian basilicas; returned to favor during the Renaissance.

Collegiate church Church served by a chapter, consisting of secular clergy and canons and under the jurisdiction of a bishop.

Colonnade A range of columns carrying a horizontal entablature, surrounding a building, an open square etc. Bernini's colonnade in front of St. Peter's, Rome, is a well-known example.

Columbarium Latin: a dovecot or pigeon house. Roman or Early Christian sepulchral chamber, usually underground, lined with niches in which were placed urns containing the ashes of cremated bodies.

Column A round pillar comprising a base, shaft and capital. May be monolithic or composed of several separate drums. To be distinguished from the pier, which is square or rectangular in section. *See Orders, classical.*

Composite capital A Roman development of the Corinthian capital. The acanthus decoration and the volutes under the angles of the abacus remain, but the intervening volutes in the center of each side give way to a band of egg and dart, as in the Ionic.

Composition The grouping of buildings or the parts of a building, to form a unified work of art.

Coffered ceiling of a Renaissance room, sixteenth century

CORBEL CAP

COUPLED BAYS

COSMATI WORK

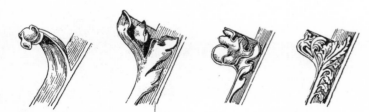

Development of the crocket, thirteenth—fifteenth century

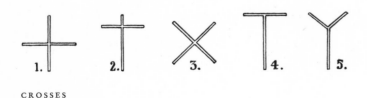

CROSSES

Concrete A building material (first used by the Romans) composed of sand, small stones or gravel and cement mixed with water. It is poured into a timber framework and allowed to set. When strengthened by the introduction of steel bars, it is called reinforced concrete.

Confessio In early churches, a small crypt for the burial of saints and martyrs below the high altar. Surrounded by a passageway and accessible by staircases at the sides of the sanctuary.

Console A block of stone or bracket consisting of two reversed volutes projecting from a wall, to carry a cornice. It may also (as in the baroque period) be used as a decorative motif on keystones, windows or portals.

Corbel A block of stone, with its sides plain but the face sometimes elaborately molded, projecting from a wall to support some horizontal feature.

►**Corbel cap** A capital, usually molded and carved, to carry an arch or vaulting ribs.

Corbeling Projections from the vertical plane of a wall, the stones being advanced in successive courses, one above another.

Corinthian order *See Orders, classical.*

Cornice In classical architecture, the upper portion of the entablature. Also used as the term for any projecting feature at the top of a wall, arch etc.

►**Cosmati** A Roman family of mosaicists (thirteenth century) and their school. Cosmati work is to be found in many churches in Rome and southern Italy, on altars, ambos, chancel screens and pavements.

►**Coupled** Denotes the grouping of architectural elements in pairs. Thus two bays or openings embraced by the same relieving arch are coupled bays; or two columns side by side under one entablature are coupled columns.

Cour d'honneur A grand forecourt contained between the advanced wings of a Renaissance or baroque palace composition.

►**Crocket** Foliated hook-shaped ornaments used in thirteenth-century Gothic for decorating capitals or the sloping sides of gables, pinnacles, spires etc. They lose their hook form by the end of the thirteenth century.

►**Cross** The symbol of Christianity. The main types are: 1. Greek cross with four arms of equal length; 2. Latin cross; 3. St. Andrew's cross; 4. Tau cross of St. Anthony; 5. Forked cross, a Gothic form.

Crypt An underground chamber, usually below the chancel of a church, containing the relics of a saint. A development of the small *confessio* in Early Christian churches.

Cubiculum The bedroom of an ancient Roman house. Term also used to denote the large chambers of the Christian Catacombs.

► **Cusps** In Gothic architecture, the pointed members projecting from an arch toward its center, to form small subsidiary arches. Used in tracery to produce the trefoil, quatrefoil, cinquefoil, multifoil patterns. The point of the cusp may be left plain or decorated with foliated carving.

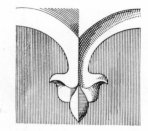

CUSPS

Cyma A molding with an outline of two contrary curves: *cyma recta*, with upper projecting part concave and lower part convex, the usual profile of the gutter of a temple; *cyma reversa*, with upper part convex and lower concave. The cymatium denotes the crowning member of the cornice in the entablature of classical temples.

Decorated Name given to the phase of English Gothic architecture beginning about 1270 and ending toward the mid-fourteenth century. Characterized by the wider use of decorative forms in tracery etc.

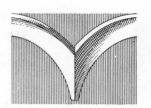

DIPTERAL TEMPLE PLAN

Diaconicon In Early Christian and Byzantine churches, a small chamber adjoining one side of the sanctuary, in line with the side aisle, and serving as a sacristy. Corresponds with the *prothesis (q.v.)* on the other side.

Diaphragm A transverse wall carried across the nave of a church on an arch, and sometimes pierced with small decorative openings, to lighten it. Found in the Romanesque churches of Normandy, Auvergne, the Rhineland.

► **Dipteral** A temple surrounded with a double range of columns.

► **Dome** A hemispherical structure placed over a circular, square or polygonal compartment or bay. When a dome is to be raised over a square bay, there are three possible methods for effecting the transition from the square to the circle:
1. *The pendentive dome.* The diameter of the dome coincides with the diagonals of the square. The portions of the hemisphere outside the square are as it were cut away, leaving four spherical triangles (pendentives) which merge into the dome above.
2. *Dome on pendentives.* This begins as a pendentive dome but — at the level at which the spherical triangles meet — a smaller dome is raised, its diameter coinciding with the sides of the square base.
3. *Dome on squinches.* An arch or system of concentric arches, called a squinch, is thrown across each angle of the square to form an octagon on which an eight-sided dome may be raised.
Domes are occasionally provided with a circular opening at their apex which is often surmounted by a small turretlike structure, the lantern. Usually a circular or polygonal vertical wall called a drum and pierced with windows intervenes between the pendentives and the dome.
The dome was used by the Romans — that of the Pantheon, Rome (c. 120 A.D.), remains one of the largest ever built — and was taken up by Byzantine and Romanesque builders. Domed construction played no part in the development of Gothic architecture, but again became popular in Italy during the Renaissance and baroque periods. The dome of St. Peter's, Rome (Michelangelo, from 1547), is one of the best-known examples. (*See illustration, page 412.*)

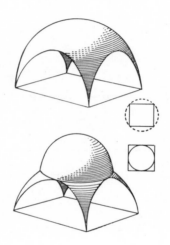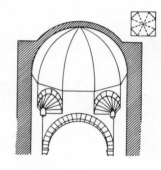

DOMES:
upper left, pendentive dome;
lower left, dome on pendentives;
right, dome on squinches

Domes on pendentives, St. Pierre, Angoulême, twelfth century

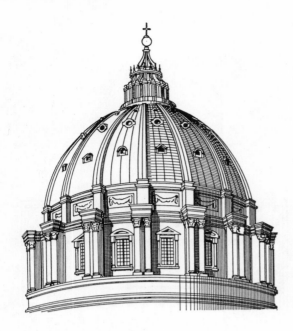

Dome with drum and lantern; St. Peter's, Rome, sixteenth century

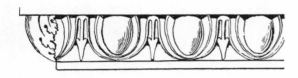

EGG AND DART

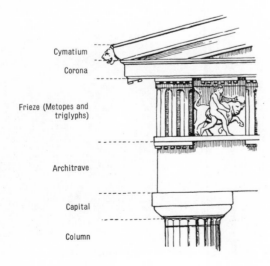

Cymatium
Corona
Frieze (Metopes and triglyphs)
Architrave
Capital
Column

ENTABLATURE

Donjon or keep The massive principal tower or stronghold of a fortress, round or rectangular in form. Used as a last place of refuge in time of siege. Early donjons were invariably entered at first-floor level, by means of a ladder.

Doric order *See Orders, classical.*

Dormer A window vertically placed in a sloping roof. Much used in the sixteenth century.

Dosseret A square block which widens toward the top. Placed on a capital in Byzantine architecture.

Drums *Of a column:* the circular stones of which a built column is formed. *Of a dome:* the circular or polygonal vertical wall, pierced with windows, on which a dome is sometimes raised.

Echinus The convex molding under the abacus of the Greek Doric capital.

▶ **Egg and dart or egg and tongue** The conventional enrichment of an ovolo (convex, egg shaped) molding on cornices, capitals etc.

Elevation The upright projection of a building or part of a building. In medieval architecture, the elevation of a church generally consisted of three stages: nave arcade, triforium gallery and clerestory. Occasionally (particularly in Early Gothic) there are four stages, with a tribune gallery between nave arcade and triforium.

Empire Term used to denote a style in France during the time of Napoleon I (1804–1814), particularly with reference to the decorative arts.

Engaged column A column attached to a wall or pier from which it stands out as a half or three-quarter column.

En suite An arrangement of rooms with communicating doors on the same axis, providing long vistas.

▶ **Entablature** The upper part of an order of architecture—between the capitals of the columns and the roof. The entablature comprises: 1. *the architrave*, resting immediately on the capitals; 2. *the frieze*, resting on the architrave; and 3. *the crowning cornice* consisting of corona and cymatium. These three main features vary in proportion and decorating according to the order employed.

Entasis In Greek architecture, the slight swelling of a column shaft, to counteract the optical illusion that gives straight lines the appearance of curving inward.

Epistyle Synonym for the architrave or beam in Greek architecture.

Exedra Greek: outdoor seat. In Greek architecture, a small, isolated, semicircular alcove with raised seats for disputations. Term extended by the Romans to denote any semicircular or rectangular recess with benches, opening off the peristyle of a house, palaestra or thermae. Also applied to an apse or niche in a basilica or church.

Extrados Outer surface of an arch.

Eye The disc or button at the center of a volute spiral.

▶**Façade** The front or external elevation of a building, with the main entrance. Often with elaborate decoration. In churches, due to the orientation, the west front constitutes the main façade.

Facings The inner and outer surfaces of a wall; or the masonry which forms the face; or any applied cladding.

Festoon Carved garland of foliage, flowers and fruit, suspended at both ends.

Figured capital Capital carved with human figures, animals etc., illustrating legends or scenes from biblical history.

Fillet Narrow, flat band dividing one molding from another or defining the limit of a molding.

▶**Finial** An ornament comprising bunches of foliage resembling crockets arranged around a vertical stem. In Gothic architecture, employed as a termination to pinnacles, gables etc. Introduced at the same time as crockets (*q.v.*), during the thirteenth century; follows a similar course of development.

▶**Flamboyant** Strictly, the latest phase of French Gothic architecture (fifteenth century). The term derives from the wavy, flamelike forms of the window tracery of this period.

Flèche Slender, pyramidal wooden spire on the ridge of a roof, often over the crossing.

FAÇADE, *St. Pierre, Angoulême, 1130*

FINIALS
Left: thirteenth century
Right: fifteenth century

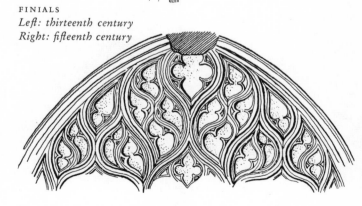

FLAMBOYANT WINDOW TRACERY

FLYING BUTTRESSES: *left, Early Gothic;*
right, late thirteenth century

Gothic tracery using trefoil patterns.
Maulbronn, Württemberg, thirteenth century

GABLE

Fluting The vertical channeling on the shaft of a column or pilaster.

Flying arch An arch flying across a nave below the vaulting, to stiffen the wall or piers.

▶**Flying buttress** A quadrant arch transmitting the oblique lateral thrust of a nave vault over the aisle roof to an exterior vertical buttress. The flying buttress was a Gothic development of the Romanesque system whereby the thrust of the nave vault was counteracted by massive walling with few window openings, by continuous semibarrel vaults over the triforium galleries, or as at Durham, by quadrant arches in the triforium chamber concealed by the lean-to roof.

▶**Foil** The lobe formed by the cusping of a circle or an arch in Gothic tracery. Trefoil, quatrefoil, cinquefoil or multifoil indicate the number of lobes.

Formeret or wall rib In a medieval vault, the rib against the wall, parallel with the main axis of the nave. A cross vault is thus defined by two wall ribs and two transverse ribs on its four sides.

Fresco Italian: *fresco*, fresh. Mural painting in which the colors are laid on the wall when the plaster is still wet, so that they sink into it while drying. This method is thus more permanent than painting *al secco* (when the paint is applied to dried plaster). From about 1250, the fresco method of painting became very popular in Italy. During the baroque period it was practiced in all European countries that contributed to the development of this style — Italy, France, Germany.

Frieze The middle and most decorated division of the classical entablature, between the architrave and the cornice. The term is also applied to any decorative band around a wall.

▶**G**able The triangular shape formed by the enclosing lines of a sloping roof. The term is also used to denote the triangular frame given to doors, windows and niches in Gothic architecture, where the sloping sides are often decorated with crockets and crowned with a finial. In medieval and early Renaissance houses of northern Europe, it was customary to present the gable end as the street façade. It was then elaborately decorated and formed in steps to correspond to the stories of the interior.

Gallery of kings Row of sculptured figures of the kings of Israel, usually above the main portal of Gothic cathedrals.

Gardens 1. French garden design, developed during the seventeenth century. Strictly formal layout with lawns, hedges and ornamental pools arranged in geometrical precision. The park of Versailles is a famous example.
2. The English garden, developed in England during the eighteenth century. Romantic and informal, trees and carpet bedding arranged with conscious asymmetry.

▶ **Gargoyle** A projecting spout used in Gothic architecture, to drain the gutter behind a parapet and to shoot the water clear of the walls. Often carved into grotesque figures and animals.

▶ **Giant order** An order of columns or pilasters embracing two stories of a building. Used by Michelangelo and baroque architects.

Gothic Architectural style which followed Romanesque and developed in northern and central France during the second half of the twelfth century, reaching England about 1175; Germany about 1230; and Spain in the course of the thirteenth century. In northern Italy (the only part of Italy to be considerably affected by the Gothic style), Gothic architecture remained bound to Romanesque tradition, and by the beginning of the fifteenth century was already being superseded by the style of the Renaissance, inspired by the architecture of antiquity. The development of Gothic in northern Europe may be divided into three main phases: Early Gothic — second half of the twelfth to the beginning of the thirteenth century; Classic Gothic — up to 1250; High Gothic — 1250–1350; Late Gothic — 1350–1520. During the early nineteenth century there was a revival of the Gothic style and methods of construction known as Neo-Gothic.

Grille An openwork screen. In the Early Christian period, pierced slabs of marble or stone were used as an infilling to window openings. Wood or metal grilles serve to protect chapels or reliquaries.

Grotesque Italian: *grotesco*, from *grotta*, a cave. A fanciful decoration of tendrils and wreaths of flowers etc. combined with human or animal figures and fabulous creatures. To be distinguished from arabesque, which consists only of foliated ornament. Like arabesques, grotesque ornament was widely used during the Renaissance. It was inspired by antique decorative devices and owes its name to the fact that the ancient Roman prototypes found during the excavations in Rome in the fifteenth century were believed to have been grotto decorations.

Half timbering A type of timber construction in which the spaces between the structural members — posts, beams and struts — are filled in with brick or other material, leaving the timber members visible. Much used for domestic architecture in northern Europe during the Gothic period and in the Renaissance. The upper stories were often corbeled out from the face below and the beams richly carved.

Gabled Renaissance façade

GARGOYLE

GIANT ORDER

Hall church Church in which nave and aisles are of equal height.

Header A brick or stone laid so that the longest dimension is in the thickness of the wall, at right angles to its length, and only the end appears on the face. *See Stretcher.*

▶ **Herma** A rectangular pillar or pedestal surmounted by a human bust (originally representing Hermes) and used during the Renaissance as a support for a cornice or entablature.

Hexastyle A temple having a portico with a row of six columns. *See Temple.*

High relief *See Relief.*

Hipped roof Roof with sloped instead of vertical ends. *See Roof.*

Hypocaust A heating chamber under the floor of a Roman thermae. The floor was raised on small brick columns, so that the heat was circulated throughout the building.

Iconostasis In the Eastern Church, a screen hung with icons or sacred images, separating the sanctuary from the rest of the church.

Impost A block of stone placed on a pier or doorpost at the springing of an arch. It thus serves as a transitional member between arch and support and fulfills the same function as a capital.

Intercolumniation The space between the columns. In classical architecture, intercolumniation was governed by strict rules of proportion, being related to the diameter of the columns.

Intrados The inner curve of an arch or vault.

Ionic order *See Orders, classical.*

Jamb The sides of an archway, door or window opening.

Keep *See Donjon.*

Keystone The central stone of an arch or rib vault (*see Boss*), the last to be placed in position. Sometimes given a sculptural decoration.

HERMA: *Town hall, Braunschweig, sixteenth century*

Lantern A small turret, surrounded by windows, on top of a roof or dome. In medieval architecture, the tower with windows over the crossing of a church is called the lantern tower.

Lean-to or monopitched roof Roof with one slope only, usually placed against a higher wall, *e.g.*, over the aisle of a basilican church. *See Roof.*

Lierne A short intermediate rib in Gothic vaulting, one which does not spring from one of the main vaulting shafts or from the central boss, but crosses the vaulting panels from main rib to main rib, to form star-shaped patterns. *See Vault.*

Lintel Horizontal beam or stone placed over a door, window or other opening.

Loggia Italian term for a gallery behind an open arcade or colonnade. May form one of the stories in a building (Loggia del Vaticano) or be freestanding (Loggia dei Lanzi, Florence).

▶ **Lunette** Curved opening in a vault or dome, to admit light. Also the horizontal segments between the pendentives of a dome or the curved space between the lintel of a doorway and the arch above.

Mansard roof A roof with a double slope, the lower slope being steeper than the upper. Named after architect François Mansard. *See Roof.*

Mask Human or animal head carved on the keystone of an arch, on consoles, entablatures etc.

▶ **Masons' or pieceworkers' marks** Marks that medieval stone masons carved on the stones they handled, for purposes of identification and payment, each man having his own distinctive sign. Found on buildings dating from the twelfth to the eighteenth century.

Mausoleum Originally the tomb of the Carian king Mausolus at Halicarnassus (died 352 B.C.), built by his wife Artemisia and his sister. Now extended to denote any large sepulchral monument.

Medallion Circular decorative tablet like a large medal, usually bearing a figure or a narrative scene in relief.

▶ **Megaron** Early form of Greek private house. Comprised a single rectangular compartment with the side walls extended on either side of the entrance front.

LUNETTES

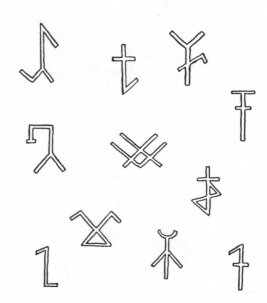

MASONS' MARKS

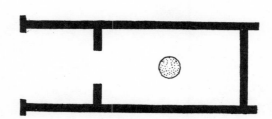

MEGARON, *Troy II, third millennium* B.C.

Metope The space between two triglyphs in a Doric frieze, filled with thin stone slabs and usually sculptured in relief. *See Entablature.*

Mezzanine A low intermediate story, between the ground floor and the first story or under the attic.

Misericord *See Stalls.*

Modillion Small bracket or console under the cornice in classical architecture.

Monastery A residence for a community of monks. *See Abbey.*

Monolith A pillar or other constructional member cut out of a single block of stone. The great slab that forms the roof of the tomb of Theodoric at Ravenna is a famous example.

► **Monopteral, monopteros** A circular temple surrounded by a single row of columns.

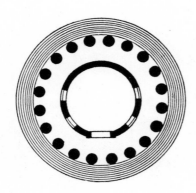

MONOPTERAL TEMPLE PLAN

Mosaic Ornamental surface of small cubes of colored stone, glass, marble or tile embedded in cement to form geometrical patterns or narrative scenes. Used by the Greeks and Romans (*see Opus tesselatum, Opus vermiculatum*) and in Early Christian churches in Italy and the East, as a decoration for walls and vaults. Byzantine mosaics provide some of the richest examples (churches at Ravenna, fifth and sixth centuries). After the Carolingian period, mosaic work was generally superseded by fresco decoration.

Mudejar style Spanish style combining Gothic and Moorish features, with a preponderance of the latter. Characterized by intricate ornamental detail. Reached its highest development in the fourteenth century.

Mullions Vertical members dividing a window into a number of lights. *See Transom.*

Mutules In classical architecture, the projecting slabs under the cornice in the Doric order. Each mutule carries 18 guttae (small cones) in 3 rows of 6.

Nailhead Ornamental motif, carved in relief, consisting of small pyramids regularly repeated. (*See Ornamental Motifs, 9.*) Used in the Romanesque period, especially in early English architecture.

Naos Greek: temple. Now commonly used as Greek equivalent to cella, the Greek temple chamber containing the statue of the deity.

Narthex In a Christian basilica, a closed vestibule or arcaded porch before the main entrance, originally assigned to penitents and those not yet in full communion.

Nave The central aisle of a church, as opposed to the side aisles.

▶ **Niche** A recess in a wall, usually for a statue or other object.

Nymphaeum In ancient Greece, a sanctuary dedicated to the nymphs, usually near a spring. Later, in Roman times and after, a water garden within a colonnaded courtyard.

Octastyle A temple with a portico of 8 columns. *See Temple.*

Opisthodome In Greek architecture, the part of a temple at the rear of the cella, a duplicate of the pronaos, but usually without a door in its back wall.

▶ **Opus incertum** Roman system of facing a concrete wall with small, irregular-shaped stones.

▶ **Opus reticulatum** Reticulate system. Roman system of facing a concrete wall with small squared stones placed so that the joints are in diagonal lines forming a lattice pattern like the meshes of a net.

Opus sectile Type of mosaic used in classical antiquity, consisting of relatively large plates of variously colored stone or marble cut in the shapes of the design.

▶ **Opus spicatum** Roman system of facing a concrete wall with stones set diagonally in alternate directions, forming a herringbone pattern.

Opus tesselatum Type of mosaic used in classical antiquity, consisting of small stone cubes of regular shape (tesserae), allowing only for geometrical designs. Most purely geometrical antique mosaics are of this type.

Opus vermiculatum Mosaic of small pieces of stone of irregular shape — some long, some lozenge shaped etc. This type is best adapted to the creation of figurative scenes, allowing for the representation of hair, facial features, drapery folds etc.

NICHE

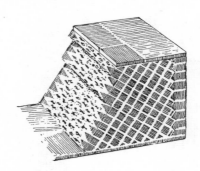

OPUS INCERTUM

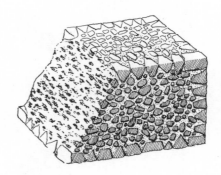

OPUS RETICULATUM

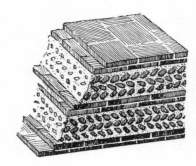

OPUS SPICATUM

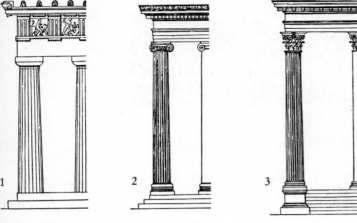

ORDERS: *1. Doric; 2. Ionic; 3. Corinthian*

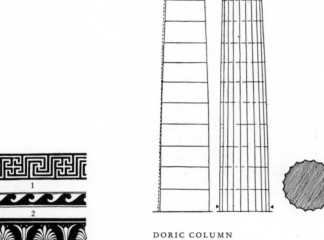

DORIC COLUMN

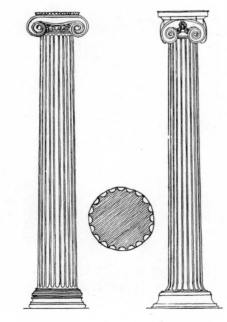

ORNAMENTAL MOTIFS

IONIC COLUMN: *Left, Attic; Right, Asia Minor*

Orchestra Space in front of the stage of an ancient Greek theatre, where the chorus danced and sang. Originally circular, later semicircular.

▶ **Orders, classical** In the strictest sense, the name given to the three architectural types developed and perfected by the ancient Greeks. These were adopted and varied by the Romans. Each order has its characteristic proportions and architectural treatment of its two principal elements — column and entablature.
1. *The Doric Order.*
Thought to be derived from timber buildings. The oldest and simplest of the orders, it was used in Greece from the seventh century B.C. The Doric column, thick in proportion to its height, springs directly from the stylobate, without a base. The shaft, usually built of separate drums, has 20 shallow flutes divided by sharp edges or arrises. It tapers from the bottom upward, the outline swelling out in a delicate curve (entasis). The capital is formed by a convex molding — the echinus — and a low square block — the abacus. The architrave, resting on the abacus, is plain. The frieze is divided by alternate metopes and triglyphs. Above the frieze comes the cornice.
2. *The Ionic Order.*
The Ionic column rests on a molded base which may be of various profiles. The most common type is the Attic base. The shaft, more slender than the Doric, normally has 24 semicircular flutes divided by narrow strips of unfluted surface (fillets). The capital consists of an echinus molding, usually decorated with egg-and-dart motif, surmounted by the volute member, the spirals dropping down on each side of the shaft. On top of this is a thin, square abacus often with a *cyma-reversa* profile. The entablature is light and slightly decorated.
3. *The Corinthian Order.*
Similar in general proportions to the Ionic. The column has the same base as the Attic Ionic. The capital, derived from the Ionic form, consists of a bell-shaped block carved with rows of acanthus leaves. There is one volute under each angle of the abacus and one under the center of each side, making 8 volutes in all. The entablature of this order is frequently richly treated.

Oriel window Bay window in an upper story, supported on masonry or timber corbeling.

Orientation The position of a building with reference to the points of the compass, particularly to the east. Greek temples stood with their main façade east, so that the statue of the deity in the cella faced the rising sun. Christian churches (from the fourth century) have generally been placed so that the altar is at the east end, the Eastern lands being regarded as the source of light synonymous with salvation.

▶ **Ornamental motifs** Almost innumerable. Among those commonly found are: 1. fret ornament or Greek-key pattern; 2. Vitruvian wave; 3. anthemion — honeysuckle or palmette ornament, in Greek and Roman architecture; 4. chevron; 5. denticulated; 6. arcuated; 7. checkered; 8. billet; 9. nailhead; 10. imbricated; 11. foliated.

Palaestra In ancient Greece, a public building for the training of athletes — a gymnasium. In ancient Rome, part of a thermae set aside for sports.

► **Palmette** Ornamental motif similar to a stylized palm leaf, much used by the Greeks. *See Ornamental Motifs.*

PALMETTES

► **Paneling** Framing — constructional in timber or decorative in plaster — applied to the walls of rooms. The example shows the elaborate type of paneling characteristic of French rococo.

Paraskenion A short wing projecting from the skene (stage) of a Greek theatre.

Parvise In medieval church architecture, an enclosed area or court in front of the west façade. Often wrongly applied to the small room over a church porch.

Pavilion Small, freestanding ornamental building, usually in a park. Also a subdivision of a building, usually projecting from the main block and surmounted by a separate roof.

FRENCH ROCOCO PANELING

Pedestal A substructure consisting of a molded base, a rectangular dado and a molded cornice. In classical architecture, frequently placed under columns or used as a support for a statue.

Pediment In the architecture of classical antiquity, the triangular piece of wall, enclosed by one horizontal and two sloping cornices, above the entablature over a portico. During the Renaissance the bowed or semicircular pediment was often used with other modifications of the classical type. During the baroque period, in both triangular and bowed pediments, the central part of the raking cornices was sometimes omitted, forming the so-called broken pediment into which an aedicula (niche) feature was often inserted. Small pediments are widely used as a decorative feature over doors and windows.

Pendentive *See Dome.*

► **Peripteral, peripteros** Terms applied to a temple surrounded by a colonnade.

Peristasis In a Greek temple, the space between the outer colonnade and the cella wall.

Peristyle An external peripteral colonnade. Also a range of columns around the inside of a room or court, as in Hellenistic and Roman houses, where the peristyle often enclosed a garden.

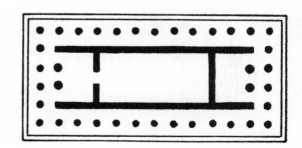

PERIPTERAL TEMPLE PLAN

Perpendicular Name given to a phase of English Gothic (*c.* 1350 – 1530) characterized by the emphasis placed on verticals and horizontals in architectural decoration.

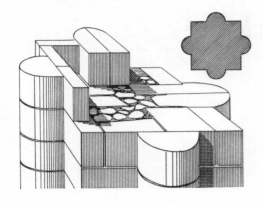

▶ **Pier** A massive support, usually square in section, as distinct from the more slender circular column. It may also be cruciform on plan or have attached shafts and moldings (compound or clustered pier). Also the wall between a pair of openings. Hence in interior decoration the pier glass or mirror applied to a wall space between two windows.

Pilaster Shallow rectangular pier, fluted or unfluted, attached to a wall and with base and capital. Not to be confused with the pilaster strip, which has neither base nor capital.

▶ **Pilaster strip decoration** Early Christian and Romanesque exterior wall decoration consisting of flat pilaster strips without bases or capitals, connected horizontally by a series of small arches.

Pillar of victory Column set up in honor of a sovereign during the time of the Roman Empire. Usually decorated with bas-reliefs and often containing a staircase. Well-known examples: Trajan's Column and the Column of Marcus Aurelius, Rome.

Pinnacle In Gothic architecture, a small turretlike feature with a steep pyramidal or conical roof, crowning a wall buttress, flying buttress, spire etc.

PIER. *Above, Romanesque Below, Gothic, Ely Cathedral, England, thirteenth century*

Plan Horizontal section of a building. A drawing of the ground plan indicates the general disposition of the parts of the building.

Plat band A horizontal course of masonry corresponding to an architrave.

Plateresque style Spanish: *estilo plateresco*, silversmith's style. Richly decorative Spanish style corresponding to Late Gothic and Early Renaissance elsewhere.

Plinth The lowest square member of the base of a column, or the plain surface of masonry forming the base of a building.

PILASTER STRIP DECORATION

Podium A high basement to a temple or other building, with three vertical faces and steps at the principal end only. Characteristic of Roman temples.

► **Portal** An elaborated entrance to a building. In medieval churches, the entrance walls are enriched with colonnettes (G), sometimes alternating with statues and carrying deeply molded arches in a series of recessed planes (A). The arch is filled with a tympanum (B) resting on a lintel (TS) supported by a central colonnette (TP). The colonnette may support a statue from which the portal often takes its name, and the theme is carried through the rich carving of the tympanum and supporting statuary. In the Renaissance, such doorways are usually more restrained, following antique example.

Portico A colonnaded porch forming an entrance to a temple, church or house.

► **Profile** In architecture, the outline of a molding or group of moldings in a base, cornice, arch, rib etc., seen in vertical section. A useful guide to the more precise dating of a building, particularly in the Gothic period. The illustration shows the development of the profile from the twelfth to the fifteenth century: 1. eleventh and twelfth centuries; 2. twelfth and thirteenth centuries (bold torus moldings); 3. thirteenth and fourteenth centuries; 4. fifteenth century.

Pronaos The part of a temple in front of the cella, often synonymous with portico.

Propylaea Monumental entrance gateway in front of a temple precinct, as at the Acropolis of Athens.

Prostyle Denotes an antique temple with a range of columns (without antae) on the façade but with no colonnade on the other three sides.

Prothesis A rectangular chamber adjoining the sanctuary and in line with one of the side aisles in an Early Christian or Byzantine church. Contained an altar and served for the preparation of the Host. *See Diaconicon.*

Pseudodipteral A temple planned as a dipteral temple but with the inner range of columns supressed so that the width of the space between the side colonnades and the cella wall is doubled.

► **Pseudoperipteral** A peripteral temple in which the columns on the side walls and rear façade are attached to the cella walls. *(See illustration, page 424.)*

Quatrefoil *See Foil.*

Quoins Dressed stones set at the angles of a building.

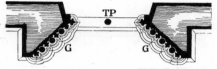

PORTAL

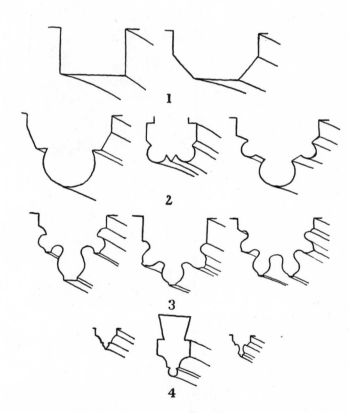

PROFILES: *development of the arch profile from the twelfth to the fifteenth century*

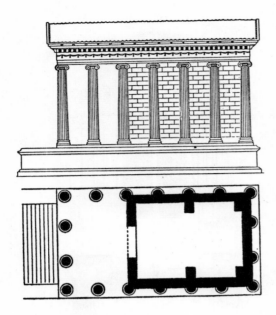

PSEUDOPERIPTERAL TEMPLE

ROCAILLE

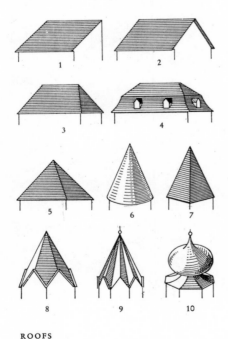

ROOFS

Raking cornice The upper cornice of a triangular pediment, following the slope of the roof.

Relief Carving or modeling in which the forms stand out from a flat surface — as distinct from sculpture "in the round." High relief and low — or bas-relief — indicate the extent to which the forms project from their background.

Relieving arch An arch built into a wall above a lintel or arched opening, to throw the weight of the upper part of the wall off the lintel or arch.

Renaissance The term applied to the architectural style that was created in Italy in the fifteenth century and that was to spread across Europe in the fifteenth and sixteenth centuries. Signifies the reintroduction of the forms and principles of the classical architecture of Roman antiquity.

Rib A projecting band or narrow arch on a vault.

Ridge The angle at the apex of a roof: the beam that usually runs along this angle is called the ridgepiece, and the tiles that cover it are called ridge tiles. In classical temples, the ends of the ridges were decorated with acroteria.

▶ **Rocaille** The type of curling, asymmetrical, shell- or rocklike ornament that signalizes the rococo style.

Rococo Latest phase of the baroque style. Current in most European countries between c. 1720 and c. 1760.

Romanesque The style of architecture prevalent in western Europe during the eleventh and twelfth centuries, preceding the Gothic style.

Rood loft or jube Balustraded singing gallery on top of the rood screen that separates the choir of a church from the nave. Used for the chanting of the Epistle and Gospel. The rood lofts and screens of most Gothic cathedrals were destroyed in the eighteenth century, but the celebrated one at Naumburg survives (c. 1250) and several later (Renaissance) examples are still extant, including those of St. Étienne du Mont, Paris, and the Madeleine at Troyes.

▶ **Roof** The most important forms are: 1. Lean-to, 2. Gabled, 3. Hipped, 4. Mansard, 5. Pyramidal (Towers), 6. Conoidal, 7. Pyramidal, 8. Rhomboidal, 9. Folded Rhomboidal, 10. Onion or Bulbous.

► **Rosette** A circular ornament resembling a stylized rose or other flower.

► **Rose window or wheel window** A large circular window with tracery radiating from the center. Introduced in the Romanesque period. Received an elaborate treatment in Gothic architecture. Usually found above the main façade of a church or over the two transept entrances.

ROSETTES

Rotunda A building that is circular in plan.

Roughcast A rough plaster for giving a light covering to the outsides of buildings. Composed of lime and gravel mixed with water unevenly thrown on with a trowel.

Rubblework, rough walling Coarse walling constructed of rough, irregular-shaped stones bedded in mortar and not laid in regular courses. Ashlar walls were frequently backed with rubble.

ROSE WINDOW

► **Rustication** 1. *Rock-faced rustication:* stonework in which the beds and joints are squared but the surfaces of the blocks are left rough or are artificially roughened.
2. *Smooth rustication:* stonework in which the ashlar blocks are smooth and separated by recessed V-joints.
Employed by the Romans and to be found in much Renaissance building.

RUSTICATION

Saddlebacked Usually applied to roofs forming an isosceles triangle in cross section.

Scagliola Material consisting of cement and coloring matter, imitating marble.

Scotia A concave molding (as opposed to the torus [*q.v.*], which is convex) in the Attic base. *See Base.*

Segmental arch Any roundheaded arch that is only a segment of a circle, *i.e.* forms less than a semicircle.

Sexpartite *See Vault.*

Shaft The portion of a column between base and capital. May be carved of a single block of stone (monolithic) or made up of several drums, and either fluted or left smooth. In some classical, Renaissance and baroque architecture, the shafts were given an entasis. In medieval architecture, the term is also applied to a slender column, usually forming part of a clustered pier, supporting a vaulting rib.

Spandrel The wall space beyond the extrados of an arch or between two arches.

Spiral staircase A staircase revolving about a vertical axis, the treads widening toward their outer ends.

Splay The slanted side of an opening, usually toward the interior, to widen the opening and admit more light.

Squinch *See Dome.*

Stalls Row of hinged seats in a chancel, for clergy and choir. On the underside of each seat, a small bracket called a misericord was placed to provide support for the occupant during long periods of standing. These misericords were frequently carved grotesquely.

▶ **Stilted arch** An arch struck from a center, above the line of the imposts.

Stretcher Brick or stone laid so that its longest dimensions are parallel with the length of the wall and its narrow side to the face.

Stringcourse Projecting horizontal band or molding along the face of a building, usually to mark the divisions between the stories.

Stylobate In classical architecture, the continuous stepped base on which a colonnade is placed. Characteristic of Greek temples.

Tabernacle Richly decorated niche or freestanding canopy, usually to contain the Holy Sacrament. The famous tabernacle at Ulm Cathedral dates from the fifteenth century.

Temple The sacred precinct (temenos) on which the Greek temple stood was surrounded by a peribolus or enclosing wall. The temple contained the cult image and was accessible only to the priests, while religious ceremonies took place at an altar before the temple, on the temenos itself. The main types of antique temple were: the temple *in antis,* the prostyle, amphiprostyle, peripteral, pseudoperipteral, dipteral, pseudo-dipteral, monopteral (tholos). In Roman examples the temple was raised on a podium. Beyond the principal entrance or pronaos, was the naos or cella where the cult image stood; behind the cella was the opisthodome, a portico with no communicating door between it and the cella.

Temples may be distinguished by the number of columns in their portico, thus: tetrastyle (4 columns); hexastyle (6 columns); octastyle (8 columns); decastyle (10 columns); dodecastyle (12 columns). According to the classical rules of proportion, the number of columns on each side of a peripteral temple is double that on the façade plus one (the columns at the angles being counted twice). The Parthenon may thus be defined as a Doric peripteral octastyle temple — peripteral because it is surrounded by a range of columns; octastyle because the portico has a range of 8 columns, each lateral face having a range of 17 $(8 \times 2 + 1)$.

STILTED ARCH

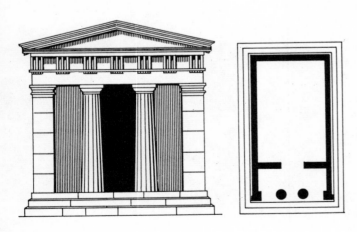

TEMPLE IN ANTIS

▶ **Temple in antis** Temple in which the portico is enclosed by the extended side walls, with columns between the ends of these.

Tetrastyle Term applied to an antique temple with a portico of four columns in front.

▶ **Thermae** Greek: warm springs — hence warm baths. Bathing establishments or thermae achieved an extraordinary importance in Roman times and were built on a vast scale and decorated lavishly. They contained theatre, palaestra, lecture rooms and libraries, in addition to the rooms reserved for the bath. The largest thermae could accommodate several thousand people and usually comprised the following main apartments within a surrounding wall with niches and exedra: 1. Palaestra for games and athletic training; 2. Apodyteria (changing rooms); 3. Natatio (large open-air swimming pool); 4. Frigidarium (covered hall with cold-water baths); 5. Tepidarium; 6. Calidarium (for warm and hot baths); Sudarium (steam bath). The ruins of the great baths of Diocletian and Caracalla are still extant.

Tholos A small Greek temple of circular form, with a circular colonnade. The Tholos of Epidaurus is a well-known example.

Tierceron Secondary rib, springing from one of the main vaulting shafts and leading to a point on the ridge rib in a Gothic vault.

Torus A large, rounded molding, convex in section, used in the bases of columns in classical architecture, where it is generally contrasted with the scotia or concave molding.

▶ **Tracery** The intersecting stone ribwork supported by the mullions, forming a decorative design in the upper part of a Gothic window. Introduced toward the end of the twelfth century. At first, only geometrical figures (circle, curvilinear triangle, trefoil, quatrefoil etc.) were used. In the fourteenth century, tracery became more elaborate; in the fifteenth century there appeared the flowing, flamboyant tracery that gives this phase of Gothic its name. Tracery is also used as a decoration for wood or stone panels, vaults, blind arches etc.

▶ **Transept** The part of a cruciform church lying between nave and choir at right angles to the longitudinal axis. The place of intersection of nave and transept is called the crossing, and the compartments projecting beyond the nave walls on either side are known as the transept arms. Sometimes, as in churches with a double apsidal ending and in some English Gothic churches, there are two transepts, one at the east and one at the west end.

Transoms The horizontal divisions or bars in a window, in some cases used to strengthen the mullions.

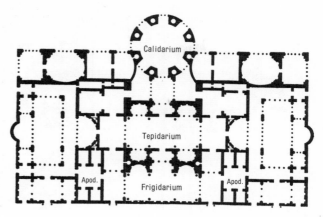

THERMAE *of Caracalla, Rome — plan*

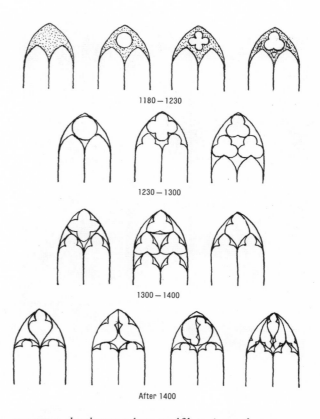

1180 — 1230

1230 — 1300

1300 — 1400

After 1400

TRACERY, *development from twelfth to sixteenth century*

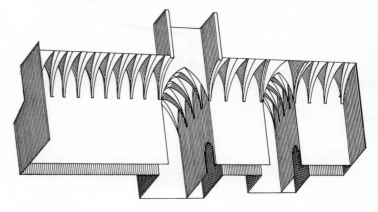

TRANSEPT

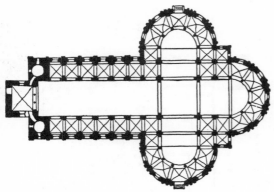

TREFOIL CHOIR PLAN:
Sta Maria im Capitol, Cologne, 1065

TRIFORIUM: *Left, Romanesque, St. Benoît sur Loire, eleventh century*
Right, Gothic, Amiens Cathedral, thirteenth century

ARCH *of Constantine, Rome, fourth century*

Transverse arch Arch spanning a nave from one lateral support to another and separating one bay of the vault from the next.

Trefoil *See Foil.*

▶ **Trefoil choir** Term applied to a church or chapel when the transept arms as well as the nave terminate in a semicircular apse, forming a trefoil pattern. Characteristic of Romanesque churches in and around Cologne.

Tribune gallery In church architecture, an upper story over an aisle, usually opening onto the nave in arches. Common in Early Christian basilicas; used in some Romanesque and Early Gothic churches. In the thirteenth century, the tribune gallery was superseded by the triforium.

▶ **Triforium** A narrow arcaded wall passage or blank arcading occupying (on the nave walls) the space between the top of the nave arcade and the clerestory windows.

Triglyphs Upright blocks placed on the frieze of the Doric entablature at regular intervals, leaving square spaces (metopes) between. Decorated with two vertical grooves on the face and a half groove at each angle.

▶ **Triumphal arch** 1. Monumental gateway with one or more openings. Triumphal arches were erected by the Romans in honor of victorious emperors and generals returning from battle, and were decorated with reliefs and articulated with columns and entablature surmounted by an attic, usually bearing an inscription.
2. The arch forming the entrance from nave to apse in a basilican church, generally bearing an image of Christ.

Trophy Sculptured group of arms, armor and standards used as a memorial of victory in Roman antiquity and taken up as a decorative motif during the Renaissance.

Tympanum In a pediment, the surface bounded by the sloping and horizontal cornices. Often richly decorated with sculpture. In a doorway, the space between the lintel and the arch. Also often given a rich decoration.

▶ **Vault** An arched covering of stone or brick. (a) and (b) show false vaults, an early form, in which the successive horizontal courses of masonry are corbeled out until they meet at the crown.
1–12: *True vaults:* those in which the stones or bricks are wedge shaped, with their joints radial to the center of the vault. The various kinds are:

1. *Barrel vault.* One continuous arch of semicircular or pointed section. Type much used during the Romanesque period.

2. *Cross or groined vault.* Formed by two barrel vaults of identical shape intersecting at right angles to produce defined edges or groins. Introduced by the Romans.

3. *Quadripartite rib vault.* Cross vault with narrow arches (ribs) projecting along the groins, and with each vaulting bay divided into four parts. Characteristic of Gothic architecture.

4. *Sexpartite vault.* One bay of quadripartite vaulting is divided into two parts by an extra transverse rib, thus producing 6 vaulting panels. Characteristic of late twelfth-century Gothic.

5 and 6. *Stellar vaults.* A type of Late Gothic quadripartite rib vault to which are added various intermediate ribs — tiercerons, ridge rib and liernes — together producing a star-shaped pattern, hence the name.

7. *Fan or Conoidal vault.* A system of vaulting peculiar to late English Gothic, in which all the ribs in each vaulting bay radiate, fanlike, from the same point and at an equal distance from each other. In the most elaborate examples, the ribs are a decorative enrichment on the surface of a solid masonry conoid.

8. *Net vault.* Peculiar to Late Gothic in Germany, and usually employed in churches of the hall type. Netlike patterns, spreading over the whole ceiling, are achieved with a complicated arrangement of ribs which serves a decorative purpose only.

9. *Honeycomb vault.* Special type employed in the brick Gothic of northern Germany. The surfaces between the ribs are folded to form individual cells.

10, 11 and 12. *Coved vaults.* A type of vaulted ceiling produced when round or pointed barrel vaults spring from all four sides of a compartment, giving internal intersections — as opposed to the groins of a cross vault. Sometimes found in Romanesque work but more familiar as a decorative form in Renaissance architecture. In the latter, the center part of the ceiling is often flat (Fig. 12).

Vaulting panels or webs The infilling between the ribs of a Gothic vault. Thus a quadripartite vault comprises four vaulting panels or webs.

Volute Spiral scroll ornament, the characteristic feature of the Ionic capital.

Voussoir A wedge-shaped stone (used in the building of arches).

Wall rib *See Formeret.*

Westwork German: *westwerk.* A rectangular construction, like an antechurch, at the west end of some monastery churches of the early Middle Ages. It usually consisted of a central tower flanked by two smaller staircase towers. Inside, above the entrance hall, is a chapel opening toward the nave. It is probable that the westwork served as a private chapel from which the emperor and his court could take part in the service on their visits to the abbey church.

Window breast A thin screen wall below a window, particularly in Gothic architecture. It carries the mullions of clerestory windows and may itself be decorated with blind arcading (fifteenth century).

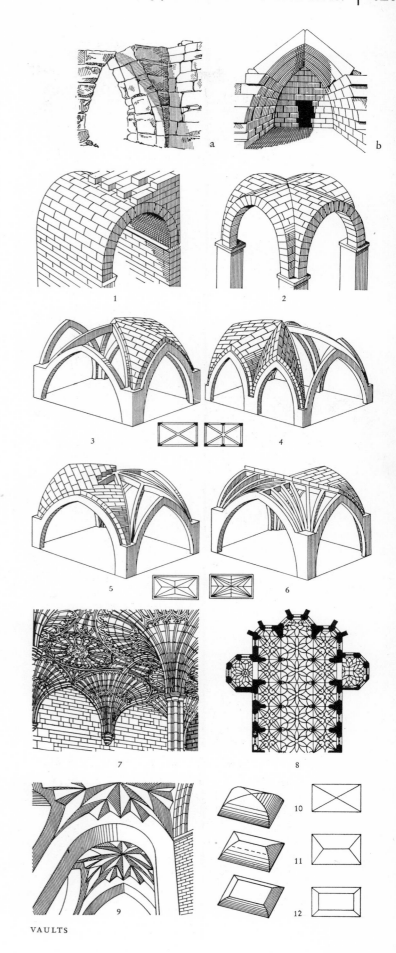

VAULTS

BIBLIOGRAPHY

Selection has been confined to books written in English and those which exist in English translation.

Chapter II — GREEK ARCHITECTURE

Dinsmoor, W. B., *Architecture of Ancient Greece*. 1950.
Evans, Sir A., *Palace of Minos at Knossos*. 4 vols., 1921–1930.
Lawrence, A. W., *Greek Architecture*. (Pelican History of Art.) 1957.
Pennethorne, J., *The Geometry and Optics of Ancient Architecture*. 1878.
Penrose, F. C., *Principles of Athenian Architecture*. 1888.
Plommer, H., *Ancient and Classic Architecture*. (Simpson's Architectural Development.) 1956.
Robertson, D. S., *Handbook of Greek and Roman Architecture*. Second edition, 1943.

Chapter III — ROMAN ARCHITECTURE

Anderson, W. J., Spiers, R. P., and Ashby, T., *The Architecture of Ancient Rome*. 1927.
Palladio, A., *I Quattro Libri dell'Architettura di Andrea Palladio*. 1570. (Several English translations, *e.g.* Ware, 1738.)
Robertson, D. S., *Handbook of Greek and Roman Architecture*. Second edition, 1943.
Vitruvius, *De Architectura*. (Several English translations, *e.g.* Morgan, 1960.)

Chapter IV — EARLY CHRISTIAN ARCHITECTURE

Davies, J. G., *The Origins and Development of Early Christian Architecture*. 1952.
Stewart, C., *Early Christian, Byzantine and Romanesque Architecture*. (Simpson's Architectural Development.) 1954.

Chapter V — BYZANTINE ARCHITECTURE

Lethaby, W. R., *The Church of Sancta Sophia, Constantinople*. 1894.
Stewart, C., *Early Christian, Byzantine and Romanesque Architecture*. (Simpson's Architectural Development.) 1954.
Talbot Rice, D., *Byzantine Art*. 1954.

Chapter VI — ARCHITECTURE DURING THE RISE OF THE WEST

Conant, K., *Carolingian and Romanesque Architecture*. 1959.

Chapter VII — ROMANESQUE ARCHITECTURE

Conant, K., *Carolingian and Romanesque Architecture*. 1959.
Lethaby, W. R., and Talbot Rice, D., *Mediaeval Art*. Third edition, 1949.
Stewart, C., *Early Christian, Byzantine and Romanesque Architecture*. (Simpson's Architectural Development.) 1954.

Chapter VIII — GOTHIC ARCHITECTURE

Frankl, P., *Gothic Architecture*. 1962.
Franklin, J. W., *Cathedrals of Italy*. 1958.
Harvey, J. H., *English Cathedrals*. Second edition, 1956.
Lavedan, P., *French Architecture*. 1956.
Male, E., *L'Art religieux XIIIᵉ siècle en France*. (Translated as *The Gothic Image* by Nussey.) 1961.
Panofsky, E., *Gothic Architecture and Scholasticism*. 1957.
Rickman, T., *Gothic Architecture*. 1881.
Simson, O., *The Gothic Cathedral: the Origins of Gothic Architecture and the Mediaeval Concept of Order*. 1956.
Webb, G., *Architecture in Britain: the Middle Ages*. 1956.

Chapter IX — RENAISSANCE ARCHITECTURE

Ackerman, J. S., *The Architecture of Michelangelo*. 2 vols., 1961.

Alberti, L. B., *I Dieci Libri dell' Architettura*. 3 vols., 1726. (Translated by Leoni, 1955.)

Blunt, Sir A., *Art and Architecture in France, 1500–1700*. 1953.

Carli, E., *Brunelleschi*. 1952.

Hughes, J., and Lynton, N., *Renaissance Architecture*. (Simpson's Architectural Development.) 1961.

Lavedan, P., *French Architecture*. 1956.

Murray, P., *Bramante*. 1963.

Scott, G., *The Architecture of Humanism*. 1914.

Summerson, Sir J., *Architecture in Britain, 1530–1830*. Fourth edition, 1963.

Wittkower, R., *Architectural Principles in the Age of Humanism*. 1949.

Chapter X — BAROQUE AND ROCOCO ARCHITECTURE

Blunt, Sir A., *Art and Architecture in France, 1500–1700*. 1953.

Blunt, Sir A., *Mansart*. 1941.

Lavedan, P., *French Architecture*. 1956.

Tapie, V. L., *Baroque et classicisme*. (Translated as *The Age of Grandeur, Baroque and Classicism in Europe*.) 1960.

Wittkower, R., *Art and Architecture in Italy, 1699–1750*. 1958.

Chapter XI — ARCHITECTURE DURING THE LATE EIGHTEENTH AND NINETEENTH CENTURIES

Clark, K., *The Gothic Revival*. Third edition, 1962.

Giedion, S., *Space, Time and Architecture*. 1941.

Hitchcock, H.-R., *Architecture, 19th and 20th Centuries*. 1958.

Hitchcock, H.-R., *Early Victorian Architecture in Britain*. 2 vols., 1954.

Pevsner, N., *Pioneers of Modern Design from William Morris to Walter Gropius*. 1960.

Chapter XII — TWENTIETH-CENTURY ARCHITECTURE

Banham, R. P., *History of Modern Architecture*. 1962.

Banham, R. P., *Theory and Design in the First Machine Age*. 1960.

Blake, P., *Master Builders*. 1960.

Le Corbusier, *Towards a New Architecture*. 1947.

Giedion, S., *Space, Time and Architecture*. 1941.

Giedion, S., *Walter Gropius — Work and Teamwork*. 1954.

Gropius, W., *The New Architecture and the Bauhaus*. 1935.

Hitchcock, H.-R., *Architecture, 19th and 20th Centuries*. 1958.

Hitchcock, H.-R., and Drexler, A., *Built in U.S.A.: Post-war Architecture*. 1952.

Hitchcock, H.-R., and Drexler, A., *Latin American Architecture Since 1945*. 1955.

Joedicke, J., *History of Modern Architecture*. 1958.

MacCallum, I., *Architecture, U.S.A.* 1959.

Pevsner, N., *Pioneers of Modern Design from William Morris to Walter Gropius*. 1960.

Richards, J. M., *Introduction to Modern Architecture*. 1949.

Smith, G. E. K., *The New Architecture of Europe*. 1961.

Wright, F. L., *A Testament*. 1957.

Three books which may be consulted freely are:

Fletcher, B. F., *The History of Architecture on the Comparative Method*. Seventeenth edition, revised by Cordingley, 1962.

Hamlin, T., *Architecture Through the Ages*. Second revised edition, 1953.

Pevsner, N., *An Outline of European Architecture*. 1943.

INDEX

Note: Figures in italic type indicate illustrations. Individual buildings, etc. generally will be found under one of the following classifications:

INTERIOR AREAM SPECTANS FACIES TOTIVS ÆDIFICII
AVLARVM CASTELLI DVLOVVRE

La face du Corps du logis a